To Jeff Grossman

With warm regards the colleague
in the Public Service

Paul Patterson

The Ring of Power

THE RING OF POWER

The White House Staff
and Its Expanding Role
in Government

BRADLEY H. PATTERSON, JR.

Basic Books, Inc., Publishers

NEW YORK

Library of Congress Cataloging-in-Publication Data

Patterson, Bradley H. (Bradley Hawkes), 1921–
  The ring of power.

  Includes index.
  1. Presidents—United States—Staff. I. Title.
JK518.P37 1988   353.03′1   88–47670
ISBN 0–465–07025–6

This book is dedicated to all those who,

serving the president,

serve the presidency.

CONTENTS

PART I
The Cabinet Government That Isn't

PART II
The Bashful Bureaucracy

ACKNOWLEDGMENTS

An admission is in order.

While this book has one father, it has a host of godparents. Authors of previous books are cited throughout the text; the work here owes much to them and is itself but one more link in a chain of continuing research on the American presidency.

Some two hundred other men and women, interviewees for over two years, were indispensable progenitors. All served at the White House; some are still there. The author's prose cannot adequately express his debt to them, nor will the nation ever know how much it owes to their years of service in public life. A few are cited, but many asked to remain anonymous. All spent hours with the author, sharing unduplicable experiences and unique memories. A few reviewed whole chapters, helping to guarantee accuracy about an institution so often hidden in misperceptions.

The author makes a deep bow to former Presidents Dwight Eisenhower and Gerald Ford, who permitted personal interviews, and sends his appreciation also to the staffs of the Truman, Eisenhower, and Kennedy presidential libraries and to the Brookings Institution.

Like most of the author's undertakings, this book has been a family enterprise. Daughter Dawn Capron and son Glenn Patterson each combed through the drafts with an independent eye. Son-in-law James Capron contributed important technical advice. Chief reviewer and tough critic, herself an experienced public administrator, full and energetic partner in this adventure as in forty-four years of marriage, has been Shirley D. Patterson.

The author warmly admires the competence and cooperation of the staff of Basic Books, and especially the project editor, Charles Cavaliere.

In the end, the buck stops with the author; if there are mistakes, they are his. The views here are his as well, their roots growing from fourteen years of White House service and their tone from a respect for a place very few have known firsthand.

—Bradley H. Patterson, Jr.
Bethesda, Maryland
May 1988

The Ring of Power

Introduction

WHY a book about the White House staff?

Because to most Americans, the staff and its work are unknown. There are studies about individual presidents, the presidency, and presidential power, but it is the men and women on the president's personal staff who first channel that power, who shape it, focus it, and wield it on his instructions. Most of them are unknown because it is very properly in the president's interest to keep them out of sight. Yet while they are curtained off in the presidency, the staff are public servants, and in helping the nation's foremost officeholder they do the public's business. The public deserves an accounting, therefore, of why the modern staff is there and what they do.

The curtain that screens the staff from view is thick with surprising contrasts, false stereotypes, and even some paradoxes. For example:

- The staff is central to the most visible person in America, yet almost all of them are cloaked in anonymity.

- There is not a word about the White House staff in the Constitution and hardly a word about it in any statute. Members of the staff have zero authority in their own right, yet 100 percent of presidential authority passes through their hands.

- If asked about his White House staff, the first inclination of a president or a presidential candidate is to minimize its role, to proclaim his belief in "Cabinet government."

- His next inclination is to emphasize how few are his staff associates, when in fact they are numerous. Veterans of past administrations typically look at the staff of the present and cluck disapprovingly, "*We* did it with a third of that number." Stung with this criticism, a sitting president tries even harder to mask the size of his personal team.

- While vowing to cut back, presidents do just the opposite: they add to the menu of White House staff services. Once created, the innovations

turn out to be truly useful, and the added functions carry over into succeeding presidencies.

- From afar, the staff appears to be a group of broad-gauged generalists.
A closer look reveals a different scene: sixteen principal offices engaged in
specialized duties. Each staff unit tells all the others: enter its guarded turf
only with its permission.

- Citizens might assume that White House staff members are cut from
the same pattern, with shared views on issues of public policy. Wrong.
Differences of experience, age, sex, race, and especially party faction arc
across the White House staff. It is an intellectually electric environment,
which is to the president's benefit unless the internal arguments become
ad hominem or are fought out in public.

- In the midst of the coterie of his own assistants who serve entirely at
the president's sufferance are, however, two major players who are not
removable by the president: the vice president and the president's spouse.
Their large and energetic staffs on the one hand reflect that sense of inde-
pendence from the presidential group, yet on the other hand have to be
tied into the whole team, else their principals may be embarrassingly out
of step.

- However intense the specializations, varieties, and controversies
within the White House staff, such differences can be misleading. When
a major presidential initiative impends, each of those specialized offices has
to play its role *in coordination with* every other one. Does this happen effort-
lessly? No, and hell no. A tough, all-seeing chief of staff, operating precisely as the president wishes, is indispensable in guaranteeing the necessary teamwork.

- While the Congress can (and usually does) micromanage every other
corner of the Executive Branch, by contrast it generally leaves the immediate White House environment alone. Scandals bring both klieg lights and
shame on parts of the staff, but when they blow over, the traditional
comity continues; presidents don't tamper with the duties or numbers of
congressional staffs, and the Congress for the most part shows reciprocal
deference.

- The senior staff are partisans of the president. Their political commitment, however, cannot be allowed to override the intellectual integrity that
they must bring to their work. Contrary to public belief, at the White
House sycophants and crusaders, if tolerated briefly, are not long welcome.

- Supporting the seniors, and invisible to the public, are the three-
fourths of the staff who are nonpolitical professionals. They serve not just
the person but the office of the president; while aiding the president they

enhance the presidency. In fact, this sense of dual loyalty permeates the senior political staff as well.

• The popular image of the White House staff is that of a barrier, walling off the president from people of different opinions or from papers presenting unconventional ideas. Often it's just the opposite; the chief of staff must insist that dissenters be heard, and must challenge those memoranda that tell the president only the welcome news.

• Shrouded as they should be by anonymity, protected as they must be by executive privilege, and necessarily immersed in matters of delicacy and security, staffers nonetheless do their work surrounded by the surveillance of an expert and unremittingly skeptical press corps. Leaks are frequent; secrets are rare. Fortunately for this democracy, the White House is a glass house, with both light and heat streaming in.

• In the White House environs, the overriding ethical standard is so strict that it is unfair. The mere appearance of impropriety is itself the impropriety. A few White House incumbents, perhaps innocent in fact, keep running afoul of that elevated criterion.

• The most exasperating paradox of all arises from the statement of a principle half a century old. Adviser Louis Brownlow said to Franklin Roosevelt that White House assistants are never to be "interposed" between the president and his department heads. But daily, yea hourly, staff members fire questions, demand information, make pointed suggestions, and convey and interpret directives—about which the harried recipients may complain, "Usurpation!" What is often unknown to both the recipient and the public is that these staff actions are *generally and sometimes specifically at the president's own instructions.* This last and most pervasive "unknown" darkly colors the view that Cabinet, bureaucracy, Congress, press, and public have of the White House staff. They are alleged to be unaccountable, out of control, pushing their own agendas. That's almost always a false view. Let there be a White House staffer who more than once (or maybe only once) misinterprets or subverts the president's wishes, and he or she will be found on the sidewalk outside.

Shrouded in this miasma of misperceptions, the White House staff is but dimly understood. The Watergate and Iran-contra scandals have strengthened the popular inclination to paint the staff deep purple if not black, to view the place as crawling with scoundrels and miscreants.

But hold on, Mr. Public! That's a bum rap.

Of course there have been staffers who were heavy-handed, boorish, on the take, even criminal. Some in the White House ring have been corrupted

by the power they were permitted to wield. The nation therefore is rightfully skeptical about how that power is used, and has become—properly—
ever more watchful of whoever are the president's agents.

Greatly outnumbering the dozens whose misdeeds have sullied their
environs, however, are the hundreds who have served their presidents, and
the public, with brilliance and with self-effacing commitment. No apologies are due to the scoundrels, but the public's very watchfulness now calls
for better illumination of the White House as a whole.

The more light that is thrown on the presidential surroundings, the more
an essential fact is revealed: the White House staff is playing an expanded
and surprisingly underestimated role in the policy processes of American
government.

This role is so crucial that the time has now come to push aside the veil
of pretense about the White House staff, to own up that it is and will
continue to be a big, tough, strong outfit, quietly but fully reflecting the
strength which is indispensable in the presidency itself. A divided nation
at home and a bare-knuckled world abroad translate into the need for an
American president who can synchronize all the resources the Constitution
and the laws afford him for leadership and governance. Many of those
resources are in his Cabinet, but it is the White House staff who are his
synchronizers; neither he nor they should apologize that they are energetic
in this role. There should be less fidgeting, therefore, about the size of the
staff, and more attention to the unique core functions that it performs and
to how the whole group is managed and controlled.

The purpose of this book is to focus this attention, to demonstrate why
the modern White House staff exists, and to afford a close-up look at what
each element of the contemporary staff is and does. "White House staff"
means the immediate group serving the president (including the National
Security and Domestic Policy offices) and the supporting White House
units. The rest of the Executive Office (the Office of Management and
Budget, the science, trade, and economic advisers) are for other authors,
other volumes.

Examples, drawn from the presidencies of Truman through Reagan, are
included not in order to retell history but to illustrate the modern White
House at work. The book does not attempt to recite a history of the staff;
there are only minimal references to the White House prior to Truman's
time. The focus here is not the presidents but the staffs themselves; not
what presidents did but how the staff supported them. It is not an objective
of this book, furthermore, to judge the wisdom or success of any president's policies; many other critics and historians are taking up that chal-

lenge. The book is designed for a general public readership, although scholars and students will learn from it as well.

The author spent fourteen years on the White House staffs of three presidents and was close to the staff of a fourth. What follows is *not* a personal memoir nor a "kiss and tell" exposé. It is the professional view of a White House practitioner speaking up. Joining with him through two years of interviews are the voices of two hundred others who also have lived through the heat and tension, the frustration and exultation of White House service. Two presidents are among them.

The overall aim is to illumine public administration at the apex of government—to open up the White House gates and describe what is within.

PART I

The Cabinet Government That Isn't

Introduction to Part I

THE modern White House is now fifty years old, and so is the environment that sired it. The twin tumults of domestic economic upheaval and world conflict that formed the background for the beginnings of White House staff development under Franklin Roosevelt have evolved into a different postwar challenge for the eight presidents who followed him.

At home, the potential actions of government are now so variegated—1,074 separate domestic-assistance programs—that coordination among their Cabinet managers is indispensable to permit their full effect. Abroad, the days have vanished when America's national security resources—diplomatic, military, intelligence, economic—could be kept in separate compartments. Vanished with them are whatever boundary lines ever existed between domestic policies and foreign affairs, or between politics and policy. The president today acts in a gigantic theater-in-the-round; he is an omnidirectional executive.

The support institutions for the modern presidency have reflected these changed environments. The president himself is not only a leader in public policy, but now is chief coordinator of a potent and intricate Executive Branch—potent because its annual outlays have reached $1 trillion; intricate because the infinitesimal specialties and advocacies of contemporary society are now duplicated within the government's own ranks. The Cabinet's government has not grown in size, but it has exploded in complexity.

The purpose of these six opening chapters is to position the reader atop the White House gates, to survey first the tumultuous environment outside, and next the ways in which, within their perimeter, all the postwar presidents have strengthened their White House staffs to counterbalance that cacophony.

"Cabinet government"—each agency managing its own affairs with the president as general supervisor—is shibboleth, not reality. It is the White House staff, the author submits, that, closely under presidential direction, superintends policy development, governs the flow of his information, monitors the implementation of presidential initiatives, and oversees crisis management.

Readers are the jury. The case begins in the White House front yard.

CHAPTER 1

Outside the Gates:
A No-Consensus Society

A zeal for different opinions . . . an attach-
ment to different leaders ambitiously contending for preeminence and power . . . have
. . . divided mankind into parties, inflamed
them with mutual animosity, and rendered
them much more disposed to vex and op-
press each other than to cooperate for their
common good. —JAMES MADISON

BRING US TOGETHER!
—Sign held by a teenaged girl in Deshler,
Ohio, during the Nixon campaign of 1968

This pair of admonitions brackets the dilemma of the American presidency. At 1600 Pennsylvania Avenue, there sits a unitary executive in the
midst of a raucously plural nation. Behind the White House fence, the
presidential policy machinery is surrounded by noisy nationwide disagreement on every policy issue.

THE PLURAL MOSAIC

Today's presidents are charged with the "common defense" and "general
welfare" of 239,000,000 Americans and are directly accountable to the
116,000,000 of them who are registered voters—a moving, throbbing mosaic of needs, dreams, interests, and pressures. Nowhere in that mosaic,
however, is there today any pattern of consensus as to what the "common
defense" should be or how the resources for the "general welfare" are to
be allocated. Merely to describe the mosaic is to see the reason for the
policy tumult.

There are dozens of nationalities represented in America (over 14 million
are foreign-born). Twenty-nine million Americans are over sixty-five and
63,000,000 are under eighteen. There are 1,275,000 with a net worth of
over $500,000 and 32,370,000 below the poverty line. Of the total popula-

tion, 203,000,000 are white, 29,000,000 black; 19,000,000 are Hispanic and over 1,450,000 are native Americans and Eskimos. Cities of over 100,000 are home to 57,000,000; 56,000,000 live in nonmetropolitan places. Phi Beta Kappa membership numbers 350,000, while 9,000,000 adults over twenty-five only finished the eighth grade. In the workforce, 3,470,000 labor in farming, forestry, and fishing, 13,630,000 in the professions; 2,500,000 drive trucks and 1,720,000 are firemen, policemen, or guards. There are 2,100,000 federal civilian employees, 750,000 postal workers, and 13,500,000 who work for state and local governments.

There are 550,000 business firms with annual receipts of $1,000,000 or more, but there are 12,000,000 small businesses (having receipts under $100,000). Each year some 670,000 new businesses start up and 650,000 petition for bankruptcy.

Approximately 7,000,000 Americans are unemployed, 4,000,000 are veterans, 970,000 are in hospitals, and 4,315,000 aged three to twenty-one are handicapped. There are 37,000,000 Social Security recipients and uncounted millions who receive the benefits of 1,073 other separate federal economic- and social-assistance programs.

Thirty-one percent of voters have Republican preference, 39 percent Democratic, and 30 percent are unaffiliated.

From this phantasmagoria of varying individuals arises—as our Federalist designers explicitly anticipated—a correspondingly dizzy welter of views on every imaginable economic and social question. Many are not merely "views"; they are quarrels.

"So strong" wrote Madison, "is this propensity of mankind to fall into mutual animosities," that many disputes erupt into litigation. Twenty-eight million other-than-traffic cases are filed each year in state and local courts. More pertinent to the president's concern are the conflicts being brought to the federal courts; 325,000 cases were filed in the 94 district courts in 1986, 33,000 in the 13 courts of appeals and 5,100 in the Supreme Court. On any typical day, 101,000 lawsuits are pending against the federal government itself.

Another measure of the plural nature of our country is the number of centers of political power across the nation. The president looks beyond the White House gates at 50 state governments, under which have been created 3,041 county governments, 19,205 city governments, 16,691 townships, 14,692 school districts, and 29,487 special districts—a total of 83,166, to which must be added 506 recognized Indian tribes and groups.

THE INSTRUMENTS OF INFLUENCE

Two hundred forty million Americans and 83,672 subcenters of governing power: on issues of federal public policy, how do they weigh in? They organize.

In 1986 the Internal Revenue Service listed 929,415 tax-exempt organizations—an increase of nearly 43,000 in a single year. Among that throng, an observer atop the White House gatepost can count over 19,000 that, national in scope, were formed in part to press their views on the federal Executive and Legislative branches. That is *double* the number that existed in 1970; new ones form at the rate of 1,000 a year. These groups act through 11,000 Washington representatives—who are regular habitués of the White House neighborhood.

Armadas of conflicting interest groups form around every issue of public policy. So inflamed become the emotions in these policy conflicts that if the leaders of opposing organizations even sit down in the same room to discuss compromise, they risk being repudiated by their own memberships.

New technologies have increased the abilities of advocacy groups to escalate their pressures. The National League of Cities, for example, has an electronic mail system that in five seconds can send a message of alert to a thousand city halls—to galvanize them into making phone calls or writing complaints.

MIRRORS OF PLURALISM: CONGRESS AND THE LAWS

The Congress is the closest target for the cascade of pressures; both its structure and its acts mirror the society that elects it. Reflecting the plural concerns of the nation, the Congress today is subdivided into some 65 committees and 248 specialized subcommittees. Members also adhere to unofficial advocacy groupings such as the Iron and Steel Caucus, the Footwear Caucus, and the Wine Caucus—69 of them in all.

The raw material of public opinion inundates the Capitol: 277,000,000 letters and telegrams a year. If a controversial issue is pending, 1,000,000 letters a day will flood into the House alone.

The vast winnowing work of the legislative process need not be detailed here, but its products—the laws—are in two important respects a further measure of the factionalism that Madison long ago described.

There are statutes enacted at different times in our history that either imply or directly induce conflict among the Cabinet executives who have to carry them out. Taken separately, each such statute mandates actions that help a given sector of America's heterogeneous society—but collectively they mandate grief for the president who has to straddle their built-in contradictions.

A 1938 law, for instance, directs the secretary of agriculture to pay price supports to growers of tobacco. Yet a 1965 statute requires every cigarette pack to carry a health hazard warning by the surgeon general. Both laws are still in the federal code, bearing their inconsistent instructions.

A second and more common reflection of the nation's and the Congress' sharp policy differences is the ambiguity written into some of those laws. Vagueness of language masks deep splits in legislative purpose but permits the necessary compromises to be struck among the quarreling Senate or House partisans. The resulting enactments, with their key provisions fuzzy and subject to conflicting interpretations, are then deposited on the president's doorstep with the expectation that they will be "faithfully executed."

Former presidential assistant Henry Kissinger dissected the series of congressional enactments that, over four years, both authorized and limited U.S. aid to the Nicaraguan contras. He summed up: "Clearly Congress provided neither continuity nor criteria to which even the most scrupulous administration could orient itself. . . . Of such stuff are institutional crises made."[1] In struggling to interpret ambiguous statutes, the president and his cabinet colleagues are in fact wrestling with the original and still-persisting uncertainties of the nation itself, and of the Congress—which faithfully represents the country's factions and its conflicting priorities. A no-consensus society produces a no-consensus Congress.

MIRROR OF PLURALISM: THE EXECUTIVE BRANCH

The other target of the drumfire of bewilderingly conflicting public pressures is the president and his Executive Branch. The president being singular, however, is it not here that pluralism comes to an end? With executive power "vested in *a* president" does not the Article II language imply that in spite of faction and dispute elsewhere, the Executive Branch is to remain a unified place? Alexander Hamilton certainly thought so:

> . . . no favorable circumstances palliate or atone for the disadvantages of dissension in the executive department. Here they are pure and unmixed. There is no point at which they cease to operate. They serve to embarrass and weaken the execution of the plan or measure to which they relate, from the first step to the final conclusion of it. They constantly counteract those qualities in the executive which are the most necessary ingredients in its composition—vigor and expedition, and this without any counterbalancing good.[2]

But no. In this area, the Federalist's admonition has been ignored. Over the two centuries since Hamilton wrote, the executive establishment has developed in contradiction to his warning.

The morning after inauguration, the newly elected presidents of 1989 and of the years to come will peer out over the White House fence at the landscape of the Executive Branch over which they will preside. What will they see out there? Not a unity, but rather a vast plurality.

Sixty-six permanent, full-time agencies will be in view. The president must set thirty-six of them apart, since as regulatory commissions (the Federal Reserve Board, for instance) or independent, multi-headed bodies (like the Tennessee Valley Authority), they are insulated from White House intervention in their decision-making.

That leaves thirty departments and agencies. Through the appointment and removal power and by exercising personal leadership, the president will have a principal influence over these thirty institutions. As he looks at them on January 21—to gauge that future influence—what does he notice?

They have the status of age. The State, Treasury, and War Departments (the last now part of the Defense establishment) and the Office of the Attorney General go back to the beginnings of the Republic. Constituent pieces of even the "new" departments have a history: the Office of Education began in 1867, the atomic energy part of the Department of Energy in 1946.

The organic statutes of these agencies convey more than authority— they radiate a sense of mission. "Leave [the national parks] . . . unimpaired for the enjoyment of future generations," the Park Service was mandated back in 1916. The Environmental Protection Agency is instructed to try to "create and maintain conditions under which man and nature can exist in productive harmony and . . . fulfil the responsibilities of each generation as trustee of the environment for succeeding generations."

For agency after agency, age and mission combine to create a pervasive culture of commitment. In the Forest Service, begun in 1905, careerists proudly claim that they wear "green underwear." In the Park Service, the password is "green blood" and there are now Park Service rangers who are the grandchildren of rangers. A retired superintendent wrote, "The programs of the National Park Service are our faith and heritage, our trust and my task."[3]

New classes of Foreign Service officers are sworn in under the portrait of Benjamin Franklin. Everyone walking into the diplomatic entrance of the Department of State sees the two large wall plaques with the 152 names of employees who lost their lives on duty.

Graven into the white marble right wall of the CIA's foyer are fifty-three stars commemorating the men and women of that agency killed in action, and into the left wall a passage from the Bible: "For ye shall know the truth and the truth shall make you free." President Eisenhower laid the cornerstone of that building in 1959, saying of the CIA's responsibilities, "No task could be more important."

The Pentagon has its Alcove of Heroes where the winners of the Congressional Medal of Honor are listed. The Army battle flag there bears 168 campaign streamers—most recently that of Grenada, but going back to Yorktown.

In Colorado Springs, the Air Force starts early to convey its institutional pride: at lunchtime the cadets form up into forty-two squadrons and, with the chapel and the Rocky Mountains towering overhead, march into the dining hall, past the colors, in step with the playing of the "Air Force Hymn." In the principal classrooms, Air Force generals' pictures are on the walls, each with the implied message "Emulate me!"

Throughout the entire Executive Branch, agencies and services, military and civilian alike, are infused with that sense of history, mission, and commitment. Award and retirement ceremonies reinforce the pride and dedication that motivate the great majority of the nation's public employees. Most of the presidents themselves help generate that dedication; they are incredibly well served by the men and women who work with such enthusiasm.

There is only a thin line, however, between loyalty and parochialism. Former Marine Commandant P. X. Kelley, referring to the need (emphasized by many presidents) to promote joint service capabilities and to damp down interservice rivalry, said, "Asking a man to be as loyal to the other services as he is to his own is like asking him to be as loyal to his girlfriends as he is to his wife."[4]

The president will also notice the twenty-four different and separate personnel systems of the Executive Branch that help to put iron cladding on parochialism. These individual administrative cages have been stuck into place as if Article II had never been written. Except for the White House staff, there is no such thing as a presidential service. Even the president's political appointees belong to the departments, and only departments hire, evaluate, promote, or fire the 2.1 million civilian and 2.1 million military personnel. The Senior Executive Service claims to facilitate flexible use of top civil servants, but the president has no role in this and most of the transfer assignments are within the walls of the respective agencies. Ask a federal employee, "For whom do you work?" and the answer will always be "the Bureau of Land Management" or "the FBI" or "for the IRS" or "the Navy." It is never "I work for the president."

Looking even more closely at the Executive Branch landscape, a president would see *inside* each department a mind-boggling array of specialized bureaus, divisions, and units—an alphabet soup of acronyms. The Department of Health and Human Services, for example, lists 3,137 of them in its telephone directory.

This is hardly surprising. These micro-offices of the executive branch are, like the Congress in its own structure, a mirror of the demographic and social microvariety of the whole country. In fact, that's how they got started. Over two centuries, needs perceived strongly enough became laws, laws authorized money, money paid for public employees, personnel were organized into bureaus or minipieces of bureaus, and the work of the government proceeded, often under the attentive eyes of the original advocates who publicized the need in the first place.

The federal program to identify and assist outdoor recreation trails is an example of this process. Needled by public-spirited advocates, Congress expressed an official concern in 1958 and created a study commission. Following the commission's 1962 report, a Bureau of Outdoor Recreation was established in the Department of the Interior. In 1965 the president proposed "a national system of trails," and in 1966 the bureau produced a response: "Trails for America." The Congress two years later created a National Trails System, which now consists of 8 national scenic trails, 7 national historic trails, and 770 national recreation trails. A president looking closely at the Department of the Interior will find several Trails desks in the National Park Service, and the White House Mail Room may be hearing from the 22 national and 213 state and local organizations keenly interested in this one specific area of public policy. Among the 213 are the Western Upper Peninsula Snowmobile Association, the Texas Bicycling Committee, the Colorado Horse Council, the Alaska Motorcycle-Racing Association, the Pocatello Nordic Ski Association, the Minnesota Rivers

Outing Club, the Arizona Historical Society, the Nantahala Hiking Club, and the Wyeast Climbers. (From their very names, one realizes that the letters from these outfits will give the president or the Park Service totally conflicting advice about what kinds of trails should be built and how they should be used.)

Multiply this example by perhaps twenty thousand and the aforesaid Executive Branch landscape is revealed in its almost incomprehensible variety.

Unlike a landscape, however, the president's governmental institutions do not just sit still on the White House perimeter. Federal departments and agencies move, throb, vibrate.

Impelled by eloquent statutory injunctions, turned on by the policy traditions of decades, stung by congressional surveillance, or fired up by advocacy groups, officials in government are usually the very opposite of the stereotypical "do-nothing bureaucrats." They want to attack the nation's problems; they press for the resources to move ahead with their mandates. "We are the 'punta de la lanza,' " boasted the early Peace Corps staffers, and from Director Sargent Shriver to the lowliest typist, they glowed with zeal.

Whether a venerable Forest Service or a new Peace Corps, the agencies in the president's own Executive Branch are driven by strong and independent traditions. For each, its single constitutional duty is to help the president, but its varied program mandates impel it in directions often centrifugal to White House priorities. Through patronage and the use of White House staff (detailed in succeeding chapters), the president has some, but only limited, control over that Cabinet landscape.

THE PLURALIST PLANET

There is of course one circle of institutions on the Washington scene where the president's constitutional reach is zero. The United States recognizes some 150 foreign nations. All of them have embassies in Washington and the United States is represented in their capitals reciprocally. Foreign countries are unique because they are sovereign. Their governments' decision-making is subject to persuasion, bargaining, and even pressure. In the absence of conquest, however, their policies are their own; neither the U.S. president nor the Congress can command them.

The 150 nonetheless coexist in a world community where military, economic, and environmental challenges require multinational responses. U.S. attack-warning systems depend on bases in Greenland and the United Kingdom. Shutting off the drug traffic will be impossible without the cooperation of Latin American and Asian governments. Reducing U.S. unemployment depends on foreign consumers taking imports from us; American farm prosperity relies on other nations lowering barriers to trade.

Much of a president's so-called domestic agenda is in reality a menu for persuasion of sovereign governments elsewhere in the world. If they won't bend, he can't achieve some of his own political goals at home. Each of the 150, however, has its own priorities and desires, about which the American president and his associates must bargain.

THE WARFARE OF WASHINGTON

The landscape outside the White House fence is thus no pastoral scene, but a battlefield. It is a war zone. Long-range institutional artillery sends shells screaming in from state and local governments. Missile batteries fire throughout the Capitol. The Big Berthas of the judiciary alternate with grenades hurled from advocacy groups. Every Cabinet agency bristles with rocket launchers; mines are buried along Embassy Row. Many of the projectiles are smoke and chaff, and policy battles are sometimes clouded with the poison gas of personal vindictiveness.

Strange battlefield, though! The lines of combat shift. Alliances are formed and disband, allegiances constantly switch; hundreds of different banners are unfurled and bugles sound their clarions against an ever-changing range of objectives. Surprise attack is almost unknown; enemies today are friends tomorrow. Perhaps the most vital pieces of military equipment in the landscape are not guns but binoculars: every unit is watching every other one. Thousands of spotting scopes peer to see who is accumulating too much power, or if anyone is stepping outside of pre-ordained trenches.

One last feature of the field: it is illuminated day and night. Star shells and flares from the nation's—the world's—television and print media throw a rude light across every meadow—into bedroom and Cabinet room alike. There are practically no secrets; information is as all-permeating as the smoke in the air, and there may be more spies afoot than soldiers. There are occasional victories and sometimes defeats; more often there are merely truces and compromises—which only last until new forces have been mustered to fight again.

Secretary of State George Shultz described this war zone to the Congress recently: "Nothing ever gets settled in this town. It's not like running a company or even a university. It's a seething debating society in which the debate never stops, in which people never give up, including me, and that's the atmosphere in which you administer."[5]

The struggles never end—precisely as the writers of our Constitution foresaw. This policy warfare of a heterogeneous, free society pauses only momentarily while a new president marches for the first time through the White House gates. It then resumes, and as the new chief executive looks back over his shoulder, he may begin reflecting about that "Cabinet government" which he admired and whether he should strengthen his own resources within his own perimeter.

BRING US TOGETHER?

Outside the White House fence are a kaleidoscopic country, a judiciary swamped with conflicts, a narrowly divided Congress, an Executive Branch of 20,000 laws and pieces, 19,000 interest groups, and 150 independent nations—the lot of them in an unending and naked debate about resources and priorities. Inside is a president feeling the full force of all those needs, dreams, interests, and pressures—and a warrior himself ready for battle.

BRING US TOGETHER! urged the little girl in Deshler, Ohio—but Madison and Hamilton make us wonder if the president can do it.

CHAPTER 2

The Gates Open:
Invitation to the Cabinet

At the beginning, I decided to meet frequently with my entire Cabinet, and scheduled two-hour sessions every Monday
morning. These meetings gave all of us a
chance to . . . develop consistent policies. . . .   —JIMMY CARTER

Cabinet members are vice presidents in
charge of spending, and as such they are the
natural enemies of the President.
                    —CHARLES G. DAWES
                    First director of the
                    Bureau of the Budget

The president's menu on the morning after his inauguration is more than
melon and toast: it is the list of issues that await him on his desk in the
Oval Office. In the platform, in the acceptance oration at the convention,
in a hundred campaign speeches, and still echoing from the inaugural
address, goals have been set and promises made. Arms control, the trade
deficit, civil rights, economic health, the eradication of illegal drugs, environmental safeguards, a dozen others: the gravity of these issues is outweighed only by the realization that in just four short years the same
questions will be first on the presidential reelection examination. Now the
president searches for the swiftest and most efficient way to address these
issues—to mobilize the brainpower and resources of his executive branch
to help him with his own creative initiatives.

In December, as president-elect, he would have gone through the typical
ritual: a television spectacular introducing the new Cabinet. He would
have made the traditional pledge: "I shall rely tremendously on my Cabinet and will not permit any of my tiny group of White House officials to
intervene between these department heads and me!"

Suddenly, the president has that menu of momentous issues in his right
hand, and in his left an organization chart of those same Cabinet departments. A sobering discovery: there is no correspondence. Not a one of his
top-priority problems fits within any single box on the diagram. None can
be confined inside the old walls of an existing agency. To no one Cabinet
officer can the chief executive point a finger and say: "The trade deficit—

you, Secretary Smith, are responsible for attacking that problem. I believe in delegation and this assignment is yours. You run with it." If Smith were, for example, the secretary of commerce, he or she would run only ten yards with the trade-deficit football before crossing into the jurisdictions of State, Defense, Treasury, Labor, Agriculture, Transportation, Energy, the CIA, the Export-Import Bank, the International Trade Commission, the Council of Economic Advisers, the national security affairs staff, the Office of Management and Budget, and the U.S. trade representative. The expertise of every one of those institutions will need to be mined, their analyses and recommendations solicited.

Being peers, none of these Cabinet-level officers will defer to Secretary Smith, few of them will even agree on the questions to be studied, and most of them will come up with different sets of facts. Several of them will secretly feel that they, rather than Smith, should have been given the lead in the first place.

Here is the earliest conundrum which faces modern presidents: how to organize for analysis, for decision, and for action when the range of cross-cutting issues he faces is so thoroughly at odds with the rigid structures of his Executive Branch?

The conundrum has four possible solutions: reorganize the structures, create supersecretaries, use Cabinet meetings, or rely on option papers.

REORGANIZE

If presidential issue areas keep crossing departmental boundaries, why not change the boundary lines? "Trade" being such an interagency policy puzzle, create a Department of Trade, sweep those other agencies' trade-related functions into the new department—and *then* the president can point to one Cabinet officer and say: "You run with that ball."

This choice seems so elemental that a president is at first tempted to try it. Perhaps he has even made campaign promises to do so. As Joseph Califano explained:

> If he can reshape the government departments and agencies into sensible functional organizations, then he will have gone a long way toward consolidating his power over the executive branch and providing himself with department heads who can truly and fairly be held responsible for program areas, like manpower training or the development of natural resources.[1]

President Nixon put it this way:

> . . . the executive branch of the government should be organized around basic goals. Instead of grouping activities by narrow subjects or by limited constituencies, we should organize them around the great purposes of government in modern society. For only when a department is set up to achieve a given set of purposes, can we effectively hold that department accountable for achieving them. Only when the responsibility for realizing basic objectives is clearly focused in a specific governmental unit, can we reasonably hope that those objectives will be realized.[2]

"Human Resources," "Community Development," "Economic Affairs," "Natural Resources"—advisers to Lyndon Johnson, Richard Nixon, and Jimmy Carter all proposed or seriously considered unscrambling the older agencies and resorting them into new, broad-function departments.

Pluralist opposition, however, has defeated all such initiatives. The Congress and its subcommittees, the affected bureaus and their staffs, the advocacy groups, join hands and drown such menacing presidential ideas in a swamp of parochial goo. Johnson's "Department of Labor and Commerce" never got to hearings; Nixon's recommendations went nowhere in the Congress. The Senate Governmental Affairs Committee forced Carter's reorganization brain trust to promise that they wouldn't even come near the Congress with a "Department of Natural Resources" proposal or "anything resembling it."

An easier reorganization technique is to establish new agencies or to upgrade old bureaus into *additional* departments. Create a Peace Corps, or an Office of Economic Opportunity; remake a Housing and Home Finance Agency into a Department of Housing and Urban Development, a Federal Energy Administration into a Department of Energy; elevate an Office of Education or the Veterans Administration to Cabinet status. Such actions are easier because they involve a minimum remodeling of older agencies and no demolition of Cabinet-level skyscrapers.

By increasing the number of the departments, however, what is a president really doing? He may indeed be counting political gains, but he is making his chief executiveship harder. Instead of simplifying the management of his Executive Branch, he is adding to his own coordination burdens. The larger his Cabinet is, the more problems are raised for the White House itself to resolve.

In the cool light of the postinaugural morning, therefore, and irrespective of presidential campaign promises, thoroughgoing Cabinet-level reorganization will be discovered to be an option not worth the effort. It is his own office, and not the Cabinet, which must be strengthened. Califano concluded:

> Inevitably, Republican or Democrat, conservative or liberal, [the president] will perceive a substantial and powerful White House staff as the best means of exercising presidential power to achieve his public policy objectives and render responsive the erratically organized executive branch over which he presides.[3]

But wait. There are—apparently—three more choices.

CREATE SUPERSECRETARIES

Although President Nixon's 1971 proposals to create four new super-departments were never enacted, he still believed that his Cabinet agencies should be regrouped into more rational structures. Just before his second term started, Nixon created by fiat what the Congress would not give him in law. He established three new counselors to the president: for natural resources, human resources, and community development. The three new supersecretaries were in effect to spend half of each day in the White House and the other half back in their respective departments. Each was to chair a cabinet committee; suites were reserved for them in the Executive Office Building. No statutory reorganization was needed; three existing Cabinet officers were given White House titles, new crosscutting responsibilities, and presidential office space.

Are supersecretaries, half White House, half Cabinet, the answer to the enduring conundrum?

In the domestic area, the nation will have to wait longer to find out; the supersecretary experiment ended after four months when Chief of Staff H. R. (Bob) Haldeman and domestic policy head John Ehrlichman resigned in April as the Watergate scandal erupted. The obvious pitfalls are the distinctions which the supersecretary designation created within the Cabinet; some were less equal than others. The secretaries of commerce, labor, and transportation inevitably appeared as Cabinet members second-class.

The experiment did continue in national security affairs. Kissinger was named secretary of state and wore both State and White House hats for two years. He reflects: "It did not work. . . . For two years I was exposed to the charge that I had an unfair predominance over the policymaking process. . . . My dual position was, in fact, a handicap and a vulnerability."[4]

President Ford ended the last trial of the supersecretary idea and put the responsibilities of being national security assistant back into full-time White House hands in 1975.

CALL A CABINET MEETING

If the big items on the president's policy agenda cut across so many immutable jurisdictions, the president has a method for getting all that advice simultaneously—and having a fruitful dialogue at the same time. He can convene the Cabinet.

Before sending out the first meeting notice, however, the president may stop to consider: as he turns on the lights in the Cabinet Room, what will come in the door? Answer: a very divisive bunch.

No law specifies, but political tradition now mandates that the Cabinet must be heterogeneous. No longer may they all be of one sex, or one race or ethnic group.[5] They cannot be from one state nor of one religious faith. Dissimilar professions must be represented and, most important, the different factions of the party. Independents, occasionally even a person of the other party, may be included.

One of the predictors of Cabinet diversity is the convention at which the president was nominated. As they did in the primaries, so on that floor, faction battles faction and wounds are opened that require postelection suturing. The new Cabinet is the great first-aid station.

Eisenhower fought Taft in 1952, but when he became president, he promptly included four men from the Taft wing of the party (Weeks, Humphrey, Benson, and Summerfield) in his Cabinet. Many were the policy issues during Eisenhower Cabinet meetings that divided the secretaries along that original fault line. Party factionalism, however, is only one of the centrifugal forces that are at work around the Cabinet table. Even wider cleavages grow out of the statutory and departmental splits described in chapter 1.

What kind of arms control, how vigorous an affirmative-action effort, energy development versus environmental protection: on all those presidential issues the department heads will—expectedly and appropriately— have sharply differing views. Turf is often involved as well as policy; personality clashes are a third incendiary ingredient.

Surrounded by his Cabinet, the president is surrounded by built-in dissension. To put them all in one room together—to hold regular meetings—is this something a president relishes? To some presidents, confrontational debate is invigorating and in their view the advantages of Cabinet meetings outweigh the costs of investing presidential time and energy. This was Eisenhower's judgment, especially in his first six years.

Ike had 236 formal sessions of his full Cabinet, with 1,236 matters (some recurrent) covered in those meetings. Between the fall of 1954 (when a more systematic support arrangement was initiated) and January of 1961, 112 formal Cabinet papers were distributed for discussion and decision; 72 papers were circulated in a separate Information Series. One hundred sixty records of action were written up, approved by the president, and then dispatched to all the Cabinet members.

Why are Cabinet meetings useful to a president like Eisenhower? There are three reasons: for coordination, to elicit broad advice, and for team-building.

First, the Cabinet can perform the direct coordination role. The agendas of the Eisenhower years included subjects that cut across departmental interests, that had both foreign and domestic import and that required consideration from many if not all of the secretaries: broad economic and budget-policy questions; minerals issues, including stockpiling; user charges; employee loyalty/security programs; energy policy; the overall farm program, including the disposal of agricultural surpluses; emergency continuity of government; civil rights issues; problems of federal-state-local relations.

Second, Cabinet meetings give the secretaries the opportunity to doff their departmental hats and speak up from their own wide-ranging personal experience. In the case of men and women like George Shultz, Oveta Culp Hobby, Elliot Richardson, Caspar Weinberger, Arthur Flemming, and John Gardner, there is hardly any area of public policy, social or economic, at home or abroad, in which they have not been involved. The Cabinet has included former senators, business executives, governors, religious leaders. Christian Herter, for instance, was a valuable voice at Eisenhower Cabinet meetings not just because he was secretary of state but because he had also been governor of Massachusetts.

Cabinet members can bring broad as well as narrow perspectives to the president and in the privacy of the Cabinet Room are able to shed their departmental robes and give statesmanlike advice.[6]

The third value of Cabinet meetings is the environment of teamwork that those frequent sessions with the president can engender. When they all meet, no one is left out, no one can claim, "I wasn't consulted." There is no enviously regarded "inner circle" and even non-Cabinet agency heads are invited ad hoc. They argue back and forth, they see the president reflecting, hear him ask questions, have the chance for explanation or rebuttal. The Eisenhower style was then to make his decision in front of the whole group. He would do more than that: he would give his reasons, explain his priorities, share his convictions, always emphatic, often emotional, sometimes profane. After that kind of meeting, and regardless of whether they had won or lost an argument, Cabinet members would leave the room much closer to a common understanding of what their president was trying to accomplish. Their natural centrifugal tendencies were not eliminated, but they were diminished. Those Friday mornings helped breed a respectful collegiality.

No president in history has used his full Cabinet so assiduously and in such a systematic fashion. Was not this, then, the "Cabinet government" so often promised? It was not. At three of its key stages—the agenda, the record of action, and the follow-up, Eisenhower's cabinet system was a White House staff production.

The Agenda

The Cabinet Secretariat—a unit of the White House staff instituted as such in the fall of 1954—acted as a radar set, constantly scanning what was going on among its staff colleagues, at the departments, in the press, the Congress, the states. The deputy Cabinet secretary (the author) sat in on meetings of interagency committees, testing the ripeness of their work. Recommendations would then go to the chief of staff (Sherman Adams, later Wilton Persons) and it was he who set the Cabinet agenda. Adams and Persons may have checked with the president on occasion, but not often. Their judgments were on the mark and their score was perfect; not once in the author's memory did Eisenhower open his Cabinet meeting book and complain, "What is this doing here?"

The secretaries themselves were often reluctant, sometimes resentful, at being asked to expose their cherished ideas to kibitzing from their colleagues; they would have preferred to carry their proposals directly into the Oval Office. Eisenhower would tolerate no end runs, however; Adams and Persons knew when to insist, when to accede.

In a study in February of 1960 of thirty-six Cabinet agendas during 1958–60, the secretariat analyzed the 119 items:

- 15 came from the president himself.
- 16 originated in the Executive Office.
- 4 were proposals by White House staff colleagues.
- 1 came from the vice president.

- 69 "required strong initial effort by the Cabinet Secretariat."
- Only 14 could be attributed as coming from departmental initiatives (2 major, 7 secondary, and 5 rather trivial matters).[7]

The Cabinet agenda is a White House staff product—though it inevitably meets the test of relevance to the president.

The Record of Action

The author remembers Secretary of State Dean Acheson coming back from Truman Cabinet meetings and calling in his stenographer to give her the "Cabinet dictation."

Letting the secretary of state bear the task of being the recorder was an improper imposition on his time—yet if all eight secretaries had been as conscientious, there would have been eight different versions of what had happened.

In Eisenhower's time, while one staff officer wrote up full Cabinet minutes for the president's private use, the Cabinet Secretariat drafted a concise record of action immediately after the meeting. The draft might be checked for accuracy with the Cabinet officer most concerned; it was then sent in to the president. When it emerged with the "D.E." inscribed, the record of action was reproduced and circulated in one or two copies to each Cabinet member.

The record was always supplemented by oral debriefings—done in the White House by the staff. Each secretary had designated a trusted executive assistant; the whole group of them would be convened in the same Cabinet Room as soon as the Cabinet itself had adjourned. The Cabinet secretary and his deputy, with good shorthand notes and events fresh in their minds, replayed the discussion, usually omitting the identities of the Cabinet protagonists but always ensuring that the president's intentions and emphases were vividly transmitted.

The practice of oral debriefings stopped with Eisenhower, and each president has used the Cabinet or subcommittees thereof in a different way. What is *not* different, however, is that for thirty-five years now the White House staff has tightly controlled the preparation of whatever records are made of presidential decisions: Cabinet, National Security Council, Kennedy's Executive Committee, LBJ's Tuesday Lunches, Nixon's Urban Affairs Council, Ford's Economic Policy Board, Carter's Friday Presidential Breakfasts, and Reagan's Cabinet Councils. The preparation of the action record of formal presidential meetings is centralized, not delegated. The president makes the decision and approves the record (the two acts often being combined) but it is the White House staff which does the drafting.

The Follow-up

Just after Ike's election, Truman mused: "He'll sit here and he'll say, 'Do this! Do that!' *And nothing will happen.* Poor Ike—it won't be a bit like the Army. He'll find it very frustrating."[8] Setting aside the testiness of the one president for his successor, the issue here is: what happens *after* the action assignments are made?

Truman's jibe was improvident. As president, he himself had initiated a follow-up system for his national security decisions, and in 1948 he appointed a special committee of the National Security Council to oversee compliance—through his NSC executive secretary. Eisenhower, no novice in administration, went far beyond Truman in the sophistication of a tracking arrangement, especially on Cabinet matters.

The secretariat periodically prepared a Cabinet Action Status Report, listing for each department all of the presidential actions during the reporting period. Accompanying every assignment was a description of what had been accomplished. The Action Status Report was circulated in the Information Series to all the Cabinet members and also listed on the agenda. One such report was thirty-three pages long and listed 110 items. At the Cabinet meeting of April 18, 1958, the president looked over the Status Report and commented:

> I want to put in a word behind that. Not many of you had the opportunity as I did to be involved with the Cabinet meetings of the former Administration. [They] were the darndest bores you ever saw. . . .
>
> One of the great crosses that Secretary Forrestal had to bear was his effort to get a secretariat organized in the White House—and the White House staff kicked him clear out of the building on it. He tried again and again and again. Defense never knew the action status of any Cabinet matter—except by getting up a special order, by going in to the President and making him sign a specific piece of paper.
>
> We have made a great amount of progress. This shows how wise it is to be careful about looking through this Report.[9]

Several of the Status Reports were sent to Adams or Persons covered by a private memorandum entitled "Lagging Compliance with Cabinet Actions." Such a seven-page memo was delivered to Adams on April 8, 1958, with eight lapses identified. The margins bear the terse "S.A." notations of his telephone calls to the foot-draggers.[10]

Convening the Cabinet, then, can be merely to keep tradition warm, or the president may genuinely wish to use his departmental secretaries in a systematic way. Eisenhower chose the latter option. Every chief executive will insist on the freedom to make that choice, nor should any statute ever shrink the president's flexibility.

Reagan began his presidency by creating five (later seven) Cabinet Councils, each of which was served by an executive secretary. Reagan's first domestic affairs assistant, Martin Anderson, describes these officers:

> They were White House staff members and carried the title of either senior policy adviser or special assistant to the president for policy development. In addition I named one or two other White House staff members to serve as members of each cabinet council secretariat. . . . The executive secretaries were a superb control and monitoring instrument. . . . they met regularly with me in my office to discuss the current and future work of the councils. . . . The result was a knowledgeable White House staff with tight control of the domestic policy agenda.[11]

Eisenhower, Ford, and Reagan are the three presidents who most used Cabinet or Cabinet committee systems for advice on policy issues. Effective Cabinet advisory arrangements, however, mean close and detailed management by the president's personal staff. While the president is always the decision-maker, opening up the gates and calling in the Cabinet also means gearing up the White House staff to a quiet but quintessential role.

Some presidents are turned off—even appalled—at the prospect of sitting for hours trying to resolve delicate issues in a Cabinet "town meeting." Theodore Sorensen quotes Kennedy as believing

> general Cabinet meetings . . . to be unnecessary and involve a waste of time. . . . All these problems Cabinet officers deal with are very specialized . . . we don't have a general meeting. There really isn't much use spending a morning talking about the Post Office budget and tying up Secretary Freeman, who has agriculture responsibilities. . . . I think we will find the Cabinet perhaps more important than it has ever been but Cabinet meetings not as important.[12]

There is one very good reason for eschewing group discussion: the danger that eloquence and force of personality can tilt both the dialogue and the decision. Secretary of the Treasury George Humphrey would deliver emphatic harangues at Eisenhower Cabinet meetings, but Ike would masterfully untilt the debate by remonstrating: "Now, George . . ."

Herbert Stein, Ford's chairman of the Council of Economic Advisers, remembers another treasury secretary:

> . . . it's better if everybody writes a paper than if everybody gets in a room together with the President. John [Connally] will always win if he's in a room

with the President. But if everybody writes a paper he has a fighting chance. The point is that there is a power of personality over logic which you have to guard against or at least balance off by a certain amount of dry paperwriting.[13]

Even though he had attended the Eisenhower Cabinet meetings and had been (to the author's personal knowledge) a lively and influential participant, as president, Nixon did not want to repeat that experiment:

> I had attended hundreds of Cabinet meetings as Vice President, and I felt that most of them were unnecessary and boring. On the few issues that cut across all departments, such as the economy, group discussions would sometimes be informative. But the day had long since passed when it was useful to take an hour and a half to have the Secretary of Defense and the Secretary of State discuss the Secretary of Transportation's new highway proposal. Therefore I wanted to keep the Cabinet meetings in my administration to a minimum.[14]

COMMISSION AN OPTION PAPER

The alternative method of collecting policy advice from many agencies on a single subject is to prepare a comprehensive written memorandum. If half a dozen departments are affected and have expertise that should be contributed or opinions the president should read, the preferred device is one consolidated product. In every presidency, there are hundreds of such papers compiled.

How is a single, evenly balanced memorandum to be produced from among a group of independent, contesting agencies? If the issue is sensitive and the stakes are high (almost certainly the case, or the matter would not be at the president's doorstep) no one of the contending Cabinet departments will trust any of the others to be objective. The term "consolidation" implies—requires—a central managing agent that has the president's policy and political concerns in mind. There is one. It is central. It is the White House staff.

The manager of an option-paper decision process has a three-fold duty: to set out the issues, describe the conflicting views, and report the decision.

Framing the Issues

Declared one White House staffer: "Washington is full of answers. The president's problem is: *'What are the questions?'* " It is his staff that poses them.

President Carter decided in December of 1977 that the production of nonfuel minerals such as cobalt, aluminum, and copper needed policy review. His domestic affairs chief, Stuart Eizenstat dispatched an "Issue Definition Memorandum" to fourteen department and agency heads. Speaking for the president, Eizenstat set the agenda for the study and specified the questions, for example:

> Whether U. S. reserves, production capacities, and inventories are adequate to deal with possible supply/price interruptions, or with the economic and social consequences of such disruptions; . . .
>   Whether current government regulations adequately protect the environment, health and safety while not unduly affecting the supply and price of minerals.[15]

Specific assignments were made to several of the departments and agencies (State, Treasury, Commerce, the National Science Foundation); schedules and deadlines were established. While the memorandum was signed "Stu," its full text had been approved by the president.

The terminology may change with the years (Kissinger called his "NSSMs"—national security study memoranda), but the task does not vary. Having a single interrogator at the White House means that there will be just one set—not several conflicting varieties—of questions propounded. However much the interrogatories may be masked by White House staffers' own signatures or telephone calls, the questions are presidential.

Consolidating Conflicting Views

Policy conflicts come in all sizes.

Should women be admitted to the Naval and Air Force academies? In 1970, Deputy Secretary of Defense William Clements said "No!" while White House counselor Anne Armstrong insisted "Yes." A ten-page option paper summed up the choices for the president.

Should federal programs for Indians be contracted out to tribal governments themselves to manage? Interior and HEW recommended it; the Office of Management and Budget (OMB) was opposed. A twenty-two-page memorandum laid out this issue (and nineteen others); the result was a presidential message to the Congress.

What should President Nixon's position be on the Equal Rights Amendment? The Citizens Advisory Council on the Status of Women strongly pushed for support; Assistant Attorney General (now Chief Justice) William Rehnquist argued that the ERA "will in fact hasten the dissolution of the family." An eight-page discussion put the question to the president.

Should President Reagan engage in a stricter regulatory effort and commit more funds to curb acid rain? OMB said no, other agencies urged an affirmative answer. A working group assembled a thirteen-page paper.

Such is the daily flow into the president's in-box.

Though raised to rarefied levels, there is nothing sterile about these issues. They reek with money, power, turf, and politics. Clinging to all of them is the smell of battle—the warfare of Washington already portrayed.

Will one protagonist trust any of the others to describe the dispute in his terms alone and have that be the definitive paper to the president? No. Too much is at stake; personalities and emotions as well as ideas.

Is there a master draftsman in OMB or in one of the departments who could rise above the struggle? Why is it the White House staff that writes the final version of the option paper—as they did in the four cases just mentioned?

From different presidencies former White House staffers themselves speak (or are described) with impressive similarity:

> [President Ford] wants to have around him a few people who have the responsibility to see these problems from *his* viewpoint. Therefore, I think it's inevitable, however you organize, that there will be a White House staff with some kind of second guessing of . . . the Cabinet members. Cabinet members don't act presidential. . . .[16]

> Were we [the Kennedy staff] performing political functions? Of course we were, from beginning to end. The presidency is a political office. I don't make any apology for that. It's intended to be a political office, and the President's senior staff must keep politics in mind at all times. I'm talking about politics in its broadest sense, not necessarily partisan or even presidential politics, but politics in sense of bearing in mind how far out in front of the country you can move.[17]

> ". . . he [Stuart Eizenstat] has a pervasive influence on every major White House policy proposal, both as interagency coordinator and as presidential adviser. In this dual capacity, he wields more authority and enjoys a closer relationship with Carter than does any domestic Cabinet secretary. . . . 'Carter generally follows his advice because he knows that *Stu is looking after his interests*' said a Domestic Policy Staff member.[18]

Reagan senior staff adviser Edwin Harper summed it up: "Cabinet members are not in a position to make the *trade-offs* which have to be made in drawing up priorities. Some departments gain or win and some lose. . . . And you need creative policy people to do this, not "manager" people or "numbers" people or "keepers of the score."[19]

The views and memoranda of Cabinet officers are almost never kept from the president, but if there is a complicated, crosscutting issue on the table, such contributions are usually attachments in a consolidated package that has the White House staffer's memorandum on top.

Honest broker? Yes, but more. Senior White House staff are especially capable of making sure that the policy package contains what Harper considers indispensable: "creative judgment—creative policy ideas which are in line with the president's policy thinking."

Reporting the Decision

In the late afternoon of March 11, 1971, there was a tense gathering in John Ehrlichman's White House office. The subject was in effect the future of the forty-ninth state. The discovery of oil on the North Slope and the need to build the pipeline were illuminating a central issue that had been sidestepped ever since Seward's purchase, and again left unsettled when statehood was legislated: who owned the lands in Alaska?

In their 206 villages, the 60,000 native Alaskan people (one-fifth of the population) had been asserting "Indian title" (based on aboriginal use and occupancy) to 340,000,000 of the state's 376,000,000 acres. Their specific demand in 1971 was for 60,000,000 acres. Several federal courts had already held that non-Indian title was clouded; one court had, for this reason, issued a preliminary injunction against the pipeline construction. Congress was at last going to *have* to settle the lands issue, and the administration had to take a position.

A stingy 1969 administration bill had been proposed without any consultation with Indian leaders. In January of 1970, special counsel Leonard Garment and his assistant (the author) had forced the reopening of the issue, for three months had studied the debate carefully, and had invited the native Alaskan leaders to Washington to present their case. Garment was persuaded that a peaceful and prosperous future for Alaska depended on a land and monetary settlement that was fairer to the natives. The senior officials of the Office of Management and Budget, however, argued against liberalizing the 1969 offer.

The author had written a twenty-five-page option paper and the protagonists were summoned to a meeting with domestic policy chief John Ehrlichman. They sat in a circle that afternoon as Ehrlichman had the author go through the uncontested items. The confrontation then loomed.

At this point, Ehrlichman interrupted and told the group that he had discussed the matter with the president (very briefly, he later acknowledged) and Mr. Nixon "wanted to continue to be forthcoming on Indian affairs." "Well, hell," said Secretary of the Interior Rogers Morton, "let's make it forty million acres and a billion dollars!"

No one objected.

Within minutes of the end of the session, the author had drafted a page-and-a-half decision memorandum, quoting the president's "forthcoming" language and encapsulating the Morton conclusion in precise terms. That memo was circulated to all the participants early the next morning.

Had it not been both precise and prompt, the "decision" would have evaporated. Within days, Interior's legislative drafters were trying to back away from the agreement, and had to be jerked into line by Ehrlichman and Garment. Some weeks later, a leading OMB official met the author at a White House doorway. "You didn't really mean that, did you? You *couldn't* have been serious!" He was told the decision was firm.

The new bill was released in a White House ceremony; the native leaders publicly praised the White House. Congress enacted the bill with little change and the Alaska Native Claims Settlement Act resolved the pipeline issue and much of Alaska's future.

But it might not have happened except for a page-and-a-half memorandum.

Another such example is the acid-rain issue, already mentioned. In February of 1986, White House special assistant Ralph Bledsoe reshaped the original thirteen-page option paper from an interagency working group to ensure that it covered the questions fully. He insisted that additional important background material be included.

After the first meeting of the Domestic Policy Council (without the president), Bledsoe wrote and circulated the minutes and—more important—the three-page decision memorandum that the chairman (Attorney General Edwin Meese) sent to the president. With the president presiding on February 18, 1986, the Domestic Policy Council met again. Thirty-three officers and staff filled the Cabinet Room.

The choices involved big price tags: one option was to accept the urgent recommendations of a high-level U.S.-Canadian policy-review team to take tough steps against sulphur-dioxide emitters and to put up $2.5 billion in scarce federal dollars to do both research and enforcement. The alternative option was more modest: endorse the team's report but spend no additional money. With senior advisers split both ways, the Cabinet Room that day was being watched by the world: by the anti-government-regulation conservatives, by the environmental community, by the budgeteers, by the midwestern states and their coal-burning power plants, and especially by our friendly northern neighbor, Canada.

The president chose the first option (with a qualifier on the funding side) knowing that he had to meet soon with the Canadian prime minister.

The final decision memorandum was again a Bledsoe product, was signed by the president and deposited with the staff secretary. Bledsoe composed the decision-reporting notice that Chairman Meese sent to the erstwhile divided advisers.

Presidents Carter, Ford, and Reagan have favored a combination of written papers and then meetings with the officials most directly concerned.

Washington the battlefield is a war zone of discontent and distrust. Madison was not, nor will today's observer be, surprised that this is so. The sentries of separate advocacy, as they should, question every White House action. If the president's decisions are not put in writing and then guarded by his White House watchmen, his intentions may be warped or even lost. Depending on memory alone delivers the president into the hands of unreliable or even hostile interpreters—and makes him their captive.

This chapter has described the president when he is a gate-opener: when he reaches out to his Cabinet either in person or through memoranda. Each new president will set his own style for seeking coherent Cabinet advice— urging reorganization, creating supersecretaries, convening meetings, commissioning option papers. A president will insist on the freedom to choose—and then to change—across that range of methods.

There are occasions, however, when the acrid smoke of controversy will stifle his trust in consultations beyond the White House walls. Reorganization will be a hopeless option, Cabinet meetings unwelcome, and even the prospect of participative papers viewed suspiciously.

The president will want to move in private, and the gates will be locked.

CHAPTER 3

The Gates Shut:
White House Staff Exclusive

A President is not bound to conform to the advice of his ministers. He is even under no positive injunction to ask or require it. But the Constitution presumes that he will consult them, and the genius of our government and the public good recommend the practice.

—Alexander Hamilton

We could always go out and find an expert on meat prices or special education or health economics to help our people analyze and understand a specific issue. But loyalty, versatility and reliability were Nixon's first criteria, and he counted on his own campaign people to take charge of his major projects.

—John D. Ehrlichman

Presidents launch initiatives—their most dramatic role in the policy process. The more controversial the subject, the more electric its political fallout, the more will a president insist that his initiative be protected. Premature exposure of his decision lays it bare on the Washington battleground, its leadership value stripped off; counterattacks begin even before the presidential position is final.

Presidents do not take kindly to such upstaging. If they think it could happen, they will sharply alter the decision-making procedures. White House staff, not anyone else, will be put in charge of the project and the White House gates shut to all but minimum opinion-gathering from the Cabinet or others outside—not only shut but locked if the president senses that elements within his own Cabinet may be opposed to his aims.

An illustration of this tight, exclusive approach came in 1970 when Nixon faced what he called "the most explosive of the civil rights issues during my presidency"—school desegregation. Paradoxically (when compared to his two final years), on this occasion there was nothing malicious or underhanded in all the secrecy; his decisions and actions were among the most statesmanlike of his entire time in office.

A year after his election, two unforeseen events forced White House action. On October 29, 1969, a unanimous Supreme Court surprised those in charge at the Department of Health, Education, and Welfare by rejecting their requests for delay in desegregating Mississippi schools that fall, and mandated that "the obligation of every school district is to terminate dual school systems at once, and to operate now and hereafter only unitary schools."[1]

In February of 1970, Vice President Spiro Agnew had accepted a speaking date in Atlanta in which he planned to go public and emphasize his "disfavor with the apparent consequences of recent court decisions."[2] The first draft of that address, written for him by conservative White House speechwriter Patrick Buchanan, was half-jokingly going to refer to southern unhappiness with impending school desegregation as justifying another attack on Fort Sumter.

White House special counsel Leonard Garment sensed the political catastrophe in the making. He persuaded Nixon to order Agnew to cancel the speech and to issue a presidential statement of his own. Preceding a policy declaration, however, a lengthy and thoughtful option paper would have to be assembled.

Who would get this assignment? Anyone in the Cabinet?

Not HEW's Office of Education. Its head, James Allen, was about to be fired for making overly aggressive statements in favor of integrated schools.

Not HEW's Office of Civil Rights. Its directer, Leon Panetta, was on the verge of suffering the same fate for the same reason.

Not Secretary of HEW Robert Finch. He also was soon to be moved out of his Cabinet post for not being able to control Allen and Panetta. As John Ehrlichman put it, "The president didn't think he was getting any help from HEW at all; he was getting problems from HEW."[3]

Not the Justice Department. The sentiment there was that the department was an enforcement agency and should not be on the leading edge of policy-making for politically hypersensitive issues. (Although Attorney General John Mitchell himself was a close confidant, Nixon was convinced that both the HEW and Justice civil rights professionals were out of control and were badgering the southern school districts unfeelingly.)

And not the vice president—even though he had just been made chairman of the Cabinet Committee on Education. His Atlanta speech gambit marked him down as not on the president's wavelength.

The presidential arrow pointed inward: the option paper and proposed policy statement would be a White House enterprise from beginning to end.

Garment was put in the lead. He was a lawyer and not an ideologue. He had been Nixon's partner in their New York law firm and one of the principals in the 1968 campaign. Now he was there on the spot in the White House. The president ordered that there be no administration speeches or congressional testimony until he himself had spoken. Garment was told to "drop everything else" for two months and do nothing but this project. A "drop-everything-else-for-two-months" command is the kind of assignment most White House staff officers are able to accept, but Cabinet officers simply cannot.

Garment knew that the president needed answers to troubling and difficult questions:

- While the Supreme Court had demanded "unitary schools" immediately, how was a "unitary" system to be defined? And what was the state of the law on busing as a remedy? The lower courts were divided.
- Would schools segregated de facto as a result of individuals' residential choice be caught up in the courts' mandate as much as those schools segregated by official school-board action?
- Would it be wise to put some kind of school-assignment amendment into the Constitution? Congressman Norman Lent had introduced one—but it was vague and subject to contradictory interpretations.
- If not constitutional change, could legislation be enacted to guide the courts and the schools? If so, what would it say? Yale law professor Alexander Bickel (a friend of Garment's and an informal consultant) considered this a promising approach.
- What were the existing policies being followed by HEW's Offices of Education and Civil Rights, and by the Department of Justice? Deadline dates for fund cutoffs in segregated Dixie school districts had been relaxed in the summer of 1969 but were still the target of southern outrage.
- Were there real educational advantages for children in integrated classrooms? Or psychic harm in busing them away from their neighborhood schools? What environments *were* the keys to learning in the first place? The educators needed to be consulted.
- Civil rights leaders had conflicting views about school integration and busing. Was any consensus reachable among them?
- Four thousand southern communities had moved into compliance with the original *Brown* decision of 1954. How did they manage to do this peacefully? Was the president going to retreat and undermine them by attacking the courts?
- How could other school districts under unwelcome court orders be helped? If help meant funds, how many millions of federal dollars should be allocated?
- There was crisis in the air. The coming fall was a deadline; some courts had even specified the approaching mid-term in the school year as the due-date for desegregation. Parents and students were demonstrating in the streets; elections were approaching in November and the "big referendum" in 1972. How was desegregation enforcement going to be reconciled with the Republican "southern strategy?"

Next to foreign policy, this boiling stew of crosscutting social-legal-political questions was probably the most sensitive and demanding challenge of the pre-Watergate Nixon years. It was too explosive to be assigned anywhere except the White House staff itself.

Garment brought in a second experienced lawyer as temporary consultant (easily arranged at the White House) and then turned to other colleagues close to him. The most indispensable associate was presidential speechwriter Ray Price who synchronized his drafting with the research and analysis going on in Garment's suite. In crisp intellectual tandem, Garment's answers became Price's eloquence.

Keeping total control, Garment did reach out to pull in some unusual resources. There was a small technical assistance program for public schools, run by the Office of Education. Garment had the program manager into the White House for a detailed conversation. Could that modest authority be stretched to meet this gigantic new demand?

How did black leaders feel about busing? He met with a dozen of them in long, quiet sessions over lunch. (Some of them were more interested in political control of the school boards than in busing the students.)

Garment learned about some courageous statesmanship being shown in Greenville, South Carolina. Faced with a court deadline of February 16, instead of taking to the streets, the leaders of Greenville organized a Citizens Committee of the Greenville County School Board. Sponsored by the local paper, the committee took up the task of explaining and defending the school board's desegregation plan to the whole community. A paragraph from their flyer shows their objective:

> Your Citizens' Committee, your Ministerial Association, your Chamber of Commerce, your Human Relations Committee—in cooperation with school officials, civic clubs, churches and other Greenville organizations—urge all citizens to work together for a greater Greenville County. Together we can create superior public schools in Greenville. Together we can be a model community that leads the region and the nation in education, in economic progress, in spirit.[4]

Garment located the leaders of the Citizens Committee, invited them to Washington, had them for dinner in the White House Mess, spent hours in behind-the-scenes dialogue: what made this effort so promising? How could the federal government help? What governmental mistakes would muck it up? The group came and talked willingly because the White House called.

There were meetings, but only in the White House, which HEW's former general counsel and Justice's assistant attorney general attended. Even Fort Sumter rallier Pat Buchanan was consulted as well.

The product, on March 5, 1970, was a ten-page memorandum for the president—in a black notebook with eighteen attachments. The eighteenth was the preliminary Price draft of the presidential statement.

In Eisenhower's time, this would have been on the Cabinet agenda—the memorandum circulated to each member, the president perhaps not reading it thoroughly but carefully absorbing its substance from an oral presentation. But this was Nixon, not Eisenhower and—as is proper from president to president—a very different style prevailed. Nixon scorned Cabinet meetings on subjects as sensitive as this, wanted to comb through policy packages that, even though bulky with supplementary tabs, were well organized. He took Garment's black book to Key Biscayne and studied it minutely.

Ehrlichman now controlled the rest of the process and at this point even the inner gates slammed shut. Not only did no drafts of the statement leave the White House, but when some of the conservatives within the staff worked up alternative versions, even Garment had to go to Ehrlichman's sanctuary to look at them. He heard reports of these other attempts and fired a shot at the inner sanctum: "Not knowing what revisions are proposed, I can't comment on them. . . ." Price himself complained to Ehrlichman: "Whatever editing is done over there, I think it is vital that I get a final crack at it *afterwards*—and that I have the *last* crack at it before it's finally approved by you or the President."[5]

Not only were there no Cabinet meetings on the school-desegregation message; neither were there any internal face-offs where the disagreeing staff protagonists debated in front of the president. Nixon worked entirely from the written arguments, wanting to avoid confronting either personal eloquence or personal emotion. "Papers don't bleed," Garment commented later when describing the Nixon preference.

The eight-thousand-word statement, eloquent, orderly, almost scholarly, was released March 24, 1970. Then and only then did his Executive Branch, the Congress, and the country read it—in all its balance and with all its impact.

With the Greenville model very much in mind, Nixon stressed the importance of local community leadership. He asked the Congress for $1.5 billion to help the affected school districts; the Congress approved an initial $75 million.

The purpose of this example is neither to analyze or praise the policy but to show how it got put together: by high-tension preparatory work concentrated in the White House.

President after president has acceded to the temptation to rely on his personal staff to be the energizers and craftsmen of his policy initiatives.

This is especially true when outside crisis events throw the raw glare of lightning on the stodgy machinery of routine interagency clockwork.

In Eisenhower's time, for instance, a presidential staff member found himself under that kind of pressure. For a decade, a creaking, ponderous interdepartmental contraption—the Air Coordinating Committee—had been grinding its gears while aviation needs soared. "God, it was the most unsuccessful, abortive conglomerate of conflicting interest you could possibly imagine," said one observer, "it became the instrument of stopping anything that anybody wanted to have stopped."[6]

In 1957, jolted by the nation's worst civil air disaster when two planes collided over the Grand Canyon, Eisenhower appointed a White House special assistant for airways modernization. Retired Lieutenant General Elwood R. (Pete) Quesada stepped in. He organized a staff of eight and spent thirteen months drawing up the final design for a new and independent Federal Aviation Administration. He built on the report of a previous special assistant (Edward P. Curtis) and on an earlier Bureau of the Budget study. Quesada's task included drafting legislation (with advice from the affected agencies) and helping write a presidential message to the Congress.

Quesada ran into determined resistance from the Departments of Commerce and the Air Force. Commerce, then the home of the thirty-five-thousand-person Civil Aviation Administration, would lose all that turf and personnel to the new Federal Aviation Administration. The Air Force, jealous of its needs for reserved air space, distrusted any civilian air-control systems. At one point, Quesada had to appeal to the White House counsel to call in the senior Commerce resisters and to tell them to cooperate or else.

Upon signing the bill creating the FAA, whom did Eisenhower appoint to head up the new agency? Reaching into his own staff, he sent Quesada himself to be the first administrator.

Jimmy Carter's energy program is another example of closing the White House gates. Just before inauguration, Carter announced that within ninety days he would submit a comprehensive energy program to Congress.

Energy policy is another crisscross of bailiwicks: it prickles with problems of production and consumer economics, taxation, science, the environment, foreign relations. As usual, outside the White House the Cabinet giants were scrimmaging and behind them cheered turbulent choruses of interest groups.

"Cabinet government" though Carter had proclaimed, no one giant could possibly handle that whole playing field. He looked within his own perimeter and named James Schlesinger as White House energy adviser; it was known in advance that Schlesinger would become the new secretary of energy. The new energy adviser then brought in additional temporary staff: fifteen professionals and other support helpers; now they were an "Energy Group."

Then came the presidential order: the Energy Group was "to refrain from contact with other parts of the government—both Capitol Hill *and the Executive Branch.*" Looking back, Stuart Eizenstat recalls:

> The reasoning behind the order was to protect against press leaks which could damage the plan before it was launched, by prematurely mobilizing opposition to its most controversial parts. Carter wanted dramatically to present the NEP [National Energy Plan] as a whole to Congress rather than have it trickle-out in pieces, undercutting the dramatic effect of his announcement.[7]

Even at a Cabinet meeting, Schlesinger spoke only in general terms.

The plan went to Carter in a big black notebook on March 22. Carter asked Eizenstat to review it, but instructed *him* not even to show it to his own staff.

It was not until April 6—a short two weeks before publication—that Carter convened a meeting at which Schlesinger unveiled the National Energy Plan to the vice president, the budget director, the chairman of the Council of Economic Advisers, and the secretaries of the treasury and the interior. They attacked it. Five days later, it was exposed to the president's political and legislative aides. They were apprehensive as well and counseled postponement. Carter refused that, but finally authorized interagency discussions. Result: just as Carter feared, it was leaked and published in the *New York Times.*

The Cabinet as a whole and others of the White House staff were briefed on April 20—the day *of* Carter's evening presentation to a joint session of Congress.

The Congress approved the creation of the new Department of Energy. Schlesinger was appointed secretary, following which he and his Energy Group departed the White House. The lead responsibility for energy policy coordination was then switched to Eizenstat and his domestic policy staff.

The baldest examples of freezing Cabinet members out of presidential policy and action took place while Henry Kissinger was the assistant to President Nixon for national security affairs. In Kissinger's own words:

> ... Nixon increasingly moved sensitive negotiations into the White House where he could supervise them directly, get the credit personally, and avoid the bureaucratic disputes or inertia that he found so distasteful. . . .

In May 1971 the Secretary of State did not know of the negotiations in White House-Kremlin channels that led to the breakthrough in the SALT talks until seventy-two hours before there was a formal announcement. In July 1971 [Secretary of State] Rogers was told of my secret trip to China only after I was already on the way. In April 1972, the President gave Rogers such a convoluted explanation for my trip to Moscow—which had been arranged secretly and which Rogers opposed when he was told at the last minute—that it complicated the negotiations. Such examples could be endlessly multiplied.[8]

One is tempted to close this chapter by studying those locked White House gates and asking: is that a good or a lousy method of presidential public administration? Kissinger looks back and reflects that if a president trusts a Cabinet officer so little, he should replace him rather than "supervise him with a personal aide."[9] But Nixon wasn't that kind of a president—and the country has just one president at a time.

The examples given here and in the chapters to come, however, reveal that the "White House Staff Exclusive" technique is not the aberrant deviation of some one chief executive. The occasional but steady favor shown for that method ranges across the modern presidents. They are aware of, and accept, the risks that inhere in acting secretively.

As the tumult outside the gates increases, the centralization within intensifies.

CHAPTER 4

What Should the President Know and When Should He Know It?

. . . he shall take care that the laws be faithfully executed. . . .

—U.S. CONSTITUTION

. . . the government's version of the law of gravity: that bad news never flows up. The only times I saw anyone struggle to warn his superior of impending trouble . . . were on those occasions when the superior was sure to find out anyway. . . . When this is multiplied over dozens of departments and hundreds of thousands of employees, the result is a vast conspiracy of self-protection, benign in origin but devastating in effect.

—JAMES FALLOWS,
Former Carter assistant

Under the president, 4.2 million military and civilian assistants are helping him "execute" the thousands of laws. He needs to know: "How faithfully?"

Between the Constitution's eloquence and Fallows' warning hangs a problem of balance: keeping the president informed but not inundated, ferreting out the important though unwelcome information as well as screening out the unnecessary. Streaming into Washington from around the country and around the world come vast flows of information. Judging—Is it the right information? What should be extracted that is being hidden in that "conspiracy of self-protection"? How much of it should be given to the president? And with what priority?—is another of the central tasks of the White House staff. Emplacing too fine a filter isolates a president and cuts him off from the ability to fulfil the constitutional requirement. Opening up the mesh may drown a president in trivia and bring about the same failure.

Presidents vary dramatically in the degree of detail they want to absorb: Johnson, for instance, demanded minutiae as contrasted with Reagan who did not. Only their personal staffs are close enough to discern just where the balance lies.

No matter who is occupying the office, the dictum in Article II is peremptory. It doesn't say "some of the laws," it doesn't say "on most occasions," and it doesn't exempt the most secretive of the presidents' retinues.

Constitutionally, the president is held accountable for *everything* his 4.2 million employees do. In case he has any doubt about that, he need only wait until his next press conference. Was that general's speech too bellicose? The president will be queried. Why were the veterans' checks late last month? Ask the president. Were funds diverted to the contras? The president is expected to know.

As the White House staff view it, such press-conference heat melts the cool "delegation" theories that assert "he's above all that." Not only the press, but the Congress, the president's political foes, the Constitution, and the citizens themselves are holding the president accountable for what happens in the most unforeseen corner of his Executive Branch. The staff are therefore driven to invent systems that will suck information into the White House, in the right quantity and at the right time.

Presidential information systems have three intertwined objectives. The first is early warning: to spot pattern-breaking "error signals" in events happening anywhere in the world: military, economic, domestic, political. The second is educational: to give the president facts together with the seasoned evaluations of trusted people who may be far from Washington but close to the problem. The third is preventive: to identify actions that others within the Executive Branch intend to take—and to spot them in time to have them tested against presidential policies.

Information systems exist in the White House to accomplish one or all three of those purposes. They are designed or monitored—some are directly operated—by presidential staff.

The most sophisticated of the president's information networks is that set up among the national security departments. Some five hundred thousand cables are generated each day in this community, to or from Washington and U.S. embassies or posts abroad. This telegraphic traffic has one accidental feature that makes controlling it manageable: the messages go through the narrow gateways of code rooms. The cryptographic units report to operations centers that were established at State, Defense, the CIA, and the White House in the sixties. Skilled intelligence and watch-officer teams staff these operations centers around the clock. Connected by secure conference lines, they can talk among each other and add their personal judgments and telephoned alerts to supplement the traffic on the video screens.

Telegraphic messages bear a variety of captions. For precedence there are FLASH, IMMEDIATE, PRIORITY, and ROUTINE; sensitive or specialized messages carry other opening code words. The caption CRITIC alerts the entire national security community that a crisis may be upon them.

The essential few of the half million cables are switched electronically to the White House Situation Room, one floor below the Oval Office. Most of the switching is done automatically, according to preset criteria. If State receives NODIS (no distribution) telegrams, its executive secretary will make a personal judgment, on a message-by-message basis, as to which should be relayed to the White House. Are any held back? Perhaps those few in which the ambassadors are bitching "Who was so stupid as to send me those instructions?" when it was the president.

Daily, some three thousand messages flow through the White House filters. The Situation Room staff can move the intake threshold up or down, vacuuming in hundreds of messages from a crisis area or raising a stricter standard against those deemed routine. As computers can overwhelm the human receptors, so they can also be used to help: the intake or search instructions can be programmed to admit or look for cables containing only certain words, names, or phrases.

The Sit Room alerts the White House national security assistant of messages that are of presidential significance; the computer blinks when a CRITIC alert zips into its innards. If an individual cable from or to a U.S. ambassador is actually sent to the president, the secretary of state is notified so that he can be prepared for a possible presidential phone call.

The twenty-five-person Situation Room duty staff are more than mere receivers; they pull together "Sit Room Notes," summaries from the heavy flows. They will spot incomplete data and tell a distant post to wake up and get more—in order not to expose the president to misleading information. Their work fits together with the special morning reports from State and the CIA that are in turn used by the national security affairs assistant in his daily intelligence briefings with the president.

While State, Defense, the CIA, and the National Security Agency share some of their messages and reports with each other, no one of them gets everything. Only at the White House does it all come together. Only the White House staff is in a position to prepare the most complete digests, to judge what should move upstairs and how quickly.

But the staff never forgets: presidents come before systems. If the boss says, "Gimme everything," he will get it—the whole pile. President Johnson at times demanded: "I want that report—now!"—and he would be given it—raw. Presidents can—and do—manipulate their institutional systems, or bypass them altogether.

The president may read instantly the latest from Kabul or Chad, but what about Chicago? The secretary of health, education and welfare was cutting off education funds to Mayor Daley; the Office of Economic Opportunity was on the point of awarding a community-action grant to the Blackstone Rangers street gang. In New York, the administrator of general services put Ellis Island up for sale; in Washington the secretary of the interior was about to criticize the Beach Boys and the FBI was starting an internal investigation of its own director's alleged acceptance of improper gifts. In Oregon, the Food and Drug Commissioner seized 2.5 million pounds of cranberries just before Thanksgiving.

Who alerted the White House to any of those prospective bombshells? Nobody. The four presidents involved in those examples all learned of them after the fact and in the middle of public uproar.

Where among the domestic agencies is there a network akin to the foreign-affairs communications? Where is the "Internal Affairs Situation Room" and a computer blinking with early warnings? There isn't any—at least not yet for ordinary domestic business.

Except for disasters or law-enforcement purposes, there are good reasons for not setting up an automated, central White House system for domestic information. There are too many agencies, no code rooms, no national security urgencies, and there are legislators and party leaders on the loose nationwide who absorb and pass on information to the White House. There is abundant media coverage and a national aversion to "big brother" snooping.

The White House has not—yet—reached out to include itself in the electronic mail networks that domestic departments use between Washington and their field offices. The Cabinet heads would likely resist any such move. There is now an "executive data link" between the secretaries' offices and the White House Office of Cabinet Affairs, but it is used chiefly for the exchange of agendas and an occasional Cabinet speech; it cannot today handle classified or privileged material.

Lacking the kind of wide window into each department which the national security systems provide, presidents have searched for alternative ways of casting a domestic dragnet.

Eisenhower initiated a system in July of 1956; it was called "Staff Notes." The head of each major agency was instructed by staff secretary Andrew J. Goodpaster: The White House wants "brief informational notes on items within your field of interest which may bear upon past presidential decisions *or which may flag especially important up-coming problems.*"[1]

The agencies were told that this was not an action channel, nor was it for news already released; the White House wanted *anticipatory* information. As Goodpaster's assistant put it, "One of our criteria for rejection would be that it was in the *New York Times* yesterday morning. Once something would appear in the public domain, by our standards it was declared legally dead".[2]

Did the departments spring into action and fill Goodpaster's basket with voluntary submissions?

In most cases quite the contrary. Treasury entered the system by sending over copies of its press releases. Goodpaster's staff had to remind, needle, and at times kick their agency contacts to jar them into concentrating on what the president wanted.

> You did not just have a Cabinet Agenda item and send out a memo, however authoritative, and sit back and wait for things to happen. All this business of phoning and visiting and trying constantly to keep the material moving and fresh, was an indispensable part of the process.[3]

Gradually, the intake burgeoned; Goodpaster hired two assistants—who had to be bird dogs as well as editors. Executive Office units and White House staff elements were all canvassed for raw material. Even in the White House Mess:

> . . . we got a chance to do a lot of missionary work at noontime. We were always waiting for people to drop into our net. . . . And of course we would never let a Cabinet officer who was unwise enough to sit at the same table with us go without trying to pump him for something or other. I think it helped us insure good coverage for the President.[4]

So assiduous did the staff's follow-up have to be that they made a monthly graph of each agency's submissions. When Treasury dropped to ninth place in the Cabinet contributions ranking, Goodpaster sent the secretary another memo: a blunt rocket wrapped in silky language: "There may be some possible areas wherein coverage from the Treasury could be extended." In case the Cabinet officer missed the point, Goodpaster clipped out and sent him a news story about a Treasury action that had caught the White House unawares.

A few department heads recognized that the Staff Notes channel could really be of high value to them: a guaranteed way of getting an important piece of information straight in to the president. As a Goodpaster assistant explained:

> The government's a very big place and any given member of it who is subordinate to the President doesn't have much time with the President with his problems. "Staff Notes" gave the smart ones a chance to raise his level of understanding and consciousness of their problems and efforts.[5]

Editing the intake often took as much White House staff effort as collecting it in the first place.

> . . . we . . . were faced with the problem of taking sometimes as much as five pages of single-typed prose and boiling it down into . . . maybe nine or ten lines . . . . this was editing with a vengeance. And yet I don't really think that we failed to communicate the kernel of the essential information in more than one or two cases.[6]

Every evening (sometimes oftener) a terse page and a half with six or seven items would go into the Oval Office. On occasion, it would zoom out again with a presidential query, and at least once even the supplemental answer was shot back with a further question.

Seven senior staff officers received copies of this extraordinary newsletter, as a help in their own coordination duties.

In four and a half years, ninety-six hundred items were submitted as raw material and some seventy-five hundred went to the president as Staff Notes paragraphs. Ike read every one of them.

While disparaging Eisenhower's staff system, Kennedy replicated some of Ike's processes. Eighteen days after inauguration, special assistant Frederick Dutton sent all the agencies a letter remarkably similar to Goodpaster's four and a half years earlier. "The President . . . is particularly interested in having major problems of the agency flagged for his attention," Dutton instructed. Two "incisive" pages were due on the first Tuesday of every month (later changed to a weekly requirement).

What Kennedy wanted, Dutton explained, were "personally composed, letting-hair-down memoranda" with "naked candor."

What did he get?

"Some were eight to twenty pages long," he recalled, "mostly fluff. They were institutional, stilted, protective—as if written by a committee."[7]

Dutton had directed that they all come to him. His Tuesday lights burned late with the work of editing.

The package would come back from Kennedy full of marginal notations: "I don't want to do this"; "Set up a meeting"; "Stop this in its tracks!" Dutton would relay the president's requests.

Why fluff—from the president's own people?

The author (then executive secretary of the Peace Corps) remembers, from the sending end, the first response of that agency to the Dutton dragnet. Two pages were prepared, candidly flagging "the major problems of the agency" (the Peace Corps being very new, it had some unusual ones).

Director Shriver took pen in hand, then stopped short. "I don't want to tell Jack all my problems," he exclaimed. "I want to let him know our *accomplishments!"* A new draft was ordered and the White House got two pages of good news.

White House staff know they are being bamboozled by such gamesmanship. Their irritation will sometimes flare into suspicions that the agencies out there not only have "containing" strategies but are withholding information intentionally.

Realizing the risk that formal information systems may produce "stilted, protective" reports, presidents and staffs are also eager to set up techniques that circumvent official channels. There are two such techniques: one begun by Nixon, the other decades old.

Since 1969 an arrangement has been devised for the White House to tap into the most comprehensive information-collecting system on the planet: the world's news media. It is the White House News Summary.

As early as 1959, when Nixon was vice president, a staff officer had begun a practice of abstracting journal and magazine articles for him. Later she summarized major newspapers and then the evening news broadcasts. By 1968 she was editing a daily digest of eighteen to twenty pages. Nixon liked it and the idea grew. "That's how Nixon got his bad news," Bob Haldeman commented. During the 1969 campaign, wire-service reports were added to the product.

Nixon brought the News Summary system with him into the White House. Ford, Carter, and Reagan have all found it indispensable, and the News Summary Group is now a regular element of the White House staff.

At 7 A.M. weekdays, along with whatever morning papers the president reads directly, he picks up a twenty-page digest (Nixon's was forty pages at times): TODAY'S HEADLINES, NATIONAL NEWS, INTERNATIONAL NEWS, NETWORK NEWS, EDITORIALS/COLUMNISTS, AND FOREIGN MEDIA REACTION. The items are each usually two paragraphs long. They are terse and tightly packed précis of public-affairs stories—with an occasional human-interest piece.

If it is Friday, a seventeen-page, blue-covered supplement will be attached: the "Friday Follies"—sixty or more cartoons.

Four hundred fifty duplicates of the News Summary are distributed in the White House. Cabinet members send their drivers over to pick up their own copies.

Three updates follow: at 11:30, 3:00, and 5:30.

If the president is traveling, the News Summary is called the Air Force One Edition. If he is in Europe, it arrives via facsimile by 6 A.M. on his clock; if he is in China, it is the only source of American news anyone has. A correspondent along on the trip may discover that the News Summary has sent a brief of his newly printed story to the president's plane so the chief can see how he is being covered.

The dragnet is impressive: 7 East Coast newspapers that are procured by 6 A.M. or before (when the president is out of town the *Washington Post* is picked up at 10:30 nightly), all the U.S. TV networks, 7 wire services, 500 papers a week from every corner of America, 350 foreign papers, and 75 major foreign radio and TV stations, covered through the "Foreign Media Reactions" reports from the U.S. Information Agency.

A staff of five in the White House, working in shifts, puts all this together; the production group is on duty from 11 P.M. to 7 A.M. One News Summary staffer comes in on Sundays to catch the morning talk shows. It is a humbling experience for the all-night crew, putting together twenty pages for the president, with perhaps only a night watchman dropping by in the wee hours.

The News Summary is probably the only document in the White House that goes directly to the president unreviewed by senior staff filtering. Knowing they have that kind of access, what is to prevent the White House editors from slanting it toward flackery?

There are two inhibitors. The primary assurance is the staff's own integrity. Raise this query to any of the recent editors and they respond fiercely: their job for the president is to put that summary together with professional honesty. If bad news is news, it's included. In the last year of Watergate, "it was like writing a daily obituary," said Nixon's editor. He even suggested to Nixon and Chief of Staff Alexander Haig that it be discontinued, but they both told him to keep it coming. Do the cartoons lampoon the president? They are nonetheless in Reagan's "Friday Follies."

So determined was the Nixon editor to be beyond reproach that he insisted the News Summary Group be attached neither to the Press Office nor to Herbert Klein's communications staff. He was afraid he would then be under pressure to feature what the White House itself was saying—and News Summary readers would then only be "listening to their own voice." (The Reagan editor was switched to the Press Office but is as emphatic as his predecessors about his objectivity.)

The only criteria are importance and timeliness. The cartoons lose their pertinence slowly; the hundreds of local papers are valued mostly for their editorial positions.

There is a second checkpoint for the summary's accuracy. Of the 449 other White House readers, some have tall egos and short tempers. If a News Summary item is critical, and especially if it mentions their own names for the president to read, a challenge is always possible—and the summary's own reliability is then put to the test.

The editor can easily wound a fellow staffer by including in the News Summary an item critical of what a colleague is working on, even if the name is not mentioned. This rile-up-the-president technique was used by Patrick Buchanan when he was supervisor of the News Summary under Nixon. Leonard Garment and John Ehrlichman were among his targets.

Like any of the presidential information systems, the News Summary provokes action as well. That is one of its purposes. Nixon's marginal scratchings resulted in three hundred Haldeman memoranda in the first White House year. They would begin, "The President has noted. . . ."

As an illustration, Nixon put a big check mark opposite one item: a brief news report about a group of young people that had met at the invitation of the American Revolution Bicentennial Commission—and were critical of the commission's planning. Garment was ordered to find out more. After a testy phone call, the full text of the report was extracted from a reluctant and embarrassed commission staff.

Reading his News Summary, Reagan had a soft spot for human-interest items. When the summary relayed a story about a young man who was late for and thus flunked a job interview because he had stopped to do a good deed, the president called the employer. The boy got the job.

Day in, day out, and throughout the long nights, the News Summary groups in each White House produce these briefs for the modern presidents. They wrote 15,000 pages in Nixon's 67 months. An experiment of the sixties has now become a standard feature of the contemporary staff. The personnel of course change, but the challenges of achieving accuracy and balance continue. The editors work within that narrow margin of judgment: between the thick torrent that floods in and the thin pipeline of what is important to go on to the chief executive.

Finally, there is the ultimate—and oldest—White House information system: the personal antennae of the staff.

Sticking up, figuratively, from the White House roof are several hundred "radar sets." Each staff officer has one, or more, and they hum with electropolitical currents. These beams focus on the issues of presidential and staff interest, but their targets touch a vast range.

Presidential appointees can have their signals bounced into the White House, but so can civil servants and the lowliest assistants in a field office. Legislators, ministers, reporters, Indian leaders, and business executives, authors and artists, candidates and local officials: if they are actors on the policy horizon, the White House "radars" will pick up their emanations.

These high-frequency beams pay no attention whatever to institutional chains of command; Cabinet members can neither stop nor even discover the traffic—though they sometimes try.

As an example, for five years the author represented a White House interest in American Indian affairs. There was no officer of the federal government, no lawyer anywhere, no tribal councilor—who was not welcome to knock at the door. The author attended Indian conferences, flew in helicopters over reservations, rode a horse at the Crow Fair, met with dissidents from the Hopi, Sioux, and Menominee.

The product of all this networking was intelligence. What was brewing? Who knew what answers? What were the issues of concern? Who was credible and who was flaky? Who had support and who was a wild man?

Radars pick up chaff—and so do White House assistants. Almost every message on those networks is skewed with self-serving arguments; the knocks on the door bring in biased advocates. The intelligence is fragmentary; additional analysis is always needed before one involves the president. The early warning, however, is invaluable and the hard nub of fact can be screened out from the sparks and static.

Multiply the countrywide range of a single staff officer's network by the large number of White House assistants, and one senses the nearly infinite horizon of *informal* intelligence the president's personal staff is scanning as supplement and test against the formal, official reporting.

The practice is at least a half century old. Arthur Schlesinger, Jr., described FDR:

> Roosevelt's persistent effort therefore was to check and balance information acquired through official channels by information acquired through a myriad of private, informal, and unorthodox channels and espionage networks. At times he seemed almost to pit his personal sources against his public sources.[8]

Roosevelt told James H. Rowe, Jr., one of his early assistants: "Your job is to be a bird dog. . . . Just run around town and find out what's happening." In Truman's White House, Clark Clifford had an informal network for matters affecting Israel: members of the Jewish community in New York who kept bringing him up short whenever they thought that even Secretary of State George Marshall was departing from the president's policies. Johnson aide Harry McPherson described LBJ's desire: "That's why he has a staff around him of people who have big ears and listen and meet with people all the time and will send him memoranda and will talk to him on the phone and tell him what they think is going on."[9]

The White House staff is a microchip in macrocosm—a pulsing transformer between information streaming in and action aiming out. Poor information means poor action—no matter how well intentioned a president or how analytical his assistants.

Like its actual gates, information filters and barriers have to be installed at the White House to screen out the biased or incomplete assertions that bombard the Oval Office perimeter. Yet even more important: sophisticated intake gear must be operating—ferrets, magnets, and radar receivers—to pull in essential bits from reluctant respondents. It is the White House staff who operate the last ring of filters and radars; it is only they who most accurately reflect each president's wishes as to how capacious those instruments shall be.

Throughout the nation and the world, as the cacophony of voices and forces has grown in volume and intensity, the demands on the White House's filtering and ferreting mechanisms have multiplied correspondingly.

What should the president know and when should he know it? Each succeeding one of the modern presidents has no choice but to commit heavy staff resources in the struggle for the answer.

CHAPTER 5

Monitor on the Potomac

... You surround yourself with the best people you can find, delegate authority, and don't interfere as long as the overall policy that you've decided upon is being carried out. —RONALD REAGAN

... The best way to run a business ... is to do it as you would cook on a wood-burning stove. ... Because you cannot control all the elements ... you keep your eye on everything at all times. ... You sprinkle here, pour there. And then you watch it cook. *You keep your eye on the pot.* You look at and check it from time to time. You sniff it. You dip your finger in and taste it. ... You let it brew awhile and then you taste it again. And again. If something is wrong you correct it. But, whatever you do, the most important thing is to keep your eye on it. You don't want it to be ruined when you are off doing something else.

—HAROLD S. GENEEN
Former president and chief executive officer of ITT

The only decision a president carries out himself is to go to the bathroom. Every presidential telephone call, record of action, finding, speech, statement, or message is only words. The implementation is in the hands of persons outside the Oval Office, and predominantly outside the White House itself. Such is the dilemma of presidential dependency.

After the most elaborate information system has been plumbed, the most electric Cabinet meeting concluded, or the most brilliant option paper initialed, the decision is pushed through the White House gates into the tempest of conflicting priorities outside. Chapter 1 described that tumult, unavoidable in our contentious country, but frustrating to a president determined to rack up accomplishments before his time runs out. If the accomplishments he has in mind—if the decisions he has made—imply sharp change, a U-turn, a drastic break with the past, the tumult intensifies and the dependency dilemma deepens.

What president, especially one newly elected, does *not* aim at change? His platform, his acceptance speech, his campaign, his inaugural address all have promised that things will be different.

But what will be the fate of a new presidential policy or order that means dramatic departure from past practice? Can it be left to run on its own energy, naked in the tempest of contending interests? It cannot.

Nixon put it succinctly:

. . . I learned early in my administration that a President must keep a constant check, not just on the way his orders are being followed, but whether they are being followed at all.[1]

Kennedy had spoken similarly:

The President cannot administer a department, but at least he can be a stimulant. . . . There is a great tendency in government to have papers stay on desks too long. . . . One of the functions of the President is to try to have [the system] . . . move with more speed. Otherwise you can wait while the world collapses.[2]

Califano described the Johnson perspective:

Seated atop this bureaucratic Tower of Babel, a president who seeks to fulfill his enlarged mandate for the faithful execution of the laws . . . will strive for control and policy direction of the executive branch. . . . And the President needs some help from his own cabinet and agency heads, which is rarely forthcoming.[3]

Former domestic policy assistant Martin Anderson expresses the viewpoint of the Reagan White House:

What we needed was a policy implementation unit in the White House, a group of people who would try to keep the policy effort focused on those things that Reagan wanted done, and in the order he wanted to do them. We needed to control, channel, and monitor a whole truckload of policies we had already developed. . . . We also needed to make sure that Reagan's issues stayed at the top of the policy agenda, and we needed some way to make sure we could choke off less important and less relevant ideas that could only use up valuable time and keep us from accomplishing the big policy goals we already had on our hands.[4]

To help mitigate the dependency dilemma, therefore, presidents turn to an instrument close at hand and easy to wield: their White House staffs. If a decision is important but also precedent-breaking, presidents find it necessary to mount an in-house surveillance over its implementation. On top of the staff's policy development and information-management responsibilities, an additional task is added: monitorship.

Deputy domestic policy chief Kenneth Cole, for instance, wrote a warning note in April of 1970 listing seventeen departmental and White House officers.

Each person listed is responsible for knowing and being in control of all of the details involved in his particular program area. It is possible that any one of these men could receive a call at any time of day or night from the President requesting specific details on his program—such as the exact status of the publicity effort or the current situation in the Congress or anything else related to the passage of the program.[5]

How is the monitorship conducted? Why can't it be delegated to the action-taking agencies themselves? The author offers an illustration from his personal White House staff experience.

On July 8, 1970, after eight months of work by special counsel Leonard Garment, the author, and others, President Nixon issued a remarkable message on the reform of American Indian policy. Its recommendations did not just change precedents—they broke 180 degrees from the past.

Among the several policy declarations in the message was the promise to Indian tribes that since "the United States Government acts as a legal trustee for the . . . rights of American Indians . . . [it has] a legal obligation to advance the interests of the beneficiaries of the trust without reservation and with the highest degree of diligence and skill."[6] This policy statement meant a transformation in the government's attention to the protection of Indian water, grazing, and fishing rights set out in treaties long overlooked. Such rights are held in trust by the secretary of the interior for Indians in the future. The federal government owns these rights as a trustee and should have been performing a trustee's duty to guard them against encroachment.

For years the government had failed to do so. In Puget Sound, for instance, the federal government in effect had left the protection of Indian salmon and steelhead fishing privileges to the State of Washington. The federal responsibility languished and the state regulators usurped the Indians' rights. There were dozens of other examples of federal laxity, injuring the Pyramid Lake Paiutes in Nevada, the Pueblos in New Mexico, the Quechan tribe in Arizona, and others.

President Nixon's statement was emphatic: such laxity was to end; Indian trust rights would be defended. Nixon even proposed that a special, independent office be established for that purpose.

A year later, the author's "radar set" received a "ping" from a lawyer handling Indian cases. An Indian named Bryan L. Stevens had trust land in Montana and earned grazing fees from it. By law, income from trust land is exempt from federal income taxes. Some of Stevens' land, however, was of a slightly different character, "purchased into trust," and the Internal Revenue Service believed that the difference meant a case of tax evasion. Stevens had been convicted in the tax court; his case was on appeal in the Ninth Circuit.

His lawyer asked: "Your Mr. Nixon made a statement about guarding

Indian trust rights. Well, where is the federal government's *defense* of my client? The only federal presence we see is the prosecution."

Garment sent the author to a meeting in the Department of Justice. The officials there considered this a routine matter and had no plans to alter their established procedures. The department would, as it always had, speak to a court with only one voice, its own, and in this case it was against the Indian. The author came home empty-handed.

Garment then called a session in his office with the solicitor of the Department of the Interior and senior officials from Justice and the IRS. He asked the solicitor if the latter could draft a legal statement in defense of Mr. Stevens' trust rights. Yes, he could.

Garment then turned to the assistant attorney general and reminded him about the president's message of a year earlier. "You are to take that Interior Department defense statement," he said, "and attach it right along with your brief for the prosecution."

"To the same judges? In the same court? Our one federal government giving them *two opposing* briefs? Why, that's never been done!"

The presidential dependency dilemma lay exposed.

It was solved in this instance by a quiet but very tough White House staff officer who in effect told the resisting agencies that that's what presidents are for: to break with the past and to set new directions. And that's why White House staffs are there: to remind both political and career officers of the Executive Branch that presidents mean what they say. He ordered the Interior statement included.

The Indian won the case, the three circuit court judges repeatedly citing Interior's arguments in composing their decision.[7] If Stevens had lost, if the federal government had failed to do what the president had promised was his policy, Indian citizens would say once more that "white men speak with forked tongues."

What makes such dilemmas poignant is that the departmental officers are not usually scheming miscreants, plotting to undermine the chief executive, although presidents often think so. On the contrary, they are almost always honorable men and women—political and career alike—acting according to established professional traditions. What they fail to realize is that presidents are tradition-*breakers*. For White House staff, who see their president beleaguered on so many fronts, who look beyond the gates and hear such cacophony, who know that the Executive Branch is constitutionally the president's branch, departmental reluctance translates into insubordination.

Referring to some 1969 Nixon decisions on East-West trade, National Security Affairs Assistant Henry Kissinger recalls:

No sooner were these instructions issued than the departments began to nibble away at them. Departments accept decisions which go against them only if vigilantly supervised. Otherwise the lower-level exegesis can be breathtaking in its effrontery. It falls on the President's Assistant for National Security Affairs to do this policing in the field of national security. I soon had my hands full.[8]

Zbigniew Brzezinski adds his experience under President Carter:

... policy was controlled through supervision of implementation. [Brzezinski's White House Deputy] ... participated in ... activity designed to make certain that presidential instructions were implemented faithfully. Much of policy is made by the bureaucracy through implementation of policy, often deliberately skewing such implementation in directions that the bureaucracy would prefer to go.[9]

White House monitorship ranges from formal, comprehensive arrangements to small, quiet actions, accomplished behind the scenes. Chief of Staff Bob Haldeman set up a special office with the responsibility of appending to each major legislative proposal a "game plan" for publicity and for legislative follow-through. For example, the "game plan" to support the precedent-breaking proposals for general and special revenue-sharing in Nixon's 1971 State of the Union message filled 158 pages. Every element of the White House staff was involved in putting it together; it included a color map of the nation's regional media markets, and a list of the dates and places of the planned 1971 national conventions of sixty-eight nationwide organizations.

Kennedy abolished the Operations Coordinating Board, which was the formal follow-up mechanism for Eisenhower's National Security Council decisions. He claimed he was favoring "an increased reliance on the leadership of the Department of State."[10] But a bare month after his inauguration, White House National Security Assistant McGeorge Bundy addressed a memorandum to (among others) Secretary of the Treasury C. Douglas Dillon:

The President has asked me to start to keep track of directives and requests which he makes in the area of national security affairs. Such requests and actions may come from memoranda of his, from phone calls which he makes or asks any one of his assistants to make, or they may come from discussions which he has directly . . . in private meetings . . . or [in] the National Security Council. Wherever they come from, he is eager to keep track of the things which he personally initiates. Accordingly we are beginning a series of National Security Action Memoranda. The first in this series addressed by the President to you is Number 18. . . .[11]

It was Bundy also who increased both the size and intellectual horse-power of the president's National Security Council staff. His February 20 memorandum went on to add: "It is not our intention to pester the departments and agencies with untimely follow-up messages. . . . *At the same time* it is obviously important to [the president] to have some orderly procedure for follow-up. . . ."[12]

When President Nixon declared in 1970 that he wanted to strengthen minority-owned banks by having federal agencies move some of their deposits to them, the circular memorandum from the White House turned out to be next to useless. What it took was a dozen or more needling telephone calls from the White House staff, each agency being told that the specific dollar amount of its newly shifted deposits would be reported directly to the president.

Most White House staff supporting actions are of much lower visibility. Nixon, no lover of modern art, was annoyed when the first thing he saw as his limousine left the White House grounds through the southwest gate was a jolting, bright orange, twenty-nine-foot-tall abstract steel sculpture outside the Corcoran Gallery. The artist named it *Adam.* Garment, twisting the arms of the National Endowment for the Arts and the National Park Service, quietly got Adam moved to a lowlier paradise in another part of the city. He sent Nixon a "before" and "after" photo.

Multiply that example by hundreds.

There is one important qualification to the thesis that White House staff must often lean on the departments to ensure implementation of a president's wishes. The desired actions have to be legal. The Watergate convictions, and those which may follow from the Iran-contra indictments and trials, are unforgiving reminders that the laws and the courts always—and necessarily—limit the president's and the staff's freedom of action.

Within those limits however, the two presidential management styles conflict: "Delegate and don't interfere" or "Keep your eye on the pot." Mr. Reagan is only the latest president to assert the first but have his staff practice the second, as evidenced by the recent retrospective bleat from his own former director of the Office of Personnel Management, Donald Devine:

Perhaps my biggest disappointment was the inefficiency created by a bloated White House staff . . . Cabinet members and agency heads in the Reagan administration spent an inordinate amount of time answering inquiries from low-level members of the White House staff and OMB, many of whom had different agendas than the president's. It would be better for the president to choose individuals he knows can be trusted for major executive positions, give them a few clear directions, and allow them to make decisions without daily, counterproductive interference from the White House budget and policy staffs.[13]

Devine's irritation is typical, understandable, but in vain. In their struggle within the frustrating dilemma of presidential dependency, presidents will permit—indeed insist—that officers close to them keep their eyes on the pot of policy implementation.

The primary pot-watchers, sniffers, finger-dippers, tasters, sprinklers, and monitors are the White House staff.

CHAPTER 6

Crisis Management:
Command Center at
1600 Pennsylvania Avenue

After a whole series of pedantic suggestions from the Emperor Napoleon III had poured into French Headquarters [in the Crimea], Marshal Jean Baptiste Vaillant curtly wired back, "It is impossible to discuss strategy by telegraph." Whereupon the Emperor replied, "I do not discuss. I give orders." To this Vaillant's terse report was, "You cannot command an army from the Tuilleries."
—Major R. Hargreaves

President Ford personally took command of the military operation, directing and supervising the diplomatic, political and military phases of the effort to free the crew and ship.
—*Mayaguez* Incident Exhibit at the Gerald Ford Museum, Grand Rapids, Michigan

The contrast between Major Hargreaves' account of Marshal Vaillant on the one hand and President Ford's actions on the other reveals not just a difference in management style but a difference in history.[1] For our country, warfare in the older sense is an anachronism. The prospect of a "standard" war—declared by the Congress and waged by five-star generals in the field until there's an unconditional surrender, probably disappeared in 1945. Even large-scale, limited wars like those in Korea and Vietnam may be passé. For America now, there *are* only crises.

What is the role of the modern chief executive in crises—those abroad and those at home? How much supervision should he and his personal staff exercise when the use of federal force is contemplated or has begun?[2]

The metaphor of a battlefield has been used to describe the public policy disputes in our society. It is apt, but of course not literal. The weapons are ideological, the ammunition of the battles is in almost all cases words and pictures and the money to pay for them.

Except when violence is used or threatened. Then the civil limits are breached; clashes of ideas are transmuted into menacing contests where lives and property are at stake. Laws are violated and police—the agents of government—appear. A crisis has begun and government is in the middle of it.

When violence exceeds state capabilities for containment, is directed against federal lands or laws, or if an international emergency arises, the federal executive power is engaged. The crisis then has the potential for presidential attention.

When does that potential become real? What elevates a particular federal crisis all the way to the White House? What impels a president and his staff to become crisis managers? Three elemental apprehensions conjoin to push the White House into the tactical management of crises:

1. The recognition that most crises are unique and cannot be handled by the departments simply following routine patterns of response or preordained "contingency plans" (if such even exist).
2. The sense of the potential for catastrophe from lower-level actions that are well intentioned but wrong.
3. The knowledge that only the president is the constitutionally accountable decision-maker, being the commander in chief as well as the ultimate bearer of executive responsibility.

Other factors will accelerate the advent of White House command: if the threatened violence is massive, if it is bizarre, if there is nationwide media attention with political fallout, if U.S. armed forces could be involved, and especially if there is any aspect of the crisis that affects U.S.-USSR relations.

At the White House, crisis management is a very special form of public administration. There is no rule book, but there are rules. And in crises, everything that has been said in earlier chapters about White House behavior applies in triple strength.

There is always more than one federal agency directly affected: several domestic departments at once or, in foreign emergencies, the entire national security community—diplomats, soldiers, spies, scientists, economists, propagandists. Only the White House can impose the tight coordination of plans required among all those action points. Mixed with the expertise that the professionals provide, political judgment—in the sense of calculating congressional and public acceptability—must also be injected; that is a unique White House task.

Information cascades into the system through both official and informal intakes. (The rolls of film taken for Kennedy by the U-2s and other reconnaissance aircraft over Cuba on October 25, 1962, were 25 *miles* long.) The information is usually in fragments, often not the most important fragments. The need for all-points evaluation escalates. Kissinger recalls: "One is forced to react to scraps of information in very limited spans of time; longing for full knowledge, one must chart a route through the murk of unknowing."[3]

If the crisis involves military moves, such as Carter's hostage-rescue attempt, secrecy becomes a life-or-death concern. As the shield of protection thickens around the commander in chief's initiatives (Kennedy's Cuban missile crisis tactics or Reagan's arms-to-Iran decision), the ring of his advisers shrinks. An "Executive Committee" is summoned or a "Washington Special Action Group" is called to meet in the Situation Room. Normal decision-making channels are contracted, limited to those in whom the president has special confidence.

The margin for error narrows drastically; the costs of a mistake in implementation, however well intentioned, are prohibitive. White House surveillance over implementation therefore becomes minute. Kissinger emphasizes: "To manage crises effectively, the agencies and departments involved have to know what the President intends. They must be closely monitored to make certain that diplomatic and military moves dovetail."[4]

Perhaps most potent of all these centralizing factors is the public's own perception. In times of crisis, citizens expect their president to be personally on duty and in charge. When a tactical exchange of fire took place with Libyan planes over the Gulf of Sidra in August 1981, his staff let Reagan stay undisturbed in California for six hours. Pulitzer Prize–winning columnist Haynes Johnson wrote: "Here's one citizen who says: At the very least, wake him up next time."[5] Together these factors act to concentrate crisis command where the American public expects it to be: in the president's office.

A few military officers still proclaim their preference for the dictum of Sun Tzu (a Chinese adviser 2500 years ago) who said: "He will win who has military capacity and is not interfered with by the sovereign." Crisis management today, however, requires vastly different procedures.

As the potential for conflict escalates, immediate facts are demanded direct from the crisis scene: What's happening block by block in Santo Domingo? Who shot first in the Gulf of Tonkin? How many Indians have guns in the Bureau of Indian Affairs Building? Precisely how far is each Soviet ship from Cuba? Is it the *Mayaguez* crew huddled in that Cambodian boat?

While those schooled in the Sun Tzu tradition may blanch at such operational inquisitiveness from on high, their communications colleagues long ago tipped the scales toward the president; electronic gadgetry lets him, if he wishes, hover right over the crisis arena. The modern soldier who has the ANTSC-85-a field radio is able, from his vehicle and via satellite, "to reach the White House," said an Army briefing officer recently. In the future, the whole terminal—satellite dish, keyboard, printer, and all—for instantaneous, secure, written communications worldwide, will fit on his back.[6] Lieutenant Jones should be prepared: if he has unique information about a crisis in front of him, the White House may call him first.

Impelled by these reasons—the need for coordination, for policy judgment, and to meet the public's expectations—and equipped with those capabilities, the modern presidents have inched—some have jumped—into elevating *tactical* crisis command into the White House. They forswear it, but they acquiesce; they deny it, but they do it. The record makes the case.

President Truman personally authorized the bombing of the Yalu bridges in Korea in 1950 and disapproved the hot pursuit of MIG aircraft over the Manchurian border.

When the CIA needed just two more P-51 fighter-bombers during the U.S. action in Guatemala in 1954, the request was brought to Eisenhower, who authorized them. In a 1965 interview with the author, Ike acknowledged that whenever military operations are bound up with diplomatic, economic, and psychological initiatives, a president must be a close and detailed manager.[7]

International crises in today's times are always military-diplomatic-economic mixtures, forcing even operational control upward into the hands of the nation's political leader. Long before the crisis development in 1960, Eisenhower had taken personal charge of the U-2 enterprise. Michael Beschloss' account describes what went on in the Oval Office when U-2 flights were being approved:

> Goodpaster ordinarily stood over the President's shoulder as [the CIA's Richard] Bissell laid out his maps on the desk, lecturing on the expected risks and rewards. Eisenhower sometimes said, "I want you to leave out that leg and go straight *that* way. I want you to go from B to D, because it looks to me like you might be getting a little exposed over here."[8]

When the pictures came back, the Oval Office scene was the same: "Asking his usual volley of questions, Eisenhower put on and snatched off his reading glasses as his eyes darted up and down the pictures of factories, railroads, highways, bomber fields and submarine pens."[9]

After the first few U-2 flights had brought a Soviet protest, Eisenhower declined to delegate authority to the CIA to fly the plane even during specified periods. Each individual takeoff had to have his personal approval.

When the U-2 was shot down in the Soviet Union in May of 1960,

Eisenhower was faced not so much with a crisis as with a question: should he reveal his personal role? The government's first defense (approved by Ike but issued at the Department of State) was to say, "A flight over Soviet territory was probably taken. . . . aircraft have made flights along the frontiers." Hearing that, the press took dead aim at the White House.

American political columnists attacked the man in the White House. In the *New York Times,* James Reston said "The heart of the problem here is that the Presidency has been parcelled out, first to Sherman Adams, then to John Foster Dulles, and in this case to somebody else—probably to Allen Dulles, but we still don't know." Eisenhower's "institutionalized Presidency" removed him from key decisions and left "the nation, the world and sometimes even the President himself in a state of uncertainty about who is doing what."[10]

Ike changed his mind. Two days later came a new statement: "The President has put into effect directives . . . to gather by every possible means . . . on occasion by penetration."[11]

"Plausible deniability" died that day.

It was given its legal burial in a 1974 enactment. The Congress wiped out the last distance between a president and even the most secret operations of an executive agency when it mandated a presidential "finding" for every CIA covert operation.

Kennedy's strategic *and* tactical direction of the Cuban missile situation is more well known—it was a quantum jump on the crisis-command road along which the contemporary presidents are traveling. His detailed supervision was "unparalleled in modern relations between American political leaders and military organizations," commented one author, who went on to add:

. . . for the first time in military history, local commanders received repeated orders about the details of their military operations directly from political leaders—contrary to two sacred military doctrines. This circumvention of the *chain of command* and the accompanying countermand of the *autonomy of local commanders* created enormous pain and serious friction.[12]

Neither Kennedy nor his advisers made any apologies for that tight presidential control. Just the opposite. Twenty years afterward, a group of them listed the lessons they had learned. Among them:

. . . restraint was as important as strength. . . . We avoided any early initiation of battle by American forces, and indeed we took no action of any kind that would have forced an instant and possibly ill-considered response. . . ."

The gravest risk in this crisis was not that either head of government desired to initiate a major escalation but that events would produce actions, reactions or miscalculations. . . .

[Kennedy kept] continuously attentive control of our options and actions. . . .[13]

President Kennedy experienced a domestic crisis as well. When black student James Meredith tried to enroll in the all-white University of Mississippi, Governor Ross Barnett's state police failed to provide the needed protection. Kennedy federalized the National Guard and then sent U.S. Army troops to the campus. "On that Sunday, the White House was more or less the command headquarters," Ted Sorensen observed. In fact, Kennedy was so annoyed at the poor response time of the Army that he ordered a log made of precisely when each White House telephone call was placed to the Defense Department and when each Army unit moved.[14]

President Johnson continued the Kennedy command style, adapting it during the Vietnam War years into a constantly tight control of the bombing operations over North Vietnam. Under Secretary of the Air Force Townsend Hoopes remembered:

The Joint Chiefs of Staff argued stoutly that both [ground and air] elements of the war should be left to the field commanders, but they gave way to presidential insistence on detailed White House control of the bombing. And tight control here was prudent, for the "Rolling Thunder" campaign, as it steadily expanded, carried an ever-present risk of military confrontation with Russia or China.[15]

Nixon disapproved of the "Situation Room syndrome" of his predecessor; he did not, according to Kissinger, want to pretend that he was a commander in chief "by nervous meddling with tactical details or formative deliberations." The former White House national security affairs assistant then adds, "He left the shaping of those to the governmental machinery *under my supervision.*"[16] If not in the Oval Office, the tactical supervision of crises remained with the Nixon White House staff.

This chapter opened with the evidence of President Ford's pride in dramatizing his personal command role in the *Mayaguez* crisis of 1975. An entire exhibit wall in the Gerald Ford Museum in Grand Rapids recounts the story. At one point, a young Air Force pilot is flying an A-7 attack aircraft over the waters near the Cambodian shore, spots a small boat, and prepares to sink it with his 20-mm cannon. But he discerns Caucasians huddled on the deck. The young pilot radios back to make sure of his instructions, and his voice comes all the way to the Situation Room in the White House. While he circles and waits out there in Southeast Asia, his request is taken to the president in the Cabinet Room. The president wastes little time to give the order: "You get a message to that pilot to shoot across the bow but do not sink the boat." The chief of naval operations runs downstairs from the Cabinet Room to the Situation Room and the radio call goes back twelve thousand miles. "It's goofy the way technology has put a president in that position," Chief of Staff Donald Rumsfeld later exclaimed.[17] But the technology gets more capable every year.

Later accounts of the *Mayaguez* affair were critical of Ford, alleged he overreacted with force, did not give diplomatic efforts enough of a chance. A president *is* responsible, and history's verdict will be given when all the facts are known. There would be only one intolerable judgment: that he had not been in charge.

Events in Tehran in 1979 drew President Carter and his staff deeply into crisis management for fourteen months. At a climactic period in November, when the shah was tottering and mobs were in the streets, the president lost confidence in his ambassador on the scene, and in the State Department's staff in Washington. Carter preempted his bureaucracy and instructed his national security assistant personally to telephone the shah and urge him to act forcefully.[18] During the ensuing months, Carter constantly employed the skills and energies of two of his most trusted White House aides, Hamilton Jordan and Lloyd Cutler, to try to discern a way out of the Iranian crisis and to arrange for freeing the hostages. Jordan himself spent an entire year in this effort, travelling, sometimes in secret and once in disguise, to be the president's man-on-the-spot in meetings in Florida, Texas, Panama, London, Paris, and Bern.[19]

In April of 1988, when a Navy pilot, flying patrol over the Persian Gulf, spotted three Iranian speedboats attacking oil rigs below him, he radioed for permission to bomb the boats. The request went swiftly up the chain of command, reaching Reagan's national security assistant, who put the question to the president. Reagan gave his approval and the orders were sent back to the pilot. Elapsed time: reportedly less than three minutes.[20]

Up to this writing (May 1988), the Reagan presidency has been spared the trauma of war or major international crisis. As is discussed in chapter 7, however, the Reagan national security affairs staff has continued the precedent of tight supervision of—even personal participation in—sensitive enterprises abroad. Reagan's own policies for such enterprises (in Iran and in Nicaragua) were exceedingly controversial and the actions of some of the staff were bizarre if not in fact unlawful. Historians and juries yet unnamed will make the final judgments on the Reagan national security operations, but the record of eight presidents is too continuous to permit any but one conclusion: strategic and often even tactical crisis management is centered in the White House.

This principle holds for some domestic crises as well, when they affect federal laws, and especially when the perpetrators act under the banner of a cause which evokes widespread public sympathy—in America and overseas. The use of force may be threatened, and sometimes employed, but the confrontations are staged rather than waged, and it is mob leaders rather than marching armies who are raising hell. There is an element of guerilla theater in such face-offs; the substantive cause or historical grievance may often be displaced or overwhelmed by the sheer drive for publicity for its own sake. The players then become actors on a world stage. Lenses, microphones, and newswires project the leaders' "demands" and all the on-scene developments to an intercontinental audience, but only if the tension is kept high, only if the drama and suspense are daily renewed. If the desperation index goes down, if the "minutes to midnight" syndrome is relaxed, press attention wanes and the television cameras may move to another assignment. The result: pressure on the perpetrators to keep inventing yet another shocking development, to threaten apocalypse anew.

Because of nationwide—in fact worldwide—attention, and because of the genuine danger that well-intentioned but misguided responses could make the confrontations much worse, such crises-as-theater, when they involve federal issues, also escalate to White House control.

How do White House staff manage a crisis of this sort? What do they actually do?

A first-hand illustration of the staff's role can be seen in three on-the-home-front instances in which the author was personally involved. They are the trilogy of American Indian crises during the period 1969 through 1973: the seizure of Alcatraz Island, the occupation of the Bureau of Indian Affairs building in Washington, and the siege of Wounded Knee. It was a three-act drama.[21]

November 19, 1969: during the night a group of eighty Indian men, women, and children occupy long-vacant Alcatraz Island in San Francisco Bay. They issue a statement challenging the federal government: you can prove your title to Alcatraz by committing "genocide" against us, or you can send the secretary of the interior to meet with us in person *after* he agrees to give us the island and enough money to "construct, maintain and operate a major university and research and development center there for all Indian people." Apocalyptic threat; theatrical demand.

Considering this to be simply a trespass, the real titleholder to Alcatraz, Administrator Robert Kunzig of the U.S. General Services Administration, issues orders to his West Coast staff: get U.S. marshals to take the Indians off at gunpoint "by noon tomorrow."

Then the White House intervenes. Presidential special counsel Leonard Garment recognizes that this escapade is much more than an ordinary trespass, sees the GSA plan as pugnacious overreaction likely to spill blood and stir up enormous public revulsion, and is sure that he has the support of the president. Garment telephones Kunzig and flatly instructs him to call off the marshals. Furthermore, the White House will need up-to-date information and will therefore want to be talking with GSA West Coast regional administrator Tom Hannon directly, for situation reports, but will keep GSA's Washington office informed.

Kunzig is furious; this is an unconscionable intrusion into his turf and his responsibilities; he finally tells Garment to deal with anyone he wants but never to speak to him again.

Garment's office promptly establishes communications with Hannon in San Francisco, keeping a Kunzig aide au courant as well. Why Hannon? Because he is the person on the front line of the crisis. It is Hannon who leaves his downtown office, takes the boat over to Alcatraz (bringing candy and cigarettes to the Indians), and meets and talks with the occupiers and of course with the beleaguered GSA custodians resident on the island. When Hannon comes back to his office phone, only he has the kind of immediate intelligence for which the crisis managers thirst.

As a rearguard action, Kunzig calls another White House officer known for his interest in law enforcement, who empathizes that the Indians would have been yanked off the island PDQ were it not for "that asshole Hannon in San Francisco." It is not known whether or how they characterized Garment, but in the public-policy jousting lists, the contestants are often members of the White House staff aiming lances at each other.

Six days later, a conciliatory statement issues from the GSA press office, abjuring force and urging the Indians to leave the island to talk about their "true needs for educational and cultural facilities" with a federal inter-agency group in San Francisco. The statement is drafted in Garment's office but—a typical crisis maneuver—is released elsewhere to mask the White House role. Secretary of the Interior Walter Hickel issues a similar release; he would meet with Indian representatives but without preconditions.

An interagency group is then organized to discuss the needs of Bay Area urban Indians and what negotiating position to take with the Alcatraz bunch. Who is on this task force? The Departments of Labor, of Health, Education and Welfare, of Interior, of Housing and Urban Development, the Office of Economic Opportunity, the GSA, the Bureau of the Budget, and the vice president's office. Each of these agencies has some interest, authority, facilities, staff, or money that could be contributed to a possible negotiated solution. But no one of them can do it alone, or even could be said to have the "lead." The White House chairs the meetings.

The twelve-year-old stepdaughter of the Indian occupation leader, Richard Oakes, falls through a stairwell in the old prison and is terribly injured. Garment telephones Hannon to go from his home to the hospital that very night and express the concern of the White House to parents and relatives. He does, for three hours. When the little girl dies the next morning, Garment sends a personal note of condolence to Oakes. Public administration is people. Across whatever the great gulfs of policy dispute, there are human bridges to be built.

In a few weeks, a special White House emissary, Robert Robertson of the vice president's staff, makes the first of several trips to Alcatraz, meets with the Indians there, and tries to set up a negotiating arrangement. His comings and goings have a dramatic air, but much of this whole escapade *is* theater. . . . The Indians attempt some countertheater: they put mescaline in Robertson's coffee just before he is to hold a press conference. He avoids that trap, but the Indians reject his proposals.

News media everywhere carry the Alcatraz story. The country is watching and, remembering U.S. history, is sympathetic to the Indians. Congressional mail into the White House favors "giving the island to the Indians." Republican Bay Area Congressman William Mailliard says the Indians are "dramatizing some real problems," and San Francisco Mayor Joseph Alioto is of like mind. Conservative Republican Senator George Murphy of California recommends making Alcatraz an "Indian National Park." Donations of food, clothing, and money arrive at the island. Entertainment stars Merv Griffin, Anthony Quinn, and Jane Fonda visit the Island; political activist Bernadette Devlin and actor Jonathan Winters express support. Nor is politics ever absent: Ethel Kennedy goes out to Alcatraz and then in a long telephone conversation needles Garment to be more forthcoming.

Concerned for the safety of the GSA custodians, the government withdraws them, then cuts off power to the island and takes away the water barge. The Indians destroy the lighthouse controls, and maritime interests then begin to complain about the resulting danger to Bay shipping. The editor of the San Francisco Chronicle loans the Indians generators (an example of how the press not only covers a dramatic story but helps keep it alive). The government gives a small planning grant to an ad hoc group called the Bay Area Native American Council (BANAC), but there is estrangement between the Bay Area Indian leaders and the Alcatraz occupiers.

Sixteen months and countless palavers later, a Time feature story characterizes the occupation as "Anomie at Alcatraz":

The invasion force became a thoroughly disorganized society . . . infighting has caused most of the original invasion leaders to leave Alcatraz. They have been replaced by homeless‚ apolitical young Indians more concerned with finding a pad where they can "get their heads together" than in sustaining any kind of significant political statement . . . mainland Indian groups . . . are somewhat at a loss as to how to deal with their recalcitrant brothers.[22]

Other press interest declines correspondingly and the Alcatraz remnant turns to stripping metal from the prison equipment for peddling to scrap dealers in San Francisco. The drama has diminished, the audience is nearly gone, the klieg lights are dimming; the stars of the cast are on leave. Act 1 must end.

On June 11, 1971, thirty-five marshals peacefully take the remaining fifteen Indians off the island. In a final curtain-closer, the GSA brings in a photographer to take snapshots of the mess left behind. The *San Francisco Examiner* editorializes: "The federal government wisely let the Indians play out their string."[23]

Unforgettable, though, has been the intervening event halfway through the occupation. On May 4, 1970, in another crisis scene two thousand miles to the east, restraint mechanisms were absent. Ohio National Guardsmen had live ammunition in their rifles as they faced taunting campus demonstrators; they fired their guns and four students died on the lawn of Kent State University. The following Saturday, eighty thousand demonstrators converged on Washington, surrounded the White House (itself walled off by buses parked bumper-to-bumper), and screamed at the president who remained cooped up inside.

These two antiphonal face-offs—Alcatraz and Kent State—portray the contrast between a crisis managed and a crisis out of control. Under pressure it is much harder to use restraint than to pull the trigger. Hard even in the councils of government; extremely difficult when agency heads— and their egos and prestige—are personally involved.

Principal lesson one for the relatively new Nixon staff: crisis management is a White House function; it takes a special combination of guts and compassion, and when needed, a mailed fist, from the top.

Act 2 opens up just a week before the presidential election of 1972 when several hundred Indians from both cities and reservations converge into a "Trail of Broken Treaties" in Washington and crowd into the auditorium of the Bureau of Indian Affairs Building on Constitution Avenue. As the day ends and the employees leave, the Indians decide to take over the building. Their request to meet with the president is denied, but an "administration representative" has been promised; they ask for John Ehrlichman, but Ehrlichman's office instructs the author to meet with them.

At eight o'clock in the evening on November 2, a hyped-up and angry group of Trail leaders (mostly activists in the American Indian Movement) is allowed to cross the street and jam into the conference room of Assistant Secretary of the Interior Harrison Loesch. They are especially offended by Loesch, who three weeks before had issued a menacing instruction to the entire Bureau of Indian Affairs "not to provide any assistance or funding, either directly or indirectly" to the demonstrators. While superficially correct, that memorandum in substance was inconsistent with the informal help other government agencies were rendering; in style it was puerile and inflammatory.

Before the evening session even opens, therefore, the Indian leaders demand that their host leave. Over White House remonstrations, Loesch is ousted from his own conference room and forced to wait outside. Bob Robertson (from the vice president's staff) and the author are left to face the visitors.

The drama escalates: across the street at the BIA Building, gasoline and typewriters are being stacked at the top of stairwells; outside the building the civil-disturbance police are putting on their special helmets with plastic visors; in the conference room the excited leaders are declaiming that tonight is to bring their martyrdom. *"You know, Mr. Patterson,"* they assert, *"we are going to die tonight!"*

What does a White House staff do with that? It listens, and through listening, buys time and cools tempers.

For hours that night, the two staffers let the impassioned young men denounce the past, boast of the present, threaten the future. Each one, around the table, spits out a froth of incantations, frustrations, threats, and sorrows—something like vomit: ugly when coming up, but bringing a temporary catharsis afterward. A local black leader joins the group, raising the specter of the Washington black community's making common cause with the Indian occupiers.

The representative of the Community Relations Service of the Department of Justice (supposedly expert in damping down crises) rushes into the room to announce that the police now have surrounded the BIA Building next door, a stupid thing to blurt out right at that time. The catharsis disappears and the high-pitched demagoguery begins anew. The only long-range promise that can be made is then made: that the twenty "demands" of the Trail leadership will be studied and that the government will respond directly to each of them. The tension diminishes.

Finally, there is a recess. In a hasty private caucus, the government officers learn that a short-range conclusion must also be reached: they must decide immediately whether to use the police to storm the building, otherwise the Civil Disturbance Unit will disband for the night. There is internal disagreement. Loesch and Robertson, seeing this as an issue of law, demand a law-enforcement solution. The author's own advice is for continued restraint. He telephones a White House colleague responsible for law-enforcement issues, tells of the dispute, makes his own recommendation, and later gets the answer (which has come from the president): no police power that evening; the government will go to court in the morning for a restraining order.

In the next seven days, the government appears eight times before two federal courts, is granted one temporary restraining order and one order for arrest and show cause, but five times asks for delays to permit the hard, actual negotiations to proceed. Finally, the arrest order proves moot when the Indians clear out of the building and leave town.

Principal lesson two: the courts are not the place for crisis management. Courts make decisions, issue orders, specify deadlines. Law-enforcement officers as representatives of the courts are mandated to enforce those deadlines. But crises require discussion, the give-and-take of promises, the crafting of words of compromise. Neither judges nor police can perform those functions. Setting deadlines only plays into the hands of the perpetrators; as the final minutes tick off, tension rises, the klieg lights turn brighter, the network cameras roll.

The negotiations themselves were conducted under direct White House auspices with special counsel Leonard Garment, Deputy OMB Director Frank Carlucci, and the author heading a large interagency team on the government side. One of the promises that sped the negotiations was that an interdepartmental task force made up from twenty-one separate offices in eleven different agencies would be formed to review Indian policies and Indian needs. Only the White House could assemble, organize, and give guidance to such a disparate collection of officials, all of whom would have to work together to produce a result.

Two sticky questions remained. First, would the Indian occupiers be prosecuted? On behalf of the White House, Garment and Carlucci made a difficult decision: no. Not for the act of occupying the building, they promised, but the Indians would be liable for criminal vandalism in the building or theft of any of its contents. Second, could the government help pay travel expenses to get the Indians home? Again a novel and controversial answer: yes, and $66,500 in cash was handed out. (One of those court orders had asked the government to provide alternate sanitary and commissary facilities for the Indians at a nearby federal hall. Carlucci wisely reasoned that a one-time going-home payment would be much less expensive than an Alcatraz-style, months-long encampment.)

The Indians left, there *was* vandalism and theft (but few successful prosecutions), and a congressional committee called hearings, yet made no recommendations. No one "died that night," but side by side with the gasoline and the Molotov cocktails there had been a nursery on the third floor with at least one six-month-old among the many children.

In the aftermath, the conservative weekly *Human Events* assailed Garment for "this disastrous, disgraceful truckling to lawlessness," but a month later Carlucci reminded the Congress: "To those who question our administrative procedures, let me assure you that this was no situation for modern textbook management practices . . . we avoided a bloody confrontation."[24]

Carlucci was right: there were no textbooks for crises, no procedures manual, but reliance instead on judgment, compassion, improvisation, finesse, and experience. And to be candid about it, the White House finds it has to impose this approach on departmental experts who, well motivated, try to "go by the book" when the book is irrelevant.

The third act of the Indian trilogy began on the evening of February 27, 1973. Two hundred armed Indian militants in a sixty-car caravan on South Dakota's Pine Ridge Sioux Reservation, en route from one hamlet to another there, drive through Wounded Knee Village. On the spot, they decide to break into the trading post, then into homes in the village, and end up holding eleven residents hostage and occupying several buildings and the Catholic church. Some three hundred U.S. marshals, FBI agents, and BIA police set up roadblocks around the village, and shots are exchanged.

The White House is immediately notified, and again Garment is point man for the decision-making process at that level. Again, knowing the president's views, he sets the policy (especially in view of the reported hostages): no violent counterattacks. The well-trained marshals, agents, and police act with professional restraint.

The script has familiar elements: the Indians' portentous dare—"Wipe out all the old people, women, children and men, by shooting and attacking us"—followed by their publicity-laden request: Chairman William Fulbright must call Foreign Relations Committee hearings on the violation of Indian treaties, Senator Ted Kennedy must start a Senate investigation of the BIA, and Senate Indian Affairs Committee Chairman James Abourezk must initiate an investigation of all the Sioux reservations.

This time, however, the violence quotient is greater: the Indians apparently have at least one M-60 machine gun along with all their rifles, and the three hundred federal police have fifteen armored personnel carriers, a hundred M-16s and, as an observer, the chief of staff of the 82nd Airborne Division.

The press come in droves, first in low-flying planes, then on foot at night, escorted by the Indians on trails through the ravines. Three hundred newspeople cover the story, among them reporters from a dozen foreign countries, including the USSR. A Harris poll is published, disclosing that 93 percent of those questioned are following the Wounded Knee events and that 51 percent favor the Indian occupation.

Back in Washington, the crisis-management machinery is collegial but totally under White House direction. Garment and the author ride over to the deputy attorney general's conference room and meet with a group representing the several parts of Justice, of Interior, and sometimes a Defense officer. A telephone call is placed to the assistant attorney general who is in charge of the federal forces—and of the negotiations—out at Pine Ridge; the speakerphone is activated and there is a long-distance staff meeting. Garment's word carries the most weight. The White House men then return to their offices, prepare memoranda for the domestic policy staff chief, Ken Cole, or for President Nixon, and get whatever answers are needed for the next decision session.

The government stays away from the courts, imposes no deadlines, and insists on restraint (although on some nights thousands of rounds are exchanged). The 82nd Airborne tells the government group how they could, if the president ordered it, overwhelm Wounded Knee with a massive attack. The Army wants no part of such an undertaking and the White House vetoes any thought of it.

Just how far-flung is the attentive public becomes clear in a memorandum from the U.S. Information Agency: "If Indians are killed, we can surely expect sharp and widespread foreign condemnation of this U.S. Government action. It would come at a particularly unpropitious time, giving Arab governments an excuse to fog up the terrorist issue."[25] Even a distant South Dakota crisis is being watched by the world.

It took seventy-one days of patient, persistent, trying negotiations before the last Indian crisis wound down. The ending was as theatrical as the beginning: upon the government's promise to send five "White House representatives" to the reservation, the Indians evacuated Wounded Knee. The author led the delegation (two were from the White House; the other three "White House" officials were actually from Justice and Interior).

Under the pine boughs at Frank Fools Crow's camp, the five from Washington listened to the impassioned accusations. They patiently explained how the Congress did indeed violate the Treaty of 1868, after Custer's defeat and the discovery of gold. When "Chief" Fools Crow demanded that the Black Hills be returned to the Sioux forthwith, the author had to tell him that even if he were the president of the United States, the answer would be no. Only the Congress could undo—or compensate for—the ancient injustice. Thus closed the crisis part of the trilogy. Lengthy letters were later exchanged between Garment and the Sioux militants, but the latter were not representative of the elected tribal leaders who wanted to continue to pursue their long-standing monetary claim through the courts.

Nine years later, those residents who had lost property at Wounded Knee asked a commissioner of the Court of Claims to find that the government's actions during the BIA Building occupation and during the Wounded Knee crisis were both negligent and improper. After a full-blown trial, Commissioner Thomas Lydon rendered his opinion on how the White House and its associates had behaved:

> The government . . . acted reasonably, with praiseworthy restraint and concern for the lives of all involved and with remarkable imagination and constructive creativity in handling the occupation and dispossession of the BIA building. . . . It is my opinion that the government's actions, both before and during the civil disorder at Wounded Knee, were at all times reasonable, responsible and proper. . . . Federal officers were persistent, determined and reasonable in their efforts to effect a peaceful resolution of the occupation crisis . . . a testimonial to the reasoned perseverance under difficult, trying and dangerous circumstances, of the government officials involved.[26]

Even today the White House officials who managed the three minicrises remember those tense days with feeling and read the commissioner's commendation with pride.

Crises strip away whatever fantasies may linger that the American Executive Branch is "Cabinet government." Textbook notions of delegation, of relying on precooked contingency plans, of a White House that only sets broad policy and leaves the details to experts—all are scrapped in the hot reality of presidential command. Experts *are* always on the scene and working, but in a crisis the stakes are so high that the decisions—even the important tactical ones—are elevated into the White House.

To the White House staff, the sense of central command and central responsibility is in the air they breathe. *But it is always the president's command; they only amplify him.*

The staff's most urgent crisis role is first to get the fullest possible information directly from where the crisis is happening, bypassing intermediaries if needed. The second is to preserve presidential options, that is, to fend off—even to countermand—lower-level actions that, however well intentioned, would exacerbate the crisis or narrow the president's choices in the future. After they help him and his Cabinet advisers frame the choices and debate them, the staff must, third, make sure the presidential decisions are recorded and transmitted. Finally, the staff must monitor every important detail of implementation.

Superb communications gadgetry makes this White House role possible; the Constitution, it is argued, makes it necessary.

PART II

The Bashful Bureaucracy

Introduction to Part II

T HE chapters of part I are the needed obituary for the shibboleth of "Cabinet government." It is the White House staff on whom modern presidents rely to coordinate the development of their important policies, to control the flow of sensitive information, to keep a close watch on Cabinet responses, and to manage crisis actions.

Just what is the White House establishment?

The reader now is asked to leave the gates and come inside the door.

The White House staff is a continuing enterprise of the American presidency. Its continuity, though, is masked by constant movement.

The people there change—frequently. Their titles change. The names of the units alter, as well as the chains of supervision. At the end of a presidency, there is a mass exodus of the political staff; most of the files, too, are removed.

Survey groups and transition teams then typically call for even more changes, for a "leaner" and "streamlined" White House staff. The new president agrees, vows to slice the "overgrown," "bloated" White House establishment, and raises his hatchet to chop. His arm stays in the air. He discovers that there is a set of elemental White House functions that cannot be severed from the presidency, nor can they be implanted elsewhere.

What are the core responsibilities of the modern White House staff? What are the major subgroups of the staff family?

There are twenty. Fourteen serve the specialized policy and political needs of the president. One staff office belongs directly to the first lady, another to the vice president. The other four are centripetal; they tie the sixteen whirling miniworlds together.

In addition to the principal twenty, the White House has a professional staff of twenty-five essential support units; they are described in part III.

The purpose of part II is to aim a floodlight at the major staff offices of the modern presidency and to illumine why each of these responsibilities has been given its home in the White House. The twenty are here introduced.

Policy and Political Staff Functions

1. The assistant for national security affairs helps the president interlink the largest of his Executive Branch communities: the worldwide diplomatic/military/intelligence/overseas information/foreign economic complex. Other areas such as science, space, and agriculture are often a part of the network. Within this complex, and facing the present-day world, the president can tolerate no wild-card moves; coordination, and especially presidential initiatives, are tightly held at the White House.

2. The domestic policy staff—by whatever name—is the counterpart of the security assistant for the president's policy initiatives at home. Because there are more Cabinet links in this network, policy orchestration is more difficult and White House leadership is even harder to maintain.

3. The counsel to the president is the lawyer for the White House. If the president's dog needs a license, his speech needs a legal check, executive privilege needs reaffirmation, an enrolled bill needs a review, a citizen needs a pardon, or SALT negotiators need advice, the counsel can be everywhere.

4. The legislative affairs staff is the president's link to the Congress, the informal two-way bridge that connects those formal, constitutional separates. Both houses and both parties tread that pathway, and every square inch of policy ground is within the legislative playing field.

5. The press officers are the authorized on-the-record spokespersons for the president; other staffers speak only at their signal. President and press are the best of enemies, and the press secretary is always in the middle of that tension. A skeptical White House press corps, several hundred strong, lurks outside his door.

6. The Communications Office (in some White Houses an umbrella staff over the Press, Public Liaison, and Speechwriting offices) is the lens that focuses the haze of White House activities into a beam of attention. It directs the theater called the White House, helping to keep the president in the starring role.

7. The speechwriters' pens become the president's voice—and the president's voice is potentially a unifying force in a cacophonous nation. World leaders and peoples listen, too. From "Rose Garden rubbish" to the

State of the Union address, the speechwriters aim at eloquence with accuracy.

8. The public liaison staff is the entrance foyer to the presidency for the leadership of the nineteen thousand national organizations that knock at White House gates. The Business Roundtable is in that throng; lobbyists for civil rights and the handicapped are there as well. All need (and can distribute) information, deserve a hearing, and carry crucial weight in the Congress. Some of their views merit the president's own attention.

9. The president has four years—1,461 days—to make his mark on history. Endless thousands of requesters will vie for those twelve thousand–odd weekday hours. To which will he accede? Will he fill those hours with significant achievements or mere activities? The Scheduling Office helps him balance and choose.

10. The intergovernmental affairs staff is another two-way path into and out of the not-so-enchanted forest of 22,802 state, local, and tribal governments. Governors, mayors, and tribal chairmen, partners in the American federal system, are friendly or hostile denizens; presidential policy initiatives require their support.

11. As head of his party, the president has obligations to its one national and fifty state organizations, to numerous political action committees and to hundreds of local volunteer groups. He also has reciprocal debts and credits with his party's elected officials. The Political Affairs Office helps him keep the ledgers, is an ombudsman for those on the plus side. When the president runs for reelection, his real campaign headquarters is there in the White House.

12. A new president can make nearly twenty-seven hundred Executive and Judicial Branch presidential appointments. His own reputation will ride on the quality of these men and women, fifteen hundred of whom will be subject to scrutiny and confirmation by the Senate. The president will, in addition, want to oversee the choice of some or all of the twenty-three hundred full-time noncareer jobholders appointed by his Cabinet and agency heads. Filtering the candidates, balancing the pluses and minuses, the Presidential Personnel Office prepares for his decisions.

13. If only for security reasons, the practice of impromptu public appearances has disappeared from the president's life. While his hours in the White House may afford him some flexibility, any visits outside those eighteen acres demand extraordinary preparations. Planning a presidential trip means dealing with dozens of local hosts, each of whom has his or her own agenda for the chief executive's time. The Advance Office keeps the president's priorities in the forefront.

14.   Extraordinary and consuming national issues require extraordinary presidential responses; the regular governmental machinery will often be seen as insufficient. On such occasions presidents will create superstaff offices, White House "czars," to dramatize his concerns and to galvanize old interdepartmental efforts with new presidential energy. A White House may, in fact, have several "czars" at once.

Aiding the First Lady

15.   The Office of the First Lady (all the gender terminology here could be switched in the future) is a copy of the president's staff in part and in miniature. Speeches, press meetings, trips in the U.S. and abroad, correspondence, testimony to Congress, political campaigning, the extensive White House social responsibilities—each first lady varies in her preferences but needs staff of her own to support her activities.

The Vice President's Staff

16.   Before 1961, the vice president's only office and staff were at the Capitol; now his (or her) principal headquarters is the Executive Office Building next door to the president. The vice president's staff is a mini White House but with a difference permeating everything they do: their boss is planning to be president. They are responsible not to the Oval Office but to the vice president, yet like their chief they are all part of the White House environment.

Tying the Place Together

17.   A civilian aide and two secretaries are the president's personal office, handling telephone calls, personal dictation, keeping the schedule moving. Podiums ready? Signature pens full? People standing where they belong? Perhaps a diary note is jotted down, a visitor slipped in the back door. The Personal Office, while intimate to the boss, reinforces—and cannot permit evasion of—the discipline by which the whole staff operates.

18.   The Cabinet Secretariat was described in chapter 2. It has a wider horizon now and a different title: Office of Cabinet Affairs. This group is home base for the non–national security links to Cabinet members' offices. For clearance of presidential policy papers, for coordination of speechmaking, for members' schedule requests for presidential visits and trips, the OCA is a facilitator, even an advocate of sorts, alert to Cabinet members' concerns. And they arrange Cabinet meetings as well.

19. "Is this document ready, in every sense, for the president to see? Have the right internal staff offices (Counsel, Legislative Affairs, Press, NSC, etc.) concurred or voiced their objections?" If the answer is no, the memo is sent back. For all the papers moving in and out of the Oval Office, the staff secretary is the unpopular, but indispensable, disciplinarian.

20. IS THE WHOLE SYSTEM WORKING? Is it working precisely as the president prefers—no tighter, no looser than his personal wish? Any weak spots? Any people or operations getting out of hand? What presidential guidance is there to pass on? The chief of staff is system manager. Without his backing, and the president's strong and evident support of it and of him, those sixteen miniworlds fly apart and the White House is chaos. The chief of staff function at times has been combined with being president (Kennedy, Johnson, Carter) but it was Eisenhower who asked: "Do I have to be my own sergeant major?"

In 1833, this, allegedly, was the System:

> The Gineral [President Jackson] says he likes things simple as a mouse-trap.
> . . . There is enuff of us to do all that's wanted. Every day, jest after breakfast,
> the Gineral lights his pipe and begins to think purty hard, and I and Major
> Donaldson begin to open letters for him; and there is more than three bushels
> every day, and all the while coming. We don't git through more than a bushel
> a day; and never trouble long ones, unless they come from Mr. Van Buren, or
> Mr. Kindle [Amos Kendall] or some other of our great folks. Then we sort 'em
> out jest as Zekel Bigelow does the mackerel at his Packin Yard. . . . We only make
> three sorts and keep three big baskets, one marked 'not red,' another 'red and
> worth nothin,' and another 'red and to be answered.' And then all the Gineral
> has to do is to say 'Major, I reckon we best say so and so to that,' and I say 'jest
> so,' or not, as the notion takes me—and then we go at it.
>
> We keep all the Secretaries, and the Vice President, and some District Attor-
> neys, and a good many of our folks, and Amos Kindle, moving about; and they
> tell us jest how the cat jumps.
>
> And as I said afore, if it warnt for Congress meetin once a year, we'd put the
> Government in a one horse wagon, and go jest where we liked.[1]

What is the White House today? Following, one by one, are the core elements of the bashful bureaucracy.

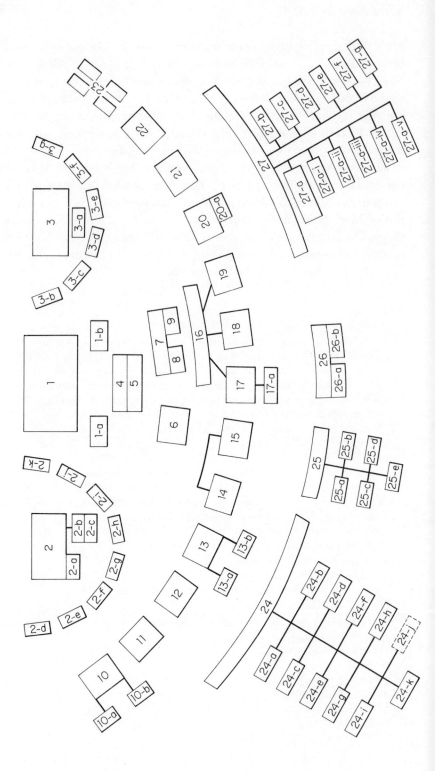

Aide with Eight Arms: The Assistant to the President for National Security Affairs

Within the area of foreign affairs, I believe . . . the Secretary of State [should] be your vicar for the community of Departments.
—ALEXANDER HAIG

The State Department is simply not equipped to handle interdepartmental machinery. . . . No department in our system will for long accept the formal preeminence of another one. It will challenge decisions that go against it, on procedural as well as substantive grounds. In the end, the result is not the predominance of one department but presidential adjudication of a disproportionate number of disputes.
—HENRY KISSINGER

The two contrasting assertions—by Haig and by Kissinger—compel a brief listing of how the last fifty years have changed the foreign affairs environment of the presidency.

- Since 1789 the president has been the commander in chief of America's military forces, and by 1988 the Defense budget has come to total $300 billion annually. Three million men and women, military and civilian, are now under his command.
- Since the Versailles Peace Conference of 1918 and especially since 1943, the president personally has become chief diplomat.
- Since 1921 he has been chief budget officer and since 1939 has had a staff in his own Executive Office to help him make the painful allocation decisions.
- Since 1946 he and the secretary of the treasury have set the policies for America's participation in the world's international monetary machinery.
- Since 1946 the two world superpowers have been in a cold war, and since 1950 the USSR has had nuclear weapons, like America's, ready to use.
- Since 1946 the president has become the country's chief economist with a group of Executive Office advisers and staff and the statutory requirement for an annual economic assessment report to Congress.
- Since 1947 a statutory centralized intelligence institution has been established

under the president's close direction; since 1974 each of its clandestine operations requires his personal, prior approval.

- Since 1947 the president has been equipped by law with a formal National Security Council mechanism for tying together his increasingly diverse national security community.
- Since 1948, statute has furnished the president with a large overseas information-propaganda capability.
- Since 1962 he has had, immediately in the White House, a diplomatic-military operations center of his own; his staff can push a button and read the latest State, Defense, or CIA cables relayed from those agencies.
- Since 1963 the president has had the capability to send and receive written messages directly and privately with the head of government of the USSR.
- Since 1975 he has been chief trade negotiator—helped by a staff created by statute in his own Executive Office.
- Since 1976 the law has made him, in effect, chief scientist for the Executive Branch—with an Executive Office staff to assist him.
- Since 1988 the total annual resource pie he has to divide—balancing his international against his domestic commitments—is over $1 trillion.

Alexander Haig is a distinguished statesmen, but his view of foreign-affairs governance reflected prerogative more than reality.

The center of that staggering (and still abbreviated) list of national security tasks is the president. In any but noncontroversial matters, no one department—no one but he—can be the principal executive agent.

The "vicar" is the president and the parsonage is the White House. Within the White House staff, one eight-handed subgod jealously guards the altar: the assistant to the president for national security affairs. The eight services he performs are in practice all wound together; in concept they can be described one by one:

1. PROCESS MANAGER

The security assistant is here a neutral broker: organizing and managing the instruments of national security decision-making. The most formal of these is the National Security Council. The NSC's four members are the president, the vice president, and the secretaries of state and defense; it has two regularly attending statutory advisers: the chairman of the Joint Chiefs of Staff and the director of Central Intelligence. Others are invited on a regular or ad hoc basis at the president's pleasure.

Unless the president imposes an unusually severe discipline, a formal NSC meeting becomes a roomful: at least thirty people, counting extras and observers. Whenever a president is willing to meet with that big a crowd (Eisenhower was—he presided at 329 of the formal NSC sessions), the preparatory staff work can be voluminous.

The security assistant spotlights issues needing council attention and orders studies or papers to be written by the participating agencies. Why is this issue-setting a White House staff responsibility?

"The departments prefer to raise just those problems to which they already have answers," explains former NSC executive secretary Robert M. Kimmitt. "It is the White House which has to demand the *jolting* inquiries—issues raised in the party platform for instance—questions about which a departmental policy officer might exclaim, 'I wish they'd never asked that!' "[1]

Carter's platform, for instance, raised a challenge: should the United States be a major arms salesman to the third world? Should not limits be imposed? Some officials in State and Defense didn't really want to get into that problem. But to Carter it was important and Security Assistant Brzezinski pursued it.

When papers have been prepared, the assistant for national security or his deputy may chair one or more of the interagency groups that first debate the issues.[2]

Hundreds of hours are spent around White House tables. In Eisenhower's time, the security assistant presided at a "Planning Board" of senior departmental representatives who would tear a paper apart, often ending up with some of its sections under three columns of views labeled STATE, DEFENSE, and JOINT CHIEFS. A paper in 1959 had nineteen such splits and took five successive meetings of the Council to resolve.

A nearly exhausted security assistant, Robert Cutler, wrote to Eisenhower in April of 1958:

> Right now, the Planning Board is at its tenth meeting in review of Basic Policy. To me, nothing done at my level is more useful than this annual exercise (killing as it may be to R.C.). All the resources, all the strong views, all the passionate advocacies, of the Executive Branch agencies meet and clash in this broad spectrum.[3]

So close were such issues to the president's own concerns that Ike insisted that the regular departmental representatives at these meetings be designated by the secretary, approved by the assistant for national security affairs, and formally appointed by the president.

Subsequent administrations have used interdepartmental groups (IGs), senior interdepartmental groups (SIGs), and other acronymic concoctions. A former Kissinger associate did some arithmetic: "Ten meetings of an IG will underlie each meeting of a SIG, and five SIG meetings will precede one meeting of the full NSC."[4] In 1982 the Reagan White House had authorized 55 IGs and 25 SIGs. The NSC staff joins—and tracks—all of those confabulations.

By 1987, in addition to the two committees that met with the president (the National Security Council itself and a more limited body, the National Security Planning Group) there were a senior review group chaired by the national security assistant, a policy review group chaired by his deputy, and perhaps fifty interagency groups, all of which were doing their work under the close surveillance of the NSC staff. So close that

> no NSC staffer worth his salt ever sees a memorandum for the first time when it hits the White House. He or she will always have been in on the preparation of the memorandum by having joined a working group or been consulted by the individuals in the respective departments who have put the memo together. This is not to say that the staffer has forced his views on the process but simply that he has been in on the gestation and maturation of the product that results.[5]

By early 1988, National Security Assistant Colin Powell was hosting intimate, 7 A.M. sessions every weekday morning in his White House office during which he and the secretaries of state and defense would briefly go over all the immediate national security issues of the upcoming day.[6]

The national security decision-making process also includes tight White House control over the CIA's covert action programs. Even in Eisenhower's administration, while CIA Director Allen Dulles could see the president directly on intelligence matters, covert-action proposals had to come in via Security Assistant Gordon Gray. For thirty-four years the national security assistant has personally chaired the intimate interagency committee (variously called "5412," "303," "40," "Special Coordination Committee," "Planning and Coordination Group") which reviews all of the CIA's unattributable operations. Like the Bay of Pigs disaster, the Iran-contra mess jolted the president and his aides, threw a glaring spotlight on White House decision-making for secret operations.

The Tower Commission then recommended "that each administration formulate precise procedures for restricted consideration of covert action and that once formulated those procedures be strictly adhered to."[7] That recommendation has been put into effect; as a result there is now an even closer staff review of covert action undertakings, those already existing as well as those suggested. After the special committee discussions, an NSC

senior director scrutinizes proposed clandestine actions prior to the required presidential finding. Later, if the methods, amounts of resources, or
risks involved for a covert action are expected to "change substantially"
from what the original finding specified, a "Memorandum of Notification"
detailing the changes must be submitted for the president's approval by
the national security assistant.[8]

Among the revelations in the Iran-contra affair was the fact that the
White House counsel himself had been cut out of any legal review of those
secret enterprises. The Tower Commission advised the president "that the
position of Legal Adviser to the NSC be enhanced in stature and in its role
within the NSC staff."[9] Reagan agreed. A new, full-time office has been
opened up on the staff. Now within the NSC group there is a legal adviser
who is a senior member in the revamped machinery—and he already has
two assistant counsels.

When wearing his hat as process manager, the assistant's role is neither
to twist nor dominate the outcome, but to guarantee that the key questions
are addressed and that all the significant alternatives are presented. Especially, he sees to it that important differences of opinion will not be bridged
or compromised—since that would give the president a false impression of
Cabinet agreement and rob him of the chance to choose.

Kennedy instructed security assistants McGeorge Bundy and Walt Rostow not even to be content with position papers coming from Secretary
Dean Rusk's office in State—but to delve below and find out what original
options had been considered at bureau or "desk officer" level before they
had been eliminated in internal review.

The White House debates can go for weeks or be squeezed into a few
days. The security affairs assistant controls the timing. He also sets the
intellectual standard for the discussion. Rather than pleading, "Let's find
some language you can agree on," Eisenhower's security assistant Gordon
Gray told the author, "More often my task was to insist, 'I will not accept
your papering over of that disagreement; the issue is important enough to
go to the president.' " Which mode of instruction he employs will reflect
his own good judgment and his appreciation of the presidential style.

Eisenhower also mandated that with few exceptions all major draft
policy papers had to have financial appendices. For each of nine program
categories (e.g., military assistance, technical assistance, development
loans, sending surplus commodities), there was a need to know what
authorities and appropriations (over the past three years) were being used
for current policies, and what new authorizations and new disbursements
(over the next four years) would be needed to carry out the policies being

proposed.[10] The staff had to do some of this work itself, and in addition consolidate the agency contributions.

With the preliminary meetings behind him, the security assistant and his staff next have a formidable task: to wrap up the presentation for the president. There may be still no State–Defense–Joint Chiefs agreement on a recommendation, on the description of the choices, or even on the phrasing of the issue.

To introduce whatever are the agreed or disagreed studies themselves, a covering "road map" memorandum to the president is required. This is invariably a White House staff product: it sets forth the problem and the options, and encloses the departmental papers for presidential perusal if wanted.

If an NSC meeting is needed, the agenda is set by the assistant with the approval of the president. At the council table, the assistant will introduce a controversial paper with a dispassionate review of the whole issue. There were 127 NSC meetings in Truman's time, 366 in Eisenhower's years.

When the council adjourns, the security assistant composes the decision memorandum, sometimes shows it to the council members, later submits it to the president, who is likely to go over it line by line. The final decision memoranda bear the president's initials.

The result is a policy statement, a who-will-do-what assignment, a marker for history. It may be called by any of a variety of names: "record of action," "national security decision directive," "presidential directive," "national security decision memorandum." In the White House, labels change but processes continue.

After the meeting, each secretary is expected to pass the necessary information down to his own agency colleagues (Eisenhower's NSC staff presented oral debriefings to the Planning Board). In the absence of that practice, the White House staffer who sat in during the council discussion may call informally to give the departmental experts a firsthand sense of the president's thinking.

The indispensable element of the whole system is intellectual integrity within the White House. If there is misrepresentation to or from the president, if communications are skewed by staff advocacy, a Bay of Pigs, a Vietnam, an Iran-contra debacle are always waiting to be repeated.

Do presidents use only the NSC formal meetings system? Emphatically not; informal alternatives are often preferred. Supplementing—for some presidents nearly replacing—the formal processes of the NSC and its subgroups, are the smaller, ad hoc sessions that are always a part of foreign-affairs decision-making. Eisenhower, for instance, held dozens of small meetings in the Oval Office, a pattern overlooked by Senator Henry Jackson in his 1960 disparagement of what he termed Ike's "highly institutionalized" machinery. Kennedy called his inner group the Executive Committee, Johnson assembled the Tuesday Lunches, Carter convened the Friday Breakfasts. Secretary of State Cyrus Vance, Secretary of Defense Harold Brown, and Security Assistant Brzezinski held weekly "VBB" noontime get-togethers ("MBB" when Muskie succeeded Vance). On sensitive national security topics, every president holds intimate meetings of a very few advisers behind closed doors.

A paradox: the graver the subject and the more secretive and ad hoc the meetings, the more vital it is to have the "before" and "after" staff work done: agendas understood ahead of time, important papers brought to hand, agreements recorded and communicated. The very presidential sessions designed to escape from procedural rigidities themselves need minimum procedures of preparation and follow-up for the president's own protection.

The Iran arms-sales failure, for instance, prompted the Tower Commission to observe:

> At each significant step in the Iran initiative, deliberations among the NSC principals in the presence of the President should have been virtually automatic. . . . The meetings should have been preceded by consideration by the NSC principals of staff papers. . . . These should have reviewed the history of the initiative, analyzed the issues then presented, developed a range of realistic options, presented the odds of success and the costs of failure, and addressed questions of implementation and execution.[11]

This was not done; the president—and the presidency—were wounded.

Two years before the NSC even got started, there were State-War-Navy meetings among Secretaries Byrnes, Patterson, Sullivan, and Forrestal. Deputy Chief of Naval Operations Robert Dennison (later to become Naval aide to the president) recalled how he and colleagues from Army and State tried to untangle what had taken place: "Well, after the meeting . . . , Peterson, Matthews and I would sit together to decide what these fellows *should* have said, who said what, who'd promised something, so that our own departments would know what had gone on. It was a lifesaver."[12]

An Eisenhower U-2 meeting began with maps carried in and ended with staff secretary Andrew Goodpaster sending a note to the CIA's Richard Bissell—in order that there would be no doubt precisely when and where that plane was to fly.

Kennedy would dictate and have his secretary dispatch personal memoranda on national security topics to State or Defense, bypassing his own staff. NSC executive secretary Bromley Smith quietly devised an arrangement whereby the recipients would send a copy of such memos *back* to him at the White House, to be recorded—and remembered—in the policy network.

When a Tuesday Lunch was called, Joseph Califano (in Defense), Benjamin Read (in State) and security adviser Walt Rostow would make up an agreed agenda; each would then assemble the needed papers for his principal. Rostow made notes of the decisions, and Smith would telephone Read to pass a reminder orally. There were "dozens of times," however, when Rostow's notes did not suffice, and three separate versions appeared of what was allegedly decided. Rostow, it was remembered, was loath to go back to LBJ and ask him, "What did you intend?" "The bureaucracy," Smith recalled, "really hated those Tuesday Lunches."

Kissinger's staff secretary, Jeanne Davis, advanced the NSC tracking system into the computer age. Today every time any document in the system moves—within the staff, to or from an agency, to or from the president—it is expected to pass through a central control point, its new position recorded. If this tracking process is followed faithfully, the touch of a button will immediately call up the status and location of every paper in the system, will produce a list of all the items wherever they are pending. Type a name into the computer: it will identify and locate every NSC document containing that name. A frantic assistant secretary from State or Defense can call "Where's my memo?" and be told within seconds.

Such responsive support warms the relationships between the White House and the departments, even as the staff must arouse agency animosities because of its tightened reviews and central control. But make no mistake: feeding such masses of data into all those computer terminals takes people power; by Kissinger's time the NSC staff group totaled 150.

In 1977 came a new president but a familiar old problem. Carter's Friday Breakfasts were limited to himself plus Vice President Mondale, Secretaries Vance and Brown, two or three senior White House officers, and Brzezinski. Have an agenda? Carter resisted; Brzezinski devised one anyway by briefing the president beforehand. Have records? Vetoed—until February of 1980 when a presidential Friday Breakfast decision was neither communicated nor understood, and the U.S. ambassador at the United Nations cast a vote that embarrassed the president. Carter forced Secretary Vance to make a public retraction. Only then did a red-faced president recognize the necessity of keeping a record of decisions; Brzezinski began to do so.

The VBB lunches were better organized from the beginning, as Brzezinski describes:

After each lunch I would prepare a memorandum listing the decisions on which we had agreed, sending a copy to each of the other two participants, as well as a report to the President. The President insisted on such immediate reporting, for he wanted to keep decisions in the area of foreign policy firmly under his control.[13]

In 1981 another new president entered the White House and the so-often-reinvented wheel again lay undiscovered. When the Tower Commission asked President Reagan about his decisions on arms sales to Iran, the president responded:

In trying to recall events that happened eighteen months ago, I'm afraid that I let myself be influenced by others' recollections, not my own. . . . I have no personal notes or records to help my recollection on this matter. The only honest answer is to state that try as I might, I cannot recall anything whatsoever about whether I approved an Israeli sale in advance or whether I approved replenishment of Israeli stocks around August of 1985. My answer therefore, and the simple truth is, "I don't remember—period."[14]

The dismayed Tower Commission described this as policy-making "in a vacuum" and sternly exhumed the wheel once more:

The National Security Adviser must also ensure that adequate records are kept of NSC consultations and presidential decisions. This is essential to avoid confusion among presidential advisers and departmental staffs about what was actually decided and what is wanted. Those records are also essential for conducting a periodic review of a policy or initiative, and to learn from the past.[15]

Spurred by the Tower Report and shaken by the Iran-contra mess, President Reagan, a long six years and two months after he took office, issued a directive specifying that the total NSC process should follow the orderly model which the Tower Commission had distilled from the accumulated experience of the previous thirty five years.[16] He sent the directive to the Congress as "evidence of my determination to return to proper procedures" and then asked the Congress not to diminish his flexibility by any further legislation.[17]

Reagan's directive brought up one additional feature of process management: "continuity of functioning of the NSC." He directed the NSC executive secretary to recommend to him "measures to ensure adequate institutional recordkeeping from administration to administration." It has been longstanding practice that the agendas, papers, and decision records of all regular, formal meetings in the NSC system, including preliminary drafts, agency comments, and even the assistant's "road map" memoranda to the president, are retained in the council's files from president to president.

They are not physically in the White House, however, but in an NSC storage depot an hour's drive from Washington. These are the only substantive national security papers that stay in the White House across administrations. All ad hoc documentation, described hereafter, is taken away to the presidential libraries. A tradition of courtesy has evolved, however, among former presidents and the one in office; when requested for national security reasons, secret papers have been made available to the sitting president.[18]

The NSC staff does keep a special record of those presidential directives that would remain in effect under a new president—until changed. President Ford's outgoing national security assistant, Brent Scowcroft, handed to his successor, Zbigniew Brzezinski, a list of what were considered international commitments from the Ford administration, and a catalog of where the documents themselves could be found.

Suppose, however, that a new president is planning for a U.S.-USSR summit conference and asks to see the records of all of his predecessors' meetings and discussions with the Soviet heads of government since World War II. Incredibly, many are not available. Not in the White House. Not in the State Department either. "No one person in or out of government today can say with certainty whether there are detailed records for each of the post-war summit meetings, including the private discussions of the leaders, or where such records, if they exist, are located."[19]

Nixon allowed no State Department interpreters during his private talks with Brezhnev; Kissinger had to ask for, but never received, the Soviet interpreter's notes. Johnson ordered State to send him its only copy of the records of his Glassboro summit session with Kosygin. Surreptitiously, State held onto a copy. Presidents Ford, Carter, and Reagan have kept better records of their summit sessions.

2. A SOURCE OF INDEPENDENT POLICY ADVICE

As presidents have used formal NSC meetings less, they have relied on the national security affairs assistant and his staff more. Long before and long since the council was created in 1947, presidents have turned to their White House staffs for private national security recommendations.

The following are two early examples:

In the summer of 1946, George Elsey, then a young Navy aide to presidential adviser Clark Clifford, spent weeks putting together a special memorandum for President Truman summarizing U.S.-Soviet relations and future prospects between the two great powers. He consulted widely with departmental experts, especially George Kennan at State, but the product was his own. Clifford later described how Truman felt about the Elsey enterprise:

> What he wanted was the opinions of the top senior personnel, all through the government, and *not* just the State Department. He wanted it to be much broader than that . . . he clearly didn't want just some Soviet expert in the State Department to get up a memo. . . . He wanted War and Navy and Justice and [presidential naval aide] Admiral Leahy and the State Department and anybody else whose activities in any way impinged upon our relations with the Soviet Union to join in this major, senior study.[20]

In May of 1949, the British mandate over Palestine was to expire and the question was: should the United States grant provisional recognition to the new state of Israel? George Marshall and Robert Lovett came to argue the negative in a meeting in the Oval Office.

Truman invited Clifford to join them, asked him to speak first and present the case in favor of recognition. Marshall "bristled," "glared" at Clifford, and asked, "Why is Clifford even here?" It was Truman who snapped back, "Because I asked him."

Lovett, then Marshall, gave the rebuttal arguments. "The suggestions made by Mr. Clifford were wrong . . . [because they were] based on domestic political considerations while the problem that confronts us was international."[21]

Two days later, President Truman granted the provisional recognition. Truman confidant Oscar Ewing later commented: "General Marshall overlooked one thing in this attitude and that is that foreign affairs are simply the extension of the politics of the Government into the external world. To attempt to handle foreign affairs in a political vacuum is an utter absurdity."[22] It's been like that for four decades.

Except for Eisenhower, presidents have sought from their national security assistants not merely staff work for meetings, but independent policy advice. Nixon wrote to Kissinger:

> If we now fail it will be because the bureaucrats and the bureaucracy and particularly those in the Defense Department, who will of course be vigorously assisted by their allies in State, will find ways to erode the strong, decisive action that I have indicated we are going to take. For once, I want the military and I want the NSC staff to come up with some ideas on their own which will recommend *action* which is very *strong, threatening and effective.*[23]

President Carter observed:

> Zbigniew Brzezinski and his relatively small group of experts were not handicapped by the inertia of a tenured bureaucracy or the responsibility for implementing policies after they were evolved. They were particularly adept at incisive analyses of strategic concepts, and were prolific in the production of new ideas, which they were always eager to present to me. I encouraged them to be unrestrained in their proposals, and consequently had to reject a lot of them. However, in the resulting discussions, we often found a better path worth following.[24]

Brzezinski appends to his memoirs excerpts from his eyes-only "weekly reports" to President Carter in which he made a great variety of substantive policy observations. Carter would scribble marginal notes in response. Brzezinski numbered each such missive; in the four years there were 159 of them.

Henry Kissinger described his responsibilities: "A security adviser serves his President best by never simply ratifying the bureaucratic consensus; he should always be the devil's advocate, the tireless asker of questions, the prober of what is presented as self-evident."[25]

Woe to the president when the prober loses his sharp point—when the devil's advocate sings only in the consensus chorus. As the Bay of Pigs planning came down to the final days, Kennedy asked the right questions but got the wrong answers. He wanted to know if the invasion brigade could succeed without any U.S. forces to join them; he was told they could. Sorensen called that a "wild misjudgment."

> Answers to all the President's doubts about the military and intelligence estimates came from those experts most committed to supporting the plan, and he had no military intelligence expert of his own in the White House. . . . He should have insisted on more skepticism from his staff, and made it clear that their courage was not to be questioned by the advocates. . . . Now the President was far more skeptical of the experts, their reputations, their recommendations, their promises, premises and facts. He relied more on his White House staff. . . .[26]

As a result of that 1961 fiasco, Kennedy made changes in staff functions—which persist to this day. Despite grumblings from the regular military hierarchy, he added a general (Maxwell Taylor) to his personal staff as a "military and intelligence adviser and representative." There has been at least one flag-rank military officer there ever since: Generals Ginsburg, Haig, Scowcroft, Odom, Boverie, and Powell, and Admiral Poindexter. In recent years, there have been special NSC staff offices reviewing military policy issues; they were called "Program Analysis," or "Arms Control and Defense Programs."

Kennedy "tightened White House review procedures under Bundy and Taylor," and no national security assistant has relaxed them since.[27]

Of course, the secretaries of state and defense and the director of Central Intelligence look nervously at the security assistant's independent policy role. The more sophisticated of them, however, understand and accept the president's insistence about it, and they establish a special understanding with the White House. Former Secretary of Defense McNamara recounts:

> Mac Bundy was absolutely superb in this sense . . . we had an arrangement under which when I sent a paper to the president . . . that paper was to go in to the president without any change whatsoever, not a period changed. Now if Bundy wanted to put a memo on top and say, 'This is a lousy paper, Mr. President, for God's sakes don't ever do what Bob is recommending,' that was his responsibility to the president. But if the president then were to take Bundy's memo and without any consultation with me reverse my recommendation . . . I would have resigned, and the president *knew* I would have resigned. And therefore he never did it. . . . Bundy also would have told me ahead of time he was going to do it. . . . He and I had that kind of relationship.[28]

Security Assistant Frank Carlucci, who took office at the end of 1986, reemphasized this decades-old viewpoint:

> My first responsibility is to be an honest broker. . . . Now, what right do I have to offer personal advice to the president? The president has every right to say to his staff: 'What do *you* think I ought to do?' . . . There's nothing in any statute or the constitution which says that the national security adviser or the staff cannot give the president independent advice if the president asks for it.[29]

The Tower Commission, referring to Carlucci's two predecessors, turned "right" into duty:

> It is their obligation as . . . advisers to the Council, to ensure that the President is adequately served. The principal subordinates to the President must not be deterred from urging the president not to proceed on a highly questionable course of action even in the face of his strong conviction to the contrary.[30]

President Reagan concurred in that recommendation as well; in the March 31, 1987, directive he specified that "As the President's principal staff advisor on national security affairs, the National Security Advisor shall present his own views and advice and, at the same time, faithfully represent the views of other NSC participants."[31]

3. PACKAGER OF INFORMATION

The security assistant's third responsibility is to make sure that the world-wide national security information systems serve the president. The chief executive is not their only customer, but his needs come first.

From crisis alerts to long-range planning, the president's NSC staff officers must fit the systems to the presidential requirements, and not the other way around. They form the link between a vast producer community and one consumer. Chapter 4 described some of the president's general information arrangements, but the national security community is special: in volume, in consequence, and in secrecy.

All those far-flung institutional systems, however, may still not satisfy a president. He may wish to go further, to test his formal intelligence materials by on-the-scene observations of a trusted personal adviser. He may want an objective, direct channel of his own to supplement what may be parochial reports from a preoccupied embassy or commander. He will use his White House staff to open one.

In March of 1955, Eisenhower needed to know how soon Chinese Nationalist forces on the islands of Quemoy and Matsu could, on their own, successfully defend themselves against a Chinese Communist attack:

> To get further information and a sensing of the problem as it appeared to an observer at firsthand, I should ordinarily have called in . . . the Commander-in-Chief of the Pacific Fleet. But in a time of such tension, with the enemy scrutinizing our every move, I could not possibly call Admiral Stump back to Washington. I therefore sent Colonel Goodpaster, the brilliant and trusted White House Staff Secretary, to Pearl Harbor to confer with Admiral Stump.[32]

Ike didn't want Stump's assessment filtered through anybody in the command chain; it was not shared until later.

In October of 1961, the South Vietnamese government began to pressure U.S. Ambassador Frederick Nolting for a very new and different kind of American support: U.S. combat troops. President Kennedy was "uneasy." "Despite the pressure of the men around him, the President himself did not like the idea. He had a sense of being cornered."[33] He sent his "special military representative," General Maxwell Taylor, and his deputy national security assistant, Walt Rostow, to Vietnam for two weeks to make a personal assessment. The resulting Taylor-Rostow report recommended sending eight thousand U.S. soldiers, a recommendation so sensitive that it was even kept from the responsible assistant secretary of state and was censored out of the document that was made public. (Kennedy held off on sending combatants, but opened up a Military Assistance Command, dispatched a lieutenant general to head it, and before he was assassinated had sent sixteen thousand American military advisory and support personnel to Vietnam.)

Jump to 1965: same scene, new president. Two weeks after his inauguration, Lyndon Johnson agreed with Ambassador Maxwell Taylor's recommendation to have National Security Assistant McGeorge Bundy come to South Vietnam to get a firsthand look. Having never been there, he was "physically detached from the local scene." By sending him out to report, Johnson could see that "we are missing no real bets in the political field," said Taylor.[34]

Bundy's trip coincided with the Vietcong attack on Pleiku in the Central Highlands. The national security assistant flew up there and visited the wounded; on the plane home he wrote a long memorandum to Johnson. His recommendation: "sustained reprisal," and Johnson followed it.

To handle information in the national security community is to be torn between two often incompatible objectives: to share it and to protect it. Share it so that those who take action will have knowledge; protect it or vital and expensive systems—some lives even—may be destroyed.

To bridge these objectives, the national security community has systems within systems and, often at the president's specific direction, special arrangements to bypass even them. President Kennedy had delicate intelligence information hand-carried only to his brother, Robert, and then to him. President Carter once specified, in a personal phone call, who the recipients of certain intelligence data were to be.

The tussle, even at Cabinet level, to acquire or preserve sensitive information borders on the bizarre. A Navy yeoman on Kissinger's NSC staff purloined copies of the security assistant's private and secret memoranda to the president, made photocopies for his Navy admiral superior, who turned around and furnished them to the chairman of the Joint Chiefs of Staff. (The chairman pleaded innocent but the admiral and all his yeomen were yanked out of the White House.)

John Ehrlichman was convinced that Secretary of Defense Melvin Laird was being tipped off about presidential telephone calls that were made from Camp David through the White House Communications Agency, a specialized segment under Laird's Department of Defense. "Did he just keep track of whom we called, or did he also know what was said?" Ehrlichman wondered.[35] Haldeman substituted the White House's own civilians for the Camp David operators when the president was up there.

Reagan ordered or permitted the director of the National Security Agency (a part of the Department of Defense) to be instructed by his White House staff not to share certain intelligence about the Iran arms missions even with the secretary of defense. The outraged Secretary Weinberger eventually got the instructions changed, but chose not to fire the director, who, significantly, was a former NSC staff member well aware of all the rules governing the employment of separate channels.

In government, as in every institution, information is blood. Clamp it off from any part and the member cannot function. At the White House, the national security assistant is a carotid artery to the president.

4. MONITOR OF WHAT HAPPENS TO POLICY EXECUTION

Chapter 5 described the dilemma of presidential dependency, the president's need to follow up on the implementation of his decisions, and why his White House staff must mount the surveillance. The national security assistant is an especially watchful monitor, because he apprehends the potent consequences of error—and because he has the tracking equipment. The NSC staff's lookout devices range from the structured to the informal.

Eisenhower, with his preference for orderliness, created a special interagency group to follow up NSC decisions: the Operations Coordinating Board. Its members, the number two officers of State, Defense, Treasury, and Budget plus the heads of the intelligence, atomic energy, information, and foreign-aid agencies met each week for a private lunch followed by a formal board session.

Almost every approved NSC action paper was assigned to the board for follow-up; forty or more informal interagency working groups (for individual countries, for functional matters) pooled their information and orchestrated their implementing actions. A twenty-four-person staff supported them. "It was the first time some of those operational level officers had even seen each other's faces" recalled Elmer Staats, the OCB executive officer (later U.S. comptroller general).[36] Every six months, a report was due from the board to the National Security Council on each of the dozens of assignments: Who was doing what? Should the policy be changed?

Ike had a special White House assistant for security operations coordination; both he and the national security assistant attended the board's luncheons and meetings. In 1957 the OCB was put "within the structure

of the National Security Council"; the whole apparatus became an extension of the White House staff network, with NSC Assistant Cutler as its
vice chairman. In January of 1960, Eisenhower completed the centralization of authority by shifting the chairmanship of the OCB to Cutler's
successor, White House Security Assistant Gordon Gray.

Kennedy abolished the OCB but at the same time enlarged and strength-
ened the role of immediate NSC staff under Security Adviser McGeorge
Bundy. He also gave that staff a potent new tracking tool: the Situation
Room, located directly in the White House.

As described in chapter 4, over the past twenty-seven years the Sit Room
has grown into an ever more sophisticated operations center for the presidency. Its principal tracking devices are computer terminals. Important
State, Defense, and CIA cables—the arterial blood flow of the national
security community—are retransmitted onto the Situation Room video
screens and exposed to White House view. Depending on the understandings that are reached between the security assistant and the affected Cabinet members, or if the president himself insists, this traffic will include:

- The Department of State's outgoing policy instructions to the (yes, they are
  the *president's*) ambassadors.
- Joint State-Defense messages to missions and commands.
- In areas of tension or upheaval, important Joint Chiefs' operational orders to
  the (yes, they are also the *president's*) regional military commanders in chief
  (the "CINCs").
- Whenever U.S. forces are in action, detailed operational military traffic; for
  example, when the B-52s are to take off, when they are airborne, when they
  have passed over certain checkpoints.

Many of the policy instructions are cleared in the White House before
they are sent, but if the national security assistant or his regional or
functional staff assistants have problems with what they see on the tracking computers, a query can be telephoned or a remedy ordered forthwith.

Carter's interest in limiting U.S. military sales abroad has been mentioned. He insisted on personally approving any transaction over $7 mil-
lion. Many were the occasions when NSC staff officers would read an
outgoing telegram with a State-Defense position concerning a proposed
arms sale. An immediate call would go to State or the Pentagon: "That's
not what the president wants." "The emphasis is wrong." "The timing is
inappropriate."

State and Defense, however, have secure telephones and special cable
channels of their own to their overseas missions and use them constantly.
Here the White House computers do not reach—with the result that secu-

rity assistants and presidents are sometimes left sitting in dismayed frustration.

President Carter, for example, had sent General Robert Huyser to Tehran to see if what the president wanted could be done: whether the shah and the Iranian military could hold Iran together and out of Khomeini's hands. The general returned on February 5, 1979, and reported to the Oval Office. Carter was so unhappy with what he perceived as Ambassador William Sullivan's twisting of his orders that he wondered out loud if he should have Sullivan removed. Huyser responded, "You should give him some instructions." He recalled:

> The President said Sullivan had had the same instructions I had had; why hadn't he followed them? My reply was: 'Mr. President, maybe you did not understand what I said; what I said was: *You* should give him his instructions.' I felt certain that the instructions I had received were exactly those prescribed by the President, but I was not so sure about the Ambassador's. I knew for some reason many of his conversations had been with lower level State Department people and they may very well have added their own gloss to the President's directives.[37]

Nine years later, Reagan's NSC Latin American officer precisely echoed Huyser's sentiments:

> I . . . learned that without an NSC advisor who assures that the President makes the major decisions and that these are indeed carried out, the constitutional authority of the President to make foreign policy will in effect be taken by his unelected subordinates.[38]

The Situation Room's window onto the cable flow is far from being the security assistant's only lookout over the pulsing of the national security departments, nor is all the scrutiny adversarial. There is much genuine teamwork among willing and honorable officers. This is particularly true among the senior professionals in both the White House and the agencies, who can thread their way around the sometimes petulant egos of their superiors. A few State-NSC relationships are so smooth that the officers involved go across town to each other's staff meetings.

Security Assistant Kissinger, accurately reflecting President Nixon's own wishes, often had only minimal communication with Secretary of State William Rogers—and the aversion was reciprocal. But the gap could be—had to be—bridged. Kissinger would order, "Don't tell Rogers," but there were senior NSC associates who would hint to their counterparts in State, "We think this is the way Henry sees it." Kissinger might demand a paper from a middle-level State official on a "don't show it to anybody" basis, but informally the senior State people had to be told—enough to inform them but not so much as to betray the White House confidence.

"These are pros working together," explains a veteran of those years. "Each one knows the role the other one is playing. Neither is embarrassed; and neither one expects the other to tell him everything he knows. . . . It is a kind of intricate ballet."[39]

In his March 31, 1987, National Security Decision Directive, President Reagan specified the NSC staff's surveillance role. While assuring his Cabinet that "execution and implementation of . . . policies shall not be the responsibility of the assistant to the president for national security affairs or of the NSC staff except as the President specifically directs," he nonetheless instructed that his security assistant "shall monitor policy implementation to ensure that policies are executed in conformity with the intent of presidential decisions," and charged that the assistant should "initiate periodic reassessments of policies and operations . . ."[40]

The new directive only affirms an old practice. At any White House, in any year, using committees or computers—and under the president's authority—the national security assistant and his staff are watching, checking, tracking, intervening.

5. AS NEGOTIATOR

In his "Open Letter to Ed Muskie," former Under Secretary of State George Ball publicly advised the new secretary:

> . . . without the Secretary's knowledge and express approval, neither the National Security Adviser nor any other White House aide should receive or call in foreign ambassadors or representatives, negotiate with foreign governments, undertake diplomatic missions, send "backchannel" (CIA channel) telegrams not seen by the State Department. . . .[41]

In *his* memorandum two weeks before inauguration, Secretary of State–designate Haig privately advised President-elect Reagan: "All contacts with foreign officials must be conducted at the State Department."[42]

That advice could not have come from more seasoned men, nor could it have been less realistic. Why? Presidents don't buy it.

All five presidents in the last twenty-three years have chosen to use their national security assistants not only as assessors of a foreign scene but as active negotiators. The negotiations take place in obscure or glittering settings overseas, in every conceivable corner of the White House—Mess Room, Map Room, Roosevelt Room—or even at Camp David.

The closer the discussions are to the president's deepest personal interests, the less likely are any officers outside the White House to be included in the exchanges. State will be informed later—sometimes much later.

McGeorge Bundy, in the Johnson presidency, was the first national security assistant to wear a negotiator's hat. At the end of April 1965, the Dominican Republic had exploded into civil war. Johnson had acted quickly, sent the Marines, then the Army—but what next? How to use that power? What kind of political solution could be engineered? Whom among the local factional leaders could the U.S. support? Johnson's own advisers were divided.

The president sent Bundy, Assistant Secretary of State Thomas Mann, and Deputy Secretary of Defense Cyrus Vance to the seething capital. Bundy himself spent ten days in Santo Domingo trying to put pieces together. The trip was not an exclusive White House enterprise; State and Defense were side by side with Bundy. But their mission was not successful; the three men came home without a solution.

Under both Kennedy and Johnson, Bundy and his successor Walt Rostow also began the practice of personally calling in foreign ambassadors and privately engaging in substantive discussions. Bundy met with the British, French, Italian, German, Soviet, Dutch, and Canadian envoys. He could tell them, quietly and authoritatively, "where the president was coming from." He would later give State officers an informal oral summary.

There are both risks and advantages in such White House conversations. The diplomats cable back: "I went to the White House today . . ."—a boost to their own stature and often a point of leverage for the U.S. ambassadors overseas who are themselves trying to pry open a better access to their host governments' leaders.

Most of the White House sessions are informational: to exchange views rather than to make commitments. If promises are made, they are reinforced; diplomats have been known to disavow the White House commitments given at the State Department. If given at the White House, they stick.

The foreign envoys themselves realize the fractured and competitive makeup of the U.S. Executive Branch; they know that adjudication of the most significant of interagency contests takes place in the White House. They are eager to hear the outcome of those decisions from one authoritative point. Diplomats, too, read our Constitution, which says that the president "shall receive Ambassadors and other Public Ministers"; they know that White House staff who are acting on behalf of the president are helping him with that mandate.

One diplomat explained categorically: "If I confine my Washington contacts to the State Department, I am dead. If my problem, for instance, is foreign military sales, I will go to Defense, State, the Office of Management and Budget, to the Congress, to the Congressional Budget Office— but the NSC contact is indispensable. It is the most important stop on my circuit."[43]

The security assistant's voice, perceived as reflecting the views of that chief diplomat, the president, resonates with special believability, special emphasis. The assistant's senior staff are guided by the same theory, follow the same practice. The staffer handling NATO affairs, for instance, will talk often with the political counselors from the European embassies.

Is State informed? Afterwards, informally, but not always.

The risks in conducting such talks are sometimes substantive, always territorial. If promises are either requested of or made by the White House, the responsible Cabinet officers must be told—or they may embarrass the president unknowingly. A sufficient number of territorial indignities will raise the core question: does the president trust his secretary?

Nixon did not, and for five and a half years he instructed Kissinger to conduct the principal presidential foreign-policy initiatives out of Kissinger's own office. Nixon said: "There could be only one person to handle some of these major issues, and where secrecy was involved, I mean secret negotiations; it had to be Henry, in the areas like Vietnam, China, Russia and the Mideast."[44]

Kissinger had private meetings at least once with almost every one of the ambassadors, regularly saw about ten of them and, most significantly, opened the direct channel to the USSR's Ambassador Anatoly Dobrynin. He later wrote: "Nixon, buttressed by me, moved the conduct of negotiations more and more into the White House. . . . The Soviet leaders soon learned that . . . Nixon had no intention to defer to others on the fundamental determination of our foreign policy."[45]

The two men met mostly in the Map Room, on the ground floor of the Residence. In case Dobrynin ever wondered whether Kissinger was speaking for the president, the security assistant would frequently let Dobrynin read the internal "talking points" memorandum with Nixon's handwritten amendments penned in. On at least two occasions, Nixon himself told Dobrynin that on important issues he should deal only with Kissinger.

With China, with North Vietnam, with Germany, with Egypt, Israel, and Japan, Nixon encouraged Kissinger to establish private links, engage in discussions kept secret within the White House. Kissinger had a telephone on his desk which rang only in his office. Dobrynin and Israeli Ambassador Yitzhak Rabin were among those who had the number.

Under Nixon, the security assistant became a traveling negotiator as well. Kissinger's series of meetings with the North Vietnamese in Paris, his first trip to China to meet with Chou En-lai and arrange the Nixon visit, his April 1972 trip to Moscow to meet with Brezhnev, were literally clandestine; his travel and logistics were managed with the secrecy befitting a 007.

Facilitating the secrecy of such expeditions is a communications capability dear to the life of the White House assistant: the back-channel. There are several modes.

To an English-speaking head of government—to any foreign leader if a staff interpreter is available—the American president may himself use the telephone; neither the embassy nor any Cabinet officer may be aware.

The White House can reach any U.S. military facility through the White House Communications Agency—and that includes the Special Air Mission planes in which security assistants fly. During his secret trip to Moscow in April of 1972, Kissinger, who was determined to stay away from the embassy, used his aircraft, parked at a military field an hour's drive from the city, as his communications center.

The principal back-channel for White House aides to use to or from overseas is through the communications of the Central Intelligence Agency. The CIA's code-room personnel, and the Agency's whole environment of tight control, are looked upon as guaranteeing far more confidentiality than using State or even military facilities. An embassy's CIA station chief will, if instructed, deliver a White House message directly to any specified officer of the host government (the ambassador unaware) or personally to the ambassador's hands (the secretary of state not knowing). On Eisenhower's orders, for instance, Japanese Prime Minister Nobusuke Kishi was informed of the U-2 flights being run out of Atsugi Naval Air Station but this information was not conveyed to Ambassador Douglas MacArthur II. Foreign presidents and prime ministers very much appreciate the back-channel: they know for sure that their return messages will go directly to the White House.

State's former intelligence chief Roger Hilsman describes why CIA station chiefs have been so favored as alternate and direct links to foreign government leaders:

> [CIA Director] Allen Dulles . . . liked to have his own man in every capital of the world, if possible, and in allied and friendly capitals, he liked to have his man on close personal terms with the chief of state, who was also in some cases

under some obligation to the CIA of one form or another. . . . In many cases the CIA's station chief had been in the country much longer than the ambassador, knew more of the nationals more intimately, knew conditions in the country better, had more money to spend, more favors to do. . . .[46]

In his early months, Kissinger did not want even the station chief reading the White House back-channel traffic, and ordered low-level CIA communications clerks to hand-carry telegrams to prime ministers' offices. Warned that this was itself a risky tactic, Kissinger later relented and allowed the station chief to be the initial recipient. Double encryption is an additional technique that bypasses everybody except code clerks and the recipient.

Ambassadors are indignant at back-channels that bypass them. Ambassador Arthur Burns remembered two instances where communications, delivered in this fashion from the White House to officers in the German government, in his view screwed up his mission. He had to "catch up from the rear" and believed that constant use of that method should be the occasion for an ambassador to resign. If it is a station chief who conveys White House messages to a host government, those officials have cause to wonder who *is* the authoritative United States representative in their country.

An ambassador receiving a back-channel instruction from the White House that appears to depart from previous positions may be tempted to turn to the secretary of state to find out if it is genuine. But what if he is instructed not to inform the secretary?

In December of 1986, Secretary of State George Shultz chastised the U.S. ambassador in Lebanon for participating in such an exchange with the White House without State's being informed. Shultz complained to the president and a "treaty" was then negotiated. Reagan addressed a letter to all American ambassadors assuring them of the secretary of state's primacy "to the fullest extent provided by law, for the overall policy direction, coordination and supervision of the United States Government activities overseas" except a CINC's military forces. Shultz then sent a covering message to the envoys:

You will receive instructions only from or through the department. All messages . . . shall be sent through regular established State Department channels. The only two exceptions to this rule are (1) if the President personally or the national security adviser instructs you to use a private channel; in such cases you should advise me personally . . . of this instruction *unless you are specifically directed not by the President;* and (2) if I . . . instruct you to use a non-State channel.[47]

The loophole is significant. Ambassadors are agents of the president, and a president will guard his flexibility to instruct them as he pleases. There is nothing to prevent a security assistant, *properly invoking the president's name,* from pushing himself through that loophole as well.

In 1977, did the habits of private White House negotiations and back-channeling disappear with the change of administration? They did not.

When he first met Dobrynin, Security Adviser Brzezinski began by reminding the ambassador that "from now on the Secretary of State will conduct negotiations." But not long afterward, Brzezinski and Dobrynin had a private lunch. The lunch grew into monthly meetings at the embassy, in Brzezinski's White House office, or at the latter's home over a game of chess.

Next came a "warm, personal relationship" with the acting head of the Chinese liaison mission in Washington, Ambassador Han Hsu. They had once-a-month meetings where Brzezinski "used each occasion to provide more and more detailed briefings regarding our foreign-policy initiatives."[48]

The normalization of relations with China was a personal interest of President Carter. Over Vance's objections, Carter sent Brzezinski to China in May of 1978 and secretly authorized him to raise with the Chinese leaders the U.S. interest in establishing formal diplomatic relations (meaning termination of those the U.S. had with Taiwan). Brzezinski's diary notes his conversation with Carter: "He says he doesn't want to play games behind Cy's back, but he would prefer to tell this to me directly. And if [when in China] I find the opportunity to move, I should move."[49]

Brzezinski did just that with Premier Deng Xiaoping, accompanied by the U.S. liaison head in Beijing and by a Chinese-speaking NSC staffer, but with State's assistant secretary excluded from the session. By the following December, Secretary Vance was so unhappy with this conduct that he called for a confrontation meeting with Brzezinski and the president. Carter confirmed to Vance, as Brzezinski describes it, that "he had wanted me to take the lead on China, especially since the Chinese trusted me." Carter went further, chided State for stimulating press attacks on his security assistant "in part as a surrogate for attacks on himself."[50]

Carter and Brzezinski had the same impulses as did Nixon and Kissinger in their penchant for back-channels to preserve secret presidential initiatives. When the communiqués announcing the normalization of U.S.-Chinese relations were being drafted to send to the U.S. liaison head Leonard Woodcock in Beijing, "the Secretary of State would leave his department and come join us while we did this work, and we communicated with Woodcock on his negotiations only from within the White House," Carter wrote in his memoirs.[51]

The White House–NSC negotiating mode continued under Reagan, his protestations about "Cabinet government" notwithstanding.

During the Falklands crisis in the Reagan administration, Secretary of State Haig had been engaging in an effort to mediate between Britain and Argentina. He was about to go over an important series of negotiating points with visiting British Foreign Secretary Francis Pym when he learned that National Security Assistant William Clark had had breakfast with Pym and had already revealed the U.S. position to him.[52]

Ambassador Dobrynin's welcome mat at the White House was lifted, however. Since U.S. Ambassador Arthur Hartman, in Moscow, had had no private access to General Secretary Gorbachev or his predecessors, the U.S. would act reciprocally in Washington.

Security Assistant Robert C. (Bud) McFarlane got on the telephone to Nabih Berri in Beirut (whom he had known earlier) to ask his help during the TWA hijacking of 1985. Later that year, McFarlane also headed a delegation that discussed the apartheid problem with South African Foreign Minister Roelof Botha in Vienna; the U.S. ambassador to South Africa and State's assistant secretary joined him on that team. It was McFarlane, however, who went secretly to Iran for the unsuccessful weapons-for-hostages enterprise, over the opposition of Secretaries Shultz and Weinberger.

The entire Iran-contra mishmash was perhaps the nadir of private and secret NSC staff conduct, although Admiral Poindexter has insisted that he and Lieutenant Colonel Oliver North acted in accordance with the president's policies. A sadder but wiser president shrank the NSC staff's charter back to a more limited role. To guarantee it, he appointed first the experienced and sophisticated Frank Carlucci as security assistant, later Lieutenant General Colin Powell.

Henceforth, should all official diplomatic contacts, and all negotiations, be left to State to handle, or are the Kissinger and Brzezinski years a proper model for the future? Where on this scale of behavior should the pendulum hang? Is there one right position?

Dr. Kissinger himself, looking back, suggests that his own style not be emulated. Does this mean that Mr. Ball's and Mr. Haig's advice is gospel? No. Former Secretary Haig himself, also looking back, alters his original precept:

My friends at the State Department will perhaps be shocked to have me say so, but it does not really matter whether the Secretary of State or the National

Security Adviser, or some other official, carries out the President's foreign policy. . . . What does matter is that the person chosen by the President must be seen to have his total confidence. . . .[53]

Haig, who had been Kissinger's deputy at the White House, makes it clear that it is the president who will choose and that he should always protect his flexibility for doing so. As presidents ponder the choice, they cannot overlook the experience of five past chief executives through more than twenty-three years. Neither Nixon nor Carter, for instance, is apologetic about how their national security assistants handled the China, SALT I, and the other personally engineered breakthroughs—of which all four men are still extremely proud.

What of the future? Will not each new secretary of state insist, with George Ball, that the security assistant must eschew the negotiating role?

Presidents now, as in the past, are not likely to accept that limitation. The security assistant, backed up by potent staff and supported by convenient facilities, is right at hand, available. Presidents, impelled by their own precedent-breaking agendas, concerned at having delicate instructions twisted by other hands, and apprehensive of leaks, are willing, often eager, to use senior White House staff as personal communicators and negotiators.

6. AS CRISIS MANAGER

Chapter 6 described why crises are managed in the White House. In a tense or emergency situation abroad, the national security affairs assistant is the White House staff officer primarily engaged. He has unique facilities.

The Direct Communications Link (the "hot line") to and from the general secretary of the Soviet Union is an official but elite private arrangement for written messages or pictures between just those two people. (It is not and never was a telephone.) While the American end of the link is adjacent to the Department of Defense's National Military Command Center, and is staffed by military personnel at the Pentagon, it is in fact an element of the White House staff itself.

Framed on the wall of the austere, windowless suite in the Pentagon is the statement of the hot line's presidential mission:

To provide a permanent, reliable and private means by which the heads of the U.S. and Soviet governments may communicate directly to reduce the risk of outbreak of nuclear war and to preclude delays, misunderstandings and misinterpretations of actions by either side which might lead to hostilities between the two countries.

The alert professionals on twenty-four-hour duty there take that charter literally. Being "reliable" means not one but six two-way circuits (three teletype and three facsimile), using two separate, geosynchronous, equatorial satellites (one American, one Russian) backed up by a cable between the United States and the Soviet Union. As many as nine color TV monitors sit on those lines, their bright blue screens, bordered in red, pulsing noiselessly in the narrow room. Every hour the teletype circuit is checked by exchanging made-up test messages; the Russians send some exotic discourses to challenge the U.S. translators; the Americans respond with short essays on volcanos, chocolate, mosquitos, and so forth. The facsimile circuits are tested every four hours with texts of all different print sizes, with maps and color pictures. Printers are at the ready to spit out hard copy.

Being "private" means that all hot-line traffic is encrypted; the coding tapes are shared with the Soviet operators. It means much more: if a genuine head-of-government message is received, it carries White House privilege; it is not shared with any person in the Pentagon outside the receiving suite and, when translated, is covered up and rushed by a team of two officers (always two) next door to the secure facsimile machines connected to the White House Situation Room. The regular machine operators stand aside while the hot-line personnel zip the message to the White House. The incoming Russian text is usually sent over as well, since some seasoned NSC staffers, like former ambassador Llewellyn Thompson, fluent in Russian, want personally to review the original wording. Once at the White House, a hot-line message from the Soviet general secretary is still private to the president; only upon a specific White House decision for each case is the message relayed to State or Defense, or for State to send to the American embassy in Moscow.

"To preclude . . . misunderstandings and misinterpretations" is the reason the whole system is only for written messages. Written text permits careful analysis of meaning, allows time for reflection and consultation. In any telephone conversation, the language difference would be a severe barrier; nuances would be missed, speech impairments might affect clarity, emotions could easily creep in. A shouting match between president and general secretary would be a bad idea.

The keyboard operator has a title: presidential communicator; the translators, too, are designated presidential translators.

It is a White House system.

In the White House itself, the national security assistant actually supervises two situation rooms. One, which the president uses, is one floor down from the Oval Office; the other is in the Executive Office Building across the street. Each consists of a single conference room for principals, adjoined by an equipment area. Both facilities are makeovers—an ironic footnote about the headquarters of the commander in chief of the world's most powerful nation.

The older of the two, in the presidential office wing, was instituted by John F. Kennedy and McGeorge Bundy, who discovered, from their Bay of Pigs experience, how woefully underequipped was the White House for crisis management. This 1962 innovation of Kennedy's was full of portent for the future role and size of the White House staff. Here began a facility with an intrusive reach into agency operations, hub of a communications net spreading worldwide, a thirsty consumer of White House personnel both technical and professional, a core magnet drawing the scattered bureaucratic iron filings into the center. The Situation Room is a powerful tool for the personal presidency—the symbol of a president-in-action.

Lyndon Johnson, with Bundy and Walt Rostow, seized the tool, used the Sit Room constantly. When the Dominican Republic crisis broke, NSC Executive Secretary Bromley Smith remembers sending the president a memorandum: "We will read over the Situation Room's daily coverage of telegrams from General [Bruce] Palmer." A note came back: "If you gents don't want to give the President of the United States the information he wants, I'll have to find other ways of acquiring the information I need."[54] The Sit Room promptly opened up a channel directly from General Palmer to the president, short-circuiting the intermediate command headquarters and bypassing the Pentagon as well. The president often telephoned Palmer directly. Smith and the Sit Room staff told Joint Chiefs of Staff chairman General Earle Wheeler that they would protect him against being completely in the dark.

Johnson, as has been described, kept a personal hand on the air operations over North Vietnam, and used the Situation Room to do so. When the North Vietnamese attacked Khesanh in 1968, Johnson had a sand table constructed and is pictured bending over it, personally examining the battlefield positions.[55] "Field Commander Johnson," Joseph Alsop wrote.

Kissinger described the Sit Room itself as "cramped, austere . . . uncomfortable, unaesthetic and essentially oppressive."[56] If principal officers are present in the conference room itself, there is space for only one assistant to be with them. Small room, perhaps, but the whole unit was a potent instrument, especially for Kissinger.

The presidential Situation Room communications equipment is in small offices outside the conference room door. These include secure telephones; the video screen terminals for telegraphic traffic, mentioned earlier; a cryptographic unit; and WASHFAX, which is the secure long-distance photocopy network instantly linking the national security agencies. An additional secure facsimile machine connects with Air Force One. Two dozen communications and intelligence experts (a fourth of them military) run the place in shifts. While the conference room itself has a text-editing gadget, there is no space in the area for the elaborate projection and electronic equipment that would permit large-screen visual displays or allow graphics to be created.

A few of President Reagan's associates were dismayed by those inadequacies and by the conference room's small size, so a supplementary complex was built, much larger and much more capable. The new Crisis Management Center (more recently termed the Situation Room Support Facility) is in the Executive Office Building's historic room 208, occupied until 1948 by the secretaries of state from Hamilton Fish to George Marshall. (It was there that Cordell Hull ejected the Japanese "peace" envoys on Sunday noon of Pearl Harbor day.) The room will hold sixty; its nineteenth-century décor has been restored but only on the surface. Opening a hand-crafted cabinet reveals television cameras and monitors; most of the east wall is a screen behind which are four more rooms crammed floor-to-ceiling with computing and projection equipment.

With the help of three VAX computers, data can be called up from any of the national security agencies, synthesized, then projected for group discussion. A digital information and display system (DIDS) can fill the screen with choropleth maps (demographic/economic data projected as colored segments of geographic units); war games can be arranged. Secure voice and video lines connect to the smaller Situation Room across the street; any displays in the National Military Command Center can be projected onto the White House screen simultaneously. Tape and television recorders are there to film every moment of a crisis situation (important for history as well as for crisis management); each message, telephone call, and decision action would be logged as well.

The Crisis Management Center can help any White House staff office make up graphic displays for top-level briefings. The Domestic and Economic Policy councils come in with raw materials, go out with hard copy ready for the president.[57]

Computers will permit telegrams the Sit Room readers have identified as important to be switched directly to the consoles of the geographic or functional NSC staff members. They in turn can print or store them; the computers will keep their files.

The president himself uses the older but closer Sit Room in the White House West Wing basement; the newer Crisis Management Center is left for senior White House and departmental staffs. Perhaps as important as the fancy computing gear outside those rooms are the plain old television sets within. The world's commercial news media are as fast on a crisis scene as any embassy officer or military attaché; no State or Defense telegram can match their color Minicams instantly broadcasting on satellite relays. Cable News Network is news-continuous—and the White House Sit Rooms tune it in.

Changes in military electronics affect White House crisis management. Data pouring in from real-time sensors—photography, thermal receptors, message and radar intercepts, underwater sound—might overwhelm an operations center. The same electronics research, however, brings a hopeful estimate as well; artificial intelligence computers are being designed that, accepting dozens of "MIPS" (millions of instructions per second), will sort out patterns of significance.

The Crisis Management Center in the Executive Office Building is one floor up from the vice president's office. What is his role in handling national security emergencies?

Near the outset of the Reagan administration came an unusual announcement. On March 24, 1981, the White House press secretary proclaimed "the President's decision to have the Vice President chair the administration's 'crisis management' team. . . . Reagan's choice of the Vice President was guided in large measure by the fact that management of crises has traditionally—and appropriately—been done in the White House."[58] As chapter 6 demonstrated, crisis management may mean that the president, or, acting on his behalf, the White House staff, must call a halt to apparently routine but actually dangerous responses. In effect, orders are given to departments or agencies to stop or alter actions about to be taken.

But the vice president is not an order-giver. He is in the line of succession, not in the chain of command. Only the president, and only staff personally responsible to him, can legitimately take up the task of crisis management.[59]

When Eisenhower in 1953 gave Robert Cutler the title, for the first time, of assistant to the president for national security affairs, the only "crisis" facility in the White House was a military telephone switchboard in a distant basement room of the Residence. The capability difference in thirty-five years is a measure not only of technological change but of management concept. The president has always been commander in chief, but now he and his assistant for national security affairs have the expanded staff and facilities to fulfil that old mandate in a world of new dangers.

7. ARTICULATOR OF POLICIES

For every president, the public presentation of his national security objectives is as important as the policies themselves.

A complicated and important foreign-policy decision does not just float out through the White House gates on its own and find itself greeted automatically by understanding and applause. A kind of world opera has to be staged. The overture of the formal presidential announcement must be followed by unfolding scenes of interpretation supporting the central theme; actors and supporting players must be cued to move and sing in precise coordination. The Cabinet, the press secretary, other White House associates, the president's party leaders in Congress, American diplomats abroad, the Voice of America: to produce a convincing performance, they must follow a single score.

The preparation of the materials, the orchestration of the whole effort, takes weeks of meticulous planning. In the contemporary White House, these staging arrangements are called "public diplomacy" and the national security assistant is in the middle of them. His own staff becomes an adjunct to the White House Press, Legislative Affairs, Communications, and Public Liaison offices in the overall enterprise of persuasion.

An example was President Reagan's May 27, 1986, decision to cease to hold U.S. strategic weaponry within the limits of the unratified SALT II agreement. The USSR was continuing to build beyond the SALT constraints, and the United States, the president felt, could no longer prudently limit itself unilaterally.

This was an important and controversial decision. It depended for its support on the public's knowing what the Soviet and U.S. strategic systems were, understanding the basic terms of the SALT II agreement itself, and understanding which weapons of both sides were going beyond the limits. What had to be produced were a lengthy presidential statement, an even longer White House fact sheet, a special report by the director of the Arms Control and Disarmament Agency, and a twenty-five-page printed booklet with color illustrations entitled *Soviet Strategic Defense Programs.*

Only through a White House–led interagency effort could these scripts be dovetailed. For this purpose, the NSC's director of defense programs had been chairing a weekly Interagency Group on Public Diplomacy for Arms Control and the Strategic Defense Initiative, its meetings including representatives from State, Defense, the Joint Chiefs, the information and disarmament agencies, plus legislative liaison staffers from the White House.

The policy and briefing statements were written up with care; facts had to be right, nuances calculated, the color photographs sanitized to protect intelligence sources. The group knew the president's audience would include an angry leadership in the USSR, an apprehensive NATO and Japan, a skeptical Congress, an American public not expert on arms-control particulars, and conservative supporters who would be pleased.

Every U.S. embassy overseas would get copies; the missions in Europe and Japan were to ask their host governments to use the materials in *their* speeches; all American military commands would receive the package. Each Cabinet officer would be expected to be familiar with the materials and draw on them when making remarks anywhere. There would have to be *one* administration emphasis, not a "soft" twist from State or a "hard" punch from Defense.

The drafting was done in the White House, checked meticulously with the small interagency team, and kept secret until release day. The whole background package was actually sent to the overseas posts ahead of time, with a "release" message flashed to them on May 27 itself. A special annex was compiled for the U.S. negotiating team at Geneva, making presentation suggestions and analyzing anticipated Soviet reactions and tactics. Another private annex discussed the best methods of being persuasive with the Congress and suggested which Cabinet officers should talk with which legislators.

In this case the NSC's "public diplomacy" effort was neither underhanded nor atypical. Similar arrangements are part of any president's premeditated campaign to explain his policies to his national constituency and to his world audience. An intricate team effort was required, and the national security affairs staff called the signals. It was only one of many.

But when, if ever, should the security assistant himself go public?

A president welcomes—in fact searches for—leaders in his administration who can explain and defend his policies. The babble of advocates outside the White House gates usually vouchsafes a degree of attention to those inside who carry the triple cachet of status, knowledge, and closeness to the president, the last of these conveying a special credibility. In the foreign-policy arena, the two individuals who most meet those criteria are the secretary of state and the White House national security assistant.

The secretary of state should always be out front. What about the security affairs assistant? If the latter is especially articulate, there will be a steady temptation to exploit his persuasiveness. If the security assistant has an ego, he will want—even rush—to accede.

Such a change from the promises that were made at inauguration time! Presidents and security assistants unfailingly begin an administration by swearing that the latter will be low-profile—will talk on background only. "You are seeing a disappearing act right now," announced Richard Allen when he was appointed in December of 1980.

Kissinger wrote, "I proclaimed at the press conference announcing my appointment that I would have no dealings with the press."[60] Brzezinski observed, "I had at the time felt it would be wiser for me to maintain a low profile with the press. . . . I would not engage in frequent formal or informal briefings but would leave the task to the White House Press Office."[61]

A White House reporter said of Bud McFarlane:

> In October of 1983, when he was named to be President Reagan's national security adviser, reporters who knew McFarlane best wrote at length about his lack of visibility. He was described . . . as 'deliberately obscure,' 'self-effacing,' 'a hidden hand,' and a 'quintessential staff man' quietly laboring in the shadow of high-powered superiors.[62]

The temptors are soon heard from. The Press Office wants the security assistant to do a backgrounder or to give a full on-the-record foreign-affairs briefing. The public liaison chief appeals for him to appear at VIP briefings in the Indian Treaty Room. Network television talk-show hosts call, and requests for one-on-one press interviews pile up.

The president signals his blessing. It is the president, and only he, who could put the OFF LIMITS sign on the security assistant's door. He usually does *not*, however, recognizing the value to himself of having an expert and vigorous defense of his objectives and of his actions.

What comes next is predictable.

Security Assistant McGeorge Bundy is featured in a cover story in *Time*.[63]

Kissinger (in his words) "learned that I could not ignore the media and I began to see journalists, though at first almost always at their initiative."[64] *Time*'s "Man of the Year" cover for 1973 is split in two: the president and Henry Kissinger.

In Washington in the spring of 1977, a full-dress Foreign Policy Association address is set up before five hundred people packed into the Statler-Hilton's ballroom. The subject is "An Overview of Foreign Policy." Brzezinski (not Vance) is the speaker.

Richard Allen "is known for bouncing back," the *National Journal* observes eleven months after his "disappearing act." Allen becomes a frequent administration spokesman, stars at congressional briefings, then is reported as making "barbed remarks at social events and to reporters that were not intended to soothe the nerves of Reagan's short-tempered secretary of state, Alexander M. Haig, Jr."[65]

McFarlane emerges "as a media figure . . . gets up early to appear on the network morning shows, gives interviews for the evening news broadcasts and has been a guest more than a dozen times on the Sunday morning talk shows." (The *National Journal* headlined that description "McFarlane's Openness Sends Press the Signal: This Bud's for You.")[66]

Carlucci appears on the national news broadcasts, speaking for the president from the Vienna Economic Summit; even General Powell is featured on "Meet the Press" and "This Week with David Brinkley."[67]

Limelight on his aides sometimes brings second thoughts to a president: might there arise a question as to who will be getting the credit for the administration's accomplishments?

In the Nixon-Kissinger White House, that question gnawed on the president. In his memoirs, he gives reasons why he installed the then-secret taping system: "Such an objective record might also be useful to the extent that any President feels vulnerable to revisionist histories . . . from within . . . his administration. . . ."[68] Haldeman was more direct: "It was a final attempt by a frustrated Nixon to pin down the opinion of Henry Kissinger and other advisers who often seemed to come up with their own versions of both their own and the President's positions. . . ."[69]

Thus, there is a limit, however obscure at the time, on the public-advocacy role of the national security affairs assistant: it is the president's own tolerance.

Eisenhower's Robert Cutler put himself at one end of the scale:

> . . . an "anonymous" Assistant to the President has no charter to speak for his Chief in public. The President and I made an early arrangement, from which I never departed except on the President's permission that as to my official duties . . . I should "keep my trap shut." No speeches, no public appearances, no talking with reporters.[70]

President Ford came under pressure to have his security assistant "go public," to demonstrate that Secretary Kissinger was not the only figure in charge of American foreign policy. He resisted that pressure; Security

Assistant Brent Scowcroft's distinguished talents were exercised only behind the scenes.

There are arguments at the other end of the spectrum. What is needed
in the White House, Kissinger reflects, is to recognize "the most obvious,
and indeed only possible strategy: conducting a serious, honest, and continuing dialogue with the hated, feared, and secretly envied representatives of the media."[71]

The "right" point on the scale will vary with each chief executive, may
often be ambiguous, may move somewhat as an administration matures.
The president will set the pointer.

8. AS AN OPERATOR

"Operations" means spending money. Neither the national security assistant nor anyone else on his staff has appropriated program funds to dispense for operational purposes.[72]

The National Security Council budget for Fiscal Year 1989 is $5,100,000,
and it is devoted entirely to salaries, some travel, and a few office expenses.
There are no secret or unvouchered funds in it from Congress. Only the
Central Intelligence Agency receives appropriated funds for covert actions,
with the close surveillance of the Senate and House Intelligence committees.

Voluntary contributions are another matter.

The Reagan White House accumulated a treasure store from profits on
the sale of arms to Iran, from importuning private donors, and even from
other nations such as Brunei. Most of those funds, it has been discovered,
were put in private Swiss bank accounts and used in part to supply the
contra forces in Nicaragua. With that kind of private money, the late
director of Central Intelligence was reported to have hoped to set up

> an overseas entity that was capable of conducting operations or activities of
> assistance to the U.S. foreign policy goals . . . 'stand-alone,' . . . self-financing,
> independent of appropriated monies and capable of conducting activities similar
> to the ones that we had conducted here. . . .[73]

Both the Tower Commission and the majority side of the Senate-House
Select committees on the Iran-contra Affair bristled at this revelation. So
does the author.

Beyond the question of money and the accountability for its use, the central issue here is whether the NSC staff is an appropriate place for operations of any kind. There are two reasons why it is not.

First, operations abroad require men and women with training and experience, require support systems that only established institutions can provide. Operations demand coordination among those institutions, which even an event as recent as the Grenada invasion showed was inadequate. A secret, macho White House unit engaged in operational activities abroad makes it even more certain that coordination will be absent—among the responsible institutions and even within the White House itself. The Tower Commission warned: "As a general matter, the NSC Staff should not engage in the implementation of policy or the conduct of operations. This compromises their oversight role and usurps the responsibilities of the departments and agencies."[74]

Second, a national security assistant and staff who are themselves personally committed in conducting operations cannot then be impartial analysts of the same national security policies that include those operations. They forfeit the very quality which permits intellectual integrity at the level of the White House: detachment. The Senate-House majority report emphasized:

> This was a dangerous misuse of the NSC staff. When covert operations are conducted by those on whom the President relies to present policy options, there is no agency in government to objectively scrutinize, challenge and evaluate plans and activities. Checks and balances are lost. . . . The NSC was created to provide candid and comprehensive advice to the President. It is the judgment of these Committees that the NSC staff should never again engage in covert operations.[75]

Reflecting again the traditional comity between Congress and the president, however, neither the Tower Commission (two of the members of which were former senators) nor the Senate-House Investigating Committees recommended that the prohibitions on NSC staff operations be statutory. As the Tower Commission put it, "The inflexibility of a legislative restriction should be avoided. Terms such as 'operation' and 'implementation' are difficult enough to define, and a legislative proscription might preclude some future President from making a very constructive use of the NSC staff."[76] The president then (belatedly) took administrative action and in his March 31, 1987, directive specified "that the NSC staff itself will not undertake the conduct of covert activities."

Once more the route leads back to the president—to his judgment, his sense of what the American people will support, the caliber of people he appoints to his NSC staff. The buck stops with him.

Can the national security affairs assistant work all his eight arms at once? If he independently proposes courses of action to the president, can he objectively assess those same recommendations? If he so closely controls the filters of national security information to the president, will he, as a protagonist of a certain viewpoint, wield those filters with neutrality? The answer in both cases is likely to be no.

A president's initial protection, accordingly, is to select a security assistant who is long on experience but short on advocacy, who faithfully reflects the president's policy priorities, while being objective enough to put even them to the test of Security Council review. In that very review is the president's backup protection against ill-considered or improper action, that is, through insisting on a process of free debate among the concerned Cabinet officers—a debate arising out of shared information.

For the national security assistant, and for the president, the first arm of the eight, therefore—process management—is the most important one of all.

CHAPTER 8

"To Summarize and Analyze . . . Refine the Conflicting Views": The Domestic Policy Staff

[Shortly before inauguration Nixon] exhorted his Cabinet to work hard, seize their departments from the dastardly bureaucracies. . . . The President made it sound as if he intended to give his Cabinet full freedom to run their departments without White House interference. At the time, that might have been Nixon's real intention.

—John Ehrlichman

[Kennedy] could not afford to accept, without seeking an independent judgment, the products and proposals of departmental advisers whose responsibilities did not require them to look, as he and his staff looked, at the government and its programs as a whole. He required a personal staff, therefore—one that represented *his* personal ways, means and purposes—to summarize and analyze those products and proposals for him, to refine the conflicting views of various agencies, to define the issues which he had to decide, to help place his personal imprint upon them, to make certain that practical political facts were never overlooked, and to enable him to make his decisions on the full range of *his* considerations and constituencies, which no Cabinet member shared.

—Theodore Sorensen

The assistant for national security affairs has a twin: the assistant to the president for domestic policy.

Pulling from the domestic cabinet departments their individual strands of policy preferences and weaving them into patterns of advice for the president are also White House tasks with a long history. What is this experience? What tasks do domestic policy staffs perform?

The Truman assistants (principally Clark Clifford, Charles Murphy, and their aides) concentrated on the messages being sent to Congress, since, as for every president, "messages, speeches, Executive Orders, and the like are not merely vehicles for *expressing* policy, they are devices for getting policy *decided.*"[1] Murphy "held the acknowledged staff lead on preparation of all the formal documents which expressed, explained, or defended the President's major policies and programs—foreign and domestic, executive and legislative, governmental and 'political' alike. Now if this did not put Murphy 'in charge' of policy and program planning, at least it got him deeply and strongly involved in the process."[2]

It was Clifford who dovetailed the policy themes of the three separate messages that Truman sent to Congress each January (the State of the Union message and the budget and economic reports). It was Murphy assistant Richard Neustadt who drafted the White House version of the 1952 Democratic platform (Neustadt's White House role was masked somewhat; the Platform Committee members, Murphy remembered, changed some of the language so they wouldn't "have a platform that somebody handed to them.")

Like Truman, Eisenhower did not label any of his White House aides "domestic policy staff," but their functions were the same. "Utility man, trouble-shooter, economic watchdog and implementer" was how presidential assistant Gabriel Hauge described his job. He was particularly concerned with trade matters. When the Tariff Commission called for protectionist barriers against lead and zinc imports, it was Hauge who sent its report to State, Commerce, Treasury, and the others, pulled their sharply differing opinions together into a paper for Eisenhower, and convened the decision meeting in Ike's office.

White House staffer Robert Merriam was a knot-untangler for Eisenhower on domestic issues crossing federal-state-local jurisdictions. Commerce's Federal Highway Administration would plan to put a federal expressway just where the Housing and Home Finance Agency was encouraging a housing development. "Here you had two federal agencies with contrary policies," Merriam observed, "Neither one would talk to the other." He called a series of meetings in the White House, and discovered "it was the first time . . . that some of these agencies had really talked to each other about urban problems." Merriam negotiated a treaty between them: they were to consult with each other before selecting land for their respective projects. He observed:

> . . . the real problem with the federal government lay in finding a means to coordinate all of these policies, and it was never going to be done by the junior Cabinet department but had to be done out of the President's office . . . or through his designated representatives. . . . The federal government today absolutely requires coordination at the Presidential level of federal policy.[3]

President Johnson's White House staff took the lead in pulling together his "Great Society" initiatives. Joseph Califano was in effect the domestic policy chief and remembers what was behind the presidential legislative program of 1966:

> There were, of course, numerous discussions during the intervening months and a healthy agenda of campaign promises yet to be fulfilled. We kept Johnson informed of our progress with scores of memos, and presented a number of critical issues for his decision. But, the whittling down of hundreds of legislative suggestions to the final hundred or so that were presented to the President in December was left to me, my staff, the other senior presidential aides like Harry McPherson and Doug Cater and Budget Director Charles Schultze.[4]

In 1970 Nixon announced that it was time to cut the White House staff; there had been "a tendency to enlarge . . . the President's personal staff." The result, he opined, was "to inhibit the delegation of authority to Departments and agencies." He would establish a Domestic Council, and "this Cabinet group would be provided with an institutional staff," those words implying the use of career professionals, not impermanent White House aides.[5] Perhaps, as Ehrlichman had commented, Nixon was sincere at the time.

What took place was just the opposite. Nixon never did like Cabinet groups for policy discussions; the "council" met perhaps twenty-two times in six and one-half years.[6] The council staff, however, rose to fifty-five; in fact, within the White House the title "Domestic Council" became a synonym for the domestic policy aides themselves. It has always been a personal, never an institutional, staff. When Reagan took office, even its secretaries were fired.

Throughout the Nixon and Ford years, the domestic policy staff, under Ehrlichman and his successors, Kenneth Cole and James Cannon, was the center of gravity for nearly all of the presidential domestic initiatives. Ehrlichman summarized what he did:

> The working groups and the Domestic Council staff exerted extraordinary care in preparing the 'option papers' that went to the President. I reviewed each one before it went 'in' to make certain it answered all the questions the President might have. Sometimes a group had worked so deeply into an issue that its paper made assumptions or skipped over basic data which seemed obvious or simplistic. One of my functions was to insist that it give us the whole picture. I'd return the paper with 'Why?' written in the margins.[7]

The year 1977 saw a new president take office, pledging, as Nixon had once intended, to rely on "Cabinet government." High among President Carter's priorities was the promise he had made to provide more effective federal assistance to the nation's big cities. Coming from a small town in the South, he did not want to be regarded as a president with only a regional—and rural—perspective. He had made a campaign speech in New York City and had won the endorsement of Mayor Abraham Beame and other urban leaders on the strength of his commitment to improve the quality of life in metropolitan America.

Perhaps none of his tall pile of policy priorities put Carter's faith in Cabinet teamwork so much to the test as his 1977–78 urban development initiative. Federal programs affecting cities were by no means confined to the Department of Housing and Urban Development; they were scattered across at least twelve departments and agencies. Nonetheless, Carter pushed the "Cabinet government" starting button—and it is revealing to trace the saga of what happened.

He began by instructing six Cabinet heads

> to form a working policy group on urban and regional development. The pur-
> pose of the group will be to conduct a comprehensive review of all federal
> programs which impact on urban and regional areas; to seek perspectives of state
> and local officials concerning the role of the federal government in urban and
> regional development; and to submit appropriate administrative and legislative
> recommendations.[8]

White House aides Jack Watson and Stuart Eizenstat were requested to "facilitate and support your collective efforts," but HUD Secretary Patricia Harris would lead the enterprise. A progress report was due by "early summer." Secretary Harris established an Urban and Regional Policy Group, and called its first meeting on April 21 in the Roosevelt Room of the White House.

It soon became obvious that each of the URPG departments had its own agenda, often at odds with the others. Treasury was not enthusiastic about the urban policy initiative if it meant changing the tax code. With tax reform on his plate, observed one veteran of that scene, "urban policy was perhaps number sixty-two on Secretary Blumenthal's list." The secretary did think that the government should establish a new Urban Development Bank. Senior Treasury officials, however, would have preferred to see the more "conservative" Department of Commerce take the urban policy lead in the first place.

Commerce would have gladly done just that; it was home to the Economic Development Administration. With all of its "development" experience, its own EDA, it thought, could handle much of the urban assistance program. Commerce liked the bank idea but of course believed it should be located in Commerce.

HUD insisted that any such bank be within its turf, and saw in Carter's new urban initiative the opportunity to increase its own development assistance programs. If there were to be new funds, they should not be in Commerce; EDA's money and experience, HUD claimed, were oriented to locations outside of major cities while the greatest need for help was in the distressed Frostbelt metropolises.

The Office of Management and Budget representatives reminded the group that the deadline for FY 1979 budget proposals was coming up, and also warned them that money was going to be a problem. Perhaps the whole project should wait another year. They smirked a bit: whatever munificent policy ideas the URPG came up with would have to be submitted to OMB's budget process for vetting anyway. And the pot wasn't going to be that big. One participant remembered that OMB was going to be on guard against creating any "noxious new programs."

Meanwhile, through its own eyes, OMB's reorganization staff viewed the whole undertaking as a rare opportunity to reshuffle the government's entire urban machinery, at last to seize the chance to link structure to policy. They would abolish the Small Business Administration, and fold EDA, HUD, and the Farmer's Home Administration into a new Department of Development Assistance.

The first lady herself put a finger in the stew; her staff did not protect her well against outside lobbyists who represented community volunteer efforts and she relayed those pressures to the White House assistants. The vice president's wife, too, had her special interest—she wanted "urban" funds put into the arts.

Secretary Harris' personal style was abrasive, "brassy" some were alleging. In spite of the president's memorandum, there were occasions at the beginning when she cut Eizenstat and Watson themselves out of some of the interagency meetings—"This is *my* project" was her state of mind. Privately, she told the White House that she "could not be perceived as coming out of this exercise weaker as a department than she went in."[9]

People were a problem. The active agents in the enterprise were the departmental assistant secretaries. Many had Capitol Hill origins, had been selected not by the president but by their Cabinet superiors; their loyalties ran the same route: not to the White House but to congressional friends and to the programs within and the constituencies outside of their departments. A former White House staffer commented: "Carter had put foxes to guard the chicken coops." Another added: "All of these activists, with ambitious spending plans in their pockets, saw the urban policy enterprise as a boat to jump on." As soon as the URPG study was announced, they headed for Capitol Hill and tipped off friendly legislators. Next they passed the good word to the thirsty advocacy groups. "Expectations exploded," said a third observer ruefully. Another summed it up: "The whole exercise turned out to be Executive Branch log-rolling."

In the late fall, Secretary Harris telephoned domestic policy chief Stuart Eizenstat. With him, she had good personal chemistry; she believed that he, like herself, was on the liberal side of the political ledger. *He* knew what Carter's campaign promises were; he had written Carter's New York City speech. Immediately following the election, he had made a summary of all the president-elect's campaign promises. Furthermore, he was supposed to "facilitate," wasn't he? Above all, he was the president's agent. "I can't do this," she complained. "I give those other departments instructions and they won't follow them. I call meetings and they won't come. I need help. A strong president would back up the chairman. *You* must get involved."

Eizenstat was torn in his own mind. On the one hand, he was concerned about getting enmeshed as a leader in a process that had already gone on for some months and which had become embroiled in interagency disputes. On the other hand, he realized that direct White House participation was the indispensable device to salvage the whole enterprise and avoid embarrassment for the president on an issue he considered crucial. A March 1978 deadline for completion and public announcement was on the horizon. "Cabinet government" by itself was not going to be enough.

Eizenstat told Secretary Harris he would move in. From then on, the urban policy development project was in large part a White House staff enterprise. Eizenstat hired additional experts in his own office to help. Then to each of nine of his domestic policy assistants, he assigned one or more of the URPG subgroups for monitoring. He chaired the URPG meetings, holding all of them in the White House.

Eizenstat had already been buffering the president from the advocates who were bringing their appeals to the White House—governors, mayors, legislators, Jesse Jackson. The governors told him: give block grants to the states. The mayors pleaded that if funds were sent to the states, they would never reach the cities; Carter should target maybe ten cities, spend heavily to make a visible difference. They estimated that $11 billion in new money was needed. County officials urged that new urban money by no means be limited to cities. Urban experts advised attracting population back into downtowns; others counseled to forget about hopeless areas like the South Bronx. In eleven months, Eizenstat's schedule had bulged with at least forty-two meetings with outside groups; as the deadline neared, he became more and more the focus of their advocacy even though he knew he could never satisfy their full demands.

Eizenstat queried, probed, sucked in information, and also soothed the crusaders, most of them politically important to his president. Unlike many a White House staff officer before and since, he had a diplomatic temperament and preserved cordial relationships with Secretary Harris. Eizenstat met with her and with the responsible HUD assistant secretary, worked up a list of the thirteen issues that demanded review, and fixed a timetable for the studies to be ready.

The first urban policy report went to the president in December of 1977. It reflected the initial pluralism. His "Cabinet government" had given him not an integrated policy but a set of departmental wish lists stapled together and Carter was disappointed with it. The URPG had merely proposed add-ons to existing programs. Eizenstat's notes underscore a presidential request: "It needs a common thrust and theme."

In late January of 1978, a new package was delivered to the president. Up front, it contained ten pages of "broad principles and objectives" from Eizenstat and Harris jointly (e.g., "Respond to the needs of all cities"; "Encourage the participation of . . . neighborhood groups, voluntary organizations.") Side by side with that was added a dissent from OMB Director James McIntyre. Those principles were "too vague . . . too all-inclusive." "Avoid promising more than we can deliver" counseled McIntyre, "long-term trends brought urban areas to the point where they are today. No 'urban policy' we can conceive of will reverse these trends overnight." McIntyre also favored major reorganization of agencies and liked HEW Secretary Joseph Califano's suggestion for a special representative for domestic assistance in the Executive Office of the president. Eizenstat covered the whole package with a six-page personal note, disagreeing with OMB on some points, promising to include OMB's views in the final report in February, but urging Carter to defer approving the reorganization proposals. Carter scribbled his approvals and comments, told Eizenstat that "Rosalynn will help actively as one of the leaders" of the voluntary organizations, and concluded with a reminder: "Stay on schedule."

Two more months of work were needed and it was now centered in the White House staff. The Eizenstat office had combed through the voluminous memoranda that had flooded in from all the agencies, and labored with HUD and OMB to prepare an encyclopedic discussion piece. Backup materials from the agencies and the experts formed a stack two feet high. A White House-HUD-OMB meeting was called in mid-March to review the mountain of paper.

The wrestling match went on all night. Each subject, each subissue, each option, each line was analyzed, questioned, costed out. Yes to this one; no to that; "That will mean another $200 million." Forty of the agencies' pet ideas were tossed out completely. Dawn came and Eizenstat's deputy went for coffee; he was first in line when the snack bar opened at 6:30 A.M.

The final product was a two-hundred-page Harris-Eizenstat option paper for the president. Lengthily but faithfully, it represented the agencies' views, described current programs, set forth "decision packages," and added the agreed recommendations. Secretary Harris came over to sign it but warned the White House assistants as she did so that they were to be damn sure to make no further changes in it before it reached the president. The paper went in unaltered, but Louis Brownlow's 1939 advice, that White House staff should not "interpose," has a flip side: no Cabinet officer can interpose herself between a top White House assistant and the president either.

It was Eizenstat who did put in the last word—a "road map" memorandum covering the massive option paper. In a thirteen-page private "not for circulation" note, he and McIntyre summarized what had been done, added up the cost, and set forth their remaining disagreement. They then discussed two "sensitive issues" too explosive to put in the joint option memorandum. Where would the Urban Development Bank be located? This was a "bitter struggle . . . between Commerce and HUD." (Their compromise recommendation: temporarily, "an interagency entity.") What kind of interdepartmental coordination should there be for urban affairs in the future? (A committee was recommended rather than a new presidential office; senior White House staff assistant Jack Watson was later to chair it.) Embarrassingly, the confidential memo leaked and Mrs. Harris was highly annoyed.

Carter plowed through the entire stack by himself, rejected many of the recommendations, approved so few that a small group of staffers later met with the vice president to gripe that the urban initiative might now turn into a "political disaster." After an eleventh-hour appeal from his political advisers. Carter relented, giving Harris and Eizenstat the go-ahead for an announcement, a message to Congress, and a press briefing on the very day of his decision. David Broder's follow-up *Washington Post* column was headlined "Chaos, Reshuffled." The staff veterans of that period agree now with the Broder comments made then:

> Harris' interdepartmental committee . . . proved mainly to be a device for protecting every program of every agency represented. . . . And in his kind of Cabinet government, with a weak White House staff, even as able an aide as Eizenstat has little authority to crack the whip on the president's behalf. . . . None of the 160 recommendations call for eliminating any single existing program—despite the almost universal acknowledgement that some of them are real losers.[10]

The urban policy story reveals as much about President Carter as it tells about Eizenstat and the domestic policy staff: *how a White House staff acts is how a president wants it to act.*

Could the Office of Management and Budget, instead of Eizenstat, have taken on the oversight task for the urban policy initiative? On reflection, one of Eizenstat's former colleagues later said no. "The urban-policy report was as much if not more a political document than it was a substantive one," he said. "OMB does not view itself as being part of such a political process." Another Carter White House veteran added: "OMB has no incentive to come up with comprehensive, interdisciplinary solutions. They are good at taking somebody else's proposals and squeezing them through the budget sieve."

A few other examples illustrate both the variety and the significance of the domestic policy staff's functions in the White House.

Like Eisenhower, Kennedy, and Johnson before him, Carter continued a system of having each Cabinet officer send him a weekly report through the White House staff secretary. In their margins, the president would scratch in questions or instructions—for example, "These are unacceptable"; or "Comment"; or "Get them to me in writing as early as possible." Staff Secretary Rick Hutcheson would make eleven copies of all the reports, complete with presidential scribbles, and distribute them to the vice president and ten White House seniors. Eizenstat and his colleagues were thus as well informed as the president about Cabinet activities and, with presidential scrawls in hand, could pursue the chief executive's requests with unquestionable authority.

With his sizable staff on top of so many fast-moving subjects, the domestic policy director sent President Carter a weekly summary from his own office. His "Domestic Policy Staff Weekly Status Report" of June 17, 1977, for instance, had sixty-one brief bulleted paragraphs. Carter would scribble on them as well.

A domestic policy staff does not serve a president well unless it sniffs out in advance every major domestic policy declaration being released from the Executive Branch. For forty years, White House staffs have worked together with Executive Office units to set up anticipatory systems.

Budget disputes were the first to be brought close to the White House, in 1939, by the new Bureau of the Budget. The review of official letters and testimony to Congress was centralized in the late forties, also by the Bureau, and the intractable arguments that surfaced were taken across the street to the White House. As shown in chapter 7, national security policy has been White House–managed increasingly since 1947. Still relatively uncontrollable are speeches given by Cabinet members in the domestic area; no White House will ever be forewarned 100 percent against all those maverick comments, James Watt's being a painful example.

One policy voice is controlled only with the application of considerable White House muscle: amicus briefs from the solicitor general to the Supreme Court. The solicitor general is a presidential appointee in the Department of Justice, serves at the president's pleasure, and speaks for the administration. Literally so: he argues in person before the Court.

The more sensitive, the more controversial a case before the Court, the more significant for the president are the views and arguments of the solicitor general. While the latter tends to take the position that he is "above politics," in the White House staff view there is no such insulation when critically important issues are at stake. Domestic policy chiefs have struggled to have him included in their arc of policy review.

Chapter 3, for instance, described how strong were President Nixon's convictions about school desegregation and about busing as an instrument. When the Supreme Court called for briefs on the *Swan* case in late 1970—a watershed case about the constitutionality of busing—White House counsel and domestic policy chief John Ehrlichman made sure that the solicitor general's brief was cleared in the White House. On similar cases, he had to keep repeating the reminder. Ehrlichman recalls one instance:

> I called in [Solicitor General] Griswold one time . . . me, a small-time lawyer from Seattle with the ex-dean of the Harvard Law School and all of his other credentials. He either refused to file a brief or insisted on some specific language and [Attorney General] Mitchell said, "I can't do anything with him." So Nixon said to me, "Get him over here." I called and said in effect, "General, get yourself over here." He thought he was coming to see the president. For a while, I thought he was coming to see the president. It turned out he was coming to see me. So I said, "The president wants you to do this." "Well . . ." he started in . . . and I said, "You didn't hear me; I said *the president wants you to do this. You are* his *solicitor general."* He said, "I am the solicitor general of the United States," and I said, "Read your Constitution, General, Article II." And he did it.[11]

In July of 1977, the same kind of issue arose, an environmental case being the trigger. Eizenstat, Cabinet Secretary Jack Watson, and White House counsel Robert Lipshutz together wrote to the president:

> There are a few conflicts, however, whose resolution entails significant policy choices for the Administration. The question is how the White House can assert the legitimate Administration interest in such matters without in any way compromising the integrity of the Justice Department. . . . We recommend that you authorize us to contact the Attorney General and request that no legal brief be filed before policy decision has been made at the White House level, and that Stu coordinate the policy analysis.[12]

The president agreed.

Eizenstat and Lipshutz had to repeat the maneuver two months later when the Court considered the *Bakke* case, a wrenching example of the affirmative-action controversy. Here it was not only the solicitor general but Attorney General Griffin Bell himself who wanted to keep the White House out of the business of reviewing briefs. Bell brought the Justice draft amicus brief with him to discuss the *Bakke* case with the president, whereupon Carter asked that Lipshutz, Eizenstat, and Vice President Mondale look over Justice's wording (which soon thereafter leaked to the *New York Times*). Bell later reflected that bringing the brief with him to the White House that day was

> perhaps my greatest mistake with regard to the power centers at the White House. Nowhere is the tug of power between the White House and a Cabinet department more apparent than in a dispute between the Justice Department and the President's staff over what is law and what is policy. If the staff had its way, no doubt every major issue that naturally fell to the Justice Department would be considered policy rather than a legal matter. Then the White House would be making all the decisions, because it is the White House where policy is made.[13]

Whether expressed in Ehrlichman's colorful anecdote, the Lipshutz-Watson-Eizenstat conviction, or Griffin Bell's rueful recollection, the point is precisely the same. The president is policymaker-in-chief and the leaders of these thirty departments and agencies, including solicitors general, are constitutionally required to have him—not them—decide the administration's position on sensitive and controversial questions. Mr. Bell's gripe notwithstanding, law and policy are inseparable.

President Reagan, like Carter, proclaimed "Cabinet government" and formed six, later reduced to two, cabinet councils. As chapter 2 illustrates, however, his White House staff were the managers of those councils and always authored the final presidential decision memoranda. The old domestic policy function was given a new name, Office of Policy Development; its director reported to an assistant to the president for policy development, of which there have been four during the Reagan years.

A principal policy focus in the second Reagan term was reform of the government's public assistance system—a morass of fifty-nine federal programs cutting across six departments which had issued some six thousand pages of regulations and were spending some $124 billion annually. No one federal agency could gather all those strands together; a system-wide approach was necessary. President Reagan wanted to encourage state governments to experiment with new approaches and to enlist private, on-the-scene organization. to manage assistance programs for the needy in their immediate areas. There were provisions in the laws which permitted cabinet officers to waive existing stringent compliance requirements and foster such "experimental, pilot, or demonstration" projects.[14] The departments however, each operating from its own unavoidably separate perspective, were found to be routinely denying such waivers, blocking state officials from trying what the president believed would be valuable new approaches to reduce rather than perpetuate dependency.

The domestic policy leaders on the White House staff saw that there was a need for much closer coordination; they elevated the review process to the White House itself, created a special interagency "Low-Income Opportunity Advisory Board," chaired by presidential assistant Charles Hobbs. The word went out to governors: send in new proposals for experimental programs. No single "lead agency" could encompass the system-wide reform at which the president was aiming; even the Office of Management and Budget was considered "too budget-oriented" as one White House staffer explained. The Board itself would pass on the state waiver-requests. At Board meetings, Hobbs saw senior departmental officers, engaged in the same area of federal activity, introducing themselves to one another for the first time. "We wanted to ensure there was better cooperation among those departments and with the White House," Hobbs recalled, "there had to be a central focus and that would have to be the White House itself." Hobbs headed a White House staff group of nine; they supported the Board and spurred the governors to propose the kind of innovations for which the president was searching.

The tradition of domestic policy staff work continues, varying with each president but constantly near the center of every White House. What grew up from Clifford and Murphy, through Eisenhower's aides and into Sorensen's and then Califano's hands, was followed by Ehrlichman and his successors, Ken Cole and James Cannon. Eizenstat personified that tradition for four years; Reagan's quartet (Martin Anderson, Edwin Harper, Jack Svahn, and Gary Bauer) succeeded him.

Over forty years, the enormity of the changes in policy masks the similarity of the White House staff operation. Johnson may have told Califano to shape a Great Society; Reagan may have instructed his aides to shrink it. Cabinets, councils, boards, or working groups may meet or not. Like its national security counterpart, each succeeding domestic policy staff continues, in Sorensen's words, to "summarize and analyze . . . refine the conflicting views."

CHAPTER 9

The "Just-us" Department: The Counsel to the President

In the Truman administration, the Justice Department tended to be evasive, sometimes downright unresponsive in providing the Executive Office with forthright legal guidance on legislative or operational issues. This left a vacuum into which the Presidential Counsel was pressed to move, and on a number of occasions—particularly concerning controversial legislation and Executive Orders—Murphy's views were, in fact, decisive. —RICHARD NEUSTADT

We certainly did not want some young, faceless twenty-five-year-old White House staffer taking issue with the attorney general of the United States, who was an officer nominated by the president and confirmed by the Senate, and then taking the issue to the president in a memo which might set forth two paragraphs and "Mr. President, check the box below."

—A former member of the Justice Department's Office of Legal Counsel

For four decades, presidents have set up in the White House what Eisenhower counsel Gerald Morgan used to call "the Just-us" Department—an immediate staff office of independent legal advice for both their policy and their personal affairs. Over at the institutional Justice Department, attorneys general and their associates have been skeptical. "The Attorney General views *himself* as the president's lawyer" was the warning that Truman's attorney general passed to Edward McCabe, Eisenhower's newly announced special White House counsel.[1] "They are not equipped to do painstaking legal research over at the White House; they tend to skim the surface" comments one former Justice officer. "In Justice nobody is overawed by our environment, nor are we subject to the kinds of pressures which abound at the White House. Some of those younger White House lawyers have views of their own which can color their legal judgment." Justice veterans are afraid that presidents may "shop around" for the legal advice they prefer, with resulting inconsistency in administration judgments.[2]

The view from the White House is different. The Department of Justice is "too remote," "twenty blocks away." White House legal staffers know they must answer the "How do I do this?" question with a speed that matches the president's urgency. "Nothing propinqs like propinquity," former counsel Lloyd Cutler observed.[3] The Department of Justice, White House officers emphasize, has parochial interests of its own in the areas of civil rights, antitrust, and law enforcement; setting up the attorney general as a presidential counsel would appear as giving unfair preference to one Cabinet officer over the others.

A White House–Justice treaty is usually agreed to; each White House counsel renegotiates it with each new attorney general. Advance consultation is promised in both directions. The White House pledges not to exert improper pressure on Justice, especially when prosecutions are involved; agrees that all White House calls to the department will come only through the counsel's office; and promises to exempt the attorney general from campaign politicking.

For their part, Justice officers are glad to know that there is an officer in the White House who, on most occasions, will insist on bringing the department's resources into a legal issue and who will stick up for those views in tight policy arguments. None of them asserts that the first family's own legal business should be handled outside the White House fence.

The counsel's resources are not limited to White House and Justice circles; he establishes links to every agency. Each department has its own general counsel, and before any of those officers is appointed, he or she has an interview with the presidential legal staff. In this fashion, and by regular meetings with the group of them, the counsel has a hand on the legal network of the entire Executive Branch.

There are some twenty people in the counsel's office. What do they do? The security assistant may have eight arms; the White House counsel is a millipede. He can be everywhere, may leave a thousand footprints.

His first step is to try to establish exclusive turf, not for selfish reasons but to ensure orderly conduct.

To enforce his "treaty" with the attorney general, the counsel notifies all other White House offices that he will be the only channel from the White House to the Justice Department. But there are large holes in that barrier. On basic legal-political issues like civil rights, it is the domestic affairs adviser who will play a central role.

The counsel's next task is to send a second warning to his White House colleagues: stay *away* from the independent regulatory commissions. His injunction does not have to recall Sherman Adams' grief (he had telephoned the Federal Trade Commission asking for the status of the case of a friend); even today most White House staffers remember it. The same caution is raised with respect to procurement agencies; not even any "status" calls are allowed, "to avoid the appearance of conflict and subsequent embarrassment."[4] This pair of sober admonitions echoes down the years; Reagan counsel Peter Wallison's May 1986 memorandum is a verbatim repetition of John Dean's proscription of January 1971.

A routine but ancient responsibility fills up every counsel's in-box. The Constitution gives the president the power to commute sentences and grant pardons for those convicted of federal crimes. Some four hundred petitions are received each year. The first-cut analysis is made by the pardon attorney in the Department of Justice. An assistant attorney general gives a second review, and sends a "letter of advice" to the president for each case, accompanied by a three-to-fifteen-page summary of the background. The counsel's staff must look at every one. The White House usually follows the recommendation from Justice (some 10 percent are granted), but on occasion reverses it in favor of denial, "to protect," in a former counsel's words, "the reputation and integrity of the office of the President."

The counsel is among those White House seniors who are asked to review draft presidential speeches. Here deadline clocks tick insistently; a new version will arrive even before the counsel staffer has finished inspecting the one before. "Those speechwriters aim for soaring rhetoric," said one staff veteran, smiling; "we want to minimize error."

Hundreds of gifts pour in to the first family from Americans and from abroad; counsel staff advise on the proprieties for acceptance. In selfish calculation or in innocence, entrepreneurs and advertisers will use the president's name or the White House label as a magnet for sales. A magazine runs a picture story about "Ronald Reagan's Secret Stag Film"; a glove manufacturer wants to announce a Nancy Reagan white-glove special; a friend of the first lady makes up several thousand "Betty Ford" scarves. The counsel will try to warn them off.

Charities are wont to trade on the presidential image, presumably for more noble purposes. A Nancy Reagan Benefit Tennis Tournament is scheduled with the proceeds destined to go to her for the war on drugs; the counsel suggests a more indirect arrangement.

Organizations supporting the president will use his, or a well-known White House staffer's, name to raise funds—perhaps implying access or some other favors in return. The Heritage Foundation employed counselor Edwin Meese's name and the counsel found even the appearance to be troublesome. Donors to the Nicaraguan contras were promised entrée to the president; the legal staff apparently was bypassed on that one.

In a presidential reelection campaign, the legal binoculars are focused on the linkages between the reelection "committee" and the White House staff. Which one pays the plane ticket for a staffer's speech? How are the expenses of *Air Force One* to be apportioned between campaign and government ledgers? Any misjudgment could mean a dangerous political embarrassment.

Demonstrators or protesters will stream into town and head for the White House gates, petitions in hand. Should White House staff members accept them? In previous administrations, such sessions had resulted in White House sit-ins. Chief of Staff Haldeman addressed an advisory to his colleagues in May of 1972; the counsel was to be informed in advance of the petitioners' arrival so that staffers could be briefed about the group's background if necessary, and Secret Service or other law enforcement teams forewarned.

Criminal matters are hypersensitive. When Teamsters Union President Jackie Presser was under investigation, counsel Fred Fielding admonished the staff to keep him "at arms's length." If a staff member personally has transgressed, White House counsel can be of no help; a statute requires all government lawyers to report any knowledge of crimes to the attorney general.

If a flood decimates a county's bridges or crops, petitions for federal disaster relief roll in. The counsel reviews them before presidential action is considered.

The conduit from the White House to the Congress runs not only through the Legislative Affairs Office; it often snakes across the counsel's desk as well. Congressional investigating committees will demand documents, especially any addressed to or coming from the president. Two centuries of precedent protect such communications from scrutiny by the other branches, unless the president volunteers them (as in the Iran-contra investigation) or if a criminal process is underway (as was happening at the time of the Watergate tapes case). The Cabinet departments, however, cowed by their congressional oversight bodies, tend to cave in to such requests, willing to sacrifice a little bit of their president's executive privilege to save themselves a large measure of grief. "We had to watch them like hawks," observed Lloyd Cutler, "We, more than they, were the protectors of the presidential office."[5]

If the committees are delving into intelligence matters, as did the Church and Pike investigations during the Ford administration, the White House counsel must sit with the national security assistant and representatives of the Central Intelligence Agency, balancing the congressional need for secret materials with the equally important requirement to protect intelligence sources and methods.

In many of these instances, counsel staff will meet with committee staff to mediate the differences, perhaps tone down the congressional requests. The tension can go both ways; the White House once sparred with the chairman of the House Ethics Committee to get information for the White House which was in the committee's possession about individuals being considered for appointment.

White House public liaison officers will ask the counsel: when they prepare briefings for outside groups, how far can they go to convert audience enthusiasm into pressure on the Congress? There are statutory limits and the lawyers must temper commitment with caution. Lists of "targeted legislators" have sometimes been drawn up—but not on White House letterhead.

The counsel is at both ends of the legislative pathway. The office clears draft statutes which are to be sent up in the name of the president. At the other end of the process, when enrolled bills are sent to the White House, the counsel is on the short list of reviewers who, within the ten-day deadline, must examine them before the presidential decision to sign or veto. This responsibility goes back at least as far as Eisenhower's time. His personal secretary, Ann Whitman, jotted in her diary: "The President is upset because of 'bad staff work' on bills presented to him for signature. He asked that henceforth Jerry Morgan okay all bills sent to him for signature."[6]

If there is to be a veto, will it be a "pocket veto" or an explicit rejection? If there is to be a signature, should there be a signing statement? When a bill before him is generally acceptable but contains a provision invading presidential constitutional prerogatives, a president may sign it but issue a formal statement announcing his refusal to be bound by the language in question. The counsel reviews each instance with exceptional care. He and the Department of Justice support the practice by arguing that such statements represent appropriate guidance to implementing agencies. Democratic Congressman Barney Frank called them "the gravest usurpation of legislative prerogative I can think of."[7]

Always present is the issue of presidential power. For two centuries since the framers wrestled with that question, courts, Congress, and the White House have verbally assaulted one another as to the extent of presidential authority. How far can it be stretched? More recently, the question is: what are its proper limits? Outranking perhaps all of the counsel's other duties is this one—to represent the office of the president in that continuing constitutional debate.

Before the Supreme Court ruled the legislative veto unconstitutional in 1983, such veto provisions were perennially inserted into bills for the president's signature. Counsels would occasionally recommend presidential disapprovals; at other times the chief executive would say, "I am signing this bill but disagreeing with the congressional veto."

For contemporary presidents, there is constitutional debate about their commander-in-chief role. Is the 1973 War Powers Resolution unconstitutional, and absent an intent to challenge it through the courts, how much military power can a president bring to bear abroad without bowing to its provisions?

When U.S. forces are to be in action overseas, the White House counsel immediately convenes the general counsels of State and Defense and representatives of Justice and the NSC staff. Are the forces heading for "situations where imminent involvement in hostilities is clearly indicated by the circumstances"? If such is unambiguously the case, Congress must be notified and a ninety-day clock starts to run. State usually argues in favor of notification; Defense almost always opposes. The counsel will try to widen the area of presidential flexibility. If notification must be made, the president's letter to Congress may say he is acting "consistent with" rather than "pursuant to" the resolution—a hint that the White House continues to have reservations on constitutional grounds about that 1973 enactment.

The *Mayaguez* and Iranian rescue missions, the invasion of Grenada, sending Marines to Beirut and naval escorts into the Persian Gulf—all were "presidential powers" issues for the counsel. The same question arises in each such case: would the War Powers Resolution apply? Advance operational secrecy is imperative, yet the counsel must be forewarned so he can prepare the president to respond instantly to congressional assertions. (The Iran-contra debacle only underscored the risk of ignoring that rule.)

Any illness of the president causes a quiver on the counsel's voltmeter. If presidential surgery with general anesthesia is in prospect, the counsel must interpret the Twenty-Fifth Amendment: is anesthesia a presidential disability? The vice president would need a legal briefing. After the traumatic experience of the March 30, 1981, assassination attempt, the then Counsel Fred Fielding hastened to complete an "emergency book" which would spell out "what do you do about X, Y, Z events concerning the President's health?" Fielding later confirmed to the Miller Center Commission on Presidential Disability and the Twenty-Fifth Amendment that

The book is now finished. Whenever I would travel with the President there are two copies. I would always carry a copy with me of the book. There was always one back in my office in the safe. The book basically is every situation you can imagine that has occurred to the president or the vice president: it is, for that matter, scenarios.[8]

Policy issues demand the counsel's attention, many of these being heavy with political as well as legal tonnage. The Selective Service Act, for instance, came up for extension during the Carter administration and with it the issue of whether its registration requirement should continue to apply only to males.

Tempers rose within the White House. Some staffers opposed any registration. A member of the counsel's staff vehemently objected to a men-only draft and personally pressured the Justice Department to come up with a finding that the all-male registration was unconstitutional. Within the department, a hot debate then flared up. Justice's conclusion was that the courts would uphold men-only registration, a position applauded by the Department of Defense but scorned by "women's lib" advocates in the White House. In the end, Justice was proved right; the Supreme Court validated all-male registration. As for the advocacy-tinged counsel staffer, one of the participants in the debate recalled, "It was hard to take her seriously after that."

When Iranian students applied to the National Park Service for a permit to demonstrate in Lafayette Park, opposite the White House, presidential counsel Lloyd Cutler argued for a denial (but held out the alternative of permitting the gathering in McPherson Square, a few blocks away). Iranian television, he warned, would show pictures of U.S. Park Police standing over students lying prone (with the White House in the background). Such scenes would inflame anti-American anger in Tehran and cause further possible harm to the American hostages. The Department of Justice disagreed; demonstrators in America, they argued, should have First Amendment rights. The Park Service of course acceded to White House instructions; the permit was refused and litigation ensued. The district court agreed with the Justice position, but Cutler persuaded the Justice lawyers to take the case to the U.S. Court of Appeals. This time his position was upheld. "The White House was just as sensitive to First Amendment rights as anyone at Justice," Cutler later recalled, "but we had an even broader perspective: the international scene."

A civil rights issue that ensnarled the Reagan administration was whether contributions to private schools practicing racial discrimination (specifically Bob Jones University in South Carolina) would be tax-exempt. Nixon counsel Leonard Garment had handled the same issue in 1973 and the answer then was no. When President Reagan was badgered by Mississippi congressman Trent Lott to relent in favor of the Bob Jones institution, counsel Fred Fielding's warnings were ignored. The reversed decision was reversed again, but only after public attack and White House embarrassment.

Like any other merry-go-round, the White House carousel changes its riders frequently; in fact, at 1600 Pennsylvania Avenue many new ones jump on between stops. Rocking up and down with the lights and music, how aware are new staffers of the public attention they draw and of the rules of propriety that inexorably govern in that environment? In other words, what are the ethics of White House service? Setting and enforcing standards of conduct is one of the counsel's constant preoccupations.

"Newcomers bring strange baggage with them," observed Ford's counsel Philip W. Buchen; "they have rather cloudy views of the ethical standards needed in the White House."[9] The principal standard is very simple and very tough, best put in Buchen's own words in 1974: "Employees must be ever sensitive to avoid the *appearance* of acting on behalf of some private interest or of a conflict or other impropriety which can be fully as damaging as the real thing."[10] No White House rule has been stated so frequently—in ethics manuals and in separate memoranda from the counsel. Unfortunately, it has been often violated.

The proximate policeman is the counsel. The ultimate standard-setter is the president. Eisenhower set a model in his years: "If anyone ever comes to any part of this Government claiming some privilege, even to as low as an introduction to an official he wants to meet, on the basis that he . . . has any connection with the White House, he is to be thrown out instantly."[11]

Ike's private conduct was as fastidious as his public declaration. At one point, his counsel, Bernard Shanley, was called by movie magnate Spyros Skouras; he wanted to see Eisenhower to plead for tax relief for Aristotle Onassis. Onassis was apparently delinquent in paying his taxes and the Internal Revenue Service had immobilized some of his shipping fleet. The president told Shanley: "Call Skouras and tell him I would be delighted to see him, but if he raises the Onassis case, he will never come into this office again." Shanley made the call.[12]

White House aides who also look for advice from the counsel are those in the Presidential Personnel Office. When a presidential appointment is pending, two streams of sensitive data converge at the counsel's desk: FBI reports and tax-compliance summaries. Conflict-of-interest declarations are sent there as well, but are then relayed to the Office of Government Ethics. It is the counsel who will then give the green, yellow, or red signal to the personnel staff. Personnel Office recruiters may have a "pride of authorship" in the candidate they have found; the counsel must be arms-length and neutral.

The counsel's office is not passive, even with FBI material. If a file contains questionable data, the counsel may call in the candidate, give him or her a chance to rebut; some informants pour merely personal spite into their statements to Bureau agents. The candidate may supply such convincing exculpatory rejoinders that the counsel will instruct the Bureau to include them in its file.

In advance of confirmation hearings, a member of the counsel's staff will hand-carry the FBI summaries to the Capitol, show them to the chairman and the ranking minority member of the confirming committee. No copies are made; no aides look on.

If the personnel checking system fails, it is the president who is submerged in embarrassment. In 1978 President Carter nominated David Gartner to be a member of the Commodity Futures Trading Commission, a body that regulates the grain and other futures markets. The chairman of a major grain company had donated seventy-two thousand dollars worth of its stock as a trust fund for the education of Gartner's children, creating an obvious conflict of interest. Gartner informed the White House staff of the gift, "but they didn't seem concerned," he later told the Senate Agriculture Committee. No one told the president, nor was the committee informed. Reportedly at the vice president's urging, the nomination was sent to the Senate, rushed through the committee and then to the Senate floor, where it was approved by unanimous consent on the same day.

When Gartner's conflict-of-interest problem was later questioned, the president at first defended the appointment, then publicly called for Gartner's resignation. He refused, but two years later did resign and endorsed Carter's Democratic primary opponent, Ted Kennedy, for president.

In that instance, and today, and always, the counsel's desk is a powder magazine piled high with mines, grenades, and bombshells. When a warning Klaxon is needed, the counsel must lean on the button.

Judicial selection is now an additional responsibility in the counsel's territory. The counsel's office itself interviews candidates for District of Columbia judgeships. When federal district judges are to be nominated, the counsel goes over the attorney general's recommendations; for appellate or Supreme Court nominations, the Department of Justice prepares a detailed analysis of the judge's past opinions and the counsel will review these with especial diligence. The counsel chairs a Federal Judiciary Selection Committee, inviting the attorney general and the White House Personnel and Legislative Affairs offices to join in the screening. When President Carter's counsel, Robert Lipshutz, embarked on such a White House group review process, Attorney General Griffin Bell later termed it "such an outrageous intrusion into the prerogatives of the attorney general and such a politicization of the process of selection that I thought of resigning."[13] But the practice went forward anyway and the Reagan White House has repeated—and solidified—the precedent.

Reagan's nomination of Judge Robert Bork for the Supreme Court demonstrated—if demonstration were needed—that for such judicial positions politics and policy are inseparable. The president must be able to depend on his personal staff to help him ascertain not only what kind of legal philosophy he is underwriting in making judicial nominations, but what the confirmation politics are likely to be.

As a president contemplates the end of his service, he plans his presidential library; the counsel draws up the agreement specifying the rules of access to his papers. Instructions are also issued to staffers that all originals of their memoranda are to be sent to the archival repository. When Nixon left office and Ford replaced him, staff members were told immediately to segregate their files as of the changeover moment at noon on August 9. If some papers were "necessary for the purposes of current government business," counsel Buchen permitted staffers to duplicate them, but they would constitute a "new set of files for President Ford." There was to be "no intermingling."

The counsel's office is one of the few White House staff units that has begun the tradition of building a file of nonprivileged reference materials to be handed down from one administration to the next. Starting in 1974, Buchen compiled thick notebooks codifying the law and the precedents for the kinds of issues just described. The Carter and Reagan counsels have updated them; a minilibrary of procedural guidance has now been established and the presidential office has thereby been made more efficient.

No one counsel uniform fits all, nor can one chapter describe the totality of his duties. The "Just-us Department" is a flexible resource; each president will employ it in a variety of ways. White House counsels Leonard Garment and J. Fred Buzhardt defended Nixon in the Watergate litigation; Lloyd Cutler was asked to be a major player in the SALT negotiations and spent uncounted days involved in the international financial footwork preceding the release of the U.S. hostages from Iran.

Some presidents short-circuit their lawyers; the Reagan Iran-contra enterprise was not checked with the president's counsel at all. While the counsel function is a fifty-year-old tradition, it is still supple, still "very unstructured," as Cutler observed, and always subject to the president's management style.

The counsel is an intergenerational person—protecting the chief executive in office, summoning past precedents to do so, and being a steward for the presidency of the future.

CHAPTER 10

Legislative Affairs: "An Ambulatory Bridge Across a Constitutional Gulf"

Of all the lurid features . . . most revealing is the behavior of the Republican Party Establishment . . . Chairman This and Senator That. . . . With a few exceptions . . . the whole damn pack has headed for the tall grass. . . . In recent years, Republican candidates have taken to prattling at election time about their devotion to "family values." But among the first of those values is family loyalty. And when a mob shows up in the yard howling that the head of the household be produced, the sons do not force the Old Man to sit down at a table and write up a list of his "mistakes." You start firing from the upper floors. —PATRICK J. BUCHANAN

We may never agree on an issue, but legislative affairs people always discuss, even with their opponents, why the disagreement is there, get their views, and they realize that while they don't agree on a given question they may agree on the next issue coming up. —Reagan White House aide

That Democratic congressman invited me to be the principal speaker at the annual reception in his district for his major supporters. The theme of my speech was how two opponents were committed to help make the system work. —Reagan White House aide

The gulf is not always the constitutional one between the Capitol and the White House. As revealed in the epigraphs above, it yawns within the White House itself. Fire across or reach across the partisan boundaries?

The winners in that venerable debate are usually the president's legislative affairs leaders, the "ambulatory bridge" as the late respected Bryce Harlow described them. As long as the Congress is closely divided (and especially if the party opposing the president controls either house), the system has to work with two-way cooperation. (Less than two months after publication of the op-ed broadside from which the above quotation was taken, Buchanan left the White House to fire his rounds in private life.)

THE LEGISLATIVE LIAISON OFFICE AT
THE WHITE HOUSE

The legislative liaison work of White House staff has a long history but began with specific designations in 1949. Truman appointed Charles Maylon and Joseph Feeney to assist his appointments secretary, Matt Connelly, in tracking House and Senate affairs respectively. The two aides, however, reportedly did only minor chores and were criticized for their ineffectiveness. It was Eisenhower who elevated the legislative affairs function to top rank in the White House, and appointed his deputy chief of staff, retired Major General Wilton B. Persons, to take charge of it. Every president since has kept the leadership of that responsibility in the hands of personal staff at 1600 Pennsylvania Avenue.

Chief of legislative affairs is the president himself; the first task of the liaison staff is to support that personal role. The Big Ritual in every White House has been the formal meetings with the congressional leaders, held nearly weekly in some administrations. The liaison staff sniff out the agenda from Capitol, White House, or Cabinet sources.

A caution about the staff's visibility was expressed as early as 1948 when counsel Charles Murphy was recommending that Truman have regular evening meetings with congressional leaders. He thought that two White House staffers might rotate in to "furnish clerical and other assistance" but warned that "one of the principal benefits to be achieved from these meetings is to dispel the notion that the President is insulated from the Democrats in Congress by his White House staff. Consequently, staff members should not take a conspicuous part in these meetings." He added, however, that no decision should be taken unless "advance consideration based on adequate staff work has pretty well explored the field."[1]

What Truman actually hosted were weekly sessions with the "Big Four"—the vice president, the speaker of the house, and the majority leaders of both houses. "Conspicuous" was hardly the word for the staff. While Murphy, with his assistants from the Bureau of the Budget, made up the agenda for the Big Four meetings, no staff attended, nor were any records made. Murphy waited outside, recalling that "The president . . . purposefully decided that he wanted to conduct these meetings by himself and he did not want staff there."[2]

Eisenhower convened the legislative leaders regularly on Tuesday mornings. The formal sessions were sometimes preceded by intimate breakfasts. At the plenary meetings in the Cabinet Room some fourteen staffers attended and full minutes were made privately for the files. Cabinet members would be invited in to make ad hoc presentations; an agenda might list eleven items.

In 1964 Lyndon Johnson convened an exceptional White House legislative meeting: a special session of the National Security Council with one senator invited as a guest: Wayne Morse of Oregon. All the council members lectured the senator in defense of Johnson's Vietnam policies. In vain; his opposition only grew.

Every president has countless small, informal gatherings with legislators, hosts social events, and makes telephone calls. The informality only masks the rigorousness of the prior preparations. Presidential spontaneity is itself almost always a staff calculation.

For Reagan, for instance, each proposed phone call to the Capitol was preceded by "talking points" enclosed in a distinctive orange folder. He scratched in marginal notes for follow-up: "Send the Senator more information"; "Follow up on point 3." Such instructions, fed back to the legislative affairs office, permitted even lower-ranking staff to act accurately in the president's name.

There are small rituals as well. A president usually boasts that he and the first lady are inviting every last congressman and senator (with spouse) for informal buffets. The staff makes sure that each receives the tangible voucher thereof—the autographed picture of "the four of us" to impress visiting constituents from its place on the office wall.

The ultimate presidential effort is a personal lobbying trip to the Capitol. The Reagan staff advised against his going to meet with the group of Republican senators in April 1987 in the effort to get a thirty-fourth vote in defense of his veto of a highway bill, but he went anyway and failed. A staff can warn, but only a president decides.

What kind of men and women are legislative affairs staffers and what do they do?

Under Eisenhower, General Persons' group together had nearly a hundred years of service in or with the Congress. One of them, Jack Anderson, had been a congressman for twelve. His passion for face-to-face contact was spurred by his memory that during his own six terms in Congress he had never once been approached by a member of the White House staff, even though he was one of the only thirteen Republicans that helped Roosevelt pass the draft-extension bill in September of 1941 by a vote of 203 to 202. Kennedy's legislative chief, Lawrence O'Brien, had exactly the same experience; when he served as an aide to a Massachusetts congressman during 1949–50, neither he nor his boss was given any attention by the Truman White House.

The Persons tradition continues; every officer and assistant in the Reagan legislative staff had worked on the Hill before. Many had previous White House experience, too; one woman who was a special assistant to the president in 1987 served in the legislative affairs office under each Republican president, beginning as a back-up secretary in 1969.

The staff is usually divided into a House group and a Senate group, with individual officers assigned to follow specific committees. One officer often concentrates on the Senate confirmations of the fifteen hundred presidential nominees who have to run that gauntlet. For some of them, it takes extra boosting.

The assignments, however, are never so tight as to shut a liaison staffer off from any congressman's or senator's concerns. Each of those generalists is alert enough to all the presidential priorities that he or she can talk to any member about every major issue. Contacts are rotated, furthermore, so a congressman is not as likely to look up and exclaim, "Oh, it's you again!"

Congressional mail to the president is snared in a special net; when opened in the White House Mail Room, it is logged into computers, then sent exclusively to the Legislative Affairs Office, first for acknowledgment, next to be summarized for the president, and then for response. Wherever a letter goes, to an agency or within the White House, a blue tracking sheet—and the computer—trace its path. Congressional correspondence is often loaded with controversy, so interagency meetings are sometimes required to balance competing departmental preferences for response. "They tarry over every word," one staffer commented. A recent month saw 633 congressional letters arrive addressed to the president.

The chief of legislative affairs faces a daily dilemma. There are two whirling universes—the White House and the Congress. How much time should be spent in each place?

Each is crackling with information, electric with meetings, pulsing with individual preferences and requests. Stay close to the president and the White House colleagues? Or be at members' elbows in the Capitol? Where to sit—Cabinet Room or Committee Room?

Although a "management team" is always on base at the White House to field the day's exchanges, the experienced legislative affairs seniors usually decide that the Hill is where they should spend much of their time.

DAYS AT THE CAPITOL

After the morning rounds of staff meetings (beginning at 7 A.M.), the liaison staffers, beepers in pockets or purses, their official cars tuned to "Crown" radio (the White House transmitter), head for Capitol Hill. Their first priority: to move the president's agenda.

They are not strangers to those presidential proposals; by sitting in on Cabinet Councils and budget reviews, legislative affairs officers will have practiced "reality therapy" with administration policy-planners. Their "this will not fly" warnings will usually have made a difference.

Nor in some cases have the presidential messages even been put in final form until the budget director or Cabinet officers are brought up first to the Capitol to give advance briefings. Unless the president demands secrecy, the legislative affairs staff goes by the rule of no surprises.

Is a Caribbean Basin Commission being planned? The opposition leadership is likely to have some useful views, may recommend acceptable experts for commission membership. If a congressman or senator who counts has advice to give or disagrees with a Cabinet secretary's actions, "we want to be sure that the member gets a fair hearing," one staffer emphasized. "But we have to preserve the ability to look them squarely in the eye, cut through the superficial stuff, and get to the nub of a matter."[3]

The White House has no office in the Capitol. As an informal command center, the Reagan staffers used the vice president's suite on the Senate side, the minority leader's rooms in the House. In each place, television monitors are giving live coverage of the floor action in the chambers, so the White House staffers can, if need be, follow every speech and every vote.

The House and Senate floors are off limits, so are the cloakrooms. Experienced staffers, however, can be inventive.

The "dean" of Republican legislative affairs officers, Max Friedersdorf, when he served during the Nixon years, found a hallway just outside the men's room off the House floor. During extended debate, there was constant opportunity to intercept gentlemen members of both parties and urge them to support the president. After seeing a Nixon veto override fail by only two or three votes, however, Majority Leader Thomas (Tip) O'Neill was irate. "He stormed out of the Chamber and said, 'Friedersdorf, you are never going to lobby out of this place again!' and barred all of us from getting in there any more," Max remembers.[4]

If a crucial vote impends, the indispensable intelligence is gathered: who is for and who against? Since the presidential party leaders don't know the opposition's head count and the opposition leaders won't share it, the White House staffers have to make the rounds of the opposition and dig it out themselves. They must relay a very precise estimate back to the management team on home base, so that possible last-minute presidential calls can be made—in time—to those considered amenable. When fence-sitters are identified, the legislative affairs officers want to go past the members' staffs and talk directly with the congressmen or senators. Only thus can they be the most confident that their head counts are accurate and can they create a final chance for personal persuasion. If it is a Cabinet member who is to make the phone contact, the White House switchboard is used to place the secretary's call to the Capitol; then the first voice will be "the White House calling."

One Republican White House veteran recalled that when the vote-buzzers sounded

> I would station myself by the door which the Democrats used. There might be ten to fifteen people lined up on each side of the entryway—mostly union lobbyists. The congressman might have a last question before going in, or I could remind the member that I had come to his or her office beforehand. Maybe I could convince them to hold their votes until the very end. At the very least, my standing there was a signal to them that I was watching the members, that I cared enough to stand out there and be there. I would go around later and say a personal thank you for a vote, or remind them that they had promised me but had backed down. If they had not shown up, I could ask, "Where were you?" But standing in that throng was an intimidating experience. . . .[5]

For the legislative affairs staff the end of the day in Congress is only another beginning. Their East Wing offices then become an "elves' factory," producing briefings and bios of members coming to see the president in the near future, writing up one-pagers for the presidential phone calls, or inquiring in the agencies about the status of an issue or project.

From the White House end, what are the resources available to the legislative affairs team? To answer that question is to reveal why the Legislative Affairs Office is in the White House in the first place.

THE PRESIDENT AS PERSUADER

Access to the president is the first resource; the staff needs repeatedly to demonstrate that when they speak, they speak for him. In the Eisenhower period, General Persons would, at the right stage, lead senators or congressmen into the president's office. The legislator would go back to the Hill and say, "I talked with the president"—which confirmed Persons' believability and added to the lawmaker's own stature.

The legislative affairs chief on occasion needs such access just for himself. He, too, must be able to tell a senator, "I spoke with the president a few moments ago." If all he can say is "I talked with the chief of staff," that is not good enough.

In October of 1981, the Senate was debating whether to prevent the president from sending AWACS planes to Saudi Arabia. With only a brief time before the roll call, and still short five votes, Friedersdorf stationed himself at a telephone in the president's private living quarters at the White House. He kept an open line to the Senate cloakroom. Majority Leader Howard Baker would bring individual senators off the floor, and Friedersdorf would talk with each, then add, "You know, the president is right here and he'd like to have a word with you," at which point President Reagan, well briefed to handle any questions, would get on the line. The president achieved a hairbreadth victory: 52 to 48.

Reagan personally met with senators who were "leaning against" or on the fence prior to the AWACS vote. The Legislative Affairs Office made the arrangements for each visit. "We were moving people in and out of this building like we were showing it for sale," remembered one of Friedersdorf's assistants.

Written exchanges from the staff to the president flow back and forth as well, and the chief puts his stamp on them. Carter's legislative affairs head, Frank Moore, sent him a "Weekly Legislative Report," which often came back with presidential comments—for example, "Make it clear that I will veto"; "Don't push it"; or "Move on him; I can help."[6]

Except for being longer, Moore's paragraphs to Carter were much like the "Legislative Notes" which the Persons office sent Eisenhower twenty-one years before. Presidential needs, and staff responses to those needs, continue across the decades.

THE STAFF AS COLLABORATORS

The second set of backstops for the Legislative Affairs Office are the collective resources of the White House itself. At the seniormost staff level, priorities have to be set and decisions swiftly made on when to compromise, when to stand firm. Especially in its first term, the Reagan White

House used a Legislative Strategy Group, chaired by the chief of staff; the head of legislative affairs was always a member. Cabinet secretaries and other White House officers were called in quickly as needed. The president could be reached easily to confirm or change the group's consensus.

In late October of 1981, as the vote on the AWACS sale came closer, the Legislative Strategy Group, with minute care, finished the draft of a crucially important letter from the president to the Senate majority leader. The letter described the detailed U.S.-Saudi agreements that had been made to ensure the security of the planes' equipment, where they would fly, how they would be operated, under what conditions the resulting intelligence could be shared, and why the planes would represent no threat to Israel.

For ten days, drafts of that letter had been done and redone, taken up to individual doubting senators for comment, then taken back—to State, to Defense, to the Joint Chiefs, to the NSC, "four, five, and six times," Friedersdorf emphasized. The letter was signed, sent, and used in the Senate debate on the very day of the roll call vote; it was essential in tipping the result in the president's favor.[7]

Few examples reveal so well the tightly supervised orchestration of effort—within the Executive Branch and within the White House—that is indispensable for successful executive-legislative cooperation on vital issues. In fact, for any policy debate, the closer a senior White House staffer is perceived to be involved in the decision-making loop, the more likely is he or she to be asked by the legislative affairs chief to contact the Capitol in person. Kissinger, for instance, helped lead the successful Nixon administration fight in 1971 against the Mansfield Amendment, which would have compelled reductions of U.S. troops in Europe. Eizenstat, for Carter, was a frequent persuader on the Hill for domestic issues; his colleague Brzezinski tells of his "many trips to the Hill" in 1978 just before the Senate narrowly voted to approve the Panama Canal treaties. Chief of Staff James Baker negotiated Reagan's 1981 budget and tax compromises. Security Assistant Bud McFarlane called on senators during the AWACS debate; his successor Frank Carlucci briefed members of Congress on arms control.

To glue such connections in place, OMB and NSC congressional-relations officers often join the legislative affairs team at the latter's morning staff meetings. One of Kissinger's staff members spent 30 percent of his time on Capitol Hill, working jointly with his White House legislative colleagues in meeting and talking with members.

Other principal offices in the White House collaborate to magnify the legislative staff's efforts. The Office of Public Liaison can dovetail its constituency briefings with current legislative priorities. If a member has an important group coming to Washington from the home district or state, special policy briefing sessions can be arranged in the White House Indian Treaty Room. The visitors are impressed and the congressional sponsors grateful.

If a congressman or senator, "leaning favorable," will, after a chat with the president, make the jump to open support, the Press Office will shepherd the member into the White House Briefing Room, there to have his endorsement confirmed on camera and to lock in the commitment.

The staff secretary will see to it that the speechwriters invite the legislative affairs staff to comment on the drafts of presidential addresses. Unless secrecy is paramount, it is neither wise nor fruitful for presidential policy declarations to ignore the lawmakers' concerns.

The congressional affairs chief will sit with the Scheduling Committee so that presidential events can be designed to support the legislative initiatives. A half hour or even an hour every month may routinely be reserved as "photo opportunities" for lawmakers with the president. The Legislative Affairs Office will recommend which supporters will be so favored and will brief the president to put in a persuasive word when the photographer has finished shooting.

The Social Office will normally reserve several places at each state dinner for couples from Congress. "You can't *imagine* how important that is to senators and congressmen," Friedersdorf commented. The Legislative Affairs Office recommends who the invitees are to be.

A small group of seats will be saved on Air Force One for favored members, even from among the opposition, to accompany the president when he travels. A Legislative Affairs officer joins the advance teams that plan those trips.

Each of the three Kennedy Center halls has a presidential box, that in the Eisenhower Theater seating twelve, the others eight, each one complete with anteroom and stocked refrigerator. In 1981 when conservative Democrats were being courted to support President Reagan's tax and budget cuts, the Legislative Affairs Office was given "total control" of those seats for a year. Friedersdorf remembers:

I worked our staff and myself to death taking congressmen to those Kennedy Center performances. Some weeks I saw the same performance three times; often I went five nights. I exhausted myself. But it made a big difference. You had a chance to talk, you became friends with them. They would invite you to some of their receptions. I still have friendships established during that year.[8]

Presidential messages and greetings can be sent to dinners and conventions. Legislators' offices are also allocated tickets to the special morning guided tours of the Residence.

Patronage is both an extra lever and an extra duty for the legislative affairs operation. The office head attends the small internal White House committee, chaired by the chief of staff, to which the director of the Presidential Personnel Office brings his recommendations. The names of those rejected are also available. Using experienced judgment (and perhaps some informal soundings), the legislative affairs director supplies the meetings with an estimate of congressional "viability" for each first-place candidate.

The extra leverage comes in the Legislative Affairs Office's ability diplomatically to "draw a picture" for the lawmaker who is thirsty for patronage: "If you can't help the president on this vote, that's going to make it awfully hard for the president to help you on that appointment."

The extra duty is in the two-step follow-up. Between the time of the president's conditional approval of a nomination and the actual White House announcement, security and other checks are made, including informal consultation with a few in the Senate: the president's party leader, the candidate's home-state senator (if of the same party), and the party's senior member on the committee of jurisdiction. The three of them have five days to respond. If problems are flagged, negotiations are undertaken. As the nomination papers go in, one last call is made to the Legislative Affairs Office: is everything cleared? When the president signs the nomination papers, the ranking opposition committee member is notified and also the nominee's own congressman (the latter is not "consulted" since the confirmation process is exclusively a Senate responsibility). After the announcement, the further duty arises—to nurse the confirmation through what may be a narrowly divided Senate.

THE CABINET AS AN INSTRUMENT OF LEGISLATIVE PERSUASION

The departments and their secretaries are relied on as participants in the work of persuasion. Cabinet members' speaking engagements are a kind of leverage for the White House Legislative Affairs Office; by going—or refusing to go—to a senator's state or a congressman's district, such VIP appearances can be tools of reward or disfavor.

Each of the departments and agencies has a congressional relations office and they add up to a thirty-position network, instantly available to the White House. Their alacrity is a product of their appointment; the heads of all of those thirty offices are approved, if not chosen, by the White House legislative chief. Many of the several hundred people on their staffs are also noncareer men and women placed there with the blessing of the White House Personnel Office. The network is close, personal, and fast.

If a congressman complains to the White House, "I'd like to be with you on this, but I am having a problem with Interior," the query zips through the network. The Interior liaison officer is told to look into the problem, give the congressman a prompt status report, and if possible work out a favorable response.

Snags can be negotiated, but there is little tolerance for foot-dragging. In the Nixon period, a Treasury liaison officer was discovered on the Hill undercutting a presidential initiative. The White House Legislative Affairs Office pulled him up short and even had to remind a petulant secretary of the treasury that whether Treasury liked it or not, the president supported the bill in question. On another occasion, a Reagan staffer found a Defense representative lobbying against the president; the White House banished him from the Hill. A Reagan Cabinet officer was found to have no interest in a piece of presidential legislation; the White House ordered that the deputy secretary take over for the issue involved. Is this hard-nosed behavior? Certainly, White House staff are disciplinarians when they find that presidential decisions are being undermined.

The network leaders are usually called together for team meetings in the White House. In Eisenhower's presidency, the favored time was Saturday morning, when General Persons would meet with the agency liaison chiefs in the Cabinet Room and serve hot coffee, sticky doughnuts, and strict advice.

O'Brien in Kennedy's time would require weekly reports. Their group met about every six weeks in the Roosevelt Room (then called the Fish Room); the participants were made

to feel that they were indeed members of a team headed by the president with O'Brien as lieutenant—that there was a program in its totality and that they should be interested in the RB-70 [bomber], or they should be interested in the farm program . . . for those broad reasons that were given. . . .

There were certain highly capable people in certain agencies . . . we would call them over to meet in a little conference room off O'Brien's office. . . . One or more of us would sit down and go name by name and say, "Where can you help us on this bill with these guys? Now, Kenny, this guy is, you know, big on the Agriculture Committee." He might say, "Well, I think maybe I can move him

or get him to take a trip or whatever." . . . When their congressman had a
problem, we would call in and say, "Look, we've got to do it for John McFall.
Can you get it done?" If it was "doable," it'd get done.[9]

President Johnson, with his long Capitol experience, was in effect his
own legislative chief; nonetheless, his principal liaison head, Barefoot
Sanders, convened similar interagency meetings in the Roosevelt Room on
Monday mornings. Perhaps fifty attended from the various agencies. Subject: "the bill of the week," that is, the piece of legislation Johnson most
wanted pushed at the Capitol. There were briefings by experts. Each of the
fifty had been assigned ten members of Congress. They were then expected
to call on all ten to urge support for the bill in question; in this way all
the lawmakers were "covered." For each of them, every week, a different
bill but the same ten calls. There was no choice about it; a weekly report
was made to the president and Johnson himself would often join the
Monday meetings to remind the group that Sanders was carrying out his
instructions and they should do likewise.[10] Years later, Carter's team met
Fridays at three—same room, same purpose.

The Reagan staff added an innovation: supplementary weekly meetings
of just the State, Defense, CIA, and NSC congressional relations officers.
They would try to look ahead to what was happening on the Hill, next
week, next month. "In the absence of those meetings," observed the staff
member who chaired the sessions, "such interagency contacts would
happen only by chance."

On occasion, the legislative teamwork frays. A White House alumnus
recalls the squabble between Treasury's Bureau of Customs and Justice's
Drug Enforcement Administration over turf and appropriations. "Members of Congress will seize such opportunities to shop around," he said.
"They will try one assistant secretary, then another, to get the answer they
want, and only the White House can settle it."[11]

SCOREKEEPING, PUNISHMENTS, AND REWARDS

In the total legislative ball game, scores are kept. They are not "enemies
lists" but the factual count: Who voted how? Who supported the president
how much of the time?

White House assistant David Lloyd was Truman's scorekeeper; in 1949
he made up a nine-page summary of Senate and House votes on twenty-

two key measures. Senator James E. Murray (D., Mont.) rated a perfect 100; Senator Kenneth Wherry (R., Neb.) came in at a minus 84.[12]

Even the allegedly "nonpolitical" Eisenhower was eager to keep track. In July of 1957, Ann Whitman noted in her diary: "The President is distressed at the Republican Members of Congress who vote against him; he asked to be sure that anyone that asks a favor for a constituent or himself . . . his voting record is attached to the request as it comes to him for decision."[13]

For Kennedy, Larry O'Brien "maintained a card file on every senator and representative, complete with personal and political data and information on their districts."[14] Johnson, it is said, practically memorized the roll calls. It may be the Political rather than the Legislative Affairs Office that operates the scoreboard, but congressmen and senators can depend on it: somebody in every White House staff is keeping the count.

Are brass knuckles used sometimes? Never admittedly, but one recalls the warfare of Washington. Strong-willed men and women contend. When Senator Frank Church acknowledged to Lyndon Johnson that he sympathized with columnist Walter Lippmann's views opposing Johnson's Vietnam policies, the president leaked his own pointed version of the exchange: that he had advised Church to call on Lippmann for his next dam in Idaho.

One brand of White House pressure is called the "hot foot." If a legislator of the president's own party is "leaning against" the president, calls may be made back home to the state party chairman and to major contributors to the offending lawmaker. The message is: "Look what your man is doing to our president! You'd better counsel him."

In 1976 White House legislative aide Vernon Loen reportedly threatened Congressman Larry Pressler (R., S. D.) with "political trouble" in his district if he voted, as the AFL-CIO was urging, against a natural gas deregulation bill favored by President Ford. When the negative vote was cast, Loen allegedly left a telephone message in Pressler's office that if he "wanted any future favors from the White House, he should call the AFL-CIO." Pressler complained to the president and Loen telephoned him to apologize.[15] Pressler's allocation of White House visitor passes had also been cut off, and were restored only after President Ford himself intervened.

Carter's legislative chief Frank Moore in 1979 allegedly denied a Democratic congressman's request for a routine greetings message because of an adverse vote. Moore was quoted as commenting, "We're learning how to play this game."[16]

One area of leverage is kept in the president's hands—whether he will assist in the lawmaker's reelection campaign. If the president is himself popular, coattails may help and a speech in the state or district can be scheduled—or declined.

The tension of the 1981 AWACS debate has been described. One of those fifty-two supporters of the president was Iowa Republican Senator Roger Jepsen. White House aide Edward Rollins later was reported as having commented that the White House "beat his brains out." Jepsen complained to the White House, which issued a statement emphasizing that "the senator's vote was cast without coercion from the White House and was, in his words, 'a vote of conscience.' "[17]

Then there are lost causes. Beyond the reach of Cabinet or White House staff or presidential persuasion, some fights are not worth precious ammunition. It is the task of the Legislative Affairs Office to gather the intelligence and pass the assessment to the chief of staff and the president. There must be a guarantee that their unvarnished views will go forward so that the president can weigh the odds and not, in ignorance, simply issue the order "Go out and run up those votes."

Fire away or reach across? The legislative affairs staff are more peacemakers than warriors. One staffer stressed: "If you remembered every slight, and kept count, you would never have anyone you could rely on for a vote." Said another:

> We had to deal with both sides of the aisle—with the waverers and skeptics and with Democrats as well as Republicans. We had to establish a trusting relationship with both sides. There were always shifting coalitions, and the legislative affairs staff had to be absolutely professional. . . . The Buchanan blasts make the legislative affairs task much harder.[18]

Larry O'Brien himself summed up the White House legislative affairs experience:

> It becomes a way of life in which you are engaged in human relations and constantly working out compromises. You listen to and solicit support from everybody on the Hill. You cajole, urge and plead. There's always the hot breath of opposition; don't resent it, understand it. You have to appreciate that at times there are those, even among your friends, who can't go along with you, that there is a line that they can't cross. Just remember, there is always tomorrow.[19]

It is a thirty-five-year tradition.

CHAPTER 11

Power Wheel or Pinwheel: The Press Secretary

I don't mind a microscope, but—oh boy—
when they use a proctoscope, that's going
too far.
—RICHARD NIXON

I'm not tired. I'm just tired of you people.
That's exactly what I'm tired of.
—LARRY SPEAKES

It's a reporter's job to challenge a president—
every president—to explain and defend his
policies whether you agree with them or not.
—SAM DONALDSON

A White House press secretary sits where three worlds intersect. In front of him is the White House press corps of several hundred, fifty of whom are barking regularly on his doorstep.[1] In back of him is the president demanding that the secretary follow only his wishes. Beside him are his staff colleagues, frequently helpful, at times maddeningly uncooperative.

If he has the stature, the time on his own schedule, and personal closeness to the president, the press secretary can be a power wheel in the White House policy machine, acting as a "reality check" within its internal councils, interpreting the president authoritatively to journalists. If he and the president are more distant, he may be, as one press secretary was described, chiefly a "pinwheel," showering only prepackaged sparks and smoke. He may be capable of both roles; it is the president who will determine which kind of wheel he will be.

The three worlds around the press secretary not only intersect but collide. "The newsman's job," former CBS reporter George Herman declared, "is always to be skeptical, always to look at the people in power and think to yourself 'What are they doing wrong? Why are they doing this? In what way does [sic] the American people, do my readers, need protection from this man if, in fact, they do at all?' "[2] Presidents for their part interpret that skepticism as hostility. According to John Ehrlichman, "Nixon was convinced that the vast majority of reporters and commentators would

be unfair to him if left to their own devices. . . . The small group of
. . . regulars in the White House press room were so jaded by their years
of covering Presidents that they constricted the outward flow of news."[3]
Jimmy Carter said: "The news media were superficial in their treatment of
national and international events and tended to trivialize the most serious
problems with a cynical approach. . . . I could not win a war with the
press."[4]

From their corner, the staff resent the journalists who probe for information they would rather keep under wraps. In the end, the staff's objective
is "to make them [the press] use what we want them to use, not what they
want. That is what we are trying to do, and it works often."[5]

The spears from all three directions land on the press secretary's bull's-
eye. When he steps to the podium for a press briefing, he often has a
shouting match on his hands. If he should attempt to slake a columnist's
thirst for substantive interpretation in private, he runs the risk of not
having enough expertise to be informative. If he asks the counsel or the
national security assistant to fill him in about some especially sensitive
matter, he may not even be told. (Press Secretary Jerry terHorst was kept
in the dark about Ford's pardon of Nixon—and resigned on that account;
Press Secretary Larry Speakes was told by Security Assistant John Poindexter that the idea that the United States would invade Grenada was
"preposterous." Speakes later complained that his senior colleagues "had
a built-in attitude that the press office is the press.")[6]

The president will expect the press secretary to absorb the heat of these
collisions all by himself. Eisenhower's press secretary James Hagerty recounts:

> Many times after he sought my personal opinion . . . President Eisenhower
> would say, "Do it this way." I would say, "If I go to that press conference and
> say what you want me to say, I would get hell." With that he would smile, get
> up and walk around the desk, pat me on the back and say, "My boy, better you
> than me." I would go out and get hell.[7]

The conjunction of pressures puts any press secretary in an uncomfortable squeeze. Little wonder that after only a year as Gerald Ford's press
secretary, Ron Nessen wrote in his diary, "The White House had become
all work, pressure and tension."[8] Larry Speakes remembers: "The potential
for screwup was greater than it was in almost any other job in the world."[9]

Sitting at the edge of these three worlds—of the press corps, of the staff,
of the president—the press secretary's responsibilities are multidirec-
tional.

FACING THE PRESS

First, facing outward, the press secretary is normally the only on-the-record White House staff source of news for the journalists assigned to cover the president. He guards this exclusive privilege energetically. During the TWA hijack and hostage incident in June of 1985, national security assistant Bud McFarlane persisted in making morning television statements from the White House front steps. Speakes complained to Chief of Staff Regan: "Bud has got to stop talking. We must speak to the world with one voice."[10]

That one voice from the press secretary sounds off, in Washington, at the formal meeting ground with the White House press corps: the West Terrace briefing room. This is a small auditorium between the office wing of the White House and the Residence, replacing what used to be the indoor swimming pool, gym, and flower shop.

Once or twice a day, the press secretary holds a briefing session with the fifty or more wire-service, television-network, newspaper-chain, and other correspondents whose "beat" is the White House. Thirty of the regulars have tiny offices immediately adjoining the briefing room. They take reserved seats up front and are joined by others arriving from outside. Lights and cameras fill a rear platform (but are not used except for special announcements or visiting VIP appearances).

For sometimes as long as an hour, the cluttered, often raucus scene is a minidrama not played in any other government headquarters in the world. The serrated edge of America's free press, sharp and rough, meets the hard bread (sometimes rock) of presidential officialdom. Irreverence collides with imperturbability.

The press secretary describes some (but not much) of the president's schedule, announces nominations, tells of travel plans. Those minima out of the way, it becomes the journalists' turn—and there is no limit to their questions. International affairs, military matters, the economy, issues of law, science, politics, technical medical details of the president's health: no subject or person escapes inquiry. Controversial statements or actions by Executive Branch officials merit a special focus. Those are the president's people; the press secretary will be asked: does the president agree with what they are saying and doing?

How does a press secretary get set for all of this?

His first concern is not to be caught unawares. He will have read the morning News Summary, looked at the principal East Coast papers, glanced at the latest wire reports. He will have had a morning conference call with the press secretaries of State, Defense, and the CIA, will perhaps have gone to the Situation Room for a summary of current traffic. He will have participated in the senior staff meeting, may have heard from the communications director what the "line of the day" is to be, and will probably have met with the president.

On some matters, his instructions will have been specific: "Say this"; or "Say nothing." To many queries, he will respond, "I'll get back to you," whereupon his staff takes on a sleuthing assignment. But for dozens of those questions shot to him in that hot hour, his only resources are his judgment, his sense of the president's purposes and priorities, and his knowledge of what is secret and what is exposable. "You get an inner ear—you cannot only hear a voice but you know how it's going to respond," commented Reagan Press Secretary Marlin Fitzwater. "The questions I get are, 'What does the president think about . . .?' A lot of it we can't say . . . but you have to have a sense because if you don't the press will know fairly soon. You can't be far off for very long."[11]

The press secretary's responses can come warm with humor, frozen with contempt, or glazed with exasperation. The briefing is an incessant sparring match between two sets of very adept professionals, the agents of an independent press and the agent of a big government. A recent 49-minute encounter, for instance, was punctuated with 109 rapid-fire questions.

White House briefings reach an audience far beyond America's boundaries; they are now recognized as a tool for shaping not only opinion but also events abroad. Two illustrations demonstrate this effect.

In May of 1975, as President Ford was ordering an air attack on the Cambodian captors of the crew of the *Mayaguez,* a Cambodian radio station broadcast the hint that the ship itself might be released. Since the United States had no diplomatic relations with Cambodia, the only fast and authoritative way to get a response to that nation was through a White House press announcement. Press Secretary Ron Nessen has described how he rushed into the Briefing Room to read a presidential statement to the reporters so that, half a world away, the Cambodians could "read it on the AP!"[12]

During the 1985 hijack incident, Press Secretary Larry Speakes realized what close attention was being paid to the reports of what he was saying. "We began to pick up intelligence . . . that every word we spoke was being picked up over there by the hijackers and others and instantly reacted to."[13] At that time, the Department of State held its foreign affairs

briefing at noon, with the White House following at 1 P.M. and concentrating on domestic matters. Speakes switched the timing, rescheduled his
White House briefing for 9:15 A.M. *New York Times* reporter Leslie Gelb,
quoting Speakes, pointed out that it was a deliberate White House decision

> to dominate the news throughout the day . . . not to let a story fester in the
> briefing room until noon or so. . . . In the TWA if we'd have been waiting until
> noon every day, basically the daylight hours would have been gone in the
> Middle East. We would have been one day behind, each day, trying to influence
> action. We were able to step out and at least get our imprint fairly early in the
> day. . . . State backed out of that thing completely; they said the White House
> could handle it. . . . That was a pattern of using my briefing every morning to
> try to shape that event. . . .
>
>   I'm trying to impress upon the State Department people that I'm speaking for
> the President, and I know where his head is because I make that my business.
> . . . We have been entrusted with virtually every major Reagan foreign policy
> development, to do it and do it from here.[14]

Thus has the White House press secretary become a key participant in the
conduct of American foreign affairs.

The press secretary also knows that he is under an additional surveillance; White House staff colleagues regularly dial him in on their internal
audio channel and even the president may be listening to him in action.
The briefing transcript is circulated widely in the White House; Nixon is
said to have read through it personally, to make sure Press Secretary
Ronald Ziegler was following instructions. Johnson reportedly monitored
the audio of his press secretary's briefings and even sent in notes with
supplementary instructions while the session was still in progress. According to Speakes, Reagan gave him more leeway:

> I go in and talk to Poindexter and Regan and the President, and they trust me
> enough, I presume, to say: "Here's what the story is," and they don't say "Say
> this, this and this." If they've got complaints they would raise heck. I don't know
> when they've ever complained. Nobody said, "Larry, you've got it wrong."[15]

At the November 1985 summit, Speakes misused—some say ruptured—
that trust. Fearing that President Reagan was coming off second best to
General Secretary Gorbachev in media attention, the press secretary had
some presidential statements manufactured and then passed out the faked
remarks on his own authority as presidential quotations. "I had been able
to spruce up the President's image by taking a bit of liberty with my P.R.

man's license," Speakes revealed, 28 months later, adding that "In retrospect, it was clearly wrong to take such liberties."[16] Speakes' gambit ("a damned outrage," his successor termed it) will cause more than temporary embarrassment; it tends to erect, for future White House press secretaries, one more hurdle of skepticism in a relationship already studded with barriers of doubt and mistrust.

However edgy the relationship, the daily briefings are by now an indispensable feature of every press secretary's task. Under Kennedy, Pierre Salinger held 1,332 such briefings; Johnson's press secretaries conducted 1,515. Ziegler, under Nixon, had some 2,000; Ford's press secretary, Ron Nessen, 583. Jody Powell, in Carter's term, conducted 1,245, and as of November 11, 1987, Reagan's press secretaries had held 2,167. The statistics are given here not to analyze frequency rates or to compare press secretaries, but to show the sheer size of the job.

The Briefing Room is an ever-ready facility. The president or a visiting newsmaker may come in for a special announcement. The press secretary will often invite a Cabinet officer or a senior White House staff member to answer questions about an especially complicated or sensitive topic.

In addition to the formal press briefings, the press secretary hosts uncounted private gatherings for reporters in his own office. Alone or with other staffers, and under rules permitting no attribution to them, they can give journalists more candid responses than is ever possible from the podium next door. One veteran remembers: "We did, every week, one-on-one or one-on-two, Wednesdays and Thursdays with magazine and newspaper people. Speakes and [Chief of Staff James] Baker would both do this. It compensated for the few press conferences. . . . You would never get into these things at the podium.[17]

There are two risks in such smaller sessions. By inviting only a select few, the press secretary may play favorites, or be accused of doing so. Accountability also suffers. Pulitzer Prize–winning columnist David Broder was once invited to an "on background only" session with Henry Kissinger but refused to talk to him on those terms. Broder is annoyed at officials who pass out information but duck the accountability that comes with putting their names on their words.

> We have been drawn into a circle of working relationships and even of friendship with the people we are supposed to cover. The distinction between press and government has tended to become erased—and that is wrong and it is dangerous. . . .
>
> We are not government. We are the permanent, resident, critical voices, questioning the people who happen to be in government at the moment.[18]

FACING HIS COLLEAGUES

Second, in the actual White House decision process, press secretaries who are confidants of the president may have inward-facing responsibilities as well. They—perhaps only they—can take up Broder's and Donaldson's and Herman's challenges and aim them inside the White House at the president and his advisers. At their best, press secretaries can themselves act as "resident critics" of proposals that would have insufficient public support, and even say, "Hold on, Mr. President!" Often, however, they are not even given this chance.

One observer describes Reagan's Strategic Defense Initiative as having been hatched in secret within the national security departments and the science adviser's office, then only on the morning of the president's speech "sprung" on the White House Legislative Affairs, Communications, and Press offices. He added:

> They kept it very closely contained; the people . . . who understood substance but asked hard questions . . . were held out of the process. . . . There is a built-in bias on the part of people in the foreign-policy area; they think they belong to a priesthood. If you're not a member, you're disqualified from knowing anything about it."[19]

Press Secretary Speakes was especially bitter at being excluded by his colleagues from meetings and knowledge about the Grenada invasion of October 1985. Only as the troops were landing was he informed—and handed the assignment to brief the press. "Not only was I furious about having been deceived, but I had been given just an hour or so to go through dozens of pages of material and prepare myself to present it to the press and to the world in some coherent fashion. That was treatment about as unfair as I had ever received."[20]

A decade earlier, Press Secretary Ron Nessen had had the same complaint:

> After . . . [an earlier] blowup . . . members of the staff were sensitive to the need to keep me informed. However as delicate new issues arose and fear of leaks grew, I was again cut out of some information. Eventually I'd explode and then the cycle would start again. It was an unending struggle to make sure I knew what was going on.[21]

Nessen's successor, Jody Powell, similarly observed, "The best way to defend an issue is to be in on the discussions."[22]

Even the redoubtable Jim Hagerty was frozen out of one closely held project: the design of the new American flag following the admission of Hawaii and Alaska to statehood. Presidential assistant Robert Merriam went so far as to have two sets of executive orders drawn up—to confuse any leakers. When Hagerty asked to see the drafts, Merriam refused to reveal them ahead of time—even to Hagerty. "Don't you trust me?" asked Hagerty. "No, nobody!" was Merriam's dictum.[23]

Upon leaving the White House in the spring of 1987, Larry Speakes affirmed his view of the press secretary's role in the substance of decisions:

> When we sit in the Situation Room and launch a policy initiative, let's judge it by how it would look if it showed up in tomorrow's headlines. . . . Let the Press Secretary in. Tell him everything. Believe him when he tells you "It ain't good policy if the public won't buy it."[24]

FACING THE PRESIDENT

The press secretary's third responsibility is "looking upward"—preparing for the presidential press conference. Telecast to the nation, those sessions may foster a double illusion: that both the questions and the answers are spontaneous. It isn't so. With 55 million people in the audience, there is little that is spontaneous on either side of the rostrum.

As soon as a press conference date is firm, the press secretary or the communications director will issue the call for briefing materials. In the Truman and Eisenhower periods, the Department of State was given the assignment to provide suggested answers to the possible foreign-affairs questions. Press Secretary James Hagerty called such assignment lists "gooser sheets." From his background in State under George Marshall, Truman's assistant press secretary, Roger Tubby, took up the practice of preparing briefing books for the president—another tradition of presidential staff work that has continued unbroken into the present. So useful have gooser sheets and briefing books been in forcing departments, staffs, and even presidents to focus on unresolved policy issues, that former Carter Press Secretary Jody Powell only half-jestingly suggests that "If I could have, I would have abolished the press conferences and made them keep doing the briefing books!"[25]

For Eisenhower, Hagerty himself would estimate the questions that might arise about domestic affairs, then test them in Sherman Adams' Wednesday morning staff meetings. The staff would try to outguess Hagerty but rarely succeeded. In the Nixon period, speechwriter Pat Buchanan helped pull briefing books together:

> I would send all the questions out that I had devised by reading three weeks of newspapers, news summaries and the rest of it. I'd ask the agencies and the various shops, they'd get me the material and I rewrote everything. I'd get it to Nixon. He would go into his study for eight hours and study.[26]

As the time of the press conference gets closer, reporters will, as one alumnus put it, "noodle around" with the press secretary,

> and it does not take great intelligence-gathering to figure out what is on their minds.... Perhaps forty questions were put down on the list [by the Press Office, for Reagan] and the list circulated. We would get answers back from the NSC, the domestic people, political people, wherever. We relied not on the departments but on the staff. A press conference has about fifteen questions and one could hit about eighty percent of them with this anticipatory system.[27]

During both Eisenhower's and Kennedy's years, reporters would at times notify the press secretary about a question they planned to ask. On other occasions, there would be an "arrangement"; the press secretary would plant questions with willing reporters that he and the president wanted to have raised. That practice has nearly ceased. Reporters do not even take kindly to their own bureau chiefs' trying to give them instructions about what questions to ask; they regard such attempts as interference with their professional judgments.

Just prior to the press conference itself, the press secretary and other staff members typically have a final session with the president. In Truman's pre-press-conference briefings, Press Secretary Charles Ross might blurt out a tough and somewhat nasty question, "like a whip across the face." Truman would fire back with a scrappy answer, often with such a snap that it rebuked the questioner. That was what Ross wanted to elicit—and, as Truman aide George Elsey observed, they would both laugh and learn.[28]

It was the same with Ike, according to Bryce Harlow. Hagerty and other senior staff members would go into the Oval Office a half hour ahead of the press conference and practice some deliberate irritation—to get Eisenhower to say things with an explosiveness which he would later, of course, contain.

Prior to his press conferences, Kennedy would have breakfast with the vice president, Secretary Dean Rusk and others from State, and the chairman of the Council of Economic Advisers. Press Secretary Pierre Salinger and counsel Ted Sorensen would join them, having "prepared lengthy lists of possible difficult questions—usually far more difficult than most of those asked—and the breakfast was customarily spent reviewing those questions and their answers."[29] In spite of the lists and breakfasts, Kennedy apparently made a number of decisions on his feet before the cameras, with his staff taken by surprise.

> The staff, the Cabinet members, may be arguing a point over and over again; the man will get up before the TV or press conference and he'll say something, and even if he has not made the decision, he can't pull back from it because of something else he said. And more damn staff work in the White House was disposed of by things Kennedy had said on TV that you couldn't retract.[30]

Carter likewise scheduled rehearsals before each news conference. His communications director, Gerald Rafshoon, together with Powell and other staffers, would throw questions at him for an hour or even longer.

Reagan's preference was to go to the White House family theater for two afternoons of two-hour rehearsals. One hour was focused on domestic issues, an additional hour on foreign policy. Staff played the role of press and, having studied the briefing books ahead of time, Reagan made up his own answers. On the spot, the staff corrected him if the answers needed to be modified. After the first hour, there was a pause for critique. The second afternoon, the press secretary had pictures of the reporters placed in the theater seats in the positions where they would be sitting during the actual conference. Questions that had given the president trouble the first time around were gone over again. The rehearsals helped not just the president but the staff as well; they came away with a more acute sense of Reagan's own judgments and priorities.

Since Harry Truman took office, presidents have held over nine hundred press conferences. The frequencies have varied with each president, but the staff work required to support this deeply established tradition has been essentially the same from administration to administration.

OTHER RESPONSIBILITIES, OTHER RESOURCES

Having faced outward to the press corps, inward to the staff, and upward to the president, the press secretary often looks in a fourth direction: ahead. When trips are scheduled, the advance teams invariably include a Press Office representative. An overseas journey requires a "Press Plan," written up in military detail. The plan specifies who in the party will meet with the press; who will do the backgrounders beforehand, the talk shows afterward; who will brief reporters during the conference overseas, and after the return home; who will talk to the newsmen on the airplane. The Press Office works out this document with all the players, the last step being a sign-off by each of them: State, Defense, the NSC, the White House—the aim being to have a minimum of misunderstandings, missed signals, and punctured egos. Immediately after returning from the Reykjavik summit, "we did something like ninety press appearances over the first three days," Larry Speakes recalled. "How could it be wrong for those of us in the Reagan administration to do our best to give our side of the story?"[31]

Foreign governments are often astounded to discover the number of press personnel who accompany an American president. The Reagan White House told the Chinese that two hundred would come; Nixon wanted three hundred to accompany him to Egypt. The Press Office makes most of the arrangements, but sometimes the president personally takes a hand in the selection of which reporters will make the trip.

The press secretary can turn to two professional groups that may give him some assistance. He usually meets periodically with the three TV network Washington bureau chiefs, primarily to discuss procedures for trips, pools, and facilities. One of these bureau chiefs is the "pool chairman" for the month; if some event arises requiring unusual press coverage at short notice, the press secretary makes one call to the chairman, who then informs the other two.

Like the assistant for legislative affairs and the counsel, the press secretary also has an "extension group" throughout government: the departmental public information officers. In theory, they are his team. They "belong" to him; he has approved them all. (The Nixon Press Office actually vetoed several proposed appointees for agency PIO positions.) Even Carter, who allowed his "Cabinet government" associates to pick their own staffs, is reported to have told his new Cabinet to clear their public information appointees with Press Secretary Powell.

Meetings of the whole group, or segments of them, are often called in the White House, to coordinate themes to be stressed in Cabinet speeches. Among an inner tier of this team—State, Defense, the CIA, and the White House—there is intense daily communication.

When the news is bad, or when he wants to put distance between the president and some distasteful subject, the press secretary will often direct that a department, rather than the White House, respond to press questions. "We won't be handling this one," he will tell the agency public information officer. "You be prepared to take it on."

Finally, the press secretary makes a private judgment as to which among the journalists on the White House beat support the president and which do not—who are "friends" and who are "enemies." As Johnson Press Secretary George Reedy explains, "The politician classifies people in terms of friend or foe and sees no reason to exempt reporters from such classification."[32] All press secretaries form these evaluations in their minds; the Nixon staff methodically wrote them down. John Ehrlichman recounts receiving "a twenty-six page catalogue of columnists, print media reporters and radio/television reporters, listed by categories. 'Those We Can Count On' was a short list. 'Those We Can Never Count On' ran two and a half pages."[33]

The three perspectives—of the press corps, of the White House staff, and of the president—all mesh, or grind, with the press secretary as wheel-in-the-middle. It is a systemic clash, particularly between press and White House. In the cacophony of contemporary society, there is no prospect that that friction will ease. The abrasion potential being so high, it is a surprise to see that in eight presidencies over thirty-five years there have been only fourteen press secretaries. (But for Kennedy's assassination and James Brady's wounding, there might have been even fewer.)

One after the other, however, even under presidents as different as Johnson and Reagan, each press secretary has continued and built upon his predecessor's techniques for surviving, if not mediating, the unending tensions. Correspondingly, staffs have been added to assist. The techniques have become traditions, the similarities from presidency to presidency being greater than the variations. The press secretary's suite of offices in the West Wing has now become a 14-hour-a-day, nonstop emergency room. In the mid-80s, Larry Speakes made a count: his 24 telephone lines typically rang 1,850 times between breakfast and quitting time.

On Inauguration Day 1977, an account appeared of a meeting between former communications chief Herbert Klein and incoming Press Secretary Jody Powell.

> Klein, looking prosperous but tired, emerged from the meeting and ran directly into a group of reporters.
> "Hey, Herb, whatja talk about?" the reporters shouted. "What's Jody going to do to us?"
> Klein took a long, almost whimsical look across the street at the White House. "I told him to get a good night's sleep before the inauguration," Klein said, "because he's going to have a very, very hard four years."[34]

CHAPTER 12

Communications Directors: The Rule of HPCQ

From the Eisenhower Administration to Ronald Reagan's, the White House propaganda machine has become an increasingly effective instrument. For . . . 34 years the president and his agents have clearly been winning the battle. . . . The White House has . . . enhanced the power of the communicator-in-chief. And it has raised to even greater importance the unmet challenge for the press to provide an alternative, non-propagandistic view of the presidency.

—DAVID BRODER

The press is on a kick, some negative response to this president or this administration. . . . Okay, what are we going to do about it? . . . We kick out various ideas from a scheduling standpoint, from a communications standpoint, to get at that. . . . You call that managing the news. I call that defending our record.

—MICHAEL DEAVER

"As you plan for any present day, you always think of tomorrow," explained a senior Nixon alumnus. You follow the rule of HPCQ. Tomorrow you know that there will be—in print and on television—headlines, pictures, captions, and quotes. The rule of HPCQ is: so to structure the White House and Cabinet activities today that tomorrow's headlines will be positive to the president, the photos and television shots will portray him attractively, the captions will be laudatory, and the quotes will encapsulate his policies."[1]

White House staffs have followed the "rule of HPCQ" for decades, at least as far back as James Hagerty's operation in the Eisenhower years.

Almost without interruption since 1966, there has been a special master of the rule present in the White House: a director of communications, in fact if not in name. The press secretary may take up some of the task, but the Press Office itself is preoccupied with its day-to-day dialogues with the White House press corps.

The communications chief has a comprehensive charter. "Communications" is the entire public presidency—the total range of possible words and deeds that can advertise to the American people that their president is doing right.

If presidential power is the power to persuade, as Richard Neustadt emphasized in his seminal work, the White House Communications Office is the central switching station for that power. Statements and actions by the president in person carry the heaviest amperage, but many a White House senior, and every Cabinet officer, is a lever on the control board. The president's schedule, the press secretary's briefings, leadership groups that could be invited into the White House, conventions wanting speakers, call-in shows hoping for spokesmen—all are part of the grid. The White House speechwriters, the trip advance teams, the Television Office, the White House photographer, the Correspondence Unit—each is an amplifier in the communications circuitry. The communications director's wires are plugged in to the national security, domestic policy, legislative, and political affairs staffs as well.

Presidential power is communications power. Viewed from the White House, not even the smallest Executive Branch generator, in or out of the White House, can be left to spin unconnected. To be a motive force, this power must be aggregated, concentrated, directed. The Communications Office is therefore a White House office, from which its lever-pullers can reach across the staff and throughout the Cabinet. In the Reagan White House, the communications director supervised not only the offices of Media Relations and Television Affairs, but the Speechwriters and the Office of Public Liaison as well. To keep all those generators of persuasive power humming at the same frequency, to have the administration speak with one voice, the communications director will operate a rack of variable control handles. The techniques are similar from presidency to presidency.[2]

The White House press corps, for instance, is viewed as a group not merely to be served, as chapter 11 describes, but if possible to be manipulated as well. A part of this communications control is exercised by the press secretary, who early in an administration typically issues a pair of aggressive instructions. To reporters: go through him to reach any other White House officer. To the staff: report to him any dealings with journalists—phone calls, lunches, private meetings.

"No staff interviews are to be given to the press without checking with Hagerty" was Ann Whitman's diary notation on September 25, 1953. CBS reporter George Herman recalled:

> . . . in Hagerty's day, if you wanted an appointment with anybody in the White House, any of the advisors, any of the staff, if you called that man's office, . . . his secretary would say, "I'll have your call transferred." And the next thing

you know, you'd be talking to Jim Hagerty's office. . . . Not always, but most of the time.[3]

Kennedy's press secretary, Pierre Salinger, on the other hand, was tolerant.

If you . . . asked Pierre, "Can I interview so-and-so?" his attitude was, in effect, "Why bother me? Go ask him."[4]

Johnson was anything but tolerant. A memorandum of June 20, 1966, laid down the law:

From now on, the president wants a daily list, submitted to him by about 5 P.M. of all press people whom you have seen or talked to during the course of the day. This list is to be submitted to [Press Secretary] Bill Moyers. If you have no contact with the press during the day, he wants a negative answer.[5]

Nixon reimposed the Johnson rule. John Ehrlichman described the practice:

Bob Haldeman told me that the President wanted all press contacts cleared with [Press Secretary] Ron Ziegler in advance, without exception.

From then on, routine requests for appointments with journalists were phoned in to Ziegler when they came in. Often it took a day or two to get Ziegler's reply. I figured that in fact, Richard Nixon himself was passing advance judgment on my contacts. . . . When I really wanted to see a reporter I just forgot to ask Ron.[6]

Such controls can have embarrassing, even traumatic outcomes. Upon joining Carter's staff in 1978, Communications Director Gerald Rafshoon proclaimed a directive to the White House staff: all acceptances of invitations to national television talk shows were to be cleared with him in advance. In July of that year, when he discovered that his colleague, Margaret (Midge) Costanza, without his knowledge, was to appear on ABC's "Good Morning, America" show, Rafshoon canceled her appearance. Carter supported his communications director and Costanza resigned a few days afterward.

In the Reagan White House, at the insistence of Chiefs of Staff James Baker and Donald Regan, logs of staff members' press contacts were collected and inspected, allegedly to "curb leaks"; Regan at one point mandated that "no member of the senior staff could talk to the press unless a member of the White House Press Office staff was present."[7] In no White House, however, can communications or press chiefs set up impermeable barriers between all the staff and all the news media, especially for off-the-record conversations. Senior staff officers and journalists swim in a symbiotic pond; social and after-hours mingling is beyond any log or registry. Unattributed stories will result, no matter how many presidential keisters are in pain. "The people who violated our controls the worst were the ones highest up," commented one Reagan administration veteran.

The "rule of HPCQ" is also a positive effort, however, not merely negative. Beyond prohibitions, it means looking for opportunities to spread whatever is the day's good news.

In January of 1971, statistics had been compiled showing how active President Nixon had been since he took office in meeting with Cabinet members, legislators, governors, mayors, and minority groups. Chief of Staff Bob Haldeman instructed a colleague: "Would you please assume responsibility for getting [the statistics] out in an exciting and interesting way. . . ." The recipient was also told to prepare "talking papers" for other senior staff members to use when *they* met with journalists.

There have been hundreds of such campaigns. From the communications director's viewpoint, however, enterprises like that have a serious flaw: their success depends on the willingness of editors to print or producers to broadcast what the White House minions have generated.

Is there a more reliable technique? How can a communications director be more confident that the presidential story will, each day, be featured favorably in those print or electronic headlines, photos, captions, and quotes? A device is indeed available, controllable, right at hand. The most potent communications tool in the White House is the president's schedule. His face and figure are—almost unavoidably—news.

The appointments secretary and the communications director therefore engage in what one aide calls "creative scheduling." Each day's appointment calendar is arranged to include one event that is calculated to "dominate the news." If it is a presidential statement, an ideal length is half a minute. Anything longer will be subject to network editing, but a thirty-second public presidential utterance will probably be used *in toto.*

A second "creative scheduling" tactic is the "photo opportunity"— pictures of the president in the Oval Office with a newsworthy visitor. The reporters and television cameramen who always accompany the president call their duty "the body watch." When the Oval Office doors swing open for a prearranged photo opportunity, they swarm in and the Minicams roll. Another communications control is often imposed at this point. The "Deaver rule" prohibited journalists from asking President Reagan any questions during photo opportunities.

When the evening television news producers request a White House report from their Washington bureaus, the thirty-second statement or the "photo opportunity" pictures are "in the can." If the communications and appointments staffers have done their job, there is only a "take it or leave it" option, that is, the one thirty-second statement or the one Oval Office picture; there will have been no other presidential newsmaking events that day at all. Explained a former Carter assistant: "We don't step on our own events." If a presidential statement is longer than half a minute, the press secretary will candidly emphasize to reporters: "This paragraph is the heart of the president's message."

To guarantee that presidential appearances will appeal to the television networks, the communications director will see to it that drama is added to the chief executive's activities. In emphasizing his concern about Soviet aggression in Central America, President Reagan was photographed inspecting an exhibit of Sandinista machine guns. To celebrate the fortieth anniversary of the Normandy landings, Reagan delivered a speech standing on the edge of France's Pointe de Hoc with the English Channel billowing below him. That is "news that wiggles," as Martin Schram put it, and it gets on the air.[8]

In the early evening, there is usually a "wrap-up" meeting; several aides gather to ask each other, "How successful was the day?" The White House journalists of course recognize that this game is being played—that their cameras and networks are in effect being used as instruments of the presidential theater. If the subject at hand is controversial, the reporters will try to escape from such one-sided manipulation. They will search out an opposition senator, an expert from the Brookings Institution, an interest-group dissident—to present an alternative voice.

In the White House, the sheer amount of staff hours taken up with "communications" manipulation is outweighed only by the elaborateness of its orchestration. In Reagan's time, there was first the "Line of the Day" meeting, later the "24–48 Hours" committee, each group representing half a dozen staff offices. Out of such sessions would come an "action memo" laying out a detailed schedule and publicity plans for the days or the week ahead.[9]

The window of "action" opportunity is often only hours instead of days in length. A colleague recalls how Communications Director David Gergen "every single day . . . called all three nets about an hour and a half before their final deadline to find out what they were going with. And then, for the next hour and a half, there was a flurry around here, trying to influence what they were doing."[10] Gergen himself observed: "Because of the immediacy of television, the White House must be prepared in advance to react quickly. Things are moving fast out there. If you're not out there in the next wave with your side of history, or your viewpoint of reality, you often are just forgotten."[11]

The "communications" game has high stakes. Carter's media adviser, Barry Jagoda, emphasized the White House perspective: "It's a way of bringing the country together. . . ."[12] "As goes an appearance, so goes the presidency," observed Nixon advance man Ronald Walker. Presidential Assistant Michael Deaver was brutally practical: "Television elects people."[13] In rebuttal, columnist David Broder declares that countering the White House propaganda machine is "a challenge we . . . cannot afford to ignore."[14]

As determined as the communications staff is to present the president in the most favorable way, for their part the journalists are equally determined not to get "suckered" into being merely the conveyors of the presidential image. The resulting inevitable tension can often turn nasty.

Informed of a forthcoming presidential trip, enterprising reporters may go to the site ahead of time, to describe a scene before the White House advance team pretties it up for television. In 1986 Jane Mayer of the *Wall Street Journal* flew down to Grenada a week before a presidential visit was to commemorate the 1983 U.S. invasion of that small island. In a candid and amusing front-page story, she catalogued the elaborate advance preparations for the four-and-one-half-hour presidential extravaganza. Even some of Grenada's roads, she reported, may have been especially repaved to dramatize postinvasion progress.[15]

Her visit was definitely not in the "action plan." White House Press Secretary Larry Speakes was not only irritated but vindictive. He telephoned members of the advance team to cancel her appointments with them and for days afterward refused to return Mayer's telephone calls. "You are on our death list," he told her later.

On another occasion, Speakes' outrage was directed against one of his own predecessors. As vice president of the Mutual Broadcasting System in 1986, Ron Nessen decided that Mutual would not automatically carry President Reagan's Saturday noon radio broadcasts, nor the Democratic response. Both items were taped ahead of time and often contained little that was newsworthy. When one Reagan tape that summer did contain a significant statement, Nessen broke the twenty-hour embargo and broadcast it early, explaining, "News is news when it's made, not when the White House says it may be released to the public." He refused "to follow the orders of the presidential PR flacks." Speakes was vindictive again. "We're going to take punitive action against your reporter. He's out of business. He'll have to figure out how to get his news some other way because he's not getting it from me. . . . He can report on Chicken Week."[16] When a reporter described to Carter's former press secretary, Jody Powell, the Reagan White House's ability to manipulate presidential scenery, his comment was, "I wish we could have done it as well."

The Reagan White House employed an especially degrading technique when the president was walking to or from his helicopter on the South Lawn. Reporters were held behind ropes, set well back from the president's path. *Marine One*'s engines were intentionally left running, blanketing the scene with a deafening whine. As the president walked past, the journalists shouted questions to him, but he waved with a grin, refusing to answer or hollering only brief rejoinders amid the screaming turbine noise. The evening news pictures then showed the smiling president being badgered by what looked like "a bunch of aggressive, ill-mannered scolds."[17] "It's an intentional technique to make the press look like a pack of animals," comments one journalist. Whether well or poorly, with class or with venom, up front or behind the scenes, every White House staff engages in the "communications" competition.

In order to minimize damage from impromptu gaffes, Reagan cut back on press conferences and allowed his staff to shield him from substantive exchanges with reporters. During a July 1984 briefing at a Maryland wildlife refuge, questions about a controversial environmental appointment were thrust aside by Press Secretary Speakes, who jumped in front of the chief executive. Explained the president, "My guardian says I can't talk."[18]

As if to compensate for the dearth of substantive presidential dialogue, the White House communications staff machinery has become even more elaborate. A subordinate unit of the communications group is the Media Relations Office. Here flourishes a channel of information from the White House to those news organizations that are not based in Washington.

White House communications chiefs have long been frustrated to see that events at 1600 Pennsylvania Avenue get into the nation's news media only through the networks' producers or through the editors or Washington bureau chiefs of the newspaper chains and major dailies. Presidents and their associates ask themselves how to get around that filter to get presidential copy to the American heartland.

The staff's answer has been to bypass the White House press corps and their supervisory editors, to "jump over them" as one aide boasted, and to place White House information directly in the hands of local papers, editorial writers, columnists, and broadcasters. Among those especially targeted are newspapers not well represented in the White House press corps, papers serving the black, Jewish, and Hispanic communities and influential nationality groups. Beginning with Nixon, a White-House-to-

local-media operation was put into high gear. Larry Speakes writes of his
role during Nixon's Watergate period:

> I assigned every public affairs officer in the government to write an Op-Ed piece
> each week telling how the government was functioning normally, and I would
> edit them and place them with papers around the country. Placing Op-Eds is not
> an easy job. But we did remarkably well. If you couldn't get them into the
> *Washington Post,* or *The New York Times,* or the *Los Angeles Times,* you could always
> get them into newspapers like the *San Antonio Light,* or the *Charleston Gazette* in
> West Virginia.[19]

Such an operation has been repeated in each succeeding presidency.

Under Carter, the office was called Media Liaison. An impending presidential legislative initiative—the Panama Canal Treaty ratification for example—would be the signal for forming a White House–chaired task force.
State and Defense public information officers would join together; agreed
assignments would be listed on a computerized printout. "It was a road
show," recalled Patricia Bario, Carter's media liaison director. Key states
were targeted, a "speakers bank" assembled, local invitations arranged for
State Department and other administration spokesmen. The task force
even provided public-speaking training for those whose articulation did
not match their expertise. Carter was a president of multiple initiatives; at
one time Bario had thirteen task forces going at once.

"Fact sheets" were written by White House editors, based on departmental raw material, and mailed to a list of "6,500 news organizations,
interest groups and individuals." Month after month, in fact, the media
liaison operation would mail out an average of over thirty-five thousand
pieces.[20] At the end of 1978, it was time for a special mailing, a nine-
thousand-word summary entitled "Carter Administration—Summary of
Accomplishments." Its editor and producer was a staffer at the White
House.

Within two years of his inauguration, President Carter had made a new
addition to the communications enterprises of the presidency; it was called
"Actualities." Audio tapes were made of important statements by the
president or others; questions about policy issues were written up by the
staff, followed by the answers, which the president, or Cabinet officers,
would record. Over six hundred radio stations around the country were
given toll-free numbers to dial into any one of five identical tape machines.
The opening message was: "Here is what happened at the White House
this morning," or "We have three feeds for you today," whereupon the
stations could select what they wanted. The five machines combined usually took a thousand calls a day. Extra staff was needed, and a former disk

jockey was hired to produce the program. Not surprisingly, the regular White House press corps objected. "They were bent out of shape," Pat Bario recalled; "they called it 'managed news.' " When President Reagan took office, the program had proved its value, so now "Actualities" has become a standard feature of the White House communications apparatus.

The Reagan communicators added still another service: electronic distribution of White House speeches and news releases. Local radio stations with automatic printers can dial into Washington and be sent the latest presidential texts. The Reagan White House had begun the system as a White House facility, but transferred it to commercial hands after complaints from the national newswire services that it was unfair government competition with them.

Under Reagan there was a Television Office on the White House staff, later renamed the Office of Media and Broadcast Relations, the director of which was a special assistant to the president. Even this unit, however, is but the most recent stage in a long White House tradition. For a brief period in 1945, Truman used J. Leonard Reinsch as a White House media adviser; in the years after leaving the staff Reinsch continued to send memoranda to Truman with suggestions about the style of his speeches. Whenever Eisenhower planned a television address to the nation, actor Robert Montgomery would fly in. He would time the speech, supervise the technical arrangements in the Oval Office, and make suggestions for both substance and delivery. "As far as television was concerned," he wrote, "no authority was to supersede mine."[21]

Early in his administration, Johnson importuned the networks to set up a television studio in the White House Family Theater. Johnson wanted to be able to go on the air live and at short notice. The networks installed black-and-white cameras and had crews on standby; Johnson came in often—to make "Great Society" announcements. This was an expensive experiment for the networks, however; when the changeover to color had to be made, the arrangement was terminated.

Through the years from Eisenhower to Reagan, as television became more and more a prized tool of presidential persuasion power, staff assistance for the White House use of television grew as well. Except for a Navy crew that tapes an internal historical record, however, the White House itself has no television production personnel. Every televised event at the White House is filmed and produced either by the national networks *because* they judge it to be news, or else commercial crews are rented to make paid spots for special groups and for campaigning. In either case, advance arrangements demand meticulous staff work, especially since television facilities at 1600 Pennsylvania Avenue are so limited.

Even though a small auditorium was constructed on the fourth floor of the adjoining Executive Office Building, presidents have preferred to hold their press conferences in the East Room of the Residence itself. It is actually a grand ballroom; getting it ready for a press conference requires eight hours of setup time. The major networks take turns handling the event, the "pool" designee sharing the "feed" with the others. The Television Office clears the way for the network producer to bring in a forty-foot van and twenty-two technicians.

A presidential address to the nation is even more disruptive. The Oval Office itself becomes the studio (the public would hardly accept anything else), and the president has to move out to let the technicians do their work.

Visual aids for presidential addresses are increasingly a responsibility of the Television (or Broadcast Relations) Office. Maps, charts, and pictures can make even a presidential presentation more convincing, but they require staff support to prepare in a professional fashion. (On one occasion President Reagan was using a marking pen during a televised talk. The hot lights dried up the felt tip and a mysterious hand was seen reaching over to supply him with a new one.) Electronically created graphics are common in modern newscasting; a president is inclined to employ visuals like that too. The White House, however, does not own one of the expensive machines needed to make them; if electronic graphics are to be used, the Television Office rents the service and orchestrates the preparatory process, which may take as much as twenty hours.

The president has a host of other television obligations. In the 1986 campaign, 150 Republican candidates paid to have presidential endorsement tapes produced. The Television Office prepared the briefing materials, checking each request with the political and legislative assistants.

Outside groups ask for video-recorded presidential messages to be shown at their major functions. The television special assistant consults with the Political, Public Liaison, and Scheduling offices, and if necessary with the national security assistant. If the request is granted, the Television Office may ask the group to supply a sample of the kind of message it would like. With the speechwriters' help, the final briefing papers and talking texts are put together, a separate set for each message. On two hours' notice, the commercial firm brings its camera into the Residence Library or the Map Room. In a single session, the president may record five or six brief tapes. The favored groups pay the seven-hundred-dollar production expenses; the staff costs are borne by the White House.

The Television Office similarly supports the first lady when she records messages and it also made the production arrangements for President Reagan's weekly radio talks.

The director of Reagan's Television Office, Elizabeth Board, looks into the future. She envisages a satellite transmission service enabling individual local television stations to receive and, if they wish, rebroadcast presidential talks. A presidential speech or message might be tailored entirely to a local or regional interest; it could be transmitted directly to the local stations, independent of the "news" judgment imposed by the national television networks.

A step further: why be limited to one-way messages? One may foresee interactive video links with local audiences, the president taking questions and entering into back-and-forth discussion. Such arrangements might lessen the need for presidents to travel, saving money and time and reducing security concerns.

Does the advent of electronic graphics presage the too-glitzy presidency? Should the White House production facilities be so much less extensive than those of a commercial studio? If future presidents answer no to both questions, the Television Office is due for even further growth.

Cabinet officers, too, are wired into the White House communications net. The White House Speaker's Bureau matches up Cabinet or sub-Cabinet officials with invitations the president has received but cannot personally accept—if the sponsors and occasions are considered important. If a Cabinet officer is anxious to make a speech but needs a forum, the Speaker's Bureau will identify one and help with the arrangements.

The reverse is true as well. Cabinet heads who are handling their own arrangements for giving speeches are usually expected to check their acceptances—sometimes their texts—with the White House, which asks for a roundup report of all cabinet public appearances. "At least they know somebody's watching," explained Carter communications director Rafshoon.[22]

Under even closer White House control are acceptances by any senior Executive Branch officials to appear on national TV talk shows. Which staffer will be allowed to "go out," which Cabinet members may "Meet the Press," is a decision monopolized by the Communications Office or by the press secretary. The unhappy example of Midge Costanza was earlier described. "When they want to talk about a subject, they can put three people out. When they don't they won't," observed Lesley Stahl, hostess of CBS News' "Face the Nation."[23]

When Jerry terHorst took over as President Ford's first press secretary, he was both irritated and bored at operating such a White House control

system; he stopped the practice of playing "traffic cop" over Cabinet
members' appearances. But looking back, he reflected that he had made a
mistake.

> I think I would have kept reins on that [traffic] because, even though I was there
> very briefly, before the end of my stint it was clear that some Cabinet people
> were already taking advantage of the opportunity not to check in with the White
> House on what they were going to say on *Face the Nation* or *Meet the Press*. The
> Monday briefings were getting to be a pain in the neck for the President if not
> for me.[24]

The terHorst experiment in laissez-faire was short-lived; the superintend-
ency has been reimposed. "The game plan for dealing with the press
. . . originated in my office," Reagan press secretary Larry Speakes emphasized. "It was up to me, in consultation with Jim Baker, and later with Don
Regan, to decide who would give which interviews and make television
appearances."[25]

Acknowledging their dependence on the White House steering operation, the networks refrain from open complaints about this form of communications control. "They're our bread and butter," one network official
admitted. Said another: "They are not doing anything that wasn't attempted before. They [the Reagan White House] have just been more
efficient about it. . . ."[26]

Following the "rule of HPCQ," the press secretary even sets conditions
for administration spokesmen on the national TV shows: no debates—the
administration representative must appear alone for his or her segment of
the program; and the administration spokesman should have the last word,
after any critics. "In fact, the White House has learned to operate the
system so well that one key participant has complained that the real
producer of the Sunday shows is Reagan spokesman Larry Speakes."[27]

The Communications Unit also reminds Cabinet and staff speakers of
points to be included when they speak. A circular memorandum of February 1974 from Nixon Communications Director Ken Clawson, for example, enclosed eighteen pages of "talking points" and sixteen charts supporting the president's recently delivered State of the Union message. "For
your use in upcoming speaking engagements," the memo explained.

Ten years later, a different staff mounted the same activity. In 1984 a
similar "talking points" memorandum was dispatched from Reagan White
House Public Affairs Director Michael Baroody, this time instructing Cabinet members how to support the presidential position on prayer in the
schools. "For your use in appropriate speaking opportunities," wrote

Baroody. The only difference in a decade: the 1984 circular was sent by electronic mail.

When Cabinet speeches are finally given, the Communications Office will close the link by reproducing the texts and sending them around the same Cabinet–White House staff circuit. That office's ties to the Cabinet departments are quick and close. Herbert Klein, the Nixon communications director, employed four staff specialists, each of whom was assigned to track the public relations activities of a specific group of departments. In every department was a public information officer, approved, if not actually recruited, by Klein, and thus bearing a dual loyalty—to the Cabinet head but also to the White House. Daily, each of those PIOs would call to inform his contact on the Klein staff about all the releases, speeches, and major public events impending in his department. Together they all formed a team, headed in the White House, reaching into every agency. Each succeeding White House has replicated such networks.

For Communications Director Gerald Rafshoon, however, the "team" theory wasn't working.

> We had these PIO meetings and I got to the point where I knew they were going to go back to their departments and ignore everything. They have different priorities. They think survival. They are interested in survival in Washington. They don't always have the same priorities as the administration. If I had been here in the beginning, I would have formed the PIO's from our [campaign] organization. To me there's only one name that's going to be on the ballot, Jimmy Carter.[28]

What is the future of the White House Communications Office? The old truth that presidents must be persuaders, coupled with the new technologies offering such potent opportunities to persuade, will convince any president that communications is an indispensable White House preoccupation. Jody Powell explains why:

> That's got to be done. Whether the press secretary should be the person to do it is a good question. I'm inclined to think that he probably should be, but he can't because I tried to do it and I don't think I was able to devote enough time to it. On the other hand, the press secretary has to have a good hand in that operation or you get at cross purposes. . . . You had literally hundreds of people involved . . . not only with "Meet the Press" and those shows but "Good Morning Idaho" and "Hello Atlanta" . . . that takes a lot of coordination. You've got to free the people up. You've got to tell them where to go. You've got to make sure that they say what they're supposed to say when they get there. . . . There's no doubt in my mind . . . that those [Panama Canal] treaties would never have been approved . . . but for that sort of operation. . . .[29]

The rule of HPCQ has thus become a governing precept in the American presidency. Is that precept mere manipulation? White House aides deny it. "Why should we not ask ourselves, 'What is our message?' and 'What, each day, will best carry that message?'" said a senior Reagan assistant. He is right; every modern president asks the same question. Communications opportunities, however, are neither seized nor used without White House staff who are watchful in spotting them—even in creating them—and who are energetic in arranging their exploitation.

CHAPTER 13

Judson Welliver and Successors: The Speechwriting and Research Office

The man who writes the President's speeches runs the country.

—Thomas E. Dewey

Speechwriters aren't supposed to make policy!

—Robert C. McFarlane

His title was "literary clerk" when the first presidential speechwriter, Judson Welliver, began his White House service under President Warren Harding on March 4, 1921. For the nearly seven decades since, there has been a speechwriting officer or group on the personal staff of the president. Over the same seventy years, the staff has expanded and the output has exploded.

In their eighteen years as presidents, Johnson, Nixon, Ford, and Carter made 5,186 speeches. Even that figure is not the real measure of the speechwriters' production. In addition to addresses personally delivered, a president issues statements (such as the eight-thousand-word Nixon declaration on school desegregation, described in chapter 3), announcements, proclamations, executive orders, and reports to Congress. The total of these items for Truman through Ford (including their press conferences) fills 34,369 pages of single-spaced print in the volumes of the *Public Papers of the Presidents of the United States.* President Carter's prose added another 9,873 pages and Reagan (through 1987), 11,321 more. The yearly average of these pages has risen from 700 in Truman's presidency to 2,468 in the Carter term. During 1976 (the Bicentennial period and an election year) President Ford spoke a million words in public.

The contemporary White House is, in fact, a high-speed prose factory.

White House speech productions come in long and short sizes, some of them rating world attention, many of them sheer miscellany.

Every presidency starts with a speech; a president's very first act is the inaugural address. Truman's "Point Four," Eisenhower's "little prayer," and Kennedy's "Ask not . . . ," each set a tone or an agenda for the four years to come. The "Ask not . . ." lines from Kennedy's inaugural speech were in fact printed on large posterboards and mounted on easels. There was one in the foyer of every agency building in Washington; for months those speech lines were the morning's first greeting to every federal employee and visitor.

Second in speechwriting importance is the State of the Union message, given by the president each January to a joint session of the House and Senate and, like the inaugural, simultaneously to a national television audience. Unlike the high-noon inaugural, the State of the Union message has been switched from daytime to evening, to place it in prime viewing hours. The "SOTU" address is the year's greatest demand on a presidential speechwriter—summing up all the president's accomplishments, cataloguing the challenges of the present, introducing the president's vision of the months to come. It is here that program initiatives are unveiled, new legislation requested. For a president with a heavy agenda of new proposals, the SOTU message may become, as one speechwriter described it, "a kind of a list, with nice sentences at each end."

The speechwriter for that message usually starts work in October; Nixon speechwriter Raymond K. Price, Jr., remembers completing fourteen drafts for the 1971 address. Price has coined a parallel to the military aphorism about planning: "Drafts are useless, but drafting is essential."[1]

At the lesser end of the scale is "Rose Garden rubbish," deprecatory slang for greetings and pep talks to special groups invited to gather at the Rose Garden steps. Here the president accepts a live turkey before Thanksgiving or congratulates Miss Teenage America. (This is not presidential statesmanship; it is presidential politics. Thanksgiving is a national holiday, and there are perhaps 9 million teenage misses.)

Author of most of the two-thousand-odd pages produced each year, also of the president's weekly radio addresses and of the hundreds of videotapes recorded as messages to favored organizations, is the White House speechwriting and research staff. Like other principal White House actors described in this book, the speechwriting director insists on his own rule of exclusivity. Other staff units may compose drafts, but it is the Speechwriting Office that demands a monopoly over the gateway into the president's office for all his addresses and statements. For his words on paper, they are the guardians of his style, his syntax, and his accuracy.

Does the formal title for that office imply a separation of authors from policy officers, a gulf between the writers and the president? Theodore Sorensen, who served Kennedy as both counsel and major speechwriter combined, has written of his concern:

> Alas, the poor speechwriter, I knew him well. Once he was a presidential collaborator . . . a Sam Rosenman, a Clark Clifford, participating in the decisions he helped to communicate, exchanging ideas with the President as well as phrases.
>
> In the last three administrations . . . he has typically been not a policy adviser but a professional wordsmith, isolated from decisionmaking and from personal contact with the decision-maker.[2]

Not true of Bryce Harlow, who crafted State of the Union messages for Eisenhower, nor of presidential adviser C. D. Jackson, who wrote thirty-three drafts of Ike's "Atoms for Peace" speech at the United Nations in December of 1953. Neither was Sorensen's description accurate for Raymond Price, under Nixon, who describes an assignment in 1970: "It was a hard-hitting speech. I worked with Nixon on it, and he spent many hours on it himself. In our usual pattern of collaboration, we swapped ideas back and forth and sent drafts back and forth, as he polished and refined precisely what he wanted to say."[3] Still, Sorensen warns future draftsmen: "Do not separate speech-writing from decision-making."[4]

How does a speech get written in today's White House?

First, the event is approved on the schedule—a process described in chapter 15. (When he was president, Eisenhower preferred to look at the first draft of a speech before he would even consider accepting the invitation itself. Sherman Adams remembers Ike exclaiming, "What is it that needs to be said? I am not going out there just to listen to my tongue clatter!")[5]

Next, a team of two is assigned to the speech, one from the writing staff and one from the research staff. (The seven-person Research Unit was formally begun under Nixon's first speechwriter, James Keogh, and has always been an immediate adjunct to the Speechwriting Office.) Before the speechwriting is started, the researcher prepares "up front" material. The event in which the president will participate is described—its history, its background, its setting.

The speechwriter soaks up this story, and an initial speech draft is then prepared, but its first routing is back to the Research Unit for a "fact check." Is there a single statement in it that cannot be substantiated? Speechwriters, explained one observer, tend to regard even their initial prose as "graven in marble"; the research staffer is expected to suggest alternative language if the factual record requires it. Is there a historical reference that didn't happen, a quotation without a source? Speech authors, the observer commented, have been known to make up quotes that they would like to believe that somebody said. To back up the Research Unit's checking system, the White House has its own reference center, full use of the Library of Congress, and computer access to commercial data banks of every variety.

If a major address is being prepared, the president may be involved early. He may insert ideas of his own, points to emphasize, anecdotes to include. "I guess he spends twenty to thirty hours on each major speech," Ann Whitman wrote of Eisenhower. "Often he caught mistakes that had gotten by everyone else."[6]

For many of his speeches, Nixon would spell out his thoughts to Chief of Staff Haldeman, who would faithfully relay them to Price. For other than nationwide audiences, Nixon preferred to speak extemporaneously, after having studied a "food for thought" memo from his speechwriting staff.

Reagan followed a different style; even his less important talks were put in writing in advance. For any president, however, a personal touch is rarely absent.

In May of 1986, President Reagan was planning a speech on trade and tax policy to the National Association of Manufacturers' Annual Congress of American Industry. The president pulled from his memory a phrase he had come across somewhere before in his life: a nation with an improper tax system would be "at sea without rudder or compass." He thought the quote came from "a Scottish economist"; could it be found and confirmed? For the research desk, that set off a two-day hunt. No luck in the White House; no luck in the Library of Congress. Finally, someone discovered a professor at Auburn University in Alabama who had written a book about the British economist Adam Smith. The research sleuth called his home. With the White House on the other end of the telephone, his wife pulled the book from her husband's shelf and found the citation: it was from an 1845 work by one John Ramsay McCulloch. The Library of Congress was then able to dig out the volume and rush it to the White House, where the full quotation was substantiated. In his speech, the president paraphrased McCulloch and used the phrase itself verbatim.[7] The documentation was later placed in the White House files in case any skeptic should ask, "What book was *that* from?"

On the researcher's desk today, every draft presidential speech, great or small, is splotched with yellow ink, each colored-over word or phrase accompanied by a marginal explanation: who that was, when it was, what circumstances. The annotated version is given back to the speechwriter, a copy kept in the "skeptic" file. Hundreds of yellow-striped pages mean thousands of hours of research.

President Reagan was criticized for factual errors in his public statements, but most of the bloopers occurred while "winging it" in his responses to press-conference queries. Pre-press-conference rehearsing helps guard against misstatements; Reagan's press conferences themselves were reduced to rare occasions. If any president's talk is impromptu, whatever meticulous staff work was done earlier is no longer controlling as soon as the first ad-lib word is spoken.

What contributions for White House speeches come from the Cabinet departments? Clark Clifford recalled the State of the Union message preparations of 1949 for President Truman:

> Every department, of course, would want the State of the Union Message devoted practically exclusively to . . . [its] problems. So quite a selection process was necessary. You might get one idea out of a departmental memorandum, you might get none, or you might get two or three. . . . We all agreed that this was very much a personal matter that belonged with the White House, and I believe we just didn't go out asking other people their opinion or informing them as to what was to take place.[8]

A decade later, Bryce Harlow was the speechwriter, but his dilemma was the same as Clifford's:

> . . . I had a Cabinet officer with me and four waiting to see me, each of them insistent that the area involving their activities be expanded in the State of the Union Message. They were unhappy that their areas had been compressed. . . . [They] were in with revised language, demanding that more space be given to their problems; to which I had to respond that the President says he wants this document kept shorter than a two-hour speech. . . .
> This happens on every State of the Union message.[9]

A major presidential address is always more than a domestic affair; unavoidably, he speaks to the world. Other government leaders, allies, neutrals, the Soviet Union, will dissect every phrase, will be impressed with what is *not* said as much as what is specified. Kennedy once commented to Sorensen: "The big difference is all the different audiences that hear every word. In the Senate and campaign we didn't have to worry so much about how Khrushchev and Adenauer and Nehru and Dirksen would react."[10]

Before an important speech is delivered, therefore, a further issue is faced: how much coordination is to be permitted within the staff and across the Cabinet? Two aims conflict. On the one hand, if a speech directly touches upon the programs and activities of a Cabinet officer or a staff member, should not that person's expertise and advice be sought or the officer at least be alerted? Yet presidents fear leaks, and if an address is controversial, teamwork may be sacrificed for security.

If coordination is permitted, the indispensable reviewing stations for important speech drafts now include the domestic policy staff, the counsel, and the economic or national security assistants, together with the Cabinet members most affected; the staff secretary may circulate the draft to as many as twenty-five separate offices. The speech itself could be the end point of months of program or budget review; it may make promises or set directions framed only after painful Cabinet subcommittee or National Security Council debates. A slight verbal nuance could set hundreds of thousands applauding but may commit hundreds of millions in resources.

Former Deputy Budget Director Paul O'Neill recalled an instance where coordination was absent. Just three weeks after having taken office in August of 1974, President Ford gave a commencement address at Ohio State University. There will be "new ways to bring the world of work and the institutions of education closer together," he proclaimed. "There will be grants for state and local initiatives," he promised.[11] Within hours, the telephones were ringing on O'Neill's desk at the Office of Management and Budget. "What did he mean by that?" "How much money is available?" O'Neill was nonplussed, unaware. He promptly started a search to find out where all those presidential ideas came from. Did the White House domestic policy staff know? They did not. Could the Council of Economic Advisers tell him? It was news to them. The deputy budget director at last tracked down the White House speechwriter. "Where did those promises get started?" he demanded. "What is behind them? What are the specifics?" The wordsmith waved him off. "We made it up. But you are taking it all too seriously," he observed. "It's only a speech. . . ."

Some presidents, Reagan having been one, prefer to stay remote from the early stages of preparing an address or statement. Even after reviewing the researcher's collection of past presidential remarks, the speechwriter may be in a quandary. What to say? "What *is* his policy on conservation?" one Reagan draftswoman once wondered. "Lacking certainty, we intuit. We are his supporters, we know his general policy approaches. We make it up." She was not the first, nor will she be the last speechwriter to use intuition in preparing presidential prose.

Whether the speechwriter is a close adviser or one more remote, intuitive language must be tested in the policy arena. Cabinet and senior White House staff—a speech draft in front of them and a deadline looming—are forced to focus on the policy issues that the proposed remarks may have opened up. Decisions are finally ground out: how much of the intuition will be confirmed, how much amended.

Peggy Noonan, a Reagan speechwriter, recalled the frustration of an author when her prose went through a twenty-five-station review. "It would come back mush or tapioca," she observed. "So I would use the 'hand grenade' technique. I would write a statement embodying an unambiguous, history-making commitment, throw it into the policy machinery, and sooner or later somebody would knock it down or pick it up. *Then* we would find out what the president's policy was."[12]

Noonan was the author of Reagan's eloquent mourning statement at the time of the *Challenger* explosion. In his talk to the nation, the president not only expressed grief, but spoke of the future: "There will be more shuttle flights and more shuttle crews and, yes, more volunteers, more civilians, more teachers in space."[13]

Noonan's original language was significantly different. She had first written: "There will be more shuttles . . . ," a declaration that immediately set off an internal policy discussion. Would the administration purchase another shuttle spacecraft—commit to spending hundreds of millions of dollars to do so? In the pressure and urgency of that morning, there was no time to check across twenty-five offices, or to engage in long policy discussions with the OMB and the preoccupied NASA officials. In record time, Noonan was given a decision: such a commitment was not in the cards. Two changed words equaled nearly a billion dollars.

A more unwelcome method of smoking out decisions is to carry the debate into the press, provoking other "anonymous" White House staffers to do the same. The resulting public shootout is messy, but even presidents have been known to fire the opening rounds.

Thus do speeches and speechwriters initiate a White House policy process, and not just come along at the end. "We are often pressured, even hoodwinked, by the policy contenders," said Noonan. "The White House can be a dangerous place to work." She echoed what one of her predecessors, Will Sparks, had observed from his White House experience two decades earlier: "Successful Washington speechwriting is one percent literary talent and ninety–nine percent political infighting."[14]

Whatever the risk, the speechwriter's task "is a fail-safe function," Price observed. "You cannot allow the president to be trapped into saying something which has a hidden meaning he did not intend. The place is full of protagonists who will try to sneak in their favorite ideas."[15]

The occasion of a presidential speech generates pressure to concoct policy goodies as a guarantor of applause lines. If the audience is large and advocacy-oriented, and if a reelection year is close, the pressure may be uncontainable.

In late June of 1971, President Nixon was to address the convention of the American Association of Retired Persons in Chicago. The AARP is a nationwide special-interest group with 25 million members. In addition to the obvious generalities, what could the president say?

His staff identified two possible initiatives of first-rank interest to senior citizens: expanding Medicare to cover the costs of out-of-hospital prescription drugs, and putting heavier federal weight into the enforcement of nursing-home standards.

White House policy officers convened special working sessions with experts from the Department of Health, Education, and Welfare. Three days before the speech, option papers were produced recommending increased federal efforts and funds for prescription drug reimbursement and for nursing-home inspections. Neither domestic policy chief John Ehrlichman nor Budget Director Caspar Weinberger approved either of the papers, however; the first was too expensive, the second had too strong a flavor of compulsion.

The speechwriter came hurrying down the White House corridor on his way to take his seat on the presidential helicopter; in effect, his briefcase was empty. "What have you got for me?" he asked his staff colleagues. The unapproved option papers were handed to him with the thought they could serve as helpful background for a generalized presidential pep talk.

The Medicare proposal died in the briefcase, but the mention of nursing homes had a different outcome; it evoked a personal presidential experience. Nixon had a ninety-year-old aunt who resided in such an institution ("a wonderful home," as he described it), but he was also familiar with substandard ones. He directed his speechwriter to bore in on the subject, and in the end, nine paragraphs in the speech were devoted to his views on nursing homes. His closing declaration rang out: "One thing you can be sure, I do not believe that Medicaid and Medicare funds should go to substandard nursing homes in this country and subsidize them."[16] While no new legislation was proposed, Nixon's statement was a policy signal to the heretofore unsung federal and state enforcement officers: here was a president who knew what they were trying to do and who supported their little-recognized efforts. It was the event that induced the speech and the speech that produced the promise, however—not the other way around.

Speeches and statements are the testament of each presidency. They are instruments of persuasion when first given, and become declarations to history as the presidential terms expire. So important are both purposes that presidential words are hardly ever left to chance; they are carefully composed ahead of time. Today the impromptu presidential speech is a rarity.

Literary presidents are rare as well, Peggy Noonan has observed. Seekers of the presidency are hyperactive politicians, not men or women who have long sat by the fire with Shakespeare on their laps, who can, or want, to orate from the stump informally yet with eloquence. "Then it's up to the speechwriters to be literary people," Noonan emphasized. "It's not enough to tell a young campaigner, 'You worked Iowa, so come be a White House speechwriter.' A president should bring in journalists, men and women who know the world of literature."[17]

With audiences now in the tens of millions, a newsworthy presidential speech is both prose and theater—the president on a world stage, recommending and defending his ideas to a fractured nation and to a divided international audience. Television on the one hand gives him enormous visibility but at the same time raises the stakes for him and for the words he utters.

It is because the consequences of a president's prose can be so important for him that the Speechwriting Office began so early and has remained so closely attached to the presidency. Judson Welliver's successors comprise a seventy-year fraternity; those still living, in fact, have instituted the Judson Welliver Society, sharing as they do a common memory of pressures, tribulations, and professional pride.

"Our victory," said Price, "is not to get the president to say what the White House staff wants; the real victory is to make sure that the president's words are what *he* wants to say."[18]

The chapter's two opening quotations are both true and false. Speechwriters do help run the country. They do share in policy-making, often are the initial prods for policy decisions. Possessing that influence, they have inevitably been, for nearly seven decades, part of the political turmoil that is both without and within the gates of the American White House.

CHAPTER 14

Representing Interests and Building Coalitions: The Office of Public Liaison

Most of the 300 groups (2000 people) represented at the eleven energy briefings this week were supportive, particularly labor, urban groups and trade associations. . . . A task force has been organized and we are working on a detailed outreach program to support the legislative initiatives.
—Weekly Activities Report from ANNE WEXLER, July 20, 1979

We have people in the White House . . . who aren't there representing the President to the country. They are representing the country to the President. That's not what the White House staff should be.
—THEODORE SORENSEN

The book's opening chapter described an American society of organized disputers; over nineteen thousand national interest groups contend to represent "the general welfare." As issues arise or disappear, coalitions endlessly form and disband. Millions of dollars are amassed and spent, and skilled managers and lobbyists wield letters, telegrams, testimony, and visits. The policy combat of the nation becomes the warfare of Washington.

What does this warfare mean to the president and his staff? It has a bipolar significance. To the lobbyists, the White House is a target. To the White House, interest-group power is presidential opportunity.

As target: the chief executive is besieged with message-carriers urging him to act or refrain from acting on any of a thousand issues. Some sit on the sidewalk with signs; millions send letters; hundreds ask to be heard in person. All of them seek a sympathetic reception—each would like to know that if not the president himself, then someone on his staff will pay attention to their entreaties. Especially do the leaders of America's major private organizations expect the White House to receive them and give weight to their views.

As opportunity: from where he sits, the president views interest-group lobbyists—on issues where they and he agree—as possible extensions of his own salesmanship. They can multiply his influence—to their memberships, and through their memberships to the Congress. With skillful staff work, the president can mobilize that extramural power; he can enlist those same organization leaders to help in squeezing out just the few votes needed in House or Senate to move his highest priority objectives.

Here are the makings of a bargain.

The president will include on his personal staff men and women who will make it their business to cultivate links to the major interest groups of America. They will be good listeners, but also willing to talk and investigate. They will be door-openers, guaranteeing interest groups a fair hearing—in the White House, in the departments, on occasion in the Oval Office, unless (as illustrated by a few cases described in other chapters) the president insists on secrecy for certain of his initiatives until they are announced.

For their part, the interest groups, even if they are skeptical, will give the president or his representatives the chance to explain their objectives, will attend briefings at the White House, will invite White House staff to their conventions. If they agree with the president, they will join his interests to their own, volunteering to do what he cannot openly ask: put pressure on legislators. Over forty years, the bargain has been struck; the White House Office of Public Liaison is its embodiment.

There is political cement in the bargain as well. As a campaigner, the president will have asked for and received endorsements from specific interest groups or from their leaders personally. Political action committee funds will have flowed into his treasury. There is no chance that, once inaugurated, he will not have officers on his staff commissioned to be attentive to the concerns of his campaign allies.

The question therefore is not whether there will be an Office of Public Liaison, but how it is to be organized and used. Will it foster genuine two-way dialogue between policy-makers and organization leaders, or merely host presentations in the Briefing Room? Will it stimulate, perhaps even orchestrate, legislative pressure campaigns, or limit itself to "making the facts available"?

At the outset, there are two techniques for setting up a Public Liaison Office: matching its staff members with client groups or focusing on issues. The White House typically includes a mixture of both.

A client group–oriented staff will have assistants labeled, or understood to be "handling" the concerns of, business, labor, women, blacks, Hispanics, Jews, youth, senior citizens, Indians, consumers, ethnic organizations, and farmers. If organized according to issues, on the other hand, a liaison staff would be a more flexible unit, its assignments reflecting the president's current legislative priorities.

Will staffers having interest-group assignments be drawn from the groups themselves? Will the Jewish adviser be a Jew, the liaison for black concerns black, the link to elderly groups himself a senior citizen? Almost inevitably. In July of 1976, President Ford addressed the Republican National Hispanic Assembly and, introducing his administration's Hispanic appointees, proclaimed: "First is my new Special Assistant for Hispanic Affairs at the White House, Tom Aranda, Jr. If you have any trouble in the White House, call Tom . . . that is his job."[1]

Instantly, for any such officer, the question of divided loyalties arises. Can the liaison staffer keep credibility, outside the White House, with the group to which he or she belongs without becoming, on the inside, a mere supplicant to the president? If, on the other hand, the person is seen as objective and dispassionate, will the interest groups entrust that person with their advocacy? Once any staffer acquires the internal reputation of being a special pleader, however, he or she will be isolated from the president's policy process—which makes even the "outside" role harder to sustain.

If, in the end, the president takes a position to which the interest groups are deeply opposed, the liaison staffer to these same groups is under intense stress. In May of 1958, Eisenhower met with four hundred prominent black leaders and counseled them to be "patient" in their campaigns for civil rights. That adjective was a dismaying term to his one black staff member, Frederic Morrow, who later wrote in his diary:

> At times it is difficult for me to hold my temper and to ride with the punches. Negroes look upon me as a symbol of disloyalty and a kind of benevolent traitor. . . . If they could only know the tides that swell within my breast twenty-four hours a day as I try to carry out the responsibilities of this office and remain loyal to the President and to my racial identity, they might be a little more charitable. There are valid arguments on both sides, but it is difficult to meet upon common ground, because of the emotionalism involved. It is a question as to how long I can remain in this uncomfortable position.[2]

Some fold under the pressure, leak accounts of internal deliberations, or pass the word to their client groups that "I supported you but so-and-so didn't go along."

At least twice during President Carter's term, White House liaison officers let their advocacy enthusiasm overcome their obligations to the president. Midge Costanza was a White House link to women's groups;

many of them were opposed to the president's policy of denying federal funds for abortions. She decided, in July of 1977, to try to change the president's mind. Her tactic was to convene two White House meetings of senior administration women. The first was held without the president, the second with him in attendance, surrounded by the advocates she had summoned. A participant in the second session recalls the lines on the president's face growing ever grimmer as the minutes wore on. The lobbying effort failed and in a year Costanza was gone.

President Carter's staff also included a counselor on aging, Nelson Cruikshank. (He had been a "must" appointment from the AFL-CIO.)[3] When Carter included in his January 1979 budget message several proposals to Congress to economize on Social Security benefits, Cruikshank accepted an invitation from the House Select Committee on Aging to testify—*against the president's proposals.* Fearful of political retribution from senior citizens groups if he fired Cruikshank, Carter let him appear. It is rare within the White House staff, but it happened in that case; interest-group loyalty became flagrant public insubordination.

The role of the "Jewish adviser" in the White House also illustrates the stresses that liaison staff endure. Leonard Garment was an informal but constant contact for Jewish leaders in the Nixon White House, although he called his responsibility "less a portfolio and more a small, manila envelope."[4] In September of 1972, three representatives of a thirty-four-agency coalition of Jewish leaders visited Garment, upset that Nixon had not been more outspoken against Soviet obstruction of Jewish emigration. The newspaper account of the meeting included this paragraph: "The meeting with Garment took place over the objection of some participants . . . one of whom said . . . that the Jewish community was always fobbed off on 'the White House Jew.' He urged insistence on an appointment with some other member of the Nixon staff."[5] One of the Jewish leaders was instantly regretful, sent Garment a telegraphed apology: "I was horrified. . . . The material may have damaged our cause. . . ."

"White House Jew," "White House black," "White House woman"—no staff officers ever want that label so baldly pinned on; if it sticks, it diminishes them with the president and in the inner circle of the White House. They themselves become mere window dressing—not a position to which any White House staffer aspires.

The Jewish advisory experience since 1977 has been especially traumatic. Both Presidents Carter and Reagan supported sales of sophisticated military equipment (F-15s, AWACS) to Saudi Arabia. The American Jewish community opposed these sales; in 1981 it narrowly missed persuading

the Senate to veto the Reagan AWACS transfer. The stress is evident; the
"Jewish adviser" post changed hands three times under Carter, four times
in the Reagan years.

As long ago as 1976, Stephen Hess of the Brookings Institution recommended that "the White House staff should have no special-interest repre-
sentation offices."[6] His advice was not taken then and is not likely to be
accepted in the future. "It is now almost cast in concrete that there will be
a Jewish liaison," commented Hyman Bookbinder, who had long been the
Washington representative of the American Jewish Committee. "The more
realistic question is, how do we make the best use of him?"[7]

One "best use" of any White House officer with ties to interest groups
is to have him act not as an automatic advocate but as a quiet ombudsman.
The person in the Oval Office is president of all Americans; no significant
groups of citizens should ever feel that they are barred from discourse at
the White House. Not that they necessarily get what they want, but that
they have a hearing.

While Nixon was president, for instance, black civil rights leaders knew
that even though most of them were Democrats, they had at least two
doors into the president's house: Robert Brown's office and Leonard Garment's. When Whitney Young, executive director of the National Urban
League, complained that the Urban League was being slighted in the award
of federal social services contracts, Garment quietly researched the allega-
tion, concluded that Young may have been right. What happened next, on
December 22, 1970, was perhaps the most unusual White House session
ever held on behalf of an individual interest group. Nixon convened a
special Cabinet meeting, with Young and several Urban League aides present. The president went around the table, querying each Cabinet officer:
"How can your department help the Urban League?" Thanks to Nixon's
obvious personal interest and Garment's quiet advance preparations,
$21,240,000 in contracts were pledged within a month.

The author had a personal "ombudsman" experience, poignant and
much less pleasant. When the Ohio National Guard shot at a group of
students on the Kent State University campus in May of 1970, four were
killed and several wounded. Among the injured was a young man who was
paralyzed from the waist down. He and his friends asked to present to
someone in the White House their petition for a federal investigation of
the incident, alleging that the state investigation had been a whitewash.
The group came in, pushing the unfortunate student in his wheelchair.
Since President Nixon had already determined that he would not take such
an action, the visit was a tense and sad experience for everyone in the
room.

Yet the appointment needed to be granted, the discussion held. The presidency is a place of compassion; it is the people's house and the voices of the public deserve to be heeded, including those that speak of discontent or tragedy.

The public liaison staff, however, has a further set of objectives: to mobilize leadership support for the president's policies. Three masters of that art have been William Baroody, Jr., for Ford; Anne Wexler for Carter; and Wayne Valis for Reagan.

Baroody began with "Wednesday Meetings." As often as three times a month, different groups of influential citizens, twenty-four at a time, were invited to the Roosevelt Room of the White House, across the hall from the president's office. Trade-association leaders, agricultural groups, and chief executive officers of companies attended. They included fence-sitters and even some opponents of the president's policies. The attendees were invited to send in, ahead of time, a write-up of their views so that attention would be given to what most mattered to them. Cabinet members and senior White House staff spoke, each on a different topic, then led the ensuing discussions.

Each group was treated to lunch in the White House Mess, then resumed its session until midafternoon. President Ford and Vice President Rockefeller would usually drop by. When the meetings broke up, Baroody's staff made written summaries and would follow up some of the suggestions. From one such Wednesday session came the proposal to increase the limit on federally insured bank deposits, a suggestion later proposed to Congress and adopted.

The Wednesday experiment was then enlarged. "Tuesdays at the White House" were initiated. A single topic was identified and seventy to a hundred leaders assembled in the White House family theater for half a day to hear a Cabinet officer or an assistant secretary discuss it in detail. Veterans, educators, the handicapped, had the chance, under White House auspices, to quiz the senior administration officers responsible for the federal programs affecting them. There were many Tuesday sessions.

Finally, Baroody proposed a series of Town Hall–type meetings in cities across the nation. His staff colleagues resisted at first, fearful of being thrown embarrassing questions from uncontrolled audiences. He was told to try one in Atlanta. Baroody flew to Atlanta, sought out a cross section of ten to twenty private organizations (the Southern Christian Leadership Conference, for one), and arranged for *them* to be the public sponsors of the Town Hall gatherings, in exchange for which he would ensure the appearance of Executive Branch leaders from Washington. In fact, President Ford came in person.

Baroody's staff quizzed the resident federal executives, and leaders of the organizations themselves, to ferret out which federal policy issues were most on their minds; he guaranteed that each of the sponsoring groups could ask the president at least one question of its choice. He sent word back to the four or five Cabinet and White House staff officers what most of the questions were going to be; they, as well as the president, were ready with well-researched answers.

The evening before the event, private dinners were arranged for the Cabinet members to meet with important local leaders. The next day, some sixteen hundred people paid fifteen dollars each to be in the audience and to help defray expenses. Demonstrators were glared down by the local sponsors; this was their own affair and they had a stake in making sure it was orderly. After the prearranged questions, there was an open question period, the president and his advisers on the receiving end. Local television stations and the PBS network covered the sessions live, but the interrogators were the citizens themselves, not the professional press.

President Ford enjoyed the occasion so much that Baroody scheduled thirteen more across the nation, calling them Public Forums on Domestic Policy. Baroody reached across lines of partisanship; the San Diego forum listed the California Labor Federation, AFL-CIO, as one of its cosponsors. President Ford went to every one of the forums; Cabinet members who originally were doubtful later felt insulted if they were not invited. As a forum concluded, Baroody's staff would study the transcript and pull out queries that needed supplementary answers; then he would write reminders to the appropriate Cabinet officers to follow through with direct letters to the questioners. Each town meeting required three months of staff work by Baroody and his associates. Soon his name became a verb; the *Wall Street Journal* whimsically asked: "Is the nation ready to be 'Baroodied'?"[8]

The Town Hall sessions naturally were of political use to Ford, even though he did not win in 1976. The fourteen forums set an impressive example of a president meeting his public in person; they also illustrated the intense White House staff work that was indispensable for him to do so.

After fifteen months in office, President Carter sought out a similarly talented public liaison chief and found her in Anne Wexler. As in Baroody's time, there were interest-group specialists on the White House staff, but Wexler built a new and parallel Liaison Office aimed at the specific issues on which Carter needed public support for congressional passage, such as SALT, hospital cost containment, the Panama Canal treaties, energy, and the urban initiatives.

Her tactic was meetings in the White House; her objective was to enlist support for legislation by inviting the interest groups themselves to help write it. She wanted no repetition of the energy program of a year before when it was, as she observed, "drafted in a closet."

The urban proposals required fourteen bills to be sent to Congress; Wexler brought in representatives from the Conference of Mayors, the National League of Cities, the National Governors' Association, the NAACP, and the Urban League. She put them together with Stuart Eizenstat and his domestic policy staff associates. "Every piece of that legislation went through group scrutiny," she recalled, and was subject to a " 'Hey, I have a different idea!' review." When the draft bills were sent to the Congress, the legislators could be told which groups already were in support; those representatives were then summoned for testimony.

Important local and state luminaries were invited to briefings along with the usual Washington representatives. Wexler would get the names from congressmen and senators (including Republicans at times). When the invitations were issued, the legislator would be notified; he or she could then call the invitees and tell them, "I put your name on the White House list," the credit then being shared at both ends of Pennsylvania Avenue. (On one occasion, an Indiana senator's list included a woman who turned out to be a hooker from Indianapolis. She let the press know of her White House invitation and explained that she had to turn extra "tricks" to earn the airfare to Washington. The White House comment to news inquiries was, "Go ask the senator!" In the end, the woman came to the briefing.)

In conducting the briefings, Wexler or her "issue" staff members would lay out the questions for discussion; Cabinet members or senior White House officers would appear for substantive dialogue. The job of the "interest group" staffers (for blacks, Jews, women, senior citizens) was to do the inviting—to fill the room.

And fill it and fill it, hour after hour. Wexler's calendar for the week of March 26, 1979, lists fifty-three briefings or interagency task-force meetings that she or her staff arranged: "SALT Strategy," "American Agricultural Editors," "Women in Timber," etc.

When the meetings ended, local press would be waiting in the White House driveway so that Bishop X or Company President Y could emerge and say, "I just told the president my views," or "Now that I have heard the facts, I support the Carter initiative." Occasionally, the statement would be "I still don't like what the president is doing," an upsetting development for Press Secretary Jody Powell, but that was a gamble Wexler took. At times, the best she could do was to have an organization stay neutral instead of move into opposition, be silent rather than speak against.

As her predecessors had done in the years before, Wexler put together unlikely coalitions for ad hoc purposes. When Carter vetoed the appropriations for an aircraft carrier, she mixed the National Taxpayers League with antimilitary activists; the ratification of the Panama Canal treaties was helped by foreign-policy groups, cities whose economic health depended on the canal's staying open, and businessmen eager for a stable government in Panama.

Even the budget process opened up a crack under her leverage. Wexler persuaded an initially skeptical budget director to permit interest groups to discuss expenditure issues at the Office of Management and Budget during the crucial fall budget season. Such sessions gave both spenders and economizers a sense of what compromises were possible, where resistance or agreement would be likely in Congress. "Some of those outside groups even went away with a feeling that they had a stake in the budget process," Wexler commented, "whereas in earlier years they only saw the budget after it had been delivered to the Congress. This was another way of following a respected principle in Washington: you don't surprise even your opponents; you don't blindside them."[9] She burned no bridges, recognizing that one's adversary today may be an ally tomorrow.

Wexler even chaired a confidential "Wednesday Group" of former Democratic Hill staffers and White House alumni. Criticism from them to her about Carter and his policies flowed uninhibitedly; it was an occasion for ruthless candor. The group agreed that if there was ever one leak from their meetings they would never get together again. They kept their promises and met in private for three years. Amid the "me too" pressures of any White House, such sessions are useful antidotes.

From the whole range of meetings that she and her staff conducted, Wexler gathered unique intelligence which she then passed to the president himself. Each week she wrote Carter a succinct "Activities Report," and while most of them were upbeat in tone, she would alert him to objections that were being raised to parts of his program, caution him about what perceptions he was generating, and request specific presidential follow-ups.

The preparatory staff work, however, was extraordinary. One memorandum to the president read: "For your information, our office had over 2000 people in the White House this week, not including Sunday's Anniversary of the Israel-Egypt Peace Treaty. This involved stuffing over 2000 information packets and [making] over 1000 telephone calls."[10] Another admitted that "we have a lot of work to do!"

Carter read each report and scratched comments and questions in the margins. Wexler and her staff were one of his important windows into the sentiments of the nation's leadership.

"I was in no one's pocket," Wexler remembers. "I never pounded the table on behalf of any group. I was nobody's person except Jimmy Carter's."[11]

In Ronald Reagan's first term, Wayne Valis, a deputy to public liaison chief Elizabeth Dole, kept his eye on one target: the Congress. He had served in Nixon's and Ford's liaison offices and knew the American business community from four years of that experience.

During the summer of 1981, the issue at the Capitol was the massive Reagan budget changes and tax cuts. In the Democratic House of Representatives, could bipartisan support be generated to vote the Reagan program into law?

The Antilobbying Act prohibits any government officer, including members of the White House staff, from urging the public to put pressure on the Congress. Every public liaison officer knows these limits; if letters, telegrams, and phone calls are to be generated, they must be the actions of private organizations.

The business community has exceptional pressure capabilities. Political action committees can send letters directed by computers to addressees in specified congressional districts. The National Federation of Independent Business can post an "action alert" to six hundred thousand small businessmen. The business community supported the Reagan program, and Valis made a survey of the potentialities he could enlist.

His first objective was to mobilize a coalition of eleven hundred business organizations. From the Valis recommendations, one thousand letters of invitation were prepared for the president's signature to individual business executives; they were asked to come to the White House to begin the campaign.

Reagan met with them. "We need your help," he reportedly explained. "I am not going to ask you for money; I want your *'blood.'* "

As the support commitments were given, Valis followed through with the Washington representatives of the same companies and organizations. When the Securities Industry Association volunteered to send fifteen thousand Mailgrams, Valis watched the mailing process, even went to congressional offices to see that the mailbags were coming in. All the coalition organizations recognized, however, that the most effective weapon was the telephone. Valis supplied the eleven hundred companies and organizations with the necessary facts, names, and numbers.

In careful step with the White House Political Office, the speechwriters, the legislative affairs staff, and with OMB and Treasury, Director Dole organized briefings for additional groups that might want to join the coalition. Doubters were invited, too: senior citizens, consumers; they were apprehensive of the Reagan proposals but would listen to White House explanations. "You may preach to the choir sometimes," said one aide, "but you always try to reach the folks in the back row of the church."

The campaign rolled to success. Valis framed the July 30, 1981, *Washington Star* account on his wall:

A TIDAL WAVE OF CALLS CARRIES THE DAY FOR THE G.O.P.

House Speaker Thomas P. O'Neill calls it "a telephone blitz like this nation has never seen." A senior White House official boasts of a "tidal wave of not entirely spontaneous origin."

Semantics aside, both agree that it was ultimately the telephone bombardment of wavering House Democrats which shattered the fragile coalition that Democratic leaders thought only 48 hours ago would produce the first major legislative victory over President Reagan.

"We had matched Reagan maneuver for maneuver until the phones started ringing off the wall," lamented one House Democratic leader. "The telegrams we could withstand, but not that damn Alexander Graham Bell."[12]

Valis played within the law, but it was a hardball game nonetheless. Some of the domestic Cabinet chieftains were told: if businessmen come to you for favors, ask first to see the note signed "Valis" which says that they have been "cooperative." When the business community presented the White House with their "ten most costly and burdensome" government regulations, Valis asked the same complainers: "What have you done for *us?*"

A much tougher challenge came in 1982. President Reagan was asking that some taxes be raised; he was taking away part of the goodies given to the business community the year before. This campaign had to have different themes. Companies could not be shown that they would benefit economically, as in 1981; now the appeal was "Tax adjustment is in the broad sense good public policy." This time the coalition was only eighty-strong.

The U.S. Chamber of Commerce was a battleground. The night the president gave his television address to the nation, Public Liaison Director Dole had invited eight on-the-fence members of the board of the Chamber to sit in the White House Roosevelt Room and watch the broadcast. She and Valis exuded graciousness, diplomacy—and power. As soon as the president had finished, he came across the hall. "Well, boys, how did I do? How did I do with *you* gents?" The eight returned to the Chamber boardroom and the resulting split weakened the Chamber's opposition. The president got his bill.

Valis was an experienced networker. The Business Roundtable would invite him to attend the meetings of its thirty Washington representatives. He would share his knowledge of the president's priorities with them; they would let him know their concerns. Returning to the White House, Valis would prepare "early warning" memoranda to Chief of Staff James Baker, alert him to problems, and suggest phoning thank-you messages to key supporters. Baker would make the calls and the Valis credibility would go one notch higher.

Even these accounts of three masters of the public liaison practice do not illustrate the full range of the techniques the office employs. In addition to the briefings already described, there are "crowd gathering" meetings in the Residence's East Room ("autographed" pictures are sent to those on the dais), "staged events" in the Oval Office (more "autographed" photos), and teas for women's groups with the first lady. Each event requires a schedule proposal, a briefing paper for the president or his spouse, and research to produce the right phrases, anecdotes, and background. Afterward, a meeting summary is prepared and letters are sent enclosing the "autographed" pictures to the dozens of participants.

Different public liaison chiefs vary in their handling of outside organizations. Some will insist that the public liaison office be the exclusive portal into the White House, but Washington-wise groups will find ways around such barriers. A quid pro quo may be enforced for briefings: the outside groups get the speakers and subjects they want, but first must listen to the White House "line" on its own priority topics, such as the Strategic Defense Initiative, or aid to the contras.

Ingenuity is always a tool of the liaison staff. If farm organizations complain about missile silos, get them together with the Air Force. To stir up business sympathy for the contras, talk about Sandinista and Cuban threats to Caribbean sea-lanes. But when the Gay Alliance knocks on the door, the meeting will be hosted over at the Department of Health and Human Services.

White House perquisites are not merely for the staff's personal enjoyment; they are instruments of persuasion as well. Lunches at the Mess, invitations to state dinners, evening viewings of the Oval Office, being asked to signing ceremonies or South Lawn arrivals, use of the presidential boxes at the Kennedy Center, barbecues at Camp David—"This is powerful stuff," one Reagan alumnus recalled; "we didn't use them enough."

The relationships are not merely manipulative, as the Wexler and Valis examples illustrate. The policy process itself may be enriched by outside comment. Business groups were invited to argue to the Reagan administration, for instance, that uniform federal product-liability standards were better than a hodgepodge of fifty state laws; the Cabinet Committee on Commerce and Trade listened to their advice and changed its recommendations. Representatives for the disabled were apprehensive about regulations limiting special education benefits; the Office of Public Liaison put them in touch with the Vice President's Regulatory Review Task Force and a new agreement was reached with the Department of Education.

For any president, public liaison staffers are a kind of outer shield, every day facing and meeting with representatives of that contentious society described in chapter 1. Most of the interactions are civil, some result in true battlefield alliances. But the public liaison shock troops occasionally absorb punishment; one White House speaker had a tomato thrown at her. "We were out on the front lines, really getting beat up pretty badly," remembered another White House alumna.

Particularly frustrating are the vehement differences *within* groups that on the surface would seem to share common ties. Native Americans, blacks, Jews, women, are themselves splintered into contending factions. The Indian "representative in the White House" is tormented by intragroup dissension among native Americans.

The experience of at least twenty years has shown that the only successful public liaison officers are those with a professional appreciation for the pluralism of American society. The zealot who divides the claimants at the White House gates into rigid categories of good guys and bad guys will end up burned out, and will even singe his or her president with the hot fumes of frustration.

An extension of the president himself, the Office of Public Liaison is a bargainer in the great American political market. Its wiser members know that they win some and lose others, are in no group's pocket, make no permanent enemies, but are at home in the turbulent marketplace. Presidents find such bargaining support indispensable; they will continue to use staff who can open the White House gates and, while negotiating alliances with some, keep listening to all.

CHAPTER 15

Achievements versus Activities: The Scheduling Office

What does a President want to do with his years in office? What is his concept of governing? We made up a four-year schedule, anticipating all the major events of his term. With that we could plan an overarching program of achievements. Without it, every day would simply fill up with activities.

—David N. Parker
Former appointments secretary
to President Nixon

Secretary of Transportation John Volpe made repeated requests for appointments with Nixon to discuss matters the president considered secondary. When he was invited to a religious service at the White House, he came down the receiving line, stopped in front of the president, pulled out a note card and began taking up business matters on the spot.

—A White House staff officer

The appointments secretary and his or her staff, known collectively as the Appointments and Scheduling Office, are much more than mere calendar-keepers. By allocating a president's time, they make possible—or impossible—the accomplishments by which he is judged; they help shape his legacy for history.[1]

There is an inevitable progression for a president, from the goals he holds to the themes he emphasizes to the events in which he participates. If there is no long-range plan against which to measure the cascade of requests, his day will surely fill up, but instead of achievements there will only be activities.

"Sixty percent of the president's time tends to be committed to engagements about which he has little choice," observed President Reagan's director of appointments and scheduling, Frederick Ryan. "Intelligence briefings, Cabinet, national security, legislative, and staff meetings are preordained. If he did just those things, however, nothing remarkable would come out of his administration. It is the remaining forty percent of his time which can creatively be used to accomplish the important initiatives and goals of his administration."[2]

Few outside the White House recognize or acknowledge the presidential priority for accomplishments over activities; even some White House staffers get it backward. Cabinet members request meetings on nonurgent matters, congressmen pressure the president to see their constituents, and political and public groups petition to stage Oval Office events or to have the president speak at their meetings. The State Department and the national security assistant, for instance, urge that the president invite not only foreign chiefs of state to the United States, but allow visiting foreign ministers to call on the president as well as on their protocol opposite, the secretary of state; they also urge that the president welcome new ambassadors who are presenting their credentials.[3]

All of these demands for time are legitimate, but most of them are not in accord with the president's own needs. "I want to be in the saddle, not saddled," Nixon would tell his aides.

It is only the White House staff, and within that circle, only the chief of staff and the Scheduling Office who, again and again, raise the more significant standard of *achievements* to fend off the daily pressures for mere *activities*. They must next translate that standard into a specific management tool: a long-range schedule. The Carter and Reagan staffs looked forward ten months; the Nixon Scheduling Office was told to draw up a four-year calendar.

The first reaction to a four-year plan was "It can't be done!" but that judgment was premature; the staff found it was both possible and valuable. First were listed the major international events that were certain or hoped for: the economic summits with Japan, Canada, and Mexico; chiefs of state meetings with the USSR and with NATO; other foreign trips; visits of foreign leaders to Washington. White House Conferences (on Children and Youth and similar precedents) could be anticipated. There were the known holidays, and there were the major national organizations' conventions at which a Republican president would be expected to speak. If they could be estimated, "preemptive" events were planned as well—presidential newsmakers that would take attention away from either domestic or international opponents. ("Creative scheduling" as a public relations maneuver was described in chapter 12.)

Each month of the four years was plotted and the whole was then judged against Nixon's personal policy priorities. Unexpected events like crises or funerals of course would arise, but the governing objective was to minimize the unknown and the unplanned.

Perhaps only in the disciplined Nixon White House could a four-year-schedule experiment be undertaken. For any president, however, a forward-looking schedule will fail without tough staff enforcement from the center.

What is the scheduling process in the modern White House?

First, a familiar instruction issues: no one on the White House staff except the Appointments Office is to make scheduling commitments. The reader is familiar with these exclusivity mandates. The scheduling process involves another one of them; it cannot tolerate more than one decision channel for the president's calendar.

To set scheduling objectives in the future, the Reagan practice had been periodically to convene a long-range planning group among staffers from domestic policy, legislative, cabinet affairs, communications, public liaison, political affairs, and from the first lady's, vice president's, and chief of staff's offices. The appointments secretary prepared a "pretend" six-month calendar block on which existing commitments were recorded. Shown also were other possible future choices that the scheduling staff grouped according to subject themes, each theme area color-coded: education, national security, tax reform, and so forth. Decisions could be made according to topic category, so that the theme chosen could be underscored by repeated presidential events, visits, photo opportunities, and personal addresses or speeches by Cabinet surrogates.

Such planning discussion linked scheduling priorities together with the staff's legislative, political, and policy assessments. The chief of staff then would go over the long-range menu monthly with the president. Wrote Larry Speakes, "Almost no news item, no speech, no trip, no photo-op whatsoever was put on the President's schedule during 1981 unless it contributed to the President's economic program."[4]

Meanwhile, in a typical day, one hundred and fifty requests would arrive. If they were oral, the originators were told to put their petitions in writing.

A superbly skilled aide (her experience in the Scheduling Office totals thirty-five years) would make the initial selection, combing out half of the requests; these would receive immediate regret letters. The deputy appointments secretary reviewed the other half, eighty percent of which were usually judged to be of inadequate priority, the planned events being of local or regional rather than national significance.

The ten percent of calendar proposals from the public that seemed to have merit would be circulated under a distinctive "yellow sheet" to perhaps a dozen senior staff colleagues; they were also entered into a computer for deadline tracking and for records. Unanimous negative votes would result in a regrets letter. If, as an alternative, a written presidential salutation was recommended, the Messages Unit would be given the file.

The twelve senior officers, including the first lady's and the vice president's chiefs of staff, then met weekly as a Scheduling Committee, chaired

during Reagan's first term by Michael Deaver. (The Scheduling Committee
was not a Reagan innovation; in Eisenhower's White House there was a
similar group of nine including the chairman of the Republican National
Committee.)

The committee would review four categories of calendar requests:

- Invitations from the public that survived the review just described.
- Requests from White House staff members (these had to be in a written
  "Schedule Proposal" format, the prescription for which has been almost iden-
  tical for seventeen years).
- Recommendations from Cabinet members for presidential events or speeches
  (these came into the White House through the Cabinet Affairs Office).
- Requests from Congress, which the legislative affairs chief brought to the
  meetings.

Perhaps forty items would be on the Scheduling Committee's agenda.
"We were glad to be inundated with schedule proposals," commented one
White House veteran. "The more we got, the more opportunities we had
to be creative." In the Nixon period, the same participant recalled, Cabinet
members were periodically circularized with requests for calendar suggestions. Asked to comment on the value of the suggestions received, he
responded with a one-word judgment: "Infertile."

At the committee meeting, a speaking invitation could be approved not
for an in-person appearance but for a videotaped message; the Television
Office would then make the follow-up arrangement. Proposals rejected for
presidential speeches but still considered worthy were often sent to the
vice president or to Cabinet members with the request that they or their
associates act as surrogates; there was a staff person in the Scheduling
Office who specialized in making such substitute arrangements.

Reject letters were signed by the appointments secretary, and with this
act it was he who absorbed the shockwaves of disappointment from the
would-be sponsors. Since the approval percentage was two out of a hundred, the scheduling job, in a sense, is 2 percent rewarding and 98 percent
frustration.

The Reagan staff learned not to inform the president himself about the
turndowns; he was too softhearted. If he heard about a Scout group or
some other deserving sponsor that didn't make the cut, he was known to
overrule the disciplined system and order that exceptions be made. So close
is any appointment secretary's relationship with the president that he can
often make final calendar decisions in the president's name. A controversial, sensitive, or split-view recommendation is always discussed with the
boss.

When finally approved as a presidential appearance, by or for the president, the calendar decisions were posted by a second thirty-five-year Scheduling Office veteran on a "narrative schedule," an hour-by-hour listing reaching out two weeks in advance. A computer memorized every action and only the Scheduling Office was privy to its all-important disks.

While necessarily methodical, the decision process is not inflexible; informal conversations among the president, the staff, and Cabinet members fill the interstices in any White House system. Cabinet members' personal requests to see Reagan were handled separately through the Cabinet secretary, while foreign-affairs appointments, as is typical in any White House, were scrutinized by the national security assistant. Procedure is always tempered with improvisation; Reagan's narrative schedule itself had to be revised twice daily.

A schedule decision, however, is only an intermediate stage in the necessary White House staff work. The Scheduling Office would dispatch a "setup" memorandum for each "approved presidential activity," alerting the Secret Service, the first lady, the press secretary, and others who needed the advance information. For each such event, a project officer on the staff was designated to be fully in charge of all preparations. (The Scheduling Office itself was the project office for events which did not have a specific contact person in the White House and for meetings with old presidential friends.) Like an airline pilot, the project officer would be given a checklist containing items such as: prepare the briefing papers, put the names of all attendees into the computer for the gate security, alert the calligrapher, coordinate with the press secretary. In each of the senior White House offices, there was a specialist who concentrated on staff work for presidential events. Each morning the Scheduling Office would call all the next day's project officers to verify that the "set up" checklists were being adhered to. Last-minute changes occurred constantly and the telephone lines would heat up among the wide circle that had to be renotified. Except for such eleventh-hour amendments, however, oral communications were eschewed; when commitments or arrangements were being made for the president, the staff had learned that the ironclad written word was much to be preferred over word-of-mouth understandings.

The afternoon before the event, fourteen copies of the briefing memorandum had to reach the staff secretary. On the preceding evening, the appointments secretary made up the final schedule, which in turn became the first page of the president's daily notebook containing the briefing papers to match each item on the calendar. The appointments secretary also made some thirty card-sized minicopies of the president's daily schedule, delivering them to the seniormost staff colleagues for insertion in a maroon, windowed pocket-holder that each carried. The staff member's own schedule could show through the back window; thus has a small new perquisite been introduced into White House practice—a cachet of inner-circleness.

Humor is a part of the job. For Reagan's birthday in 1985, the Scheduling Office played a trick of sorts. As the president was getting in his car for a breakfast across town, he was handed a "schedule" for the day. It included a "Signing Ceremony to Repeal the 22nd Amendment," a "Meeting with the Ronald Reagan 1988 Exploratory Committee," and an "Interview in Antarctica with Local Correspondent Sam Donaldson."

When a group event is taking place in the Oval Office, the scheduling staff has an additional responsibility: conniving to relieve visitors of gifts that they often bring to unload on the president. At the entrance gate, magnetometers of course have scoured each person for any dangerous articles, but enthusiastic visitors will, approaching the president, fish into their purses or pockets for "little things for you from the folks back home." A fan-club member from Reagan's Hollywood days wanted to present a trash can decorated with labels; visitors will try to hand-deliver letters; one former campaign associate brought a whole shopping bag of presents. The scheduling officers will diplomatically say, "Let me hold your purse; you don't want it to show in the picture, do you?" (In response to oral entreaties from visitors, the president finally became well trained; eschewing commitments, he would promise "to look into your problem.")

For one person in the Scheduling Office, the end of a presidential day is only the beginning. To her desk in the ensuing week come reports of every minute of each day that was. She is the presidential diarist and the unique collection she assembles is the aperture into the history of his years in office.

The chief usher and the Secret Service tell the diarist when the president arose and when he went to bed, and who if any were his guests for breakfast, lunch, or dinner. The listed schedule is in fifteen-minute segments, but no real day goes like that. At 10:02 he talked with Senator X about arms control, at 10:19 Chairman Y called him on tax reform. The meeting planned for 10:30 didn't start until 10:42; two invited participants never came but three extras were added (the gate guards send her their names). The staff secretary contributes copies of the briefing papers; the accompanying staff and the Secret Service give her minute accounts of the president's trips around town or abroad. Only sensitive national security papers are handled separately.

It all goes into the diarist's computer: the name of every person who met with the president, the agenda of every meeting, in whatever room, every telephone call, almost every topic. The computer organizes them both chronologically and alphabetically, and inside of a week she has a complete account of each day, together with the unclassified papers accompanying each session. The presidential diarist ends up with a documented minute-by-minute account of the chief executive's life in office.

These files will be the principal guides to the presidential archives to come—the tracks into history for the retired president and for the authors and scholars of the future. But they have a current use as well. Does the counsel want to know who was with the president on a given day three years ago? Did topic A come up at last year's meeting? The records are available at the touch of a button (through a tightly controlled access code).

The presidential diarist is a professional, an employee of the National Archives and Records Administration. She has been on duty continuously in the White House since January of 1974.

It was the experienced Bryce Harlow who summed up the scheduling task. The problem is always to prioritize: every presidential activity approved means some other activity forgone. The scheduling decision-making, he commented, "must be a tight process, not loosely run like a country store, because a President's got too much of too much importance clamoring consistently for his time."[5] "It's a protective job," remembered Eisenhower's former appointments secretary Bernard Shanley. Said another alumna of the scheduling staff, "I would have to say no in nine hundred ninety-nine different ways." There is even a political cost; those disappointed are regretful, even angry, and each day occasions many more disappointments than delights. Yet there is no way around the discipline that must be imposed, no way to handle scheduling casually.

In the larger sense, the appointments secretary and his scheduling staff are more than just the severe managers of the day's calendar; they are, in a tradition going back decades, pacemakers of the White House heartbeat. Their judgment and skill help make the difference, over the president's years in the White House, between a record of presidential achievements and a catalog of mere activities. In serving the man, they serve the office, helping to preserve its dignity and to ensure its proper role.

CHAPTER 16

Ombudsman for Federalism: The Office of Intergovernmental Relations

More than once I was called to Agnew's office to hear his complaints. If he were going to do the intergovernmental relations job for the President, he'd say, he had to have more help from the White House staff. . . . I tried to explain that such staff people usually were following established Presidential policy, which probably didn't please the mayor or governor Vice President Agnew had on the phone. That was why they were calling him. His job was to sell our policy to them, not theirs to us.　　　—John Ehrlichman

As governor I had been frustrated and angered by the absence of even minimal cooperation between the Nixon White House and state and local leaders. The system of federalism had almost completely broken down. . . . When I was elected President, I was determined to let the governors, mayors and county officials know that they were part of my team and would always have unimpeded access to my office. . . . I wanted them to be partners with me. . . .

—Jimmy Carter

Ehrlichman was unkind. Even the executive order that Nixon signed creating the Office of Intergovernmental Relations had no directive to "sell our policy." Nixon's instructions to Vice President Agnew in fact told him to "help make the Federal executive branch . . . more sensitive, receptive and responsive to the views of State and local officials."[1] And Carter was using hyperbole. No one gets "unimpeded access" to the Oval Office, especially when bearing complaints or advocacy. The intergovernmental relations staff is—and has been for some thirty-three years—in the middle between these two sets of expectations.[2]

It was the Kestnbaum Presidential Commission on Intergovernmental Relations that included in its 1955 recommendations the proposal that each president have

a Special Assistant in the Executive Office . . . to serve with a small staff as the President's chief aide and adviser on State and local relationships. He should give his exclusive attention to these matters throughout the government. He would be the coordinating center.[3]

Since February of the same year, former Arizona Governor Howard Pyle had been an administrative assistant to President Eisenhower working with governors and mayors; in 1956 he was elevated to be deputy assistant to the president with the specific responsibility for intergovernmental relations. Pyle experienced the continuing dilemma of the man in the middle between conflicting local advocacies:

> Fifteen [Chamber of Commerce] people would arrive at the White House to sit down and belabor you about the budget . . . and how desperately it needed to be cut . . . the taxes were . . . confiscatory. . . . You could just get lacerated from head to foot. . . . Two weeks later, the mayor of the same city would arrive in town in search of urban renewal grants. . . . I would listen very carefully . . . would say 'Now, gentlemen . . . I had a delegation in this very room from your town. . . . What am I supposed to believe? . . . The mayor would reach in his pocket for his principal supporters, and 75% of the names on his list were guys who were in last week. . . .
>
> We talk out of both sides of our mouth about what we want government to do . . . between those who want to economize and those who want to spend, and very, very often they're the same people, in a different costume each time they come. . . . You simply can't save money and spend it at the same time.[4]

Besides sweating out such an uncomfortable ombudsman role, the early and elemental task of a White House Intergovernmental Relations Office was to provide information on the specific activities federal agencies were initiating that would have a local impact, and those programs the federal government was managing that could assist state and local governments. Kennedy's White House had an intergovernmental relations staff of two, and it was they who addressed the first of those information needs. They persuaded Kennedy to sign a presidential directive to the departments that told the agencies to notify governors and mayors in advance about major federal projects so that those local officials would be informed before the bulldozers arrived.[5]

President Johnson in 1965 began the practice of assigning intergovern-mental-affairs oversight to the vice president's office. Hubert Humphrey, having been the mayor of a major city (Minneapolis), was asked to keep in touch with mayors; a year later, county officials were added to his liaison charge. Johnson's Office of Emergency Planning was designated as the link to governors and OEP's three successive directors were themselves former governors. OEP was an Executive Office organization, however, not a personal White House staff unit.[6]

Humphrey, seeing the need to meet the second of the elemental sets of information essential for governors and mayors, spurred the Office of Economic Opportunity to pull together a *Catalogue of Federal Domestic Assistance*

Programs. First published in 1967, it was a massive fact book that listed, and grouped by categories, every domestic federal-aid activity, including eligibility requirements for each, the resources available, and the office to which would-be recipients should apply. When OEO was terminated in 1981, the Office of Management and Budget became responsible for preparing and publishing the catalog. It is now a "standard text" in the hands of state and local administrators; three copies are also sent to every senator and congressman.

Nixon began his administration by assigning the intergovernmental-affairs responsibility to Vice President (and former Governor) Agnew. After his reelection in 1972, however, that assignment was transferred to the Domestic Council, a part of President Nixon's own White House staff.

It was the White House staff that, more effectively than the other offices that had been tried, could pursue the task of intergovernmental trouble-shooting. The "trouble" was usually in Washington itself.

Chapter 1 described the plural nature of the president's Executive Branch. To local administrators not familiar with the federal landscape, it is a jungle indeed. Carter's former deputy assistant for intergovernmental relations observes: "Most of the state and local government officials' view of the federal government is that it's a monstrous, impenetrable, agency-by-agency fortress that one has to fight with to get the job done."[7]

Sharing that perspective, as evidenced in the second epigraph at the beginning of this chapter, and to fulfil the promise described there, President Carter designated Jack Watson to be both secretary to the Cabinet and to track the implementation of domestic policy decisions made at Cabinet meetings, working with departments and with local governments to do so. "The only job in the White House I would rather have than yours, is mine," Carter once told Watson.[8] In August of 1978, by executive order, Carter created an Interagency Coordinating Council and named Watson as chairman.[9] To ensure no misunderstanding as to who was their contact at the White House, the president would include Watson's home telephone number in his out-of-town speeches to local leaders. The states and cities lost no time in making their way to Watson's door.

Long Beach, California, for example, had developed a plan for its waterfront, but four federal agencies (Community Development, Economic Development, the Federal Highway Administration, and the Corps of Engineers) had to dovetail their programs to let it happen. Watson's staff added some White House glue to the mixture.

The mayor of Charleston, West Virginia, telephoned to complain that federal highway funds were going to be used to build interchanges for a shopping center that would siphon jobs and business from downtown.

Knowing the priorities of Carter's urban policy, Watson convened an extraordinary meeting of the governor of West Virginia, the mayor, and federal officials. The highway plans were changed. Watson's Coordinating Council then developed a generalized interagency agreement concerning shopping centers: if any mayor was apprehensive about such a development that might weaken his urban economy, the Department of Housing and Urban Development would make an analysis of the plans. If the mayor's concern was substantiated, the White House would ask federal agencies such as the Corps of Engineers (which granted permits for dredging and filling) or the Department of Transportation (which funded new roads and interchanges) to withdraw federal support for the offending development.

The administrator of general services informed the president that in spite of Carter's urban policy statement, federal departments were reluctant to relocate their offices into central cities. Carter scrawled on the memo, "J. Watson, help with this"; at least one agency was persuaded to alter a planned move to suburbia.[10]

The South Bronx needed interagency help for rehabilitation. Watson and his staff saw to it that self-help housing, subway-station improvements, and manpower-training initiatives were combined with an economic development grant for a small industrial park. The Watson office worked out a general criterion for giving priority to otherwise equally meritorious housing-grant applications according to the numbers of jobs generated for the disadvantaged. Manpower-training funds would then be committed to supplement the housing subsidies. Often it was only the White House that could negotiate such "treaties" between the Housing and Labor departments.

The General Services Administration could choose how to dispose of excess federal properties; the Department of Transportation had abandoned railway stations available. Implementation of these and other elements of Carter's urban policy stretched into nearly every corner of his Executive Branch. Wherever they stretched, Watson and his staff reached as well.

"There are powerful statutory tools to make interagency cooperation work on an intergovernmental basis," Watson's deputy, Eugene Eidenberg, commented,

> but it requires political will and political leadership from a place that can command it. [The president] can say . . . "I want this policy to be implemented," but if there isn't somebody driving it, it's going to be another book on the shelf.
> We had the entire panoply of agencies of the United States government—

Small Business Administration, independent agencies, Cabinet agencies; trying
to glue them, work them, paste them together, in response to particular, customized program priorities, coming out of a political process at the state and local
government level—it could never have been done, in my judgment, without
senior staff leadership.[11]

An undernoticed part of the American federal system are the more than
two hundred federally recognized Indian tribal governments. Some of the
communities over which they preside are the nation's poorest places. Their
reservations are federal lands, however, defined in treaties signed with the
federal government; their water and other resource rights are held in trust
for them by the United States. For this reason, elected Indian leaders have
a special relationship directly to the federal government for their legal
protection and their welfare. The Nixon and Ford administrations began
the practice of designating a White House staff officer to keep track of
Indian affairs and to coordinate the work of the many federal agencies that
provide assistance to them; the Reagan administration located this responsibility in its Intergovernmental Relations Office. It belongs there; native
governments are not just "interest groups," but are a continuing part of the
American federal community.[12]

The policy-making role of the Intergovernmental Relations Office was
especially prominent under President Reagan when its director, Richard S.
Williamson, led the development of the 1982 New Federalism initiative.
At its meetings in 1980 and 1981, the National Governors' Association,
fortified by studies from the Advisory Council on Intergovernmental Relations, adopted resolutions calling for a major reform of the American
federal system.[13] It was overloaded, the studies found, and needed to be
decongested. Its division of labor between the national government and
states should be sorted out anew.

A new Advisory Committee on Federalism, appointed by Reagan and
chaired by Senator Paul Laxalt, had been meeting during 1981 (twice with
the president). Its membership of forty-two senators, congressmen, governors, mayors, state legislators, county officials, and private citizens was a
testing ground for ideas from on-the-scene experience. The staff work for
the committee—setting its agenda, drafting papers for its consideration,
writing its decision memoranda—was done in the White House by Williamson and his colleagues. While the Advisory Committee did not issue
a formal final report, its dialogues paved the way for the next steps that
Williamson took within the White House. President Reagan himself had
spent much time during his first year in meetings with more than fourteen
hundred state and local officials; the Williamson office initiated the sched-

ule proposals, provided the briefings and follow-up notes, and made the arrangements for these sessions.

As the time for the 1982 State of the Union message approached, the Reagan staff was looking for a "grand theme." Williamson, fortified by the Advisory Committee discussions, persuaded the private inner group of Meese, Baker, Deaver, and Stockman—and then the president—that the message theme should be New Federalism. Preparatory work was then needed on an unforgiving timetable; it was centered in the Office of Intergovernmental Affairs.

Eight policy papers were written by a Williamson-OMB team. The White House domestic policy staff did not play a central role, and even in the Intergovernmental Affairs Office only its senior members were privy to the new proposals. None of the documents were circulated to the Cabinet.

After two meetings with the president and the inner group of White House aides, Williamson drew up the final decision paper, which received presidential approval. As the speechwriters put together the State of the Union language, Williamson helped them write the crucial three pages, then reviewed their entire draft to ensure that the message was consistent with the central theme.

It was not until ten days before delivery of the message that the Cabinet members most affected were called to the White House to meet with Meese and Williamson. They were informed of what was coming, were told that the presidential decision had already been made, and were asked only for their comments on the best strategy for implementation. A paper was handed out for those present to read, then collected again as each member went out the door.

Why was this decision-making so centralized and secretive? From the start, it was clear to the White House that no one of the Cabinet departments could have carried this enterprise, even as a "lead agency," since some forty-three federal programs were involved in the intricate combination of swaps and turnbacks from federal to state jurisdiction or vice versa. As for secrecy, "We did not want any pressures from special-interest constituencies, from congressional committees or advocacy-oriented departmental staffs," Williamson commented later.[14] Health and Human Services Secretary Richard Schweiker admitted publicly that the White House "did in fact hold it very closely."[15] It was as if Williamson had studied the Carter urban policy experience and drunk in its lessons: if wholesale relandscaping of the federal turf is in prospect, only the White House can put the bulldozer in gear.

A day or two before the message was delivered, the full Cabinet was given a final description of the New Federalism, the president confirming in person that this new direction was a first-rank priority. Four days before the address, Williamson gave a detailed briefing to the two Republican congressional leaders, then a general overview to the rest of the Republican leadership. Selected state and local officials were invited to the White House for a sneak preview the day before the Message; at that point the president approved telephone calls by the Intergovernmental Affairs Office to a wider group of governors, mayors, and state legislators. On the day of the address, Williamson and Budget Director David Stockman conducted a three-hour press briefing, following which Williamson met individually with reporters from the *New York Times* and the *Washington Post.*

At least one Cabinet officer was sore about both substance and process; Secretary of Transportation Drew Lewis heard that part of the new gasoline tax he had been counting on was to be turned over to the states. He telephoned in to object. (The tax was later enacted as he had planned.) Health and Human Services Under Secretary David B. Swoap, a former California welfare director, was opposed to making Medicaid a wholly federal program. President Reagan, however, called a post–State of the Union Cabinet meeting and emphasized once again to the group how much he was committed to the New Federalism. That word, passed down to departmental subordinates, eased the follow-up task to which Williamson and his White House colleagues next turned.

Even a presidential State of the Union message is only a proposal, a generalized concept laid before the nation. For the New Federalism, the most difficult phase now lay ahead: negotiating the specifics with the state and local officials. This was also to be a White House–led undertaking.

Williamson and the president wasted no time; the first of more than twenty-five negotiating meetings took place the day following the State of the Union address. The president made three other major addresses before state legislatures.

To negotiate the specifics of the New Federalism with the Reagan White House, the governors named a team of six, state legislators selected six of their number, and county officials designated eleven for their consultations. These organizations all had large permanent Washington staffs; working papers—although still general in nature—were exchanged between Williamson's administration group and each of the negotiating teams. An internal "technical working group" made up of White House staff, the Office of Management and Budget, and six Cabinet departments was in nearly constant session.

Williamson and his deputies were at the center of the entire negotiating nexus, which lasted throughout the spring and summer of 1982. "It was a thoroughly professional operation," commented Stephen Farber, who was the executive director of the National Governors' Association at the time. "Williamson gave our views to the president and the president's perspectives to the governors, regardless of party. We both took pride in being honest brokers."[16] For his part, Williamson never forgot that Reagan had been a governor himself and would be especially willing to listen to the states' viewpoint.

The governors did not trust the Office of Management and Budget, however. They suspected that Director Stockman saw the New Federalism as a deficit-reducing device—and they were right. To them, that would be not New Federalism, but "cut-back federalism." They were suspicious of the domestic policy staff as well, perceiving that office as an ideologically slanted filter into the White House. Governor Richard A. Snelling (R, Vt) recalled the three contending White House factions:

> One [faction] believed in federalism. I think the President and Rich [Williamson] were in that group. Then there were people who wanted to use federalism to reduce the budget. And then there were people who were antigovernment. They not only wanted the federal government's influence shrunk, they wanted the local government shrunk.[17]

The three-way split, which Williamson believes President Reagan should have spent more time in resolving, blocked the administration's ability to translate its general proposals into specifics. Exactly how was Medicaid to be taken over by the federal government while welfare aid was to be assumed by the states? No draft legislation was ever put together by the Williamson-OMB team; without seeing how the proposed laws would read, the governors were not going to commit their support.

Williamson went personally to the National Governors' Association meeting in Oklahoma in August. They were about to approve a resolution calling off their negotiations with the White House, so Williamson huddled with several of them privately, then used ammunition that only a White House staff officer could detonate. He told two of the Republicans that if they wanted Reagan help in their reelection campaigns, they should throw their support to a substitute resolution "to continue discussion with the president regarding his federalism initiative." Wearing his White House hat, he reportedly reminded the Republican governors, "You guys don't have anybody else [but Reagan] to take you to this . . . and if you don't show more flexibility, we may just tell you to go to hell."[18]

The substitute resolution was approved.

This was neither the first nor the last visit of a White House intergovernmental relations chief to a governors' conference, but the 1982 conclave serves as an example of how such a presidential agent operates and how his unique White House position strengthens his bargaining power.

Without specifics and without draft legislation, the 1982 initiative in the end did not produce what its authors had hoped. It did, however, show how large a policy step could be made, as Stephen Farber observed, "with the energy and determination shown by Williamson [and] his deputies." Farber's own conclusion is the same as that of columnist David Broder: "Some future Rich Williamson will have to take up the cudgels for federalism . . . in somebody else's White House."[19]

Williamson and his associates under Reagan, and Watson and his staff under Carter, had more than just energy; they also had credibility with the nation's state and local governing officials, regardless of politics. Of course, they were partisans, as are most senior White House officers. Governors, mayors, county commissioners, state legislators, and tribal chairmen, however, are different from the other external constituencies with which the White House communicates: they exercise governmental power. It is for this reason that, ever since the Kestnbaum Commission urged it in 1955, there has been a designated White House office to respond to their concerns, at times in a completely nonpartisan fashion. Natural disasters, for instance, wear no political labels. Elected state and city leaders of both parties must have confidence that when official duties like disaster relief need White House "good offices," the intergovernmental relations staff will assure them of evenhanded treatment.

Although discretionary federal largesse, of course, is not immune from political calculations, the intergovernmental relations staff keeps all its bridges open. Williamson remembers that a Democratic governor or mayor would sometimes telephone him at the White House. "I am going to make a partisan attack on the Reagan administration," the caller would announce. "You understand the position I'm in." On occasion, the caller would even give Williamson a chance to suggest toning down passages where the partisanship was unjustified.

Throughout the American federal system, the work of governing imparts a sense of responsibility shared, even in the face of party differences. Watson, Williamson, their associates and successors aimed at conducting their White House ombudsmanship with not only the expected partisan advocacy but also with an admixture of professional respect for all the men and women who are elected to public office in America.

CHAPTER 17

Doing the Thrustworthy Thing: The Office of Political Affairs

My job is to thrust out the Democrats, and I find that a very thrustworthy thing to do. I am going to move around here and do my damndest to thrust them.

—LYN NOFZIGER

Those people around Nixon were not Republicans in the sense of trying to build the party. Their only interest was in reelecting the President. . . . As for the Republican National Committee, we were relegated to the back of the bus . . . no, the truth is we weren't ever on the bus at all.

—ROBERT DOLE
Senator and former
RNC Chairman

When political affairs director Lyn Nofziger was asked by one Reagan backer what he considered to be political, he reportedly replied, "Everything." That one-word answer is an accurate summation of the White House environment. Every presidential issue is political in the broad sense that the decisions the president makes test the limits of consensus in the country. Partisanship in its narrower meaning colors each presidential action as well. If it succeeds, there is political hay to be made; if even a "nonpartisan" national security initiative crashes, the president's electoral standing plunges with it. Johnson's policies in Vietnam forced him out of the presidential race. The Iran-contra affair damaged Reagan. The U-2 shootdown denied Eisenhower his visit to the Soviet Union, robbing the 1960 elections of what would have been the afterglow from such a triumphal tour. But Ford's popularity surged after the *Mayaguez* crisis, and yes, the picture of tots rolling Easter eggs on the nonpolitical White House lawn under the eyes of a human-sized White House rabbit leaves a warm fuzzy feeling in the national pysche.

Policy and politics are inseparable, be they in the Rose Garden or in the Persian Gulf. The president is head of his party wherever he goes, whether to the South Bronx or to the Great Wall of China.

In recognition of the political "everything," there is a White House staff group which, while specializing in "politics," reaches into the whole presidential universe; it is the Office of Political Affairs. The formal title is a recent addition, but the role goes back at least forty years.

Truman's appointments secretary, Matt Connelly, was, as he described it, "contact man for the politicians from all over the states." "I handled all the politics in the White House except for Truman . . . at his own level. . . . And we maintained a liaison with the National Committee, to see about political things—working together is part of the game."[1]

The national committees, however, whether Democratic or Republican, have not, in four decades, been the exclusive managers of the president's political affairs; the quoted remark by former chairman Dole is only a more recent expression of the tension between the committees and the White House. Former presidential assistant Ken Hechler describes the 1948 arrangements:

> Over the objections of many of the older hands at the National Committee, the White House staff engineered the establishment of an independent research division, headed by William L. Batt, Jr. and nominally attached to the committee. A seven-man staff assembled a remarkable amount of useful background data on major issues. . . . This stockpile of information, including 'local color' on key areas where Truman planned to visit, was an invaluable feature of the master plan outlined for 1948.[2]

Working in a building separate from the committee's offices, the Batt group produced "Files of the Facts," a dozen short papers on the substantive issues in the campaign, plus four to five pages of speech material for each of the dozens of whistle-stops. The customized packages were delivered to the White House and flown to the campaign train, where presidential aide George Elsey edited them for use in Truman's remarks. "We were in effect an extension of the White House staff," Batt recalled.[3]

Elsey, Clark Clifford, and Charles Murphy accompanied Truman on the campaign train. When he came to the rear platform to speak, the three would get off the train, mingle with the whistle-stop crowds, climb back on after the speech, and give Truman a critique from the audience's perspective.

In 1952 White House assistant Richard Neustadt had drafted the platform. White House staffer David Bell was sent to Springfield, Illinois, to be the link to Adlai Stevenson's campaign.

Under Eisenhower, some political-research functions began to be moved into the White House itself. During the first term, two White House aides who were veterans of the Citizens for Eisenhower Committee in 1952 managed a political affairs unit named the Executive Branch Liaison Office. They gave each presidential appointee a loose-leaf binder and kept it filled with one-page fact papers, which they wrote, summarizing administration policy on individual issues. They interviewed the responsible administration officers and checked the drafts with them. Each fact paper was revised monthly. The thousand recipients also included congressional leaders and the Republican National Committee—to keep them aware of White House priorities. One hundred fact papers were produced in this White House enterprise.[4]

Eisenhower's later campaign arrangements were, like Truman's, occasions when the White House again reached out to extend its policy discipline. In 1956 former Arizona governor and White House assistant Howard Pyle was designated as the contact person for the Republican National Committee; as early as March he asked Cabinet members to send him platform recommendations, which he and Henry Cabot Lodge reviewed.

In the 1960 campaign, staffer Robert Merriam was the White House link to the Platform Committee. Like Neustadt eight years earlier, he took a White House–prepared draft to the Chicago convention, helped platform chairman Charles Percy and others rewrite it on the scene, checking sensitive wording issues through a direct line to the summer White House at Newport, Rhode Island. At one point, Merriam put Percy on the telephone with Eisenhower to smooth out a disagreement on the wording of defense policy; on another occasion Merriam had to argue with the entire Platform Committee of "15 irate men and ladies all of whom wanted to have a real, full-blown revolt." Merriam told them plainly that Ike was not going to support any 1960 campaigning if the platform disparaged his policies. He persuaded the committee to go along with Ike's positions.[5]

When the campaign itself started, Merriam organized a White House Answer Desk; it could ferret out response and rebuttal information from anywhere in the Executive Branch and forward it to Nixon. No National Committee office could match such access.

At the beginning of his administration, Johnson designated personal aide Walter Jenkins as Democratic Party liaison, but political responsibilities were actually diffused throughout the White House.

> During the 1964 presidential campaign, the staff was fully mobilized to write campaign speeches, make advance arrangements for presidential appearances, plot strategy, arrange for advertising, and perform all of the other activity usually associated with election year politics. Johnson and his staff, rather than the national party structure, were the center of activity.[6]

After the election, Marvin Watson was the bridge to the National Committee and had regular meetings with Chairman John Bailey and his senior colleagues. Watson transmitted and enforced Johnson's requests and instructions.

In the Nixon White House, there were two officers who were specifically charged with political duties—Harry Dent (for the first four years) and Murray Chotiner (during 1970). Explained Dent, "The 1972 campaign for reelection of the President of the United States was underway from the time the Nixon team entered the White House in January, 1969."[7]

Ford, Carter, and Reagan have followed the same pattern of building up their White House staffs to manage their political leadership responsibilities. Why has this happened? The headquarters offices of each National Committee is in Washington and the president in effect picks the chairman of his own party. Does there need to be a White House political office, too?

Forty years of reality undergird the affirmative answer. The political adviser has the vast advantage of proximity to the president and to the policy discussions that take place behind White House doors. He attends staff sessions and Cabinet meetings, and is in the Oval Office frequently. "I saw the flow and flavor of everything going on in the White House," reflected Harry Dent. Party officials from around the country would call him first—"They knew where the power was."[8] If appointments or trips are to be scheduled, if information must be dug quickly out of a department, if a White House dinner invitation is requested or a patronage position is to be filled, the response will come only from 1600 Pennsylvania Avenue.

The National Committee staff, furthermore, is in the chairman's not the president's hands. Whenever sensitive or controversial matters are at stake, a president is fearful of leaks and prefers loyalties that run only to him. If need be, it is uniquely the White House that can invoke executive privilege as a shield against outside civil investigations.

The party national committees, on the other hand, have resources the White House lacks. They can pay for mass mailings, and have "electronic billboard" networks to state and local headquarters. The party offices are not limited by the Antilobbying Act; they can urge their grass-roots supporters or a legislator's major contributors to wire or telephone their congressmen, a practice forbidden to anyone on the government's payroll.

During campaigns or in between, however, modern presidents have sought both electoral and policy support from citizens beyond party membership. Reflecting that wider search, the management of alliance and outreach systems has moved from party to personal presidential control. Outside the White House, organizations like Citizens for Eisenhower, the

Committee to Reelect the President, and the President Ford Committee have paralleled or even dominated the traditional party structure. The strengthening of the White House's own political staff has not met with favor from National Committee chairmen themselves. Former chairman Robert Dole's frosty comment (quoted at the beginning of this chapter) was echoed by the 1982 Republican chairman, Richard Richards, who upon resigning sneered, "Every clerk at the White House thinks he knows how to do my job." He reportedly added that he "believes the political arm of the White House should be abolished, because it acts as a 'buffer' between Reagan and the party."[9]

From his experience, Clark Clifford comments, "I just have to say to you that I doubt that in . . . [a presidential] election either of the national committees [on an incumbent President's side] plays much of a part. They just don't. It's up to the President and his organization to run the campaign; the committee doesn't really do that."[10]

Within the White House, personal control by the president over his political activities has required personal staff to help him exercise that control; the Office of Public Liaison (discussed in chapter 14) and the Office of Political Affairs have grown up to serve that need. There are some fifteen people in the political affairs group. "But only twenty percent of our time is spent in old-fashioned politicking," explained a recent veteran of the Reagan political affairs staff. "What we really do could be called 'policy management.'"[11]

A senator who supports the president, for example, may run for reelection; he may be sponsoring an appropriations amendment that will help his state. The Political Affairs Office will get in touch with the Office of Management and Budget to ascertain if the costs of the proposed amendment are tolerable. If not, there may be some negotiation. If, or when, the amendment is acceptable, the senator will be brought in to meet the president, have his picture taken, and will then be able to march out to the White House lawn to publicize his amendment—and the president's support.

"We are not directive," said the recent Reagan political aide, "but we are directional. We don't win all the policy battles, but we do make sure that political factors are brought to top-level attention as policies are decided."

Energy problems may be on a Cabinet Council agenda, with congressmen from producing states needing an economic boost for their region. The Political Office might get together with the American Petroleum Institute or the Independent Petroleum Association of America to ascertain whether there are additional policy alternatives for aiding the hard-hit oil industry. The political affairs director attends Cabinet Council meetings and the

Monday "issues" luncheons, is able to raise such supplemental suggestions. Instead of a prematurely negative decision, the result may be to create a task force to study the new materials. " 'Policy management' doesn't mean just saying 'You must do this for political reasons,' " the former aide emphasized; "it simply permits extra alternatives to be introduced into the decision-making process."[12]

The 1983 presidential veto of a textile protectionist bill was a disappointment to southeastern Republicans. "Policy management" in this case meant damage limitation. The political affairs staff first worked with the Speechwriting Office to couch the veto message in language full of sympathy for the affected industries and states; then, it arranged for the message to be issued at night shortly before Christmas.[13]

President Carter's White House political staff were "policy managers" in the same sense as in the Reagan administration. When Secretary of Health, Education, and Welfare Joseph Califano argued for going slow on proposing national health insurance, Hamilton Jordan disagreed. Califano recounts Jordan's emphasis:

> The President has a political commitment to the UAW [United Auto Workers] and the UAW is the best political organization in the country, and the most powerful. At a time when our public opinion polls are down, we've got to stay close to powerful organizations like this.[14]

Califano lost the argument.

The same confrontation recurred when the issue arose of how quickly Carter should propose a separate Department of Education. Califano argued that a careful study be done before the campaign commitment was renewed. "Hamilton Jordan recited his familiar lines. 'I don't know anything about the merits, but I know the politics, and politically the NEA [National Education Association] is important to us and it's important for the President to keep his word.' "[15]

Jordan was correct, as Califano later acknowledged. At the 1980 Democratic Convention, 464 NEA members came as delegates or alternates for Carter. Although Califano won the argument for a study, the new department was subsequently proposed and created, and Carter himself was renominated.

Harry Dent is proud of his policy-management role for Nixon's "southern strategy." "We have to do something *big* in the heart of Dixie," he told Nixon, "and that would be the Tennessee-Tombigbee Waterway."[16] The president concurred, and the immense engineering and construction project was supported.

"Policy management" can be dressed in Republican or Democratic clothing; it may be applied informally in one White House and systematically in another. Whichever party is in power, nose-counting politics will never be absent from presidential decision-making.

There is a further array of tools available to the White House Political Affairs Office. First among them is to put a popular president on the stump. In the fall of 1954, Eisenhower had hung back from campaigning for congressional candidates because he deprecated the "barnstorming" that Truman had done as president. His staff dug into the polling evidence, however, and laid it in front of him. Ike changed his mind, and biographer Stephen Ambrose recalls that "he traveled more than ten thousand miles and made nearly forty speeches." (Republicans still lost control of both houses, but, it is believed, by smaller margins than without Eisenhower's campaigning.)[17]

Thirty-two years later, the Reagan staff faced nearly the same challenge: control of the Senate. Political Director Mitchell Daniels chaired a White House planning group; on its recommendations Reagan made thirty-seven major political speeches between mid-May of 1985 and October 17, 1986.

Political travel requests get expedited treatment; they are not delayed by the elaborate schedule reviews described in chapter 15. Days are blocked out on the schedule marked "Hold for travel." As soon as the Political Office makes its recommendations to the chief of staff, they are discussed with the president and the first lady (who, typically, is always concerned about extra demands made on her husband). When the approvals are given, the local sponsors and the advance teams are notified; there is usually only a thirty-day lead time.

For the 1985–86 campaigning, Daniels' office had queried each candidate whom the president would be helping, asking what local issues were important, where were the opponents' vulnerabilities.[18] With this intelligence in hand, Daniels and the speechwriters could compose special inserts to sharpen Reagan's attack for each individual contest. The White House advance teams displayed their skills (see chapter 19), crowds turned out in far greater numbers than the candidates could attract alone, and the thirty-seven appearances grossed over $30 million in campaign funds. (In spite of his efforts, Reagan suffered the same frustration as Eisenhower thirty-two years earlier: control of the Senate switched to the Democrats.)

Not only for trips, but for all the president's Washington activities, political calculations are indispensable. Chapter 15 described the Scheduling Committee, which reviews proposals for the president's calendar. The political director is a member, his voice given extra weight in evaluating campaign requests for photo opportunities, for taped messages to important groups, and for taped endorsements of candidates.

The Office of Public Liaison, as chapter 14 portrayed, brings hundreds of groups into the White House for briefings and organizes national campaigns to support legislative initiatives. During the election year of 1984, one participant remembers, the Political Affairs Office in effect controlled the public liaison agenda entirely. The Political Office is often host in the Briefing Room itself; Daniels recalled that political leaders—on occasion two hundred at a time—were invited to the White House, with the president dropping by at several of their sessions.[19] The political staff is always consulted when plans are laid, by the Public Liaison Office, for instance, to inundate senators and congressmen with telephone or telegram blitzes from "private citizens."

Patronage, of course, is a lever for the Political Office, especially at the beginning of a presidential term. The initial staff work on appointments is handled in the Presidential Personnel Office (see chapter 18), but the political affairs chief becomes directly involved. In the Reagan White House, there were two internal committees that reviewed presidential appointments requiring Senate confirmation—a Personnel Committee and a Judgeship Selection Committee. The former was chaired by the chief of staff, with the legislative and domestic policy assistants participating; the latter was headed by the counsel to the president. The political affairs chief was a member of both groups. A 1981 news story described Political Director Lyn Nofziger:

> He didn't come here to be a "personnel director," he says, but it has turned out that way because Nofziger, probably better than anyone else and certainly with an elephantine memory about such matters, knows who labored loyally in the Reagan vineyard and who didn't. "Goddamn near" every potential appointee, schedule C and higher, is run past Nofziger.[20]

The White House Political Office plays a direct hand in presidential campaign advertising, and may even try to influence the ads of senators and congressmen as well. At Chief of Staff Haldeman's instructions, an outside public relations firm designed "hardball" negative ads for Republican Senate candidates to use in 1970. Political assistant Harry Dent was then expected to "sell the ads to the candidates." (Dent demurred, but his colleague Charles Colson pushed the ads on the reluctant candidates.)[21]

Cabinet members' travel is a tool that the political staff is anxious to control, but such added management from the White House is often resisted. Thirty-five years ago, Eisenhower's Executive Branch Liaison Office asked each of the several hundred presidential appointees to fill out a form alerting the White House to the speaking invitations each of them was receiving. The White House aides stuck pins on a map to show the geographical pattern of planned acceptances. The Liaison Office then advised the appointees which areas of the country were "empty" and which were overly favored.[22]

Former Secretary Joseph Califano describes a Cabinet campaign-planning dinner in 1979 at the vice president's home:

> Tim Kraft [White House campaign coordinator] said that each Cabinet officer would be asked to speak at least once a month for the White House, and that each should give a travel schedule to the White House so that political events could be worked in around departmental business. . . . Blumenthal muttered, "I don't think the Secretary of Treasury should raise money for the the campaign." [Commerce Secretary] Juanita Kreps . . . said in a whisper that was meant to carry, "I never heard such nonsense."[23]

To support its tools and levers in a coordinated fashion, each Political Office has a network of designated cooperators in the departments—men and women in Cabinet members' immediate offices. Dent called them his "commissars" and summoned them every month to the White House family theater to "psych them up" for the president's political priorities. Reagan's Mitchell Daniels likewise organized a web of departmental political contacts, making sure, of course, that each one of them "had the ear of the secretary." Once in place, such networks are canvassed to discover what favors—requests for special assistance—are being asked of the Cabinet departments and by whom. "We wanted to make sure that on the same day the White House was asking for loyalty from a political leader some Cabinet department wasn't giving away the store," Daniels recalled. "The system only works when all of the offices are in harness together."[24]

Effective use of the entire array of White House political tools implies an attempt at scorekeeping, a systematic cataloging of political debts and payments. The scattering of supplicants, however—535 legislators, 50 governors, 50 state party chairmen—and the diversity of sources—30 departments and agencies, 1,074 programs of domestic assistance, a dozen different White House offices—make it nearly impossible to organize an all-inclusive system. Much of the essential bargaining over dollars and projects, for instance, takes place privately between congressional appropriations offices and the individual departments; so incestuous are those ties that the White House is not even informed. "We should have had a central computer from day one of the administration," Daniels observed.

A rough calculus is kept, but the essential question is whether the "debtors" will be disciplined. Will those calculated as "disloyal" be ostra-cized from Executive Branch favors? "Almost never was a seditious Republican officeholder denied the benefits of the administration," Daniels complains, ". . . too often the most courageously loyal went unrewarded."[25] "The legislative affairs people have to take a different view," Daniels recalls resignedly. "To them, the *next* vote is the only one that counts and bygones are always bygones." The counsel may be apprehensive as well, Daniels remembers. "They send out a memo saying 'Don't do anything.' If you followed all that advice, ours would be a nine-to-five job."

The Political Affairs Office typically sends the president a "weekly political report," to which are attached newsclips of local political stories from out-of-town papers not included in the News Summary. From "policy management" to debt-and-payment catalogues, the Political Office thrusts its priorities into a White House environment that can never ignore its admonitions. Over the years between the 1948 platform and the 1988 campaign—with some significant exceptions—the "clerks at the White House" have moved in to manage and control the president's political activities. From so-called apolitical Eisenhower to "Great Communicator" Reagan, presidents have demanded that control, objections from the party national committees notwithstanding.

An exception was the Reagan campaign of 1984. Chief of Staff James Baker closed down the Political Affairs Office for several months, not wanting to appear to mix government resources and political resources in the same federal establishment. Six months after the election, Daniels recalls, the official White House cars were still under instructions not even to discharge passengers at the building where the Reagan reelection committee had had its headquarters. The Ford Political Office in 1980 was scrupulous as well; assistant Rogers Morton and his staff were paid by nongovernmental funds.

Within any White House, while touching "everything," the Political Office has its special focus: winning.

> "I will let Mr. Meese and Mr. Baker and Mr. Deaver and all those good guys worry about Reagan being President," says Nofziger. "They like government, they want to run the government, they can run the government. I'm much more interested in making sure that we go on running it."[26]

Republican or Democrat, every White House political director echoes those sentiments.

CHAPTER 18

Control All the Way Down: The Office of Presidential Personnel

Carter asked if I had any questions. "Only one," I responded. "Will I have the ability to pick my own people?" "Yes. Many are presidential appointments, of course, but . . . you can select your own people. I intend to keep my promise of Cabinet government. . . ."

—Joseph Califano

You cannot separate appointments from policy. Appointments *are* policy. . . . Before we appointed a Cabinet officer, we sat him down with President Reagan. Ed Meese would explain: "The White House is going to control the appointment process. We're not going to shove any people down your throat, but the control is going to be right here. All the way down. Do you understand that?" They all agreed to those terms.

—E. Pendleton James
Former assistant to the president

What is the patronage universe for the president of today? How many jobs come under White House purview? As of early in 1988, the theoretical total is close to six thousand three hundred.

TABLE 1

The Patronage Universe

Presidential appointments requiring confirmation by the Senate:	
Full-time, in the Executive Branch (including Cabinet, under secretaries, assistant secretaries, ambassadors, U.S. attorneys, marshals, etc.)	873
Federal judges (appointed for life)	860
Part-time members of boards and commissions	425
Presidential appointments not requiring Senate confirmation:	
Full-time, in the Executive Branch	26
Part-time members of boards and commissions	1,140
White House staff with presidential commissions	100
White House staff appointed under general presidential authority (other than those who are detailed or assigned there)	568
Noncareer Executive Branch jobs (non-career senior executive service, Schedule C) appointed by Cabinet and agency heads	2,303
Total	6,295

For the director of the Presidential Personnel Office, the actual job universe is smaller. That office does not concern itself with choosing White House staff members, and of the 860 judgeships a president may only get to fill 200 in a four-year term. (6,295 minus 100 and 568, and minus 660, equals 4,967.) The Office of Presidential Personnel focuses, therefore, on some 5,000 available positions, 1,565 of which are the board and commission members who serve part-time, many without pay.

The 5,000 can be divided another way—those requiring presidential action and those which do not. From the point of view of the chief executive, all of the 1,565 part-timers and 1,099 of the rest—some 2,664 of the 5,000—are by law "presidential." The appointment decisions are the president's; he signs their commissions and his own reputation is thus tied to the quality of the selections.

The final 2,303 are full-time patronage positions that supposedly belong to Cabinet and Agency heads, but which are actually controlled "all the way down" by the White House—a White House, that is, which subscribes to the Reagan rather than the Carter principle of noncareer personnel management.

How does a Presidential Personnel Office control 5,000 appointments? It manages six principal tasks:

- Describing the appointee positions.
- Identifying and, after election, recruiting candidates.
- Upon inauguration, opening up the noncareer vacancies.
- Selecting and clearing the nominees or appointees.
- Providing orientation to newcomers.
- Evaluating their performance.

The first of those must begin early, even before election. While he is still a candidate, a prospective president's staff will want to be aware of the noncareer positions that a new president needs to fill promptly. The second early task, "talent-searching," can also be started as soon as the nominating convention ends.

DESCRIBING POSITIONS

What skills are needed? What talents are required, for instance, to be the assistant secretary of defense for production and logistics? Early qualification profiles need to be developed.

As part of its general transition assistance program in 1960—planned in the early fall as a help to whichever nominee won the presidency—the Brookings Institution arranged with McKinsey & Company to prepare summary descriptions of 735 noncareer jobs in nineteen agencies. The position profiles were extremely brief, however, and the finished compilation did not reach Kennedy until four days before inauguration.

In 1976, the Carter associates moved more quickly. Approximately a month after Carter's nomination at the July convention, Richard Fleming, then a member of Jack Watson's transition planning staff in Atlanta, was designated as principal talent scout for a possible Carter presidency. There had been newspaper stories about the Watson group, with the result that each day's mail brought some two hundred letters from people seeking jobs. Fleming consulted with Lyndon Johnson's former deputy personnel chief, Matthew Coffey, then recruited four full-time assistants for his Atlanta staff. The group put together a Talent Inventory Program, which consisted of job profiles for thirty-two major positions and a register of some five hundred "source references" who could recommend names later if asked. The TIP staff assembled lists of actual candidates—up to four hundred names for each job. As a separate enterprise, a women's "Talent Bank '77" was put together by several volunteers in Washington. After the election, however, Hamilton Jordan and his own campaign staff, a different bunch with different priorities for personnel, moved in and decided they had to redo the TIP; the resulting rivalries and the lack of priority-setting from the top wasted both time and effort. When Carter actually moved into the White House, a completely different person, James E. King, who had been in charge of arranging transportation during the campaign, was brought in as director of the Presidential Personnel Office.[1]

The Reagan planners began even earlier. In the fall of 1979, a year before the election, future counselor Edwin Meese approached future Personnel Director E. Pendleton James. Could James draw up a plan to pick Executive Branch leadership for a possible Reagan presidency? Meese picked James because the latter knew Reagan's associates well, was a professional in the executive search business and had also served in the White House personnel office, under Nixon. James knew what to do and how to get going. His design included two phases: what could be undertaken before the election, and before the inauguration.

As soon as Reagan was nominated, James, eschewing all publicity, and equipped with a budget of eighty thousand dollars, rented an office across the river from Washington and hired a few assistants. Three months before the election, five months before inauguration, a part of the future White House staff, it turned out, was in place in Alexandria.

James faced the familiar initial task, to identify the positions that should be filled with the highest priority. For him they were the thirteen Cabinet offices, plus a dozen or more of the important Executive Office and independent agencies. For each of these positions, James compiled a description of its responsibilities; he had two veterans of the Ford Presidential Personnel Office to help draw up the qualifications requirements.

Since the Executive Branch's principal appointed positions are all established in statute, and known ahead of time, why burden each new presidential personnel team with the same repetitive task? Here, the Reagan Presidential Personnel Office is planning to make a laudable contribution to a more effective presidency by leaving behind, in the White House computer, a data base for the next Chief Executive. A catalogue of all the full-time and part-time presidentially appointed jobs in the Executive Branch—their titles, terms, pay-levels, and in brief their current duties—is being saved for the recruiters who, serving the next president, will occupy the Presidential Personnel Office chairs.[2] The catalogue may even be available to the candidates following the conventions. Such interpresidential foresightedness shows the modern White House at its best. "I have been paid by the government of the whole United States," commented the staffer who has been setting up the system, "this material, not being privileged, belongs to the nation."[3]

FINDING CANDIDATES

The next challenge facing early-starting presidential personnel staffs is to begin to identify their own candidates for the highest-priority appointments. In his Alexandria headquarters, James put together three groups of names: "outstanding and well known," "less well known but qualified," and "long shots." He drew on the circle of Reagan's intimates, later known as the Kitchen Cabinet, men and women who themselves were not hungry for jobs but whose acumen Reagan trusted.

James was endowed with advantages that the Fleming group in 1976 did not enjoy. From the beginning, he was part of the Reagan inner circle; his lists reflected the judgments of Reagan's closest advisers. Equally important, his service was continuous—from the preconvention months on into the White House.

Recruiting is in fact the first thing on a president-elect's mind the morning after election. Eisenhower commissioned Herbert Brownell and Lucius Clay to undertake a talent hunt for his new administration; Kennedy asked Larry O'Brien and Sargent Shriver to do the same for him. Nixon had Frederic Malek, his Personnel Officer director beginning in late 1970, bring eight professional executive recruiters into the White House from the private sector.

Within days after Reagan's election in 1980, James and the Kitchen Cabinet group met in Los Angeles and compiled their final recruiting preferences, which James then discussed with the president-elect. Reagan's task of choosing was made far easier because of the twelve months of preparation that James had completed. Nearly all of the recommendations were accepted. James then moved to transition headquarters in Washington, better organized than most of the other offices there for the eleven-week tumult facing them before inauguration.

Every presidential transition operation becomes the target for thousands of job-seekers. Resumés cascade in by the mailbagful; telephones never stop ringing. James used a staff of one hundred, many of them volunteers, to breast the tidal waves of pressures. One woman sent a hundred identical resumés, each applying for a different job; an acquaintance shipped him a whole frozen turkey (not the best choice of symbols) with a resumé inserted in its neck.

Amid the winter melee in 1980–81, James stuck to his agenda: Cabinet recruitment first, next the negotiations with the secretaries-designate about second and third levels of presidential appointees, finally the decisions on the nonpresidential patronage. The Senate Governmental Affairs Committee printed its quadrennial "Plum Book"; with the head start he had gained, James never needed to look at it. The various Reagan "transition teams" invaded the respective departments; James kept them at arm's length. "I had total control," James recalled.[4]

As Cabinet members were being selected, each met with the president-elect, together with James and the future White House staff chiefs. Contrary to the Carter promise to his Cabinet (which Kennedy had also made to Defense Secretary Robert McNamara and which Nixon had repeated to Defense Secretary Melvin Laird), Reagan and Meese made it clear to each of them: "Pen James is going to control all of the appointments right here at the White House." Agreement to that was in effect a price of admission to the Cabinet; the likelihood of later misunderstanding was lessened at the beginning.

There would of course be consultation, negotiation, and compromise, but even for the lowest level of the twenty-three hundred agency patronage appointments, the White House would have an initial veto. "We wanted the receptionist who answered the secretary's telephone to have a Reagan tone to her voice," said one White House aide.

If "control all the way down" was a startling personnel principle for the incoming Cabinet, it also had enduring consequences for the new White House. It meant a bigger and more active staff in the Presidential Personnel Office.

As each Cabinet officer was picked, James handed him or her a notebook with names and backgrounds of candidates for subordinate levels of appointments. The secretaries-designate could recommend alternative names, but the White House would have the last word. James emphasizes: "In my case, I was at the table when they started to cut the pie, not after it was half-eaten and all the players were in and there's no control and you're trying to grab hold of the reins."[5]

The morning after inauguration, James was ensconced in the White House, his title was assistant to the president (equivalent to Baker, Meese, and Deaver), and his office was in the West Wing itself. Those two perquisites were potent signals of seniority and control. "That has to be the way it works," James said later; "if you're there, they can't end-run you, and everybody in Washington tries to end-run you." His staff was still a hundred strong, but the number of volunteer members slowly diminished to bring the permanent complement to forty-two.

At the initial senior staff meetings, a familiar instruction was ordered— familiar because, as the reader has observed, the same kind of edict is typical throughout the specialized White House turfs: nobody was to make or even imply commitments on patronage matters except James' Office of Presidential Personnel. President Ford voiced the same instruction at a Cabinet meeting in his administration as soon as Douglas Bennett was named White House personnel chief. "Doug is the guy you deal with," Ford told the assembled secretaries. Such an exclusivity mandate is indispensable in presidential personnel operations; otherwise one job may be promised to two people, two different answers given to the same candidate, or an applicant may be appointed without sufficiently thorough review. Senior personnel choices are the president's business; little mistakes are big embarrassments.

When new to the office, presidents themselves may slip up, however, and permit the impermissible: end runs around their own staff systems— which they later regret. In a receiving line (a bad place for decision-making), Nixon once caved in to a senator's importuning and agreed on the spot to nominate the senator's candidate to a senior position. He ordered the name sent to the Capitol the next day. Running to catch up, the personnel chief privately advised the Senate staff to go slow until at least the FBI check was done; it uncovered an embarrassing arrest record. The president withdrew the nomination.

During the early Reagan months, James himself encountered illustrations of the importance and the clout of the exclusivity rule. There was one end run around him, which he lost, and one tough Oval Office confrontation, which he won.

The end run happened at a California New Year's Eve party (another ill-advised occasion for decisions). Without consulting any of his staff, Reagan committed himself to an ambassadorial appointment. While he later rejected his staff's advice to renege on his pledge, he promised that he would fend off all such attempted circumventions in the future. The president kept his word and in effect James' control system was strengthened by the mishap. The second early test came when a member of the senate Republican leadership insisted that the White House take the senator's candidate for a regulatory agency appointment. James had recommended a better-qualified person. Although he preferred to leave congressional negotiations in the hands of the legislative affairs staff, James paid a call on the senator. No agreement; the senator insisted on coming to see the president (who had not yet made any decision). The appointment of ten minutes stretched into thirty-five, ending with the president commenting, "I understand what you're saying, but under the Constitution, I make the appointments." Reagan picked the James recommendation, underscoring the credibility of the Personnel Office's system and of James himself.[6]

James insisted on one other White House privilege: he attended Cabinet and other policy meetings of his senior colleagues. "You cannot separate appointments from policy," he emphasized. "The guy who is in charge of the appointments has to understand policy, because he can't say, 'Mr. President, for this position we recommend . . .' without knowing what the issues are."[7]

Once in office, what are the subsequent priorities of the presidential personnel staff?

OPENING UP VACANCIES

After inauguration, one of the staff's initial objectives is to see to it that the noncareer posts in the Executive Branch are in fact vacated—to make room for the new president's appointees. A change in party control of the

White House of course intensifies the search for vacancies; the experience of the Eisenhower administration in 1953 illustrates the pressures.

After twenty years in the political desert, the Republicans in 1953 rushed thirstily up to the well of federal patronage. Senators and others badgered the White House staff and even importuned Ike directly to move on the political job front. Ike's first personnel chief, Charles F. Willis, Jr., scouted the agencies for patronage opportunities, arranged frequent reminders at Cabinet meetings, and later reported to Sherman Adams that he had located 86,665 jobs for the party (most, however, were temporary positions as census workers, rural letter-carriers). Willis drew up a plan for "job-opportunity notifications" to be sent to the Republican National Committee and designed a series of reporting forms and progress charts.

The thirst then went too far; Willis invaded the career sector. His Personnel Management Program proposed a "Phase III," including "fitness reports" on higher civil-service "holdovers." Criteria were to include "loyalty to his Republican appointee superior's policies and program," and each administrator was then to be asked "would he [if it were a *de novo* action] hire this . . . holdover?" If the answer in any case was no, "steps should be taken for [the employee's] removal—within the framework of existing rules." Any resulting vacancies were to be included in the "notifications" to the Republican National Committee, who could refer new candidates to the agencies "to compete on equal terms," it was said, without any "preference."[8]

The Willis Plans—on which he had been working for a year—were leaked to the *Washington Post*, and at a press conference in the fall of 1954 Eisenhower was asked if he had approved them. "I have," said Ike; ". . . it is . . . an effort . . . to get the White House out of the channel, so far as possible . . . to get it away from the White House as far as we can."[9] Ike was in effect dissembling; the personnel operation stayed right in the West Wing.

Phase III was not put into effect, however, and Willis departed eight months later. Eisenhower's private views about filling political jobs are revealed in his diary entry for January 5, 1953: "The real fact is that no one should be appointed to political office if he is a seeker after it. . . . Patronage is almost a wicked word—by itself it could well-nigh defeat democracy."[10] He may have been the first and last president to believe that. His staff never did.

In his book *Eighteen Acres Under Glass*, Eisenhower's subsequent personnel chief Robert K. Gray describes White House impatience at department heads who were slow in making noncareer changes.[11] Nixon made the same observation: "I could remember my concern when Eisenhower . . .

failed to press his Cabinet members and other appointees to Republicanize their agencies and departments."[12] Then he reflected on the poor perform-ance of his own first-term Cabinet:

> Week after week I watched and listened while even the Cabinet members who had been in politics long enough to know better justified retaining Democrats in important positions in their departments for reasons of 'morale' or in order to avoid controversy or unfavorable publicity. . . . Once the opportunity had passed, it was too late to correct this failure during my first term. I could only console myself with the determination that, if I were re-elected in 1972, I would not make the same mistake of leaving the initiative to individual Cabinet mem-bers."[13]

Nixon had precedent going for him. In order to give every newly elected president proper flexibility, a White House tradition has long been in effect: when any presidential term ends, all presidential appointees (other than those serving statutory terms) offer their resignations. The tradition applies to reelections, too; by the hour of the second-term inauguration, the letters are expected to be on the president's desk. It is only a tradition, not a statute, and it has been unevenly applied. Distinguished White House veteran William J. Hopkins recalls that in the past, appointees had to be reminded about their resignation obligations—even when the presi-dency was changing hands.[14]

Nixon, however, went far beyond the precedent. Remembering his first-term frustrations, he demanded, in November of 1972, that *all* nonca-reer personnel, at every level in every agency, including the entire White House staff, tender their resignations. (Each staff member was invited to accompany the pro-forma letter with a personal memorandum stating what he or she really wanted to do.) Nixon's move accomplished his clean-sweep objective, but he has since written that it was "a mistake" because of its "chilling effect . . . on the morale of people who had worked so hard during the election."[15]

In 1977 it was Carter's turn to be frustrated with the slow pace of patronage. Six months after inauguration, Stuart Eizenstat and Hamilton Jordan wrote him: "Many Schedule C and Non-Career Executive Assign-ment positions have not been filled . . . the appointment process should be speeded up . . . 197 of the 358 filled jobs are filled by people who were in the jobs prior to January 20, 1977, and legally could be asked to leave."[16] They told Carter to make it clear to the Cabinet that "you will review monthly reports based on information about all noncareer jobs, on a job by job basis."

At the beginning of his second term, Reagan not only did not repeat the

Nixon housecleaning, but ignored even the older tradition respecting presidential appointees. He made no general call for their resignations. "It would have been too disruptive," one aide commented.

Johnson took no chances. Presidential appointees were to give him a signed, undated letter of resignation as soon as they entered on duty.

SELECTING AND CLEARING NOMINEES

After whatever means have been exercised to open up the noncareer vacancies, the Presidential Personnel Office continues its talent-scout operation to find and recruit the men and women who will move into the opened positions. It needs to reach out beyond the throngs of seekers and sponsors to identify those who should be brought forward. Carter's personnel chief said, "If the office initially becomes a place where only requests from the campaign are honored, a placement agency for campaign people, then this will destroy the credibility of the office as a recruiting service."[17]

President Johnson's Personnel Office was managed by John Macy and Matthew Coffey, with most of the political clearance duties assumed by LBJ's personal aide, Marvin Watson. The Macy-Coffey talent-scout operation took a jump forward in White House history when they were able to borrow a data-processing expert for a year, then to wangle time on another office's Univac computer. Automation bloomed at last; the machine was loaded with over thirty thousand names (at times Coffey would run the keypunch personally) and could sort by characteristics—for example, "black," "woman," "lawyer." It printed out nineteen books of candidates that were updated every two months.

Each Presidential Personnel Office has improved its automation services. The Ford computer was able to warn the campaigning president which states had no presidential appointees in government; the Reagan computer could immediately identify each candidate's sponsors, and could print out Senator X's whole list of recommendees. Regular progress reports are produced from the electronic storage, including statistics on how well a president has been doing in appointing women or minorities to noncareer positions. Not all automated systems have been well regarded. One personnel chief commented, "Our computer was the turkey roost. If they went into the computer, they were gone."[18]

A recruiting search can even become too systematic. The fact that Ford's Personnel Office had a "talent bank" became public, prompting one enterprising Californian to have personal stationery printed up with the caption MEMBER, WHITE HOUSE TALENT BANK.

The ultimate recruiter is the president himself. Frequent are the occasions when the Personnel Office must request the chief executive to pick up the telephone and personally cajole a reluctant candidate into public service. Surprisingly perhaps, many of them tell him no.

As the Carter and Reagan examples illustrate, the first two stages of an effective talent-recruitment program need not—should not—wait until the morning after the election; they can begin even before the convention. Qualification profiles are not merely a "personnel" preoccupation, however. Carter's patronage head, Arnie Miller, emphasizes:

> As you write that position description or write the set of objectives, there's some discretion that ends up with the writer, but it ought to be reviewed by the policy people. . . . The personnel office, if it's going to be powerful, has to be connected to all the other parts of the operation.[19]

A new wrinkle has appeared on the qualification front. Displeased by "the lack of sufficient experience and expertise by persons appointed to political positions in the Department of Defense," the Congress in 1986 imposed the following statutory mandate on the head of the largest Cabinet department:

> When a vacancy occurs in an office within the Department of Defense and the office is to be filled by a person appointed from civilian life by the President, by and with the advice and consent of the Senate, the Secretary of Defense shall inform the President of the qualifications needed by a person serving in that office to carry out effectively the duties and responsibilities of that office.[20]

If the secretary takes this responsibility seriously and provides a full statement for each civilian appointee position, the Presidential Personnel Office will indeed have the beginnings of a library of authoritative qualification profiles. In fact, in developing its permanent catalogue, the White House is securing similar information from all the agencies.

The next step is selection and clearance. Even with the vacancy awaiting, the qualification requirements stated, and one or a group of recruits in hand for a presidential appointment, the route of a recommendation from the Presidential Personnel Office to the Oval Office is roundabout.

The responsible Cabinet member is consulted. Other White House offices must add their advice. The domestic policy chief or the national security assistant compares the candidate's views with what are known to be the president's policy objectives. The legislative affairs staff estimates the congressional reception of the appointment. The political adviser scrutinizes the depth of the prospect's party loyalty—or, more precisely, the loyalty to the president's own faction of the party. The counsel makes a quick FBI name check, and the vice president may be invited to put in a word.

For each presidential appointment, a separate memorandum is sent to the chief executive. It first describes the position to be filled. Ford's personnel chief William Walker recalled: "We would always have a fairly extensive one-page description, not only of what the job was, but how it interacted with the various policies the President was trying to implement. Everybody would have a common understanding of what . . . the rationale for the appointment was."[21] The "preliminary decision memorandum" portrays the preferred candidate, relates the four or five other offices' views, and reveals who the alternative prospects are.

A small committee of White House seniors, usually chaired by the chief of staff, convenes, debates the choices, and occasionally calls in one of the several office heads to give unvarnished comments in person. At the beginning of the Reagan administration, James remembers, the senior group met every day for two years. The group coordination was necessary, but it opened up tempting possibilities for what one personnel veteran termed "shopping around." A sponsor, frustrated by a Meese disapproval, would run to Baker or Deaver; an adverse James recommendation would be appealed to Baker. "It subverted the system," the former aide recalled.

Upon general consensus, or to settle uncompromisable staff differences, the director of the Personnel Office takes the decision to the president. Douglas Bennett would see Ford three times a week; James had twice-a-week appointments with Reagan. On those occasions, the whole range of arguments had to be presented, the arguments against as well as in favor of accepting the Presidential Personnel Office's recommendation. The process seems tedious, but shortcuts, it has been learned, bring trouble and there is only one boss in the White House. In his memoir, Carter recalls:

> These decisions would sometimes develop into mammoth arguments among my staff and with others. Most of the time the contention would not reach the Oval Office, but on occasion, I would be dragged into it. For instance, because so many people were involved in the process, I personally expended far more effort in choosing a chairman for the National Endowment for the Arts than I did in choosing a replacement for Cy Vance as Secretary of State. . . .[22]

Carter's personnel director, however, found a certain advantage in the internal conflicts:

. . . the memo that Carter got would say "Eizenstat and Watson concur, Zbig prefers someone else, here's something about that someone else, but I recommend so-and-so." More often than not, he'd just throw up his hands and say you've thought it through and I'll go with your recommendation. I found our power was derived from that kind of cancelling each other out.[23]

The presidential "decision" is only a middle stage. The Presidential Personnel Office notifies the candidate of the "probable" selection and the formal clearance processes are then engaged. The FBI starts its full field investigation, the Internal Revenue Service must certify a clean tax record, and conflict-of-interest and financial-disclosure forms must be submitted to the Office of Government Ethics. More intensive checks are undertaken with the Congress (described in chapter 10) and with the local party.

Since no announcements are made at this stage (although the competing candidates are notified that they were not selected), to the public the job still appears to be unfilled; complaints of "foot-dragging" are heard, or that the White House "can't get its act together" (sometimes a correct surmise).

Only when all the investigations are evaluated—perhaps six weeks later—a final decision memo goes to the president, and even at that point there can be last-minute appeals. When signed, the nomination papers are dispatched to the Congress and the press release is posted on the Briefing Room bulletin board.

From the first vacancy identification to the last press release, the presidential-appointment saga, however prolix and bureaucratic, does not admit of foreshortening, nor can hasty or informal oral assurances take the place of written record. "Zero defects," Bob Haldeman demanded; that hoped-for ideal is approached only through the tight system that the Presidential Personnel Office controls.

Especially contentious is the White House control of ambassadorial appointments. They are all presidential appointments, all confirmed by the Senate. Secretaries of state traditionally urge the president to elevate career foreign service officers; while presidential personnel chiefs and the Political Office see some of those posts (Luxembourg, Switzerland, for example) as appropriate for major campaign supporters. There is endemic conflict.

A rough percentage, usually about 30 percent, is sometimes negotiated for the noncareer portion. Lyndon Johnson's personnel chief John Macy recalled:

In my time, we went over with the Secretary of State or his Deputy . . . to try to get some kind of understanding. . . . We were constantly looking for qualified outsiders. That was the problem. There were plenty of unqualified outsiders who wanted the job. But it was a tough job to get people who had some foreign affairs or international experience. We were much heavier on the noncareer side. But also, I found it was necessary to take a look at the career proposals because frequently the argument was that good old Joe has done this and done that and it's his turn for chief of mission. Those are the ones we really had to stop before they got through the machinery.[24]

Under Reagan, still another category of presidential-appointment preparatory work was shifted to the control of the president's personal staff. James explained: "We were the first White House in history that selected judges. We wanted to pull the selection of judges over to the White House. The set-up before was always that the Attorney General handled them."[25]

Since judges are appointed by the president for life, nominations for the federal bench require exceptionally careful staff work prior to the president's decision.[26] Judicial nominations involve not just the analysis of a candidate's policies and opinions, but, as the Bork episode illustrates, can be a first-order political decision for the president personally. Securing confirmation may require a full-blown White House effort. Little wonder that the preparations for the choice of judges has been brought closer to the chooser. The Department of Justice continues to be a major participant in winnowing judicial candidates, but the selection process itself has been put in White House hands.

As mentioned in chapter 9, the Reagan White House convened a Federal Judiciary Selection Committee, chaired by the White House counsel and including the attorney general and two of his deputies, and the presidential personnel director. The pace of the committee's work was impressive. Since Eisenhower, presidents have appointed federal judges at an average rate of one a week.

Nearly a third of the five thousand noncareer positions under the presidential personnel purview are part-time—members of statutory boards and advisory commissions. Some of these 1,565 are compensated for the days of their meetings, while others serve without pay, only their travel expenses being reimbursed. Some commissions, like the *Challenger* disaster board of inquiry chaired by former Secretary of State William Rogers, fill a unique need. Others are more prestigious than substantive, honorary if not actually honored.

To a beleaguered presidential personnel chief, the latter category of boards and commissions is a relief valve. Having only advisory responsibilities, their members do not have to be held to the standard of managerial competence required for full-time executives. The political quotient in their selection can be much higher. The more vacancies of this sort that can be found, the more potent are the bargaining and trade-off tools that the personnel director can wield in his infinitely convoluted negotiations with Cabinet members, senators, congressmen, and party officials.

A special genre of the part-time universe is what one presidential personnel chief calls the "Orient Express" assemblages: ad hoc presidential delegations.

> We did funerals, coronations and inaugurations. That sort of thing. You can imagine the royal weddings, the intense pressure from people who wanted to go, for example, to the coronation of the King of Nepal which was a wild ceremony in the mountains of Nepal. We had thirty or forty people who were elbowing each other for seats. . . .
>
> . . . for Chiang Kai-shek's funeral we put together the (Murder on the) Orient Express. Nelson Rockefeller and the China Lobby. We had a big battle over who was going to get on the delegation, but we weren't sure they would all come back alive.[27]

Like its legislative, political, press, and communications counterparts at the White House, the Presidential Personnel Office has its own network throughout the federal agencies. At each Cabinet officer's right hand is a special assistant, usually approved by the presidential personnel chief, who specializes in noncareer placement. "Our gauleiters," one White House veteran labeled them. (The assistants' location in the immediate office of the secretary keeps this area of employment decisions separate from the departmental personnel offices, which handle only the career systems.)

The "gauleiters" help manage the intricate footwork of patronage, walking on the thin edge between White House pressure and Cabinet resistance. Their lives are especially painful because of the Presidential Personnel Office's determination since 1969 (except for the Carter years) to exercise a veto right over the twenty-three hundred noncareer positions the appointing authority for which is in the agency heads' hands.

A description of the Reagan clearance system is not atypical:

> All non career/political personnel were expected to have voted in the 1980 election and to have given some level of support to the Reagan/Bush campaign or to a candidate for another office who supported Reagan/Bush. Designated officials on the White House staff had to approve each of these noncareer appointees before they were to be hired.[28]

Director James himself added, "Unless they had the 'P.J.' initials on them, nobody would process anything."[29]

The Presidential Personnel Office's "veto right" in practice translates into much more than negative screening. It means the office can put irresistible pressure on the "gauleiters" and through them the agency heads. For every sterling candidate whom the Personnel Office may recruit for an important assignment, there are hundreds of less qualified who hammer at the gates. Some are easily evaded, but others, while not rating the imprimatur of a presidential appointment, need kid-gloved treatment. Depending on their sponsors, some become "must" placements. If one of the boards or commissions won't do, if a seat at the royal wedding will not suffice, the Presidential Personnel Office will "negotiate" through its interagency network.

William Walker recalls one presidential instruction: "In November of 1974, we lost, if I recall correctly, 42 seats in the House. And the President called me the next morning and said 'I want every one of those members offered a job.' "[30] Fortunately for Walker and his Presidential Personnel Office staff, not all forty-two wanted federal employment. One who did, but who was no friend of the president, was from Pennsylvania. He was "must"-placed—as executive director of the Four Corners Regional Commission, two thousand miles from home.

ORIENTATION OF NEW NONCAREER APPOINTEES

Having arrived from Peoria or Pocatello, the president's newly appointed men and women sense a tinge of apprehension amid their exuberance. What are they getting into? What is a "continuing resolution"? Will "Circular A-95" affect them? How can they fire "foot-dragging bureaucrats"? Will they ever see the president who hired them?

Assistant secretaries remain on the job an average of only twenty-two months. If their on-the-job training can be shortened, their effectiveness for the president increases.

Out of these quite ancient concerns came, in October of 1975, an added responsibility for the White House staff; President Ford's Presidential Personnel Office began an orientation program for senior political executives new to Washington. Groups of some thirty-six appointees were invited to the White House on three separate occasions. In the East Wing Family Theater, from Friday morning until Saturday midafternoon, they went to presidential school.

Their "professors" included Chief of Staff Donald Rumsfeld, domestic policy assistant James Cannon, OMB Director James Lynn, and Civil Service Chairman Robert Hampton. House Minority Leader John Rhodes told them "How the Congressional Leadership Looks at the Policy Executive," presidential counsel Philip Buchen reminded them about standards of conduct, Press Secretary Ron Nessen described "Dealing with the Press." Each "student" was given a thick notebook with descriptions of the White House and Executive Office units with which they would have to work. At 6 p.m. on Friday, the group joined President Ford for cocktails in the Jacqueline Kennedy Garden. Later, within their respective departments, agency-specific briefings completed their preliminary "education."

The Reagan staff resumed the practice, also contracted with Harvard's John F. Kennedy School of Government to lead seminars of case studies and host larger conferences and briefings as well.[31]

Such orientation programs are not cheerleading mass meetings of hundreds, but are intense classes, helping to equip newcomers to work effectively in the disputatious policy environment that chapter 1 has already described. Interspersed are informal social times, and on occasion the opportunity to meet the president himself. Only the White House staff can produce—and can command attendance at—presidential "schools" of this caliber.

A need that has never been properly met is a counseling service for families of those appointees coming to Washington following the first notification that the president will be asking them to move to the nation's capital. Explaining the long delay before the formal nomination, preparing appointees fully for the confirmation hearings, helping find houses, schools, medical, and other community services—no White House has sufficiently provided organized assistance of this sort.

EVALUATION OF PERFORMANCE

Recruited, cleared, hired, placed, and oriented, the appointees—secretaries, under secretaries, assistant secretaries, ambassadors, bureau chiefs, public affairs and congressional relations directors—take office in their respective agency fiefdoms. On their shoulders rest the defense of the president's policies, the leadership of their career staffs in the direction the president wants to move. For any president's agenda, they are the field commanders. It should be no surprise that the officers who put them there—the president and the White House staff—often wonder to themselves, "How well are they doing?" No surprise either that they should try to find out.

For everybody except political appointees—civil service, foreign service, and military employees—there is an annual rite: performance appraisal. It is all the more important, in the view of some at the White House, that presidential appointees be evaluated, too, either informally, or perhaps in a systematic fashion. At least two presidential staffs have launched initiatives in this delicate area, but they have done it indelicately.

At a Cabinet meeting in July 1979, newly designated White House Chief of Staff Hamilton Jordan handed out a two-page form. Cabinet officers were told to fill out one for each of their assistant secretaries and deputy assistant secretaries. The form contained thirty questions—for example, "How confident is this person?" "How mature?" "How stable?" "How bright?" "List 3 things about this person that have disappointed you." Needless to say, the "White House Report Card" appeared on the front pages of the *Washington Post* two days later.[32] Three days after that, the *Post* printed an evaluation of President Carter by former Senator Eugene McCarthy, using the same thirty questions (rating his "Maturity" as "2" out of a possible "6"). A month later, the form was reproduced on T-shirts. Commented personnel chief Arnie Miller later: "There weren't any serious discussions with Cabinet members or members of the senior staff. While I thought the idea made sense, I didn't think the execution worked. . . . It was very primitive."[33]

Then it was the Reagan staff's turn to be indelicate. During a White House meeting in 1984 of some two hundred midlevel appointees, the deputy director of the Presidential Personnel Office gave a forceful talk. "You know, we are here to drain the swamp," she reminded them. "You have to keep that objective in mind. If it is not happening in the agencies where you are working, if there is foot-dragging, we need to know about it. It's getting to be report-card time!"[34]

While Chief of Staff Baker later asked that her forthrightness be softened, there nevertheless did exist a kind of tattletale system under which complaints from true-blue presidential adherents about other noncareer appointees would be piped into the Presidential Personnel Office. Sometimes the allegations arose from the familiar "personal chemistry" relationship problems; on other occasions the Personnel Director took real foot-draggers to a White House woodshed, and a few to the chopping block itself.

However indelicately they go about it, every White House staff is aware of its president's dependence on the policy loyalty of his appointees throughout the government and is tempted to institute both evaluation and discipline. Ford White House personnel chief Douglas Bennett remembered that Cabinet officers themselves would come to the White House and ask for help in moving out noncareer nonperformers. "We tried to find a soft landing for them somewhere," Bennett recalled, "maybe in Samoa."[35]

In reflecting on the role of the Presidential Personnel Office, a former deputy director, Becky Norton Dunlop, recommended that a White House staff officer should

> have charge not only of personnel selection but also of evaluating the perform-
> ance of appointees in office . . . the policy office and the Cabinet office could
> provide feedback on performance of political appointees in carrying out the
> President's policies. Such a program of systematic review during the selection
> process *and* during the tenure of appointees would improve the team approach
> . . . and regularize the evaluation of their performance."[36]

Two Heritage Foundation associates expressed their own dissatisfaction with the Reagan White House for its "absence of centralized oversight and disciplinary mechanisms for appointees once they were in office."[37]

In addition to his 1972–73 housecleaning, a Nixon technique to boost departmental loyalty was to appoint some of his own White House staff veterans to sub-Cabinet positions. Presidents have often made such transfers. "The trouble is," Ehrlichman sadly observed, "they go off and marry the natives."

There is one final service that a presidential personnel staff offers, this to its own White House colleagues. A president's departure from office finds many White House staffers at loose ends. Where to land next? If there has been a party change, government's doors are not open to them; the world outside the gates is unfamiliar. In 1976–77, the Ford Personnel Office secured the pro bono help of half a dozen private executive-search professionals who came into the White House and held a series of counsel-ing seminars with outgoing staffers. In addition, a "job bank" of private-sector offers was compiled. The autographed picture and the glamorous memories are not the only, or a sufficient, thank-you.

The Presidential Personnel Office has always been held closely under the wing of whoever is designated as White House chief of staff; the staff chief knows, as the president knows, the truth of James' observation on appoint-ments at the opening of this chapter. On one occasion, the personnel chief's hat was worn by the chairman of the Civil Service Commission: in Johnson's White House, John Macy divided his time between the two offices. The Congress signaled its displeasure with that kind of arrange-ment by specifying, in the Civil Service Reform Act of 1978, that the director of the Office of Personnel Management, even if sitting in the White House, may not recommend any person for a presidential appointment requiring Senate confirmation.[38]

It was Macy, under his Civil Service Commission authority in the Kennedy period, who removed from White House and Cabinet patronage an entire category of appointees: the student summer interns who flocked to Washington every June. Kennedy was reportedly irritated at having this large pool of jobs taken away from political discretion, but Macy insisted that they had to be merit appointments. A nationwide examination was designed with the interns certified eligible according to their exam scores.

"Personnel is policy," Becky Dunlop wrote, and perhaps several thousand times in his term, a president—or his staff with his authority—chooses the twain together. The presidential policy "tone" may be expected in the voice of the receptionist, in the pen of the Supreme Court Justice, and in the actions of all the noncareer men and women in between. Without that leverage, a president, and through him the electorate, enjoy less than their full constitutional powers.

Is patronage control by the White House a political process? Of course it is. Those who vote for a president—any president—deserve the assurance that if their candidate wins, his concept of government, and his policy priorities, will *be* reflected throughout the top level of his Executive Branch and in the judges he nominates. The White House control described here over the entire noncareer personnel universe embodies the president's pledge to his electorate that his accountability to them is direct and undiminished.

Critics who sneer "politicization" perhaps forget that the size of the senior noncareer contingent is set by law, and in fact has greatly diminished since the years when all postmaster, collector of customs, and even summer student intern positions were political plums. What the epithet "politicization" usually signifies is that the critic who utters it doesn't *like* the president's policies or doesn't approve of the "political ideology" or the qualifications of the president's personnel choices.[39] As the preceding pages of this chapter have shown, these White House choices are made not casually, but (with few exceptions) only after thoroughgoing scrutiny. Whatever the candidate's qualifications (or lack thereof), they are not ignored in the White House, but are balanced against other elements in the total presidential equation. Whatever the staff's role, it is the president who is responsible for the decisions. The critics' subsequent recourse is always open: at the Senate's confirmation proceedings, or in the next presidential election. The Presidential Personnel Office is thus part of the White House gateway, closing out those who don't measure up, beckoning in the select, doing the president's bidding to help him be chief executive in fact as well as in name.

President Carter's Personnel Office director Arnie Miller reflected:

Carter thought he could return to that earlier decentralized approach, but he failed to understand how interwoven a fabric the presidency is. You pull a little string over here and everything unravels. He tried to decentralize personnel. He tried to cut back on the size of the Presidential Personnel Office staff. He bumbled it. Midway through his presidency, he suddenly realized that he had given away the store. The expectations are still there on a President. The demands are so concentrated now. . . . in order to countervail all that out there, you've got to build your own [store] in the White House.[40]

CHAPTER 19

Manager of Apparently Effortless Success: The Advance Office

Advancing is an art! It is the exhausting, detailed planning that makes each presidential trip and event appear to be an *effortless* success. An incredible diversity of activities . . . [is] involved. . . . The Advanceman is always a manager integrating and coordinating. . . . He is the leader of a highly professional and dedicated team of White House experts . . . he must accomplish these things in an anonymous fashion—giving gladly the credit for a successful visit to the local people or event sponsors.

—*White House Advance Manual*

"Damned fine men," exclaimed Lyndon B. Johnson after shaking hands with a planeload of 82nd Airborne soldiers at Fort Bragg on February 17, 1968. He had made a special trip to praise the "bravery, skill and devotion" with which, he thought, they were about to serve in Vietnam. But he was saying goodbye to the wrong troops; the confused men whose hands he shook were returning veterans; the real departees were having a beer bust and left quietly the next day. No one ever told Johnson of the mistake that had been made.

—BENJAMIN F. SCHEMMER
Armed Forces Journal, Winter 1976

Presidents never stay home.

From Shawnee Mission High School to the Emperor's Palace, from the Kentucky State Fair to the Kremlin, the president of the United States is visitor in chief, representing now his party, now his government, here his country, here all the people of the nation. As chief of state, he has words of encouragement to the National Association of Student Councils; as chief partisan, he addresses a Senate candidate's closing rally; as chief diplomat, he goes abroad to sign a SALT treaty; as national spokesman, he stands on the cliff above Normandy Beach. The divisions among his roles of course are never quite that distinct; to each place he travels, the president is all those "chiefs" at once.

His national and political roles are public and he wants them to be so; cameras and the press are invited to witness every motorcade, film each ceremony, record all the ringing words. A presidential trip is theater, each city an act, every stop a scene. As the Secret Service recognizes, however, in any balcony can lurk a John Wilkes Booth, at any window a Lee Harvey Oswald; a Sara Jane Moore or John Hinckley may emerge from any crowd. One other presidential role is quintessential, but is usually more concealed: the American president is constantly the commander in chief, having always to be able to reach his national security command centers from any place in the world.

A presidential trip, therefore, is not a casual sojourn; it is a massive expedition, its every mile planned out ahead, its every minute preprogrammed. The surge of cheering thousands must stop just short of a moving cocoon of security; curtained behind each VIP receiving line must sit the doomsday telephone.

While each chief executive's travel style is different, every trip for any president makes similar preparations. A Nixon would tolerate only one or two "events" in a carefully measured day, while a Ford would feel lonely without a day crammed with visits. Underneath variations, however, the "art" of advancing is common to presidency after presidency.

Within any White House staff, trip-planning means intricate choreography among more than a dozen separate offices: Scheduling, Political, Legislative, Public Liaison, Domestic Policy and Intergovernmental Relations, National Security (if the trip is abroad), Press, Communications, Speechwriting, Secret Service, Social, Military, Transportation, Communications, and the first lady's staff. The orchestrator of the team and the manager of the on-scene arrangements is the Advance Office.

The White House advance staff had some of its origins in the Nixon campaign of 1960. The successful 1968 campaign led to the decision to establish a White House Advance Office in 1969. Instead of hiring an office full of paid staffers, the first advance director recruited volunteers from business and law firms around the country. He identified and, by putting them on occasional assignments, tested one thousand candidates, then settled on some fifty recruits. They were available on call and stayed on the payrolls of their companies; the White House or, in 1972, the campaign treasury paid their expenses when they were on the road.

The Reagan White House has used volunteers as well but had a full-time staff of twenty-five. (The office cannot use detailees from government agencies for political advancing; they are restricted by the Hatch Act.)

How does the White House Advance Office organize a presidential trip? A domestic presidential visit can get its start from any one of the hundreds of invitations that pour into the White House, but more likely it originates from within, as a homegrown idea. What policy themes is the president emphasizing? To which areas of American life does he wish to draw attention? Educational excellence, industrial competitiveness, athletic prowess, racial harmony, ethnic progress, minority achievement . . . ? At campaign time, of course, electoral issues are foremost—what voters is he targeting, which senators need help?

Like the daily schedule itself (discussed in chapter 15), a trip is not a casual event, but a calculated piece of a larger theme, and is designed to convey a message. A presidential trip, in other words, is an instrument of persuasion.

As soon as the desired message is framed and agreed to, through discussions within the White House, the Advance Office reviews the choices for domestic travel. Where in the country can the presidential theme best be dramatized? Which groups, which sponsors, which cities or towns? In what already-scheduled local events could the president join, transforming them into illustrations of his own policy initiatives? Local and state calendars of events are scanned; *The Farmers' Almanac* is studied. Invitations are searched, private suggestions reviewed. Long lists are vetted into short lists, tentative alternatives identified.

The Advance Office then moves out to make a quiet survey. A local volunteer may be used, more likely now a National Committee aide or a full-time White House staff member. The White House interest is masked; the surveyor may go incognito.

In the summer of 1973, President Nixon, for instance, wanted to carry a message of support for Senator Howard Baker of Tennessee. "I wore Levi's and penny loafers" remembered one White House advance man, "drove a rented car for three hours through the hollows and little towns near Carthage, Tennessee, and ended up on a dirt road to the dedication site of the Cordell Hull Dam." He wore no White House label, made no announcements, but needed a hundred answers. How could crowds get there? Where could helicopters land? Would the hilltop landing site have to be black-topped? Could the small stream bridge bear the weight of the presidential limousine? What theme event could be added to attract more spectators? The few local officials who knew who he was were warned this was only an "unofficial survey." Any premature stories would kill off even the possibility of a VIP visit. (But the local political leaders were also promised they could make the first announcement when the trip was firm.)[1]

Whether in rural or urban America, cities or countryside, similar survey visits are made, as a necessary step before the Advance Office seriously supports a recommendation. If the site survey leads to an approval for a visit, invitations need not actually be in hand; when solicited, "they will come out like raindrops," said one White House alumnus. The scheduling machinery's "go" decision is, for the advance staff, only a precursor for what they have to do next.

If any part of the trip has a political purpose, the White House counsel must be asked to advise the Advance Office where the line is drawn; when is the president a partisan and when is he just president? In scrupulous detail, all the proposed meetings, receptions, rallies, and speeches are later divided along that watershed so that mathematically precise formulae can be used to allocate expenses between the sponsors and the government. "21.7% of the trip is political, 78.3% is official" explains one illustrative memorandum.[2]

As the national press producers' pool is told to make their plans, the Advance Office orders 450 press credentials prepared. Some five weeks before the trip, the "preadvance" team assembles. It includes eight to ten officers representing the units of the White House that must be directly involved in the visit: the Advance Office person in charge, plus members from the Press Office, the Media and Broadcast Relations Office, the Secret Service, White House Communications, the *Air Force One* crew, the *Marine One* (helicopter) crew, and the Military Office, including the medical unit; the first lady may send an advance staffer of her own as well.

Each unit has its separate and very specific checklist, but they plan the entire visit as a single team. They visit the airport, draw rough sketches of where planes, helicopters, and cars will park, and review the planned arrival ceremonies. Motorcade routes are surveyed, and each event site is examined in detail. What will be the backdrop, the "storyboard" (the picture that television will capture)? Walking routes are plotted: for the president, the press, the guests, the staff, and the public (more sketches). There must be a presidential "holding room" where he meets sponsors and guests. What will be the program? What kind of audience will there be and how long will it take them to go through the magnetometers? If there is an outdoor rally, who will do the "crowd-raising"? If hotel overnights are planned, floor plans are needed. Finances must be discussed with the hosts and agreement reached on who pays for what.

No team is without its conflicts. The press advance men want to have an airport arrival, at high noon, big crowds, remarks, greetings, bands, balloons ascending, people pressing against the ropes. The Secret Service looks through different eyes. "If they had their way," commented one former advance man, "they would have the president arrive after dark, in an out-of-the-way corner of the airport, put him into a Sherman tank, lead him to a bank, and have him spend the night in a vault. They would say," he added, " 'you cannot choose that route,' and we would counter 'no, he *will* drive that avenue, you go ahead and protect him.' " Since the assassination attempt on Reagan, the Secret Service wins more of those battles.

There are conflicts with the local hosts as well: who will sit on the dais?

How many greeting speeches at the airport? One sponsoring group for a fund-raiser had sold every seat on the floor of a gymnasium; the advance-man had to insist that the same tables and seats be squeezed together to make room for the camera platforms.

The White House advance head, the instructions make clear, is a diplomat-in-temporary-residence, "the mover and the shaker, the stroker and the cajoler, the smoother of ruffled feathers and the soother of hard feelings. He is the leader of a great team."[3] The preadvance team for recent presidents has included nongovernmental companions: technical experts from the news networks, news photographers, the White House Correspondents Association. Satellite time must be reserved, transmitting "dishes" placed, camera angles planned. What will be the dramatic scenes? Where will the sun be?

The government team and the news planning team represent institutions that are different and often at odds. In this miniuniverse, however, they have a common purpose: to get the fullest stories and best pictures to the most people the fastest. "All of them know that, visually and technically, there are right and wrong ways to do things," explained one former participant, "and this is true whoever is president; it's a professional business." Such symbiosis disturbs newsman Martin Schram, however. He quotes a colleague:

> "In a funny way, the . . . advance men and I have the same thing at heart—we want the piece to look as good as it possibly can. . . . That's their job and that's my job. . . . I'm looking for the best pictures, but I can't help it if the audiences that show up, or that are grouped together by the Reagan campaign, look so good. . . . I can't help it if it looks like a commercial."[4]

Schram then adds: "That is what White House video experts . . . are counting on. Offering television's professionals pictures they could not refuse was at the core of the Reagan officials' efforts to shape and even control the content of the network newscasts."[5]

The preadvance team returns, and writes a schedule memorandum that refers back to the original purpose of the trip, describing the themes that underlie the visits and reiterating the "event concepts" that govern what the president will actually do and say. Questions are raised for presidential concurrence: will he go for a certain speech here, a group photo there, a separate, private picture taken with local political leaders? The APPROVE and DISAPPROVE boxes are checked.

Approximately two weeks before the formal departure, the White House advance team itself leaves for the event site. The same units of the staff are represented, usually by the same people that did the preadvance, plus many more, enough for one from each unit to be at each event site in a single day.

The advance team carries a wizard's menu, its twenty-six pages listing 485 items to check off. Among them: "Effect of the motorcade on normal commuting patterns"; "Lighting: 150 foot-candles on the speaker and 100 foot-candles on the crowd"; "Overtime cost estimate"; "Other appropriate music—can the band play it?"; "Toe marks" (adhesive strips on the ground to show exactly where VIP airport greeters are to stand); "Empty seats filled or draped"; "List of gifts accepted for the President"; "Bad weather alternative."[6] Each motorcade is standardized, the occupants of every car specified by name, the needed radio equipment described.

The advance team is to communicate daily with the Advance Office, and a "countdown" meeting is scheduled for the team the night before the event. Date-time stamp and file every piece of paper, the team is instructed, and "Keep Everybody Informed."

If the trip is political and a big rally is scheduled, the advance person dons another specialized hat: crowd-raiser. The local hosts must do the work, mobilizing hundreds of enthusiastic volunteers. A vast menu of techniques is systematically used, but they are all on the advance man's checklist; not a single step is left to chance. For illustration:

- Event sites should be "collapsible" so that new seats can be added or empty chairs removed.
- Ten times as many handbills should be printed as there are places to be filled—enough for every shopping-center grocery bag, door handles in parking lots, taping to public rest room mirrors, even to lay (right side up) on busy sidewalks. One last idea is suggested: "Stand on top of the highest building in town and throw the handbills into the wind." Leaflets must list the event as at least a half hour before it really occurs; a president on the platform with a crowd still at the gates is chaos.
- *Air Force One* should be mentioned in leaflets for an airport rally; some folks will come just to see the plane. News stories about the history of presidential aircraft should be used to stimulate crowd interest (but mention of their costs should be avoided).
- Bands, cheerleaders, pom-pom girls, and drill teams are to be mobilized (but the Secret Service has to check every make-believe rifle).
- Banner-painting parties are suggested, with supplies of butcher paper and tempera paint; a "hand-held sign committee" should be organized.
- Three thousand balloons are recommended, with balloon rises preferred over balloon drops. The truly experienced may try to do both simultaneously in the same auditorium, helium in the ones to go up, air for those coming down. The hall manager must be consulted first, however; the risen balloons will cling to the ceiling for two days afterwards.

No matter how rah-rah some aspects of a trip may be, White House advance staffers are forever conscious that it is the president of the United States who is there. They strive for a "colorful and mediagenic setting" but never at the expense of the dignity of the person or the office. Their instructions state:

> The President must never be allowed into a potentially awkward or embarrassing situation, and the advanceman is sometimes the only person who can keep that from happening. . . . For example, an oversized cowboy hat, a live farm animal, an Indian headdress, or a Shriner's 'Fez' could produce a decidedly un-presidential photograph. Common sense must be used to make sure that the dignity of the office of the President is never compromised by the well intentioned generosity of local partisans.[7]

And no thank you to sound trucks, bands on flatbed trailers, elephants, clowns, and parachutists.

Like crowd-raising, press-advancing is a special skill of the Advance Office team. At a major-event site, a press area must be set apart and special press-only magnetometers installed. The size and height of camera platforms and radio tables is specified. Half a dozen long-distance charge-call telephones are to be at each event site. Lighting of "presidential quality," and a proper audio system will be provided by the White House itself if necessary. Four nearby rooms are reserved (at their cost) for the three television networks to edit their tape. A filing center is needed with tables and chairs for a hundred people; the press secretary and his staff need a separate, adjoining large office area with six tables to hold their equipment. "We duplicate the White House Press Office on the scene of a presidential visit," one expert explained. "The White House press staff can do their work just as if they were at 1600 Pennsylvania Avenue." Some of the advance team stay on site, completing its prodigious checklist, until the very moment the president is to arrive.

Back at the White House, the formal press announcement is made, with the local sponsors tipped off ahead of time and the necessary congressmen, senators, governors, and mayors likewise alerted just before the White House release. The speechwriters are at work; idea notes or complete remarks are prepared ahead of time for arrivals, departures, and for each stop in between. The earlier sketches of airports, motorcade arrival and departure points, corridors, rooms, and walkways are transformed into minute diagrams, with arrows drawn in showing each presidential footstep. When its own thousand details are done, the White House Press Office writes a separate "Press Schedule Bible," which is given out to the national press representatives.

On the morning before the day of departure, the Advance Office holds a final trip briefing for the chief of staff. The guest list for *Air Force One* is rechecked (the Legislative Affairs Office will have been guaranteed four seats for favored lawmakers); the lead advance man composes the president's and the first lady's personal schedule sheets. Even when airborne, *Air Force One*'s communications desk buzzes with last-minute advice from the advance team waiting at the arrival site.

As the presidential party approaches the runway, what goes through the advance man's mind? One veteran remembers:

> There are a hundred bad variables, when you look at a situation, and go down your list. What you try to do is to reduce those down to zero. You never get them to zero, but if you get them down to six or five or four when the event occurs, then the odds are with you, and if they do go wrong, they are at least in the manageable range.[8]

If these domestic arrangements seem lengthy and elaborate, they are modest when compared to the preparations for a presidential trip abroad. Advancemen for a foreign trip must contend with two complicating institutions unique to the scene outside of the United States: the sovereign host government and the American embassy. In some countries, particularly where an American president has never traveled, neither of those establishments has any comprehension of the magnitude of a presidential visit. A multistop journey will require the support of some four hundred staff, security, and communications assistants; at an important summit conference the U.S. official group may number a thousand. What is more, the conference itself will be covered by three thousand journalists, four hundred from the American press alone. To a few U.S. ambassadors and some foreign ministers, those figures come as a shock; what was thought to be a president turns out to be an invasion.

Kissinger writes of his negotiations for Nixon's first trip to China:

> . . . even in the millennia of their history the Chinese had never encountered a presidential advance party, especially one whose skills had been honed by the hectic trips of a candidate in the heartland of America and disciplined by the monomaniacal obsession of the Nixon White House with public relations. When I warned Chou En-lai that China had survived barbarian invasions before but had never encountered advance men, it was only partly a joke.[9]

For foreign trips, the preadvance teams may have thirty-two members. In addition to the offices included in domestic advancing, the first lady's chief of staff personally is part of the team which composes the preadvance group, plus officers from the State Department (including its Protocol

Division) and from the national security affairs staff. The president's household staff, including the chef or chief steward, is represented because the president will host a formal dinner in each capital he visits. That means food procurement, and flying in a full array of as many as 150 settings of White House china, silver, and serving pieces (all of it is routinely packed in transportable cases).

With the preadvance team come the network pool producers, one for each country in which the president will stop, accompanied by lighting and sound advisers. Some of the individual network shows, such as "Nightline," send their own producers independently.

Arriving in the foreign capital, the lead advance man makes his first call on the U.S. ambassador. The latter may be stunned by the size of the group that has come, but if he or she agrees that the ambassadorial role is substantive while the White House team's responsibility is public relations and logistics, a workable division of responsibility is achieved. A few ambassadors initially insist on managing all the details of the forthcoming visit, but that is a view which promptly leads to trouble. "It is only a matter of time until the weight of what has really happened lands on the guy that tries to do that," observed a veteran of many advances. "He buckles." If necessary, a back-channel call is made to the White House chief of staff, who sees to it that the president's interests are communicated to any overambitious envoy.

"Traditionally, what happens," explained the former White House aide, "is you sort of mold the domestic professionals in with their State Department-Embassy counterparts and you work together." Still not comprehending the magnitude of a presidential movement from one place to another, the embassy officers may suggest seven or eight events for each day's schedule; the advance officers must explain that a three-event day is nearer the true maximum.

Having achieved some consensus with the embassy, the ambassador and the lead advance man then pay a call on the host government officials. Not surprisingly, the same dialectic ensues. The foreign government has its own ideas about what the president should do and how he should do it; its version of his calendar is also crammed with multiple visits and meetings.

Negotiations about the first lady's activities are often equally painful. She, for instance, will be interested in visiting hospitals or drug-rehabilitation clinics, to which the host government's answer is "The Palace must approve all such visits and there is no hospital available," or "Our country does not have a drug problem!" The first lady's exasperated advance staffers may try to shake off both government and embassy escorts and explore visiting possibilities for their principal on their own.

A host government will often impose limits on the numbers of media representatives; "crowd-raising" and prime-time television production for the benefit of U.S. audiences may not be high on the prime minister's own agenda. The American president's commander-in-chief role is not always understood and the hosts are embarrassed at the advance leader's insistence that the president use only his own limousine and aircraft. (The principal reason for this request is because of their built-in communications facilities; a U.S. military transport plane will, if several countries are being visited, bring three or four spare limousines, extra mechanics, and even the *Marine One* helicopter itself from home.)

"You have to rely on the embassy people to tell you how far you can push or how far you need to retreat to get things done," said the former advance man. "But you work off a different checklist," he added. "Generally, your objective is to have the host government as happy as possible, and you come away with more than your minimums."

Red Cavaney, a seasoned advance alumnus from the Nixon and Ford presidencies, recalled the Nixon visit to Egypt in June of 1974. The entire visit had been arranged informally; the U.S. embassy had been reopened only four months earlier. "Advance" was hardly the right word; Cavaney was dropped off in Cairo only nine days before the president was due to arrive. "I don't know what you're going to do here," said Cavaney's advance chief to him before leaving for the next stop, "but I've got to have a presidential schedule before *Air Force One* touches down!"[10]

The ambassador, as Cavaney remembers it, was not familiar with presidential visits and the tiny embassy staff had few resources. Cavaney's office had no electricity, no typewriters, no copying machines, and the telephones weren't working.

Since this was Egypt, American television audiences would of course expect to see Nixon at the Pyramids. After several days of being toured around by the cooperative Egyptians, Cavaney discovered that President Sadat had a guesthouse near Giza and readily agreed to include that on the joint schedule. By now it was forty-eight hours to go; every member of the advance team except Cavaney had come down with intestinal ailments. By using the embassy's teletype keyboard and shutting off its transmitter, Cavaney was able to produce a crude typescript. Such staff meetings as they had were all oral; nobody had papers.

The presidential party took off from Washington still having received no schedules from their Cairo outpost. Only after leaving Salzburg, a stop on the way, was the Advance Office chief able to reach Cavaney by radio. "I don't know what the hell you've got down there," he warned, "but I hope it's good!" Cavaney's only answer: "Trust me!"

The visit was a triumph. There were not only motorcades, but a notable train trip from Cairo to Alexandria with the two presidents on an open railway car. Seven million Egyptians jammed the streets and sidelines. So warm were the two men with one another that when Sadat, at the guesthouse overlooking the Pyramids, admired the presidential helicopter, Nixon gave it to him as a present. And Cavaney got his picture: the two presidents, the helicopter, and the Pyramids on the horizon.

Cavaney summed up his advancing experience:

> You look at each and every situation you become involved in and try to figure out what are all the worst things that could happen in that situation, and then develop your own little mental plan as to how you would deal with each one of those problems, before you were faced with it, so that, before an event ever came to happen, you could try and resolve them all. . . .[11]

The words are those of a professional, and the Advance Office is a professional place. Devoted, each one is, to Nixon or Ford or Carter or Reagan; in a larger sense there lies in every advance staffer a commitment to perfection. Take away the partisan names and labels—in the abstract the commitment endures.

The very words of the *Advance Manual,* while Republican in its origin, speak to a profession which is both within and beyond politics:

> This is the advanceman's reward: the challenge of the task, and the knowledge that only a few—but a very unique few—will give credit where due. Those who look for public praise and gratitude should look elsewhere for their challenges. The true advanceman settles—indeed, thrives—on a quiet kind of satisfaction, and a private kind of pride.[12]

CHAPTER 20

First-Magnitude Czars

If . . . an official is appointed with the charge to be a czar, the government organism almost always rejects him. Like thrombogenic materials introduced into the human body, czars cause clots in the administrative organism. I avoided the appellation like the plague.

—James R. Killian, Jr.
Special assistant to president Eisenhower
for science and technology

I had proposed . . . that there should be a Director of Missile Development in the Defense Department. . . . President Eisenhower immediately grabbed the phone and called Secretary McElroy to try the idea out on him, but McElroy hesitated and made various excuses, at which point the President slammed down the phone and said, "Goddam it, I'll do it through Killian then and give him all the power he needs. At least that way I won't have to worry about restrictions on his power."

—Presidential speechwriter Arthur Larson

The previous thirteen chapters have been thirteen photographs of the principal, continuing functions in the White House staff. Their origins can be traced in decades; they will be there in the future.

No president is confined by neat organization charts, however; his individual interests and priorities, changing and expanding from year to year, jump beyond the "continuing" arrangements. If he is frustrated and chagrined by yesterday's snarled interdepartmental machinery, by today's crisis, or by tomorrow's threatened political slippage, he will be pressed to make new promises, to demand novel and dramatic responses. How does a president engineer a fast, dramatic response? To alter his Executive Branch takes months (and may never happen), but he has an appealing and facile alternative: he can create a special assistant to the president and can do it in an hour.

The White House is at once the first target for trouble and the last refuge of administrative flexibility. Thus a maxim: when an overwhelming problem lands in the president's lap, his easiest reaction is administrative; he can create a White House "czar" to deal with it. Neither legislation nor confirmation need be wrestled through the Congress, little money is involved, and a suite can always be found in the Executive Office Building next door. Political momentum can be regained, and a large interest group, perhaps an apprehensive general public, assuaged. Of course, the "czar" may really be needed; it is even possible that he or she can match the rhetoric of the opening press release with the substance of some closing accomplishments.

Never mind that such a new White House special assistant will probably be a pain to the Cabinet and will appear to them to fuzz up their direct lines to the president. And don't mention that the problem against which the czar is aimed may be incurable by administrative fixes anyway. A czar conveys the flavor of action, will be publicized as the superman who will "knock heads," "cut red tape," and "mow down" resistance. The president can collect some praise for his "initiative"; the very fact of the czar's appointment will help rebut the political attack that the beleaguered chief executive is "doing nothing about" the problem at hand. None of the recent presidents has withstood these temptations.

As has already been described, the White House staff has a center of continuing offices. But the staff is—and always will be—the mirror of the president's priorities; as they surge and expand, it will change to reflect them. Flaring out from that center, therefore, will be a corona of ephemeral luminaries.

Eisenhower, for example, created special White House offices for Personnel Management (Young, followed by Ellsworth), Airways Modernization (Curtis and later Quesada), Disarmament (Stassen), Cold War Planning (Jackson), International Understanding and Cooperation (Rockefeller), Public Works Planning (Bragdon, followed by Peterson), Agricultural Surpluses (Francis), Foreign Economic Policy (Dodge and later Randall), Science and Technology (Killian and later Kistiakowsky), and Atomic Energy (Strauss). He also appointed Meyer Kestnbaum on his White House staff as a special assistant to follow up the reports of the two Hoover Commissions and of the Commission on Intergovernmental Relations which Kestnbaum himself had chaired.

Except for the Science and Technology Office, which finally became an institution in the Executive Office, Kennedy wiped them all out and started new ones of his own: Food for Peace (McGovern), Mental Retardation (Warren), Latin America (Mann), International Trade (Peterson), Transport Mergers (Prettyman), and Military Affairs (Taylor). Johnson established czars of his own, for the War on Poverty (Shriver), Alaskan Earthquake Rehabilitation (Anderson and Ink), the Arts (Stevens), and he reappointed Maxwell Taylor as a consultant for Military-Diplomatic Strategy. President Nixon, in addition to his extensive Public Liaison Office with its links to consumers and to minority groups, installed White House special assistants for Energy (Love and later DiBona), Physical

Fitness (Wilkinson), the Academic Community and the Young (Heard), the Business Community (Flanigan), and Manpower Planning (Hershey). Ford created czars for Labor-Management Negotiations (Usery), Urban Affairs (Fletcher), and Human Rights and Humanitarian Affairs (Wilson). Carter initiated a counselor for Aging (Cruikshank), and special assistants for Inflation (Strauss, followed by Kahn), for Reorganization (Pettigrew), for the Middle East (Strauss), Drugs and Health (Bourne and later O'Keefe), Information Management (Harden), White House Administration (Hugh Carter), and the Iranian Hostages (Ball). President Reagan has had his own assistants for Drug Abuse Policy (Turner, followed by Macdonald), for Private-Sector Initiatives (Ryan), and for Agricultural Trade and Food Aid (Alan Tracy)—this last a position ordained in statute.[1]

Not even counted here are the dozens of special ambassadors and envoys (such as Averell Harriman, Walter George, Donald Rumsfeld, Hamilton Jordan, Philip Habib, Ellsworth Bunker, Robert Strauss, and Cyrus Vance) whom presidents have sent for brief and sensitive missions to inflamed corners of the country and the world.

Beyond the catalog of czars created in fact, there have been others proposed but not deployed. Eisenhower ended his presidency arguing for a "first secretary of the government" to help in the "formulation of national security objectives." A 1964 Johnson Task Force recommended a "secretary at large" for "interagency program coordination." (Both would have required Senate confirmation.)

White House veteran Joseph Califano, while Secretary of Health, Education, and Welfare for Carter, suggested a White House "special representative for domestic assistance," while arts advocates called for a presidential Office of Cultural Affairs. Senior Reagan staffers reportedly urged him to create an "arms-control czar," Senator John Glenn proposed a White House assistant for "nonproliferation," and Reagan himself vetoed a bill that would have forced him to appoint a statutory, Cabinet-level drug-enforcement czar.

The few proposals that did not make it to White House status are outnumbered by the legions that did. What opens the door to such appointments? What conditions produce new ad hoc special presidential assistants?

Presidents are spurred to appoint czars when three incendiary elements converge: if action is needed, time is short, and several federal agencies must contribute to the urgent enterprise. If there is a hint of failure having occurred, and if political flak is exploding, the White House is doubly pressed to dramatize the president's personal concern and to center the needed initiative within his own perimeter.

Of the many that are possible, three illustrations are offered.

The Russian launch of *Sputnik I,* the first earth satellite, on October 4, 1957, generated a "climate of near hysteria" in America.

As it beeped in the sky, *Sputnik I* created a crisis of confidence that swept the country like a windblown forest fire. Overnight there developed a widespread fear that the country lay at the mercy of the Russian military machine and that our own government and its military arm had abruptly lost the power to defend the homeland itself, much less to maintain U.S. prestige and leadership in the international arena. Confidence in American science, technology, and education suddenly evaporated. . . . there were few Americans who were not caught up in a mood of chagrin and concern, with a desire to see prompt action to ensure the nation's security.[2]

Eisenhower's political opponents took good advantage of his new vulnerability. Senate Democratic Majority Leader Lyndon Johnson, for instance, predicted a dire future from the Communists' "foothold in outer space."

Not yet being able to send up a satellite of our own (our Vanguard vehicle blew up December 6 on its launching pad), Eisenhower did the next best thing: he orbited a new special assistant to the president. "Through him, I intend to be assured that the entire program is carried forward in closely-integrated fashion," the president told the nation; there was not to be "even the suspicion of harm to our scientific and development program."[3]

James R. Killian, Jr., was brought from the presidency of MIT to the White House. KILLIAN NAMED MISSILE CZAR, blazed the headlines. Killian himself recalls one staff associate commenting, "Apparently I had been hired as a miracle worker."[4]

Killian urged that he not be called a czar but soon heard the president tell congressional leaders that "I would be clothed with all the power that he held." He himself later observed, "Thanks to being a protégé of the president, I was made to feel that I had the confidence of powerful men at the apex of government."[5] "During the last years of the Eisenhower administration," another observer remarked, "Killian, Kistiakowsky [Killian's successor] and PSAC [the President's Science Advisory Committee] reviewed virtually every important high-technology program of the Department of Defense. . . . Few programs or ideas that did not meet with their approval got very far."[6]

The president included Killian in Cabinet, National Security Council, and other more intimate, secret meetings, giving him a policy role to match both his own skill and the resources that he mobilized. Killian, however, was no czar lifted into the White House merely for appearance' sake; he was truly a substantive adviser.

He was also in the middle of conflict. In 1958 the president had to decide whether there should be a single space agency and if so which one. The Army, the Air Force, the Defense Advanced Research Project Agency, the Atomic Energy Commission, and the National Advisory Committee for Aeronautics all competed, but none so vehemently as the two military services, each with what Killian called its "special brand of fantasies." It was, he remembered, an "anvil chorus of contestants." Killian reached for outside advice, worked with the Budget Bureau and with the president's Advisory Committee on Government Organization, and composed a long memorandum for the president that analyzed and evaluated the alternatives. More important, however, he had talked informally with Ike ahead of time and was assured that the president wanted civilian rather than military direction of the overall space effort. The creation of the National Aeronautics and Space Administration grew out of that memorandum.

Killian was also in the middle of the nuclear-testing controversy, a sharp debate among the president's advisers as to whether the United States should join in an international test ban. Killian observed:

> . . . the President needed technical views independent of those coming to him from the Department of Defense and the Atomic Energy Commission. Up until my appointment . . . the President was largely limited in his technical advice on nuclear matters to . . . elements associated with the Atomic Energy Commission and the Department of Defense, all strong opponents of a test ban.[7]

Killian again assembled panels of the nation's most distinguished scientists; their advice helped Eisenhower when he initiated the negotiations with the Soviet Union that culminated in the Test-Ban Treaty of 1963.

Succeeding Killian in 1959 was George Kistiakowsky, himself an eminent scientist, who continued to be the principal link between presidential policy issues and advice from the American scientific community. Like his predecessor, Kistiakowsky observed how centrifugal to the president's outlook the cabinet agencies are. He chaired the interdepartmental Federal Council on Science and Technology, which, as he recalled, "remained a gathering of individuals who represented frequently opposing agency positions and just were unable, unwilling . . . to think on a national, federal level."[8]

What began as a "missile czar's" office in 1957 became, in 1976, a statutory unit of the Executive Office. By that time, the Congress, supported by President Ford, insisted that scientific advice be regularly provided to every president and through a continuing institution, not an ephemeral personal adviser, however distinguished.

Sometimes a presidential czar will have neither office nor a title in the White House, but will have a presidential mission of extraordinary urgency. An example occurred in the spring of 1964. In the early evening of March 27, an earthquake of 8.3 to 8.7 on the Richter scale devastated southern Alaska, killing 115 people and causing $400 million in property damage. Sixty percent of Alaska's people lived in the disaster area. Normal communications, food supplies, water and sewer facilities were severely disrupted. With only a short summer ahead for repair and reconstruction, there was real fear for the survival of much of Alaska's population.

In six days, President Johnson signed an executive order creating a Federal Reconstruction and Development Planning Commission of eleven federal agencies, and named Senator Clinton Anderson as its chairman and Dwight Ink (then the assistant general manager of the Atomic Energy Commission) as its executive director. The last written paragraph of the Executive Order told the federal departments that the commission had no legal authority over any of them; the unwritten message was that Anderson and Ink were the president's personal deputies—the agencies were to follow their instructions. "We have to save Alaska," the president told Ink. "You've got to go do things that have never before been done in peacetime."[9]

Anderson and Ink roped in virtually every agency of government and took off for Alaska. Anderson announced the policy guidelines under which reconstruction would proceed; Ink organized a field committee and set up nine task forces. When Anderson returned to the capital to push the needed emergency legislation, Ink was left in administrative charge, shuttling between Juneau and Washington. Weekly reports from each task force were combined into a single statement that went to Johnson as well as to commission members. "Information was flowing up to the president faster than it was flowing through the agencies," Ink recalled. When Johnson at one point read critical comments about agencies that were slow in responding, he personally leaked them to the papers, a stark method of injecting his cabinet with the presidential message. Johnson signed letters of appreciation to Ink and Anderson; copies circulated to all the commission and task force members. The federal and state executives got the word: Lyndon was watching every detail, and Ink was Lyndon on the spot.

The Corps of Engineers' first estimate was that the job couldn't be done in one summer. It balked at incorporating high-incentive and stiff penalty clauses in the reconstruction contracts—which Ink knew would be needed to finish before winter. Ink then paid a visit to the deputy secretary of defense.

Wherever in the Executive Branch Ink needed to push or spur, he acted, and wherever he acted, he bore the easily decipherable warning: "Do we need to go back and tell the president that you . . . ?"

In the end, the task was accomplished and Anderson could tell the president:

> It has been said that the Federal Government has grown so large that it has lost its capacity to function quickly and effectively in response to domestic problems and that its great size has left it cold to the needs of the American people.
>
> No surer refutation of this misconception comes to my mind than the manner in which the Government acted in the aftermath of the Alaska earthquake.[10]

Were Anderson and Ink presidential czars for Alaskan reconstruction? They were. Did they call themselves by that name or even have a White House title? Indeed not. No agency would be "subject to the authority of the commission," Johnson had written—the same Lyndon Johnson who let it be known that Anderson and Ink were in reality clothed with his own authority. That is every White House czar's not-so-hidden secret: outwardly, they abjure the power that inwardly they carry—and that power is the president's, not their own.[11]

President and Nancy Reagan spotlighted drug abuse as a priority subject for federal (as well as state, local, and voluntary) action. On June 24, 1982, heads or representatives of eighteen federal agencies were summoned to the White House. The president said: "We can put drug abuse on the run . . . we're running up a battle flag . . . we must mobilize all our forces to stop the flow of drugs into this country. . . ."[12] Reagan signed an executive order and named Carlton Turner as "the person responsible for overseeing all domestic and international drug functions. He'll head the new campaign against drug abuse."[13]

Warring on drugs would be a more elusive objective than rebuilding southern Alaska. It would be a task of human rather than physical engineering: working with many other nations, strengthening law enforcement, supporting medical research, aiding detoxification and treatment, educating young people, establishing testing programs in the military services and for selected federal civilian employees.

Would there be any budget increases? Which Latin American countries were to be pressured? How was turf to be divided among Customs, the

Coast Guard, the FBI, and the Drug Enforcement Administration? This
was not a seven-month spurt but a years-long effort.

At the June 24 meeting, the president instructed the eighteen agencies:
"I'd like to ask you to report back to Dr. Turner within two weeks with
what suggestions you may have for continuing and for our strategy."
Turner followed up to collect the agencies' suggestions; he and his seven-
person staff wove them into a seventy-five-page strategy document, twisting Cabinet arms to pin down their final concurrence. Everywhere he
found conflicts of priorities. The Army saw drug-testing as a deterrence to
voluntary recruitment; the Department of State and some of its ambassadors resisted turning the screws on sovereign foreign governments; the
budget director wanted to trim rather than expand research; one Cabinet
officer fought to install as a bureau head a person Turner considered poorly
qualified. Turner struggled with all of them.

He foreswore the use of any title or stance that suggested a czar, but
when necessary he relied on Chief of Staff James Baker, and on occasion
the president, for support. He also allied himself with the vice president
and his South Florida Task Force, and with the first lady. When his differences with Cabinet members grew painful, Turner made it clear to the
president that he could easily be relieved. "You have to go to work every
day willing to lay your job on the line," he later observed.[14] Turner left
after six years, feeling "burned up," a common occupational hazard in
White House territory.

Drug abuse is still an issue, still such a crazy quilt of multiagency
jurisdictions that no one member of the Cabinet can manage the overall
enterprise. A new director of the Drug Abuse Policy Office took Turner's
place in the White House; like his predecessor, he himself has little more
to go on than the strength of the president's own commitment.

There is a contrast in administrative style between the two "ends" of the
federal Executive Branch. At the one end are the Cabinet departments and
agencies, specified in statute, organized for the long term, staffed by men
and women with tenure and continuity. With predictable repetition, they
respond to the recurring needs that fit within their jurisdictions. At the
other end is the White House, with neither tenure nor organization chart
enduring longer than the president's personal determination. The White
House's very malleability permits the president to react to the unpredict-
able, to improvise out-of-the-ordinary responses to extraordinary circumstances.

Even within the presidential staff, there are units with limited flexibility.
None of the three missions illustrated in this chapter could have been
assigned, for instance, to the Scheduling or the Press or the Personnel

Office. The president preserves an ability to jump beyond the rigidities of even his personal staff and to summon temporary and ad hoc advisers. First-magnitude czars, they could be called—who might mobilize a fractured Cabinet, underscore the president's concern for an issue bothering his countrymen, and damp down the political fires that would singe him if he relied on business as usual.

CHAPTER 21

First Special Counselor:
The President's Spouse

Traditionally what the West Wing wants from the East Wing is nothing: no waves, no problems, no bad publicity. "The East Wing has always been a pain in the ass to the West Wing. They make no policy; there is no substance. It is damage control", said a former West Wing official.
—*The National Journal,* December 14, 1985

I don't think there will ever be another First Lady who will act only as . . . a hostess. One thing you realize when you get to the White House is that the First Lady has influence and resources. You see the problems that come to the President's desk and see how far short governmental programs fall in meeting the needs of the people. It made me want to do what I could while I was there and had that platform.
—Rosalynn Carter

If the President has a bully pulpit, then the First Lady has a white glove pulpit. It's more refined, more restricted, more ceremonial, but it's a pulpit all the same.
—Nancy Reagan

Besides being a wife, the first lady is a senior counselor to the president, perhaps his closest and best. She has no constitutional duties, but like other high-ranking assistants, she can speak for the president with a special credibility.

The past half century has shown that the president's spouse has the broadest turf of any White House counselor. If she wishes and the president agrees, the first lady can attend Cabinet meetings, participate in his political strategy sessions, give press conferences, speak at the United Nations, discuss matters of state with national and foreign leaders, address political rallies, write newspaper columns, convene a world conference of first ladies, have weekly business lunches with the president, host television specials, and testify before congressional committees. Rosalynn Carter even rode with the president on the National Emergency Airborne Command Post. She was there as a passenger, but very few of the White House staff have ever been in it.

Mrs. Carter recounts her first fourteen months as first lady:

. . . I visited 18 nations and 27 U.S. cities, held 259 private meetings and 50 public meetings, made 15 major speeches, held 22 press conferences, gave 32 interviews with individual journalists, had 77 hours of briefings, attended 83 official receptions and social functions, held 26 special-interest and group meetings at the White House, spent more than 300 hours working in mental health, received 152,000 letters and 7,939 invitations, signed 150 photographs a week, and made 16 public appearances around Washington, D.C.[1]

Like any other senior counselor, the first lady can—and does—express strong opinions to the White House chief of staff and to the Presidential Personnel, Speechwriting, Domestic Policy, National Security, Scheduling, Advance, and Press offices. According to her former close associate Michael Deaver, First Lady Nancy Reagan

> lobbied the president to soften his line on the Soviet Union; to reduce military spending and not to push Star Wars at the expense of the poor and dispossessed. She favored a diplomatic solution in Nicaragua and opposed his trip to Bitburg. . . .
>
> It was Nancy who pushed everybody on the Geneva summit. She felt strongly that it was not only in the interest of world peace but the correct move politically. She would buttonhole George Shultz, [then-National Security Assistant] Bud McFarlane, and others, to be sure that they were moving toward that goal. . . .
>
> Nancy took care to pick her spots. But once into an issue, she was like a dog with a bone. She just didn't give up. . . .
>
> She will wage a quiet campaign, planting a thought, recruiting others of us to push it along, making a case: Foreign policy will be hurt . . . our allies will be let down. . . .
>
> Nancy wins most of the time.[2]

A first lady therefore can pick out causes, encourage their advocates, and even bring her concerns to meetings of government advisory committees. In showing favor to special groups, however, she takes the same risks as any White House officer; if not alert she could become their captive.

An active presidential spouse thus needs help, as surely as the president did when Louis Brownlow diagnosed the chief executive's requirements fifty years ago. Pursuing her own priorities in public affairs requires staff support; in addition, there are the more traditional East Wing responsibilities of supervising the Residence and managing the social obligations of the first family.

Can the first lady tap the president's staff for extra duty? Mrs. Carter relied on officers from the State Department and the National Security Council for her trip to seven Latin American countries in 1977. Mrs. Reagan has been closely supported by the special assistant for drug abuse. The presidential speechwriting group can be asked to prepare draft remarks for the first lady, although that arrangement has not always been satisfactory, as President Nixon noted in his diary in 1972:

I am going to . . . see to it that the [speechwriting] shop does a better job in
preparing material for Pat and the girls, and [son-in-law] Ed, in the days ahead.
It just seems that they won't really buckle down and get something done unless
they think that they are doing it for me, which is a grievous error.[3]

There are limits, however, to the hours that the first lady can ask the
presidential assistants to give her, and her own perspectives and style may
be different from theirs. The first lady therefore, has a separate staff of her
own.

"Assistance and services" to the president's spouse are in fact sanctioned
in law when the spouse is helping "in the discharge of the President's
duties and responsibilities."[4] Her staff numbers approximately thirty.

Their separateness is a consequence of the presidential spouse's own
unique status in the White House hierarchy. All the men and women of
the White House staff are instantly removable by the president and she,
of course, is not. The gilt of her special position rubs off on her staff; they
are answerable first to her. President Ford remembers a discussion on this
subject with Chief of Staff Donald Rumsfeld:

One problem involved cuts of East Wing employees. That was Betty's area—
traditionally the First Lady's domain. Rummy would enter the Oval Office, show
me a list of people we could trim from her staff and ask me to talk to her about
the changes. . . . "Oh, no," I'd reply, "I'm not going to do that. You are Chief
of Staff. This is *your* plan. You go up and settle it with her." Predictably, the size
of the East Wing staff hardly changed at all.[5]

What is the first lady's establishment?

Since Mrs. Kennedy's time the first lady has her own press office that
responds to the questions and interview requests from the group of some
forty-five reporters who specialize in writing about her activities and those
of her children. She may hold press conferences, requiring advance briefing
materials, and will typically make remarks and answer questions at her
public appearances, such as those by Mrs. Reagan on the subject of drug
abuse. Meetings like the Nancy Reagan/Raisa Gorbachev "summits" or
world conferences of first ladies are of enormous media interest.

The first lady's press secretary is her staff support for all these newsmaking encounters. Mrs. Nixon's press secretary held press briefings twice a
week for the East Wing reporters. Press secretaries for first ladies attend
the presidential press secretary's daily briefings to keep informed of how
the president's own judgments are being both questioned and defended.

A new first lady may receive over ten thousand letters a month, her close
friends are given a code to guarantee direct delivery to her office. If the first

family's sons or daughters are living in the White House, as was the case during President Ford's term, they, too, get mail from the public. The central White House correspondence office has a designated unit to help with this deluge, but the first lady has her own correspondence assistants in the East Wing.

A director of scheduling and advance (this office was instituted by Mrs. Nixon) plans her calendar, synchronizes her engagements with the president's, and joins the presidential advance teams when the first lady is to accompany her husband on domestic or foreign trips. She needs her own advance representatives because it is they who guarantee that the side trips and events planned for her will match her own interests rather than the well-meaning irrelevancies that are often proposed for her by others. (In Mrs. Reagan's case, often her chief of staff personally did the advancing.)[6]

The first lady's social secretary is at the center of the tension-filled task of White House entertaining. There are an average of 300 occasions each year, and during the fall-winter-spring season, major White House social events occur almost once a week. A state dinner is a classic production. The State Dining Room seats 130; another 150 guests are invited to the musicale that follows. The Social Office is the heat sink for the incandescent pressures that burn in from the State Department, the rest of the Cabinet, the Legislative and Political and Public Liaison offices—all arguing that the guest list should make room for one more of their favored clients. Explained one veteran of the legislative affairs staff:

> We constantly fought with the Social Office about more seats at the dinner table . . . for more state dinners for Congressmen and Senators, but of course that is a never-ending debate, because the Political Office wants to bring in his pols, the Press Office wants more for the Press, and so forth on down the line. But we used those dinners to good effect.[7]

Former First Lady Betty Ford gave her side of the guest-list controversy: "The State Department used to send over proposed guest lists, and they were so dreary we hardly ever used them, because State tried to hold back all the glittering people for themselves. . . . I wasn't going to take . . . leftover guest lists."[8] In the end, the president and first lady personally approve the guest list, and often specify the table seating as well.

The Social Office puts forward the suggestions for menus, programs, the entertainment, and for the artists who will perform. It arranges their hotels and sends cars to meet them at the airport. The office instructs the chefs and has the invitations, programs, and menus printed. (The admission cards are coded to prevent counterfeiting or gate-crashing; one young gentleman tried and was caught.) The musical selections, flower arrangements, wines, and guests' attire are specified in advance. The social secretary keeps track of acceptances and regrets (with a computer), assigns and briefs the thirty-five social aides who are brought in from the armed forces, and then composes a final "scenario" memo for the president and first lady.

Gifts to the visiting head of state are purchased (by the State Department), toasts are written, and reporters and photographers invited. The receiving line is picked, and mikes, lights, and pianos are supplied. Even a portable stage may have to be assembled in the East Room.

The fine art of calligraphy is alive and well at the White House. The envelope for each formal invitation is hand-inscribed by the first lady's Graphics and Calligraphy Office; countless other gift and acknowledgment cards are created there and then engraved from the original handwork. Sanford Fox, a veteran of twenty-nine years on the first lady's staff, designed the certificate for the Medal of Freedom. The graphics staff makes the final walking diagrams for presidential trip arrivals and suggests gift ideas for official luncheons. Fox's talents have ranged from hand-lettering the inside of a gift tortoiseshell for Truman to painting a placard that read WELCOME HOME FROM THE HOSPITAL, BETTY FORD. (Campaign posters, though, are off limits.) Every day brings a different challenge to the calligraphers' creativity.

The presidential seal is a familiar motif, but only the White House can sanction its use; those approvals come from the Graphics and Calligraphy Office. If a private donor, for instance, wishes to engrave or inscribe the seal on a gift to the president, that is permissible. If the objective is to use the seal commercially, it is forbidden, since the seal implies presidential endorsement. The office, supported by the counsel, is strict in its guardianship.

Under Mrs. Reagan the practice was begun of hiring substantive officers on her staff to give her expert advice on issues which she has elevated as personal priorities. She had a "Director of Projects" within her East Wing group and later employed Ken Barum, himself a reformed drug addict and leader in drug rehabilitation endeavors, to help her with her campaign against drug abuse.

The first lady has had a chief of staff, in function if not in name, at least since the Eisenhower period. In the Reagan administration, her staff chief has also had a West Wing title, assistant or deputy assistant to the president. Attending senior staff and Scheduling Committee meetings, joining the advance teams, her staff chief is the link between the two separate but interdependent White House universes. The president and the first lady may share the same suite at night, but by day their institutional apartheid can cause mischief. A White House press secretary's graphic description of presidential surgery may offend the first lady as an invasion of privacy. On the other hand, a Betty Ford remark on "Sixty Minutes" about premarital affairs may jolt her husband's campaign strategists; Rosalynn Carter's advocacy of more funds for the mentally retarded could undercut the president's budget stance. The more that first ladies speak, testify, travel, and write, the greater will be the need for East Wing/West Wing synchronization.

Scheduling priorities provoke staff differences. Commented a former presidential chief of staff:

> There was a lot of second-level conflict between the two staffs as we got into scheduling and event-planning that I had to arbitrate. . . . There is an East Wing/West Wing clash and you have to live with it. . . . Our scheduling people would suggest that the first lady do something, and her staff would argue against it.[9]

"It was like living in two different worlds," commented one of President Kennedy's secretaries,[10] and Sorensen recounts a Kennedy remark to one of his wife's aides: "Sometimes I don't think you people in the East Wing have any understanding of our problems over here in the West Wing."[11] Chiefs of staff at both ends of the presidential corridor have to mute if not squelch the antiphonal disharmonies.

As the twentieth century ends, the office of the presidential spouse may find itself in different circumstances. A first lady in the future may be much more like a Rosalynn Carter than a Bess Truman. She may be a professional woman who wishes to continue her career. She may have come from active political life in her own right, with strong positions publicly stated. The president may be a woman, with a first gentleman in the supporting role. Any of those eventualities points to more rather than fewer East Wing staff responsibilities and will demand even closer ties between East Wing and West Wing environments.

CHAPTER 22

Second Special Counselor: The Vice President

The chief embarrassment in discussing his office is, that in explaining how little there is to be said about it one has evidently said all there is to say.

—WOODROW WILSON

. . . we agreed that he [Vice President Mondale] would truly be the second in command, involved in every aspect of governing. As a result, he received the same security briefings I got, was automatically invited to participate in all my official meetings, and helped to plan strategy for domestic programs, diplomacy and defense. . . . Our staffs cooperated without dissension, even in the most difficult times.

—JIMMY CARTER

Within the White House environment, the president's second special counselor can be—and since 1977 has been—the vice president. Only in the last three presidential terms has the vice president been welcomed into such a principal advisory role and been afforded the aides, the facilities, and the access to support it. As a result, the Office of the Vice President—a staff of over ninety persons—is a significant new center of participation in White House decision-making.

The postwar beginnings of the president's regular use of vice presidents for policy advice came in 1949. The vice president was made a statutory member of the National Security Council; Alben Barkley also came to Cabinet meetings and to Truman's "Big Four" legislative leadership sessions. Barkley was seventy-one, however, and considered that the Capitol was where he belonged. Truman evidently viewed Barkley in the same way; when the president was absent, it was Secretary of State Dean Acheson, not Barkley, who chaired Security Council meetings. If Acheson was also away, Acting Secretary James Webb presided.[1]

Richard Nixon's policy-advisory role as vice president was more substantive in that the Cabinet and the National Security Council, which he attended, were systematically used by Eisenhower for policy discussions. He spoke up often at these sessions; the author remembers one Cabinet debate on federal aid to education in which Nixon's arguments helped swing the president away from a less liberal position he had earlier taken. Nixon was present at over 171 Cabinet meetings and chaired at least 20 of them in Ike's absence. He attended more than 217 NSC meetings and presided at some 26 of those, joined 173 legislative leaders' meetings, chairing two of them. The Cabinet and the National Security Council papers were sent to Nixon; his policy assistant attended both the post-Cabinet debriefings at the White House and the meetings of the NSC Planning Board. Eisenhower's privileged daily Staff Notes information memoranda were also taken to the vice president.

Nixon suffered under limits, however. His office was on Capitol Hill; he was only a visitor at the White House. A veteran of that period (when there was no private reception area in the West Wing of the White House) recalled Nixon even looking for a place to sit while waiting for meetings. He would plop himself temporarily into a chair in the doctor's office, tucked away near the downstairs entrance. Up at the Capitol, under 1953 Senate rules, Nixon's office budget was no more than that of a senator from a one-district state (Delaware or Vermont, for instance), much smaller than his allowance as a senator from California, and, said aide Robert Cushman, "Nobody in the office had any training in handling classified material."[2] A White House assistant recalled a conversation with Cushman:

> . . . he said that it was terribly difficult to keep the Vice President informed because of the attitude of executive branch departments towards Vice Presidents. . . . the State Department refused to provide the Vice President with the Top Secret daily cable summary. Indeed it was like drawing water from a stone to get any information from the State Department at all for Nixon. . . . he struck a deal with the CIA and they bootlegged State Department cables to him. . . .[3]

Another observer was present at meetings with Secretary of State John Foster Dulles when Vice President Nixon participated. Dulles, he remembered, would remark, as an afterthought, "Oh yes, let's hear from our vice president."[4] Ike's biographer Stephen Ambrose wrote, "Nixon wanted to do more, be more visible, shoulder more responsibilities, but Eisenhower would not let him."[5]

The White House staff environment itself began to change in 1961 when Kennedy brought Vice President Johnson into the Executive Office Building, next door to the White House. As author Paul Light put it, "No longer would the Vice President belong to Capitol Hill."[6]

Johnson of course continued to attend the three series of White House meetings in which Barkley and Nixon had participated; he was "intermittently" a member of the Executive Committee of the National Security Council that met for the thirteen days of the Cuban missile crisis. Yet he was not a close policy adviser to the president. Kennedy, in the words of one of his aides,

> did not involve Lyndon Johnson in some of the major things that Lyndon wanted to be involved in. . . . their relationship was not close and he had never assigned to Johnson a major substantive responsibility. . . . What he assigned to Lyndon were things that Lyndon would come to him and ask for. And he would give them to him because . . . Kennedy always wanted to keep peace in the family and . . . because he did think Lyndon had some capacity for organizing things—getting things done.[7]

Added a Johnson intimate: "The years as vice president were the most miserable years of his life."[8]

With Johnson, however, came staff: thirteen from the Senate payroll, perhaps ten others detailed from agencies or advisory commissions.

The ebullient Hubert Humphrey was also housed next door to the White House, but was not any closer to the inner circle of policy advisers under Johnson than Johnson had been under Kennedy. Humphrey, for instance, was not a regular member of the Tuesday Lunch group that set the strategies for the war in Vietnam. As historian David Halberstam recounts,

> At the time of Pleiku he was called in for one of the smaller meetings, and he expressed himself forcefully . . . against the bombing. . . . from then on he was kept on extremely short rations by the President. . . . Humphrey was not invited to meetings, not informed of important memos or the drift of the policy. He was, in effect, frozen out.[9]

Former Agriculture Secretary Orville Freeman observes: "It isn't the principals as much as it's the staff people who report things. The Humphrey staff and the people in the White House were at each other's throats."[10]

The author had a personal encounter with the apprehensions about Humphrey in the Johnson White House. In the early spring of 1967 the National Advisory Commission on Selective Service (a public body of twenty distinguished citizens) was readying its final report on reform of the draft—an incendiary subject in those months. A presidential message to Congress was being written; legislation would be recommended. Humphrey asked for a private briefing about the commission's work. The word from the White House was "no." The request was repeated a few weeks later and the answer finally was, "Wait until the day before the release;

he's too leaky!" The author spent an hour going over the report and its recommendations with the vice president, who had many comments about both substance and legislative strategy. All in vain; the report was in concrete and the message set. The vice presidential comments were welcome only to an embarrassed executive director.

Johnson himself was literally crude. When Humphrey gave an enthusiastic speech on education in November of 1964, "Johnson," recounts Halberstam,

> was furious; this was his terrain and Humphrey was told this in no uncertain terms. Just so there would be no mistake about it, Johnson called in the White House reporters who were with him on the Ranch and told them, "Boys, I've just reminded Hubert that I've got his balls in my pocket."[11]

The many commissions of which Humphrey was chairman were nonetheless a convenient device to staff his office. Light quotes one of the Humphrey aides: "We used those commissions as a hiding place for Humphrey's staff. I'm not sure Johnson would have been so willing to have Humphrey on all those councils if he'd known what Humphrey was doing. We managed to collect a fairly large staff through the device."[12] By the time he left office, his staff numbered thirty.

In Spiro Agnew's vice presidency, the man shrank but the office expanded. Although Agnew resigned in disgrace in 1973, in February of 1970 the Budget of the United States contained a small but historic new line: "For expenses necessary to enable the Vice President to provide assistance to the President in connection with specially assigned functions, . . . $700,000."[13] The title of the appropriation was "Special Assistance to the President." (That title persists today; the amount requested for FY 1989 was $2,199,000.)

The Nixon White House interpreted that appropriations title literally; some of Agnew's staff were Nixon people, their loyalties belonging first to the president. At first, as Nixon put it,

> I told Agnew that I wanted him to assume policy-making responsibilities, and I suggested that he have an office in the West Wing of the White House, the first time in history that a Vice President would do so. I asked him to draw on his experience as a state official by taking the major responsibility for federal-state relations. . . ."[14]

The high-sounding plans did not last in practice. Agnew was moved back into the Executive Office building, and the intergovernmental-relations task was taken from his hands in December of 1972. According to Ehrlichman, he showed "mental constipation" rather than resourcefulness in conducting a study of health policy.

> Nixon found early that personal meetings with Agnew were invariably unpleasant. The President came out of them amazed at Agnew's constant self-aggrandizement. . . . Agnew's visits always included demands for more staff, better facilities, more prerogatives and perquisites. It was predictable that as Agnew complained and requested more and more, Nixon would agree to see him less frequently.[15]

Ford as vice president changed that understanding; he brought in his own men and women—and had seventy of them by August of 1974. They were specialized like a mini White House: counsel, speechwriters, a national security assistant.

In February of 1975, President Ford named his vice president, Nelson Rockefeller, to be vice chairman of the Domestic Council and gave him what looked like a limitless charter for:

- Assessing national needs and identifying alternative ways of meeting them.
- Providing rapid response to Presidential needs for policy advice.
- Coordinating the establishment of national priorities for the allocation of available resources.
- Maintaining a continuous policy review of ongoing programs.
- Proposing reforms as needed.[16]

An accompanying "Statement by the Press Secretary," however, flashed Rockefeller both a green and a yellow light. It said that the president "wants the Vice President to have a major substantive role in his administration, and he wishes to use Vice President Rockefeller's talents, energies and experience to the fullest," but it added, "The President considers the Domestic Council an integral part of the White House staff."[17]

For nine months, Rockefeller tried but failed to squeeze between these two instructions. His talents spurred him into the very advocacy that the White House staff found irreconcilable with the president's budget priorities. He had good personal access to the president, but strode into the Oval Office more as a salesman than an analyst. Light quotes a Ford aide from the Office of Management and Budget:

> There is something inherently difficult about the Vice-President wanting to be an advocate. Unless his views and programs are amazingly coincident with the President's, he will be cut down. The President can't submerge his ideas to

accommodate the Vice-President. What Nelson had in mind was to control domestic policy, as if he was saying "I know everything there is to know about domestic policy and Ford will have to listen." What Ford was thinking was "I'll listen to Rocky's ideas and make my decisions on the basis of what I think is important."[18]

Carter's plans for Vice President Mondale are summed up in the quotation at the beginning of this chapter. Those plans worked, but only because each man contributed some indispensable ingredients. During the campaign of 1976, Mondale installed his personal staff in Atlanta, where his group worked side by side with what turned out to be the future White House staff. There was cooperation from the start, instead of the usual endemic rivalries. On taking office, Carter added a potent increment to the vice presidential tradition: he put Mondale into an office in the White House West Wing, adjoining the suite of the chief of staff. Mondale's own senior assistants were given White House passes so they could come and go easily, and Mess privileges so they could continue their Atlanta-born camaraderie.

For his part, Mondale learned lessons from his predecessors' experiences and asked Carter not to saddle him with any commission chairmanships or specific line assignments. Supported by a staff of sixty, he held himself open for giving the president confidential advice on any matter under the sun, and did it quietly and frequently. Two of his senior staff members became deputies, respectively, in Carter's domestic policy and national security offices; Mondale's staff were welcome at White House staff meetings and the latter's chief of staff, in Carter's own words, "became one of my most valuable advisers."[19]

Reagan and Bush followed the Carter-Mondale model of a relationship that was close and quiet. Regularly on Thursdays, the two men had a private lunch. Bush's own chief of staff accompanied him to meetings of the National Security Council and to the hour-long "Weekly Update" meetings Monday noons with the president. Others of his staff represented him at White House senior staff, legislative strategy, and schedule-planning conferences. As Reagan himself commented, ". . . George Bush as Vice President has been part of all we are doing. . . . Why do you let able-bodied manpower sit by? . . . I always felt that. . . . that man should be like an executive vice president in a corporation. He should be involved in what was going on and have assignments and so forth. . . ."[20]

Like Mondale, Bush had a West Wing office, but he had five others as well: working space on the first floor of the Executive Office Building, a refurbished ceremonial office on the second floor, a suite in the Capitol, some rooms in the Senate Office Building, and his campaign office in Houston. The vice presidential staff numbered over ninety, not including his campaign organization.

At the beginning of the administration, Bush was given the specific assignment of chairing a Task Force on Regulatory Reform; he delegated the heavy part of that duty to his counsel. Reagan named him crisis manager, but insiders acknowledge this was a diplomatic compromise among the secretaries of state and defense and the national security assistant, none of whom would tolerate another of the three being so designated. Crisis management in any case was not a predominant Bush role in the Reagan presidency.

Beginning in January 1977 therefore, the nation has witnessed a new scene at the White House: vice presidents who are major players in the president's policy game, respected and influential. They have been given big blue chips for playing: regular access to the president, offices in the West Wing, papers and information shared, large staffs of their own. Mondale and Bush played the game quietly, reserving their advocacy for their private sessions with the president and keeping mum about it.

A vice president's largest chip—his constitutional status of being unremovable by the president—is, paradoxically, both potent and irrelevant. Potent because it separates him (or her) from all other associates in the White House, irrelevant because any vice president's influence with the president depends not on the former's constitutional underpinning but on the trust and confidence generated in their one-on-one relationship.

That same confidence could easily have come under strain from their other unique attribute as vice presidents: the ambition each has had to become president himself. Can any vice president transform himself from being a hidden-hand adviser for three, or seven, years and then emerge from the president's shadow as a candidate advertising his "I-am-my-own-man" leadership? Bush's chief aide said of the vice president in October of 1987, "He's emasculated by the office of vice president."[21]

What will be the vice president's role in the future White House?

The practice since 1977 affords no guarantee of the arrangements in 1989; each new president will determine where the vice president fits in his policy family. But the game will not start on a tabula rasa. There has now been formed a precedent of expectations—by presidents, by vice presidents, and by the public. Office, staff, information, access—each new vice president will count on beginning with the same stack of blue chips that Mondale and Bush have had.

Former President Gerald Ford would go even further than his two successors; he would have a future president seat the vice president in the most important staff chair in the entire White House.

> I personally feel that the Vice President could, very properly, be the Chief of Staff in the White House itself. . . . In that way, the Vice President is fully informed on what is . . . transpiring in the Oval Office. I feel it is better to have an elected official in that position than an appointed official.[22]

Ford acknowledges the possible conflict between the vice president's duties in the Senate and his chief-of-staff responsibilities, and recognizes that the vice president could be torn between the anonymity required as a staff chief and the public posture of a person ambitious to be president. Ford's proposition, however, is yet another measure of the strength of the expectations about what the vice presidential role could be.

The Ford viewpoint, plus the experience in the three succeeding presidential terms, now suggests that within the White House policy family of the future, the vice president has a good chance of remaining the president's second special counselor. In the words of a presidential scholar:

> The past two decades have seen the transformation of the republic's Second Citizen from a minor political figure into an important presidential advisor. The vice-presidency now offers its incumbent the opportunity to be among that small circle of senior presidential aides and counselors. . . . with all the other demands placed on the First Citizen by the post-modern presidency, the president can use the sort of help and advice that an activist vice-president has to offer. So, it is likely that the new vice-presidency is here to stay.[23]

CHAPTER 23

The President's Centripetal Offices

Legislation should be enacted . . . prohibiting assistants to the President from issuing orders and interposing themselves between the President and the head of any department or agency or any one of the divisions in the Executive Office of the President. The legislation should include appropriate sanctions to be applied to both the initiator of such illegal orders and those officials who accept and carry them out.
—1974 Panel of the National Academy of Public Administration.

. . . the speech comes in late. Now, what's the chief of staff's job? The chief of staff has to heave his body in the middle and try to figure out a way for the . . . speech to finally reach the substantive people. . . . But what happens when you do that? That's throwing sand in the gears and it gets grindy, and pretty soon out come news stories that Cheney is having a fight with the speechwriter. He couldn't care less about the speechwriter. All he wants is for the ultimate product to accomplish what the President intended. It isn't personal . . . and yet that's where the rubber hits the ground. And if there's no rubber on the tire, it's steel, and that's sparks.
—Donald Rumsfeld

The previous pages have described the sixteen policy offices of the modern White House staff. Collectively, the place is like a racing car—its sixteen cylinders charged with political high-octane. The president climbs into the driver's seat and turns the inaugural ignition. The question is: will the engine hum or sputter?

The White House power pack hums only if there are "distributors" in the system, some signaling and control centers that will energize the heated machinery to move in synchronization and at the president's pace. There are four centralizing points in the contemporary White House: the staff secretary, the Office of Cabinet Affairs, the President's Personal Office, and the chief of staff.

Why are they indispensable?

As the preceding sections reveal, the White House staff today is a supercharged environment of capable but diverse presidential instruments. The sixteen policy domains are specialized, and necessarily so—for example, speechwriters, arms control experts, the counsel. Each of the sixteen claims exclusive jurisdiction over its share of the presidential universe. No one but the appointments secretary makes scheduling commitments; no other staff units than the Presidential Personnel Office dispense patronage; no White House officer is to bargain with senators or congressmen without the imprimatur of the legislative affairs director. Such jurisdictional separations are unavoidable; contradictory commitments in any part of the president's business produce administrative chaos within the White House and political damage to the chief executive himself.

The staff, though, is more than boxes surrounded by rules; it is a nest of brainy and aggressive people. The sixteen chiefs and their several hundred assistants are men and women of varying ages and professions, both military and civilian, from every corner of the country and from different races and religions. Of most significance, they are brought into the White House from every faction of the president's party—liberals, conservatives, moderates, and hard-liners. Like the Cabinet, the White House staff is a confederation of built-in dissimilarity.

As a result, their turf sensitivities are interwoven with policy and personal differences, making the White House home to constant friendly debates if not unfriendly dissension. In Truman's time, there were what seemed like "warring camps" of Clifford or Murphy against Connelly or Steelman.[1] Black Eisenhower assistant Fred Morrow despaired at hearing his colleague Howard Pyle assure southern whites that they had "little to fear from the Eisenhower Administration on civil rights."[2] Kennedy's so-called "egg-heads," Ted Sorensen and Myer Feldman, tangled with the Irish politicians Kenneth O'Donnell and Larry O'Brien. In Nixon's years, Daniel Patrick Moynihan crossed swords with Arthur Burns on domestic policy while Buchanan jousted with Garment on school desegregation. The issue of federalism was debated within the Nixon staff by the exchange of contrapuntal essays signed "Publius" and "Cato." The Ford term saw acrimony between Donald Rumsfeld and Robert Hartmann; Carter's Mark Siegel resigned over the issue of arms to Saudi Arabia, which Brzezinski favored. Reagan's "pragmatists" feuded with his "true believers." These are men and women of high-voltage convictions; the White House policy grids are constantly crackling with ideological if not *ad hominem* sparks.

If the electrical discharges are internal, the president benefits. In option papers, speech drafts, and private meetings, the clash of viewpoints illuminates his choices. The more heated the dissension, however, the greater is the temptation for each protagonist to evade the debate, try to run privately to the president with a skewed presentation and extract a premature commitment. Left to himself, a president may tolerate or even encourage such forays.

The more unfriendly the dissension, however, the more likely it is to break out in public; the protagonists leak their one-sided accounts to favorite columnists or reporters. Such is the end stage of White House differences, reflecting poorly on the president by implying that he is not master in his own house.

White House senior staff members are driven men and women, fired as is the president with the compulsion to change the government and its laws, frustrated by the time it takes to "turn the ship around." As he began his second term, Nixon gave every Cabinet and staff member a four-year calendar; each page torn off revealed, on the next sheet, the number of days left in his administration. In a covering message he included these words: "The Presidential term which begins today consists of 1461 days—no more and no less. . . . The 1461 days which lie ahead are but a short interval in the flowing stream of history. Let us live them to the hilt, working every day to achieve . . . [our] goals."[3] Lesser deadlines are incessant; there is little toleration for error; impatience for results is overwhelming.

While the considerable egos of White House staff are nurtured by the perquisites of office—radio cars, the Mess, *Air Force One,* the *Sequoia,* Camp David—they are further honed to a sharp edge by the realities of sacrifice. Seventy-hour weeks are the norm; Saturdays are given up and often Sundays as well; a special White House telephone rings at odd hours in senior staff members' homes. Their private lives are disrupted by presidential travel. A staffer with Truman at Key West recalled his winter week in the sunshine while his wife had to stay home with the kids in Arlington. Even the off-duty activities of White House staff are subject to media scrutiny, their spouses and children put under stress. A few receive threats to their lives.

White House staff, accordingly, are men and women who are warm in their common loyalties, but tense from the pressures of unending demands. It is a molten environment.

The White House staff parallels the Cabinet in a second essential respect. Important presidential issues are no more confined within one or two White House jurisdictional fences than they are within departmental walls. A major presidential initiative cuts across most or all of the sixteen bailiwicks of the White House community, requiring closely sequenced, multiple actions.

Assume, for instance, that the president and the first lady were to fly to Mexico City to announce a financial-aid package for Mexico in exchange for a drug-suppression agreement. Consider the elements of the White House staff that would have to involve themselves in such an enterprise:

- The national security assistant would ensure that State, Defense, Treasury, Justice, and the intelligence community are united on the substance of the agreement. He would prepare the briefing papers for the president's meetings.
- The vice president, if it were Mr. Bush, would contribute his experience from having chaired the South Florida Task Force on Drug Control.
- The drug-abuse "czar" would have helped to negotiate the agreement and would accompany the presidential party.
- The speechwriters would draft the presidential address, banquet toasts, and arrival and departure statements.
- The counsel would review the legal obligations the United States is undertaking.
- The legislative affairs staff would sound out congressional willingness to approve the aid proposal and would invite senators or congressmen to fly with the president.
- The Advance Office would send two successive teams to Mexico City to plan every detail of the trip ahead of time.
- The first lady's staff would be represented on those teams, to design complementary events in Mexico City for her.
- The Scheduling Office would allocate the president's time during the entire period.
- The Press Office would arrange briefings and announcements to coincide with maximum media coverage.
- The communications staff would plan a publicity initiative, including appearances by Cabinet officers and the sending of copies of the presidential address to hundreds of local newspapers.
- The Office of Public Liaison would begin a series of White House information sessions with the interest groups whose support is needed with the Congress.

Such a hypothetical trip is more typical than fanciful; enterprises of that sort are the regular fare of White House life. A summit with the Russians is many times as complicated; even a quiet day in the Oval Office requires support from many offices.

Will all these staff contributions be self-initiated, be completed according to specifications, arrive on time, and be in the sequence the president needs? Not in today's White House.

The necessary synchronization will not happen without a primary signaling office, a tracking and coordination center that looks ahead, anticipates the president's total requirements, specifies assignments, and imposes a production discipline on a staff that is inherently heterogeneous. Such are the three centripetal offices—the Staff Secretary, the Office of Cabinet Affairs, and the president's personal office—that directly assist the fourth, the White House chief of staff himself.

THE STAFF SECRETARY

For internal coordination, the staff secretary is the initial control point. The first Hoover Commission proposed this office in 1949; it was established under Eisenhower and has been continuously a part of the White House staff since 1969.

If an option memorandum or Cabinet Council paper is heading for the president's attention, the staff secretary circulates it among the White House offices which should see it, requiring comment within a specified deadline. (Some sensitive NSC documents and occasionally other confidential proposals are handled separately, but the Iran-contra affair illustrated the risk a president runs when his own coordination control point is short-circuited.) If a speech draft is newly prepared, it gets the same treatment. Should policy differences surface, they are flagged early for extra attention.

The staff secretary (and the chief of staff if need be) will subject papers for the president to a tough procedural scrutiny. Are memoranda verbose? Are they larded with extraneous details? Has the author slanted the options, including a favored "Option I" balanced only by three "clunkers" instead of genuine alternatives? Explained one Reagan aide, "We want to professionalize the process."

The staff secretary attends staff meetings, for example, Sherman Adams' regular staff assemblies and Reagan's Monday "weekly update" sessions, to sharpen his sensitivity about what is going on and to note down all the action assignments.

Each afternoon the staff secretary assembles the president's "Daily Book." On top is the schedule for the next day; under tabs or in folders are the briefing papers for every presidential appointment: a speech, a meeting, a taping, a photo session. (The staff's proposed "talking points" for meetings are often specific to a fault. Johnson reportedly required presentation proposals for international conferences to be written in "Texas language" so he could read them aloud; Reagan's staff went so far as to write out first-person wording for him to use at even the most mundane appointments.[4] On the scene, in person, however, presidents usually escape from the confinements of their cues and extemporize with their own personal warmth.)

Each event's "action officer" has been in charge of all the preparations, both substantive and logistical; the action officer will sit in on most of the Oval Office meetings that are held, to record the decision. "Should sit in" perhaps, rather than "will." If the practice of leaking is pervasive, this essential staff service will suffer. Former Chief of Staff Donald Regan observed that during his time at the White House, leaks "had achieved such epidemic proportions that the inner circle was afraid to take notes lest they read them next day in the newspapers or hear them broadcast over the networks." He added:

> In the past, confidential clerks sat in the Oval Office with notebook in hand, recording the exchanges between Presidents and some of their visitors. This provided a record to support or correct the President's memory of events and an aide-memoire to history. No such record can exist, however, except in conditions of inviolable confidentiality. And no such condition existed or was even imaginable in the White House that I knew.[5]

Finally, the staff secretary is the funnel for papers coming back out of the Oval Office. If a decision is marked or notes scribbled on briefing papers, he scoops up the inscribed documents, notifies those concerned of the chief executive's action, and builds the archival record.

THE OFFICE OF CABINET AFFAIRS

The external coordination circuit is managed in the Office of Cabinet Affairs; it connects with the respective chiefs of staff who are resident in each Cabinet department. Eisenhower began this system, too, in the fall of 1954.[6]

While meetings of the full Cabinet (described in chapter 2) may not always fit a president's style, the Office of Cabinet Affairs is still the primary guarantor that Cabinet members will be consulted on all presidential business (other than the separately handled NSC papers and in the other instances where special secrecy has been mandated). Working in parallel with the staff secretary, the same Cabinet Council papers, option memoranda, and draft speeches are sent by the Office of Cabinet Affairs to the affected departments.

In a "morning briefing" system, each departmental chief of staff is expected to send in a daily note alerting the Office of Cabinet Affairs what the "lead issue" is expected to be in the department that day. "The Department of Justice is the worst," commented one Cabinet affairs official, who must therefore scout behind the "nothing to report" notices with telephone calls to ferret out what otherwise might take the White House by surprise. The OCA staffers in turn keep their Cabinet "clients" up to date on planned presidential actions. Knowing what transpires at White House senior staff meetings, they share the needed information through their Cabinet circuits. "We are a sort of mother superior and they are our flock," explained another Cabinet affairs aide. "Cabinet officers know we are their helpers and guardians within this fast-moving place over here."[7]

Helpfulness, however, is backed up by vigilance. A Reagan Cabinet officer who previously had been a White House staff member smuggled a supply of the president's distinctive pale green stationery into his new office—and on one occasion put in a letter for immediate presidential signature. Only an alert OCA ensured that the policy-review process was not short-circuited.

For the Staff Secretary and Cabinet Affairs offices, the formal act of circulating papers is only the minimum. In both suites, there are personal contacts, informal meetings, telephones always in use. These coordination systems may appear to be merely bustling with small, prosaic arrangements—paper flow and all that—but the Iran-contra affair illuminates just how much hangs on having a set of presidential initials, on where papers do flow and how records are kept.

THE PERSONAL OFFICE

The president's personal office—his private secretaries and the civilian aide—is a third and very small control unit at his immediate doorstep. Stephen Ambrose's description of Ike's private secretaries, one of whom, Ann Whitman, was with him during the eight White House years, could be applied to those of any president:

> Both women were extremely competent at their jobs, highly intelligent, comfortable to be around. They knew his professional concerns intimately. He could, and often did, comment to them in detail on matters of world importance. He knew they would understand the most cryptic remark; even better he knew they would be completely on his side, because their devotion to him was unquestioning. He drove them like slaves, dawn to dusk. He made impossible demands on them—have this paper out by so-and-so—and they met those demands. . . . [They] gave him an outlet for that big, gutsy laugh, or for that terrible temper. With them, he could be as angry or as contemptuous toward another man as he wished, without having to fear that the story of his outburst would be all over town the next day.[8]

Ms. Whitman, as is well known now, kept a diary, at the president's request; among Eisenhower's papers, it is one of the most revealing and candid sources of information about Ike's daily official life and his reactions to pressures and people around him. Inevitably, the personal secretary is also a gatekeeper, since the president's back door opens into her office. Many are the White House staffers—in all the recent presidencies—who used that access (and her cooperation) to duck the scrutiny of those at the front entrance. For this reason, a chief of staff must diplomatically fashion an arrangement to enlist her gatekeeping into his intelligence network.

The civilian aide is, day to day, the schedule enforcer. "There were three dynamite cartridges I could send in to him," recalled one. " 'Mr. President, you are running late' was the first warning. 'There are a hundred fifty kids waiting in the East Room' was the next imperative, and, finally, 'Your whole day's program is being disrupted!' "[9]

If a presidential speech recognizes people who are "with us today," the civilian aide ensures they are in fact on the scene. Should a Cabinet member or other visitor petition for an oral promise from the president while walking with him through the Residence or standing at his car, the aide is there, and makes a mental note to put it into the staff system promptly. On trips, it is the civilian aide who leads the president and his party on the preselected paths, through back doors, kitchens, unused corridors. "I once led him smack into a china closet," recalled Ford's aide ruefully. In some motorcades during the 1984 campaign, Reagan's civilian aide helped enhance presidential security by riding in a decoy limousine, even donning a Ronald Reagan face-mask to confuse potential terrorists.

For the unexpected, the vexatious, the sudden bursts of presidential temper, "I was part of the ventilator," Nixon's personal civilian aide, Steve Bull, remembers. "There are always two people in that Oval Office," he said, "the president, and the human being who happens to be the president of the United States. I had little to do with the first, but concentrated on the second. There was such trust, that when he and I were together, the president was alone."[10]

In every minute of every day, these three small control offices are being shoved and challenged. If they fail, the president lies exposed—vulnerable to White House or Cabinet short circuits that can be traumatic in outcome no matter how well meaning in origin.

The opening chapter of this book noted the power of the centrifugal forces that pull the Executive Branch agencies away from their single, responsible chief. But inside the White House as well, the chief executive presides over a confederation of specialized functions and contending personalities. Pressures to bypass the coordination controls are so intense that the staff, Cabinet, and personal secretaries need reenforcement. A senior guardian there must be, standing watch for the president over the integrity of the entire decision process. This is the White House chief of staff.

THE CHIEF OF STAFF

The title may sound grandiose, even militaristic; the two presidents following Nixon avoided it. Donald Rumsfeld and Richard Cheney were designated "staff coordinators" in the Ford years. President Carter began his presidency by banishing not only the title but the function as well. He was wedded to a "spokes of the wheel" arrangement where he was the hub and each senior staff office connected to him directly. It didn't work, and his own staff told him so.

"I continue to believe that our most serious structural problem is the lack of internal White House coordination," wrote Domestic Policy advisor Stuart Eizenstat to President Carter only eleven months after they entered the White House. While the staff feels comfortable with one another, he observed, "there is no mechanism by which, on a regular basis, we can find out what the other is doing that may have impact on an area in which we are working. . . . no one has been given the directive to sort out the various priorities of our work, to coordinate our work and make sure it is all going in the same direction, before it all pours in to you." Acknowledging Carter's aversion to the chief-of-staff title, Eizenstat diplomatically proposed the same responsibility with a different label:

> . . . this White House coordination function, which is critical . . . can be done by a key "coordinator" to whom we would all look as a point of coordination between us. This would be particularly useful also in making sure that there was domestic input into foreign policy decisions and likewise that there was foreign policy input into domestic decisions.[11]

Nearly a decade later, distinguished presidential scholar Richard Neustadt agrees: "Even at [the] . . . minimum you do need some administrative coordinator . . . a modicum of administrative tidiness."[12]

"Administrative," however, is too prosaic an adjective. The chief of staff is *system manager*—the boss of none but the quarterback of everything. He commands no senior person in the White House, but the decision-making procedures he enforces leave not one of the sixteen staff centers exempt. His task is not to redo the internal work of any of them but to guarantee that when their product touches the concern of others on the staff (as it always does), the linkages are made. The chief of staff will not second-guess the national security assistant on strategy in the Persian Gulf, but if the president's legal powers are questioned, or if a congressional consultation impends, he will see to it that the counsel or the Legislative Affairs Office is in the picture. As former Ford Chief of Staff Donald Rumsfeld recalled, "You are the person who sets up the staff system so that there is an orderly flow of work, meetings, paper, appointments, thought, and action, and that it satisfies the president, and serves the president. You bring those disparate threads up through a needle eye."[13] As for the first lady's and the vice president's territories, here the president's personal word may be needed so that the chief of staff can also glue them de facto into the whole White House framework.

While the chief of staff's authority comes from only one place, his intelligence sources must be ubiquitous, his antennae tuned to every corner of the White House establishment. "It's 'walking-around management,'" Rumsfeld remembers. "You have lunch in the Mess; you talk to congressmen and senators and press people, you hear things and learn things, *and end up asking questions.*"[14]

There can be no significant enterprise afoot of which the chief of staff is unaware—be it a planned speech by the first lady or a covert action hatching in the National Security Council. Thus alerted, it is he who must be able to say, to the national security assistant or to any other senior White House staff member, "Hold everything, let's have the boss look at this once more."

While past chiefs of staff (Adams and Haldeman for instance) have hung back from positioning themselves directly in the national security affairs decision process, President Reagan—in the Iran-contra aftermath—affirmed the chief of staff role here in perhaps the most explicit fashion in all the history of that office. At the president's invitation, the chief of staff "shall attend NSC meetings," the president wrote, and he was made a formal member of the National Security Planning Group and the Senior Review Group. National security decision documents, including "all proposed Findings and MONs [memoranda of notification detailing changes in findings]" for intended covert actions were to be transmitted "to the President through the Chief of Staff." "The National Security Assistant," Reagan instructed, was to keep the chief of staff "fully informed on all matters of substance."[15]

The chief of staff must close the Oval Office door to some, open it to others—but only because he knows the president's own priorities. To one Cabinet officer "who carried a huge briefcase and had an unending flow of items to talk to Nixon about," H. R. Haldeman must have seemed a barrier. To a legislative leader whose arm Richard Cheney had to twist to bring him back *into* the Ford Oval Office to avert a misunderstanding, Cheney must have seemed a nag. The chief of staff is both, and will absorb the heat for being so. He must be as wary of the staff or Cabinet member who wants to tell the president only the "good news" as he is alert to those who avoid the Oval Office, claiming that "we mustn't bother the president." The chief of staff assumes all those unpopular postures—he's a "javelin-catcher," observed Carter Chief Jack Watson.[16]

Surprising as it sounds, a chief of staff must at times tell even the president to "go slow." A president can be tired, mad, punch-drunk, preoccupied; he needs a buffer person at whom to vent an angry command, who will perhaps say "Yes, sir" but then do nothing. Scholar Fred Greenstein quotes Eisenhower:

I told my staff . . . once in a while you people have just got to be my safety-valve. So I'll get you in here and I will let go, but this is for you and your knowledge, and your knowledge only. Now I've seen these people going out, and I've gotten a little extreme, a little white, but pretty soon one of them comes in and laughs and says, "Well, you were in good form this morning, Mr. President. . . ."[17]

Both former presidential assistants Haldeman and Califano describe their similar experiences. When Nixon issued an intemperate instruction on one occasion, Haldeman remembered, "I said nothing more, then stepped out of the office and placed the order immediately on my mental 'no-action-ever' shelf."[18] President Johnson had the same habit and Califano used the same response. Califano comments: "After three years of serving on his White House staff, he would have expected me to have some sense of how to measure his true meaning when he spoke in anger."[19]

Illustrating the importance of enforcing escape-proof coordination systems are three notable failures, from the Truman, Nixon, and Reagan presidencies.

On September 10, 1946, Secretary of Commerce Henry Wallace came into the White House to clear with Truman in person a speech about foreign policy that he intended to give two days later in New York. Reportedly, Wallace realized that the Department of State would not approve of what he was going to say, since it undercut the position being taken by Secretary of State James Byrnes, who was in Paris. Wallace, however, read his speech aloud to the president. As historian Robert Donovan's account states, "The President, either through preoccupation with other matters or simply through lack of insight as to how others might read the speech, allowed Wallace to consider it cleared."[20]

When queried by the press, Truman had to admit that he had approved the speech, and as the embarrassment grew worse, Byrnes threatened to resign. Angry at himself as well as at Wallace, Truman fired his secretary of commerce.

In letting himself be importuned to clear a speech, Truman put an unfair burden on himself. What he needed then but didn't have was an airtight staffing system, which would extract from even a Cabinet member's hands a policy statement requiring interdepartmental review, and which would insist on completing that review before the secretary even got into the Oval Office.

The second example of failure, the Watergate wiretap, occurred when a supposedly strict staffing system was in effect, in the Nixon White House. It was apparently not strict enough. If Chief of Staff Haldeman's account is to be believed, the president, through private conversations with White House assistant Charles Colson, "caused those burglars to break into O'Brien's office." Of Colson, Haldeman writes: "Even though I knew he was a potentially troublesome person and represented a real possibility for damage, I let him go ahead rather than doing something about it. . . . I dealt with what came before me, leaving the rest to others." He commented as well: "Had Watergate been handled through the usual White House staff system . . . it never would have happened in the first place."[21] Watergate, of course, was a disaster involving many other actions and people, but this one stupid move, Haldeman implies, might have been stopped cold.

The third example, the Iran-contra debacle, is another instance of a supposedly tough chief of staff who in the end was not tough enough. Under questioning by the House-Senate Investigating Committee in July of 1987, former Chief of Staff Donald Regan admitted that he allowed National Security Assistant John Poindexter to "pass papers to the President . . . getting his signature on them and having them returned . . . outside the normal way." When pressed, he acknowledged, "I sort of lost track of what was going on."[22] The Tower Commission itself was unforgiving. "He [Regan], as much as anyone, should have insisted that an orderly process be observed. . . . He must bear primary responsibility for the chaos that descended upon the White House when . . . disclosure did occur."[23]

Haldeman and Regan may be underestimating what their respective presidents personally knew and personally commanded, thus putting too severe a burden on their own shoulders. The lesson, however, seems clear.

A chief of staff cannot afford to let *any* people or information go past him without review. The hotter the enthusiast who marches toward the Oval Office, the colder must be the scrutiny.

How cold? Does this mean that a chief of staff will inevitably be tagged as an abrupt and arrogant martinet? Sherman Adams was called "the great stone face"; Haldeman "the Iron Chancellor," "with a gaze that would freeze Medusa"; Rumsfeld the "Praetorian" and "the Haldeman who smiles." A joke told about Regan was: "He's leaving to be a cardinal. For most of us it is a relief to know that we will now only have to kiss his ring."[24]

Most chiefs of staff will not escape those labels. Asked if he would have changed his style, Adams declared, "No, I could not have gotten the job done"; Haldeman acknowledged, "I should have used a velvet glove," but then reflected that courtesy could be misunderstood, that when he spoke he was not merely making a polite suggestion, he was conveying a presidential order.

Former President Ford summed up his experience:

> The Chiefs of Staff we had were on the ball, paying attention to their responsibility—which was the administrative side. They weren't worried about getting their face in a picture with the President; they weren't worrying about getting recognition themselves; *they ran the shop.*[25]

The chief of staff is system manager, but around the Cabinet and in the White House, the system he is trying to manage throbs with centrifugal thrust. While the White House is a unifying counterforce to the pluralist Cabinet, within the White House staff itself sixteen miniworlds spin in separate orbits. The central staff offices, and the chief of staff, are the centripetal forces for the lot of them.

PART III

The Professional
White House

As a new president inches down Pennsylvania Avenue in his inaugural parade, the cheers and bands proclaim an exuberant message: the changing of the guard. Unless the occasion is a second-term inauguration, the presidential and vice presidential families and their accompanying staffs celebrate the coming fresh start, the break with the past. The "empty" White House, the nation assumes, awaits the surge of new beginnings.

The reality, fortunately, is not as stark.

Throughout the modern White House are teams of men and women who serve the continuing office of the chief executive, loyal to whoever is the incumbent, proud of their unique place in American public administration. They are the professional White House, the support staffs for the contemporary presidency. Some of their heads or members will change with a new administration, but for almost all of them the morning after inauguration will be one more, albeit breathtaking, day in years of White House service.

The support staffs are large, unknown, unsung—and indispensable. No book about the White House staff is complete without a look at who they are and what they do.

THE EXECUTIVE CLERK

Every office in the White House handles "presidential papers," but one category alone is so special that it is under the exclusive care of a staff that handles nothing else. These are the original copies of the documents that, signed by the president, represent his official public actions. They include public laws, vetoes, executive orders, nominations, proclamations, commissions, pardons, treaties, and reports and messages to the Congress. For these, the executive clerk is the last stop before presidential signature and the first receiver afterward.

The executive clerk and his staff of four work in a room packed with history. A picture near the corner is of Maurice C. Latta, who joined the White House staff when McKinley was president and served in or at the head of the clerk's office for fifty years. (Latta's predecessor, Rudolph Forster, served for forty-six years; his successor, William J. Hopkins, for forty. The incumbent, Ronald Geisler, is already a twenty-three-year veteran.) The opening entry in their card file of presidential appointees is dated 1911. While the executive clerk's computer terminals blink with the urgency of the present, the surrounding shelves are crammed with the precedents of the past.

The executive clerk's office doesn't just "handle" the cascade of presidential documents; it researches them. Each appointment, for instance, is checked against the law that authorizes it, comparing the paper the president will sign with the precise requirements of the statute. In the clerk's bookcase are nineteen loose-leaf volumes specifying the legal authority for each of the over 2,600 nominations or appointments the president could make. That compilation was begun by William Hopkins in 1952; today every new law Congress passes is studied for changes that may have to be made in the loose-leaf collection. As of October 1987, President Reagan had sent 3,597 civilian nominations to the Senate.

The parchment copies of the bills passed by Congress are deemed "presented to the President" when they reach the executive clerk's doorway. The clerk keeps rigid watch over the ten-day clock that then begins to run; at the end of a Congress, there may be two hundred bills waiting in the White House at one time. The clerk's office is the president's "pocket" for pocket vetoes (bills unsigned and disapproved by the president after the Congress has adjourned). Normal vetoes, like other formal messages to the Congress, when it is in session, are delivered in person by a clerk's aide to the House and Senate chambers—the aide being the only staff officer in the White House who is permitted on the floor of either body. (The aides must stand in the back of the chamber until recognized by the chair and, the clerk recalls, "have on occasion been literally hissed and booed—usually good-naturedly—off the floor of both houses" when delivering an unpopular veto.)[1]

As of late March 1988, President Reagan had sent 1,012 presidential messages to the Congress, 63 of them vetoes (28 more stayed in the clerk's "pocket"). If, while the Congress is in session, a veto is not received within ten days, an enrolled bill becomes law; on several occasions, deliveries of veto messages have been rushed to the Capitol with less than twenty minutes to spare.

Besides messages, which are his own initiatives, the president is directed by law to send reports to the Congress. The executive clerk's computer tracks each such requirement, and its deadline; current statutes mandate seven hundred of them.

Knowing, as they do, the exact status of each bill awaiting signature, the executive clerk and his staff field telephone queries from agencies or the public. On one day at the end of a congressional session, twenty-four hundred calls were answered.

The executive clerk's office continues to be the modern end of a 130-year White House tradition; its computer records, notebooks, library, and card files are, fortunately, not cleaned out the night before Inaugural, but are passed from administration to administration.

THE WHITE HOUSE TELEPHONE OPERATORS

In 1878 it was "the Executive Mansion" and its newly installed telephone number was 1. More than a century later, the famous number, 202-456-1414, is receiving 48,000 calls a day, with peaks as high as 136,000 (when U.S. aircraft bombed Libya). Some twenty operators, including an all-night shift, staff the main switchboard in the Executive Office Building. They are professionals in their high-tension work; one chief operator retired in 1978 after twenty-nine years of service. At their fingertips is a file (going back to the Roosevelt administration) of ten thousand VIP names; any person who is in the news is a candidate for inclusion.

The White House operators are accorded the special privilege of being able to interrupt a connection anywhere, and they are famous for locating the sought-after recipient of a VIP phone call wherever he or she is in the world. The first position operator handles the president's calls, one of her first concerns being the authentication of people who call in to speak to the chief executive. The caller is put on hold while offices or spouses are checked for verification; the call is then logged for name and time.

Smaller switchboards are usually set up at presidential retreats, such as

Johnson's ranch in Texas, and operators flown out to staff them. "I always kept a change of clothes in a bag" remembered one veteran of eighteen years of duty.[2]

Caroline Kennedy (at age five) called and asked to speak to Santa Claus. With the help of a gruff-voiced gent in the Transportation Office, the call was completed, and she told him of her Christmas wish list. "John-John wants a helicopter," she is reported to have added; "he sees his daddy using one all the time."

Crank calls, children's calls, president's calls, all part of the working day. One night after midnight, the president's light went on; Kennedy had one question: "Where can I find a can opener?"

THE VOLUNTEER AND COMMENT OFFICE

As chief of state, the president is "president of all the people," say the textbooks, and it appears that more and more of the people themselves are discovering this axiom. By the 1970s, the White House switchboard operators were becoming swamped with calls from the general public. The Nixon staff designed a supplementary answering system; volunteers were invited to come to the White House to help answer the thousands of public queries. The idea worked; like other White House staff innovations, the successful initiative of the seventies has now become a standard service. The White House staff today finds itself augmented by five hundred men and women who, as regular volunteers, help the president, with little other reward than their own pride of service.

The volunteers are typically supporters of the president; a new group—equally indispensable—would join up after a turnover inauguration. They are organized in the Volunteer and Comment Office, where a director and two assistants mobilize the principal volunteer activities: answering public calls and addressing and mailing presidential cards.

Twenty cubicles have been built into a ground-floor room of the Executive Office Building. Several of them are staffed daily by volunteers who donate their time one or two days a week. On the nights of presidential speeches or press conferences, all twenty phones are covered to handle the flood of calls. A separate telephone number, 202-456-7639, has been listed to lead directly to this office; during Reagan's time, some evangelical television stations displayed it during their broadcasts, urging viewers to "call to say you love the president!"[3] They did. In fact on any typical day, five hundred calls are received by the Volunteer and Comment Office. 252,000 came in during 1986.

But love is not their only sentiment. Most of the callers comment on current issues, supporting or disagreeing with the president. "We are delighted to have your opinion," they are told, and the numbers of calls are carefully tallied: from what state, what issue, pro or con. Monthly totals are shown to the president. Many ask questions: "Why is the flag at half-staff today?"; "Has the White House always been white?"—and the volunteers consult their reference sources. A few threaten the president (the Secret Service handles these).

On some issues, hundreds will use identical wording—evidence that a campaign is being mounted. Most of the callers ask to speak to the president; he *is* the White House, he is *their* president. "I gave my dollar to his campaign; surely he can talk with me!"

Some sixty a day call with personal problems. They may be elderly or lonely, confused in what they perceive as a complicated and impersonal society. They telephone the White House and, fortunately, find themselves talking to a friendly voice.

The toughest of all to handle are the people in urgent need, men and women who are sick, jobless, homeless, with no money, no food—they call the White House as the nation's parsonage of last resort. The volunteers try to suggest federal, state, or local resources that are available—such as churches and charities. They are always sympathetic, sometimes motherly. "I have four kids myself," one will say. If, in spite of sympathy or referrals, the caller's problem seems insoluble and if the emergency can be identified as legitimate (a few are recognized as repeaters), the volunteers make up a "hardship case" note that is passed to a special desk at the White House (see below). In each day, typically, six such cases are recorded.

The volunteers will give out their first names but never their last (they don't want such calls at home). They don't say they are volunteers, with the result that some citizens upbraid them: "Why are they paying you if you can't help me?"

There is warm satisfaction when a hardship case is solved. One night a grandfather called from an Appalachian state; his daughter's baby had diarrhea, was dehydrating, had been refused admission at the local hospital. The Volunteer and Comment Office telephoned the hospital manager ("What? The White House?") and arranged for the baby's admission. They then called the grandfather and told him to have his grandchild taken to the hospital. When they called the hospital the next morning, the baby had improved.

The second principal volunteer contribution is arranging for presidential greeting cards. Birthdays over eighty (especially centennials), golden wedding anniversaries, graduations, marriages, Gold and Eagle Scout awards—to citizens young and old the president is the nation's pastor. In a tradition going back decades, he greets, encourages, and congratulates his flock. In 1986 he and the first lady reached out, in this pastoral role, 604,000 times.

The Volunteer and Comment Office keeps the written or telephoned requests in pigeonholes by date; the volunteers (some handicapped) do the addressing at home. One home worker addressed over 250,000 envelopes during the Reagan presidency. Other volunteers in the office insert the proper printed card in each envelope and complete the mailings. At Christmastime, the volunteers address the president's 125,000 Christmas cards. Volunteers also serve as docents for Saturday tours of the Executive Office Building (nine hundred people a month come through); they hand out programs at South Lawn receptions, help at the Easter Egg Roll.

During 1986 the five hundred volunteers (all but twelve were women) contributed 145,000 hours of their time. One of the staff reflected: "In everything our office does, the trend lines are up."[4]

THE CORRESPONDENCE OFFICE

Write the president! In 1986, the people did just that—4,203,467 times.[5] The yearly averages have trended up as well:

    Eisenhower: 700,000
    Kennedy: 1,815,000
    Johnson: 1,647,000
    Nixon: 2,687,000
    Ford: 2,381,000
    Carter: 3,532,000
    Reagan: 5,802,895

Some letters come in foreign languages (they are sent to State), a few in Braille (with help from the Department of Health and Human Services they are answered in Braille); visitors, especially children, leave notes behind after their White House tours.

A staff of ninety-one White House and twenty-eight Postal Service employees, helped each day by volunteers, refer some of this deluge to departments and agencies; the White House itself, however, responds in a volume that also spirals up each year. In some cases, acknowledgment cards are used (219,000 in 1985), and in response to children a special booklet is sent (189,000). In 1985 the director of correspondence signed 119,842 letters; 53,091 bore the president's signature.

About thirty letters a week—representative of the variety—are pulled from the enormous intake and sent to the president. Reagan, a softy for warm human stories, on occasion took up yellow paper and pen and scrawl-ed personal answers; after they were typed, he would often add a written postscript, might even include a personal check in a hardship situation.

Much of the White House mail is exuberant—the folks want the president to know of their happiness as well as their problems. On the wall of the Correspondence Office are five bulletin boards, every square inch of them jammed with snapshots of weddings, new babies, and anniversaries. The thousands of smiling little pictures are a daily reminder to the belea-guered correspondence staffers: the president is National Friend, sharer of joys as well as of tribulations.

Can any White House staff do justice to such a numbing volume? The Correspondence Office is confident it can, and proud of doing so—even 8 million times a year.

PRESIDENTIAL LETTERS AND MESSAGES

If events or personages deserve greater recognition than the printed card of presidential greetings, robotyped letters or even specially drafted messages are furnished—these, too, being part of the pastoral role of the American presidency. Many of the 19,000 nonprofit organizations in the nation send in requests; they arrive at the rate of 750 a month. The more attention the letter or message will attract, however, the greater is the need for careful staff checking before the presidential signature is added. There are rules and limits; none are sent to judges, for example, or to fund-raisers; commercial events are taboo. The counsel or the national security assistant often must review both the request and the message itself. Unfortunately, there are individuals or groups who try to manipulate the message tradition for selfish purposes. They are foiled only by meticulous and mature review; the two most recent staff members who have had the message-preparation responsibility served eighteen and twenty-two years respectively. Even the best of screening can fail; on one occasion a message of greeting to a testimonial dinner for a mafioso was caught only by President Johnson personally just before he signed it.

The rules, of course, can be bent. A codification of the proprieties for messages was set forth in the Eisenhower administration, which had this paragraph near its end:

> Because the White House is located on the growing fringe of precedent, and because the President is a human being—with a heart much bigger than protocol or policy—he can make exceptions to all the above rules and regulations. He can write a little girl who has lost her cat. He can write a golfer who can't control his slice. He can write anyone, anywhere, for any purpose—and the addressee is always delighted.[6]

On perhaps six hundred occasions each month, the specially drafted greetings are dispatched to organizations or events that meet the criteria. A staff of eight supports this contemporary extension of a long-observed presidential tradition.

The gracious presidential favor of yesterday, however, may have become the mere routine of today. A veteran of the message business asks the recurring question: do messages that issue at a six-hundred-a-month clip signal "the ticky-tacky presidency?" Has the pastoral tradition become too "canned," too manufactured? An even more troubling question is raised at the same time: has the auto pen to too great an extent replaced the president's hand?

THE "AGENCY LIAISON OFFICE"

Masked under this prosaic label, five staff members in an Executive Office Building room personify the latest and most elaborate extension of the pastoral presidency. To them are given the hardship cases—those requests scrawled in letters, those taken down from the telephone calls. *In extremis,* hundreds of desperate people write or call the president; for them he is the ultimate ombudsman.

The agency liaison staffers' first recourse is to refer such a hardship case to one of the Cabinet departments, or to state agencies, or to local organizations in the needy person's hometown. Each referral is registered in a computer, as is every departmental or White House action taken. The White House aides will often locate and telephone the individual citizens, get more of their stories firsthand, find out what efforts they have already made to help themselves. Repeated writers and those "milking the system" are easily identified, but the cases of real need are kept current until some answer is provided.

A twelve-year-old Indian boy wrote that his father, a veteran, was out of work; the White House discovered that a Labor Department contractor was looking for just the kind of skill his father had. A street-cleaner called; someone had stolen his broom. The agency liaison staffers found a local charity to get him a new one. On Christmas Eve, a family called from Denver; they were living in an automobile. The White House called the Salvation Army, who aided the family and helped the father find work. They later came to Washington to thank the White House staffers personally. A woman whose power was cut off was found to be owed thirty thousand dollars by a state disability office that was slow in processing her papers; a call from the White House pushed the state officials into action. A woman in Mississippi had her power cut off; the White House found a local minister who ran an extension cord from a neighbor's house. When the police objected, asking who authorized the plug-in, the answer was "the White House."

"Case work" of this sort has long been a staple of congressional offices. Now those offices themselves are referring their most intractable emergencies to the White House, which helped to push the total number of cases handled by the "Agency Liaison Office" in 1986 to 49,039, 27,000 more than in 1985.

THE GIFTS UNIT

There was a "black hole of Calcutta" once, and it was in the White House itself. It was the joking term for the storage area underneath the Cabinet Room where gifts to President Truman had piled up—"so many we didn't know what to do with them," one aide remembered.

Today the facilities are different, but the tradition of sending gifts to the president continues. To the same president who is "pastor," his "flock" is generous. Some nine thousand gifts flood into the White House each year. What can be accepted, however, is limited by the laws, and by the Constitution itself.

It is the Gifts Unit that receives every incoming gift, registers it, judges its acceptability, arranges for the note of thanks, and sends the donation to its next destination. Eight staff members handle this delicate assignment; one alumna of this office served for twenty years; another was on the White House staff from Coolidge to Kennedy.

Gifts from foreign governments are considered as being presented not personally to the president but to the nation. If they are of more than "minimal value" (currently defined as $165) they may be displayed temporarily in the White House but then are sent to the National Archives to be part of a presidential museum or for disposal. The president and first lady received 121 such gifts in 1985, 67 in 1986; the list is made public annually by the Department of State.

Gifts from private citizens arrive from everywhere in the world, principally of course from American admirers. Exactly 9,491 came to the White House in 1986. If a president has a hobby, he is deluged with gifts suitable to it. The Reagans were sent horses and boots, the Fords skis and ski clothing; Johnson was given dozens of pairs of cowboy boots, Vice President Bush got boxes of jogging shoes. Most private gifts are redonated or returned; if they are kept and are worth more than a hundred dollars, they are reported to the Office of Government Ethics, which makes the list public.

If there are children or grandchildren in the president's immediate family, toys come in by the hundreds. In 1954 toymaker Louis Marx sent over eight hundred to Eisenhower for his grandchildren; they were donated to charities in Washington and to Secret Service agents with kids.

Whoever he is, without regard to politics, thousands of Americans regard their president with benevolence and affection. An elderly gentleman wills the president his cherished grandfather clock; an excited fisherman puts his prize catch on ice and sends it to the White House. (Unfortunately, all food is destroyed unless it comes from close friends.)

Less benevolent are gifts with a selfish purpose, for business promotion or advertising, or that could give even the appearance of exploitation. The Gifts Unit calls on the counsel to help spot donations that might cause embarrassment.

For the Gifts Unit, interwoven with their never-ending judgments about laws, regulations, and proprieties, are threads of warmth and humor. Staff members come back from foreign or domestic trips loaded down with presents pressed into their hands. "Glad you visited our school today," said one donor, "Love from Andy." Which school? Who was Andy? The Gifts Unit would be sleuths so that the proper thank-you could be sent.

A retired nun knitted President Ford a ski cap, which he kept. Seeing him wearing it, on a television news clip, the donor was worried that it looked too tight. A letter came in with her further instructions: he should wet it and let it set on his head until dry.

Among the hundreds of pets sent in (they are never destroyed, always donated elsewhere), one admirer sent Nixon a fancy, live rabbit. The Gifts Unit called the zoo; yes, they would take the bunny, but please let them know ahead of time when the White House van would come; if the rabbit got mixed up with their other small animals, it would get fed to the pythons!

THE PHOTOGRAPHIC OFFICE

In most of their official hours, presidents have note-takers to write down what is said and by whom. The contemporary president also has a "visual note-taker," the personal photographer to the president (now bearing the title of special assistant to the president). With security clearance admitting him to any Oval Office session, the photographer records every meeting and every person with the chief executive. If the meetings are repetitive, with recurring attendance, one shot will do; if new faces appear, the visitors will be captured on film.

There was a National Park Service photographer on duty in Roosevelt's time (he stayed on through the Eisenhower years), but only in the more recent presidencies have photographers come into the new role of documenting the president's minute-by-minute existence. "The president would walk out of his elevator in the morning, and we'd be on his tail until he went back into the family quarters," explained an alumnus of the White House Photographic Office. "We would review the private schedule the night before, and would assign one of our staff to cover every event of his day—from the 'grip and grin' shots of handshakes to the meetings in the Cabinet Room."[7] At major presidential events, the official photographers use a zone system: the assistants are pre-positioned in the press stands; the personal photographer "comes and goes with the body."

After each presidential session, the film is dropped into a separate bag, developed, printed, and filed. The name, date, time, and place of the event and the names of VIPs attending are registered in a computer, along with the film number; the staffers of today or the historians of tomorrow can reach any photo record instantly.

Every private citizen gets a souvenir of his or her moment with the chief executive. If there have been thirty handshakes in an Oval Office ceremony, thirty prints are sent to the responsible staff action officer; White House letters go out to each visitor.

Every year, the photographer and his five assistants put 7,000 rolls of film into their cameras; some 150,000 frames are snapped, 70 percent of them producing pictures of archival quality. Assisting the group of six are a supporting staff of four and a lab group of as many as forty in a nearby military station.

Presidential trips bring a photographic harvest. The White House Photo Office is represented on the advance teams, and the presidential photographer flies on *Air Force One.* If a presidential trip or conference is three days or longer, the photographer brings a portable darkroom, a picture editor, and four lab assistants; they produce color enlargements on the spot. At the conclusion of hosting the Williamsburg Economic Summit, for instance, President Reagan was able to present each visiting chief of state, before he or she left, with a leather-bound album of color photographs of the very conference from which the group was just departing.

The photographer fills another role: source for news pictures. After the necessary approvals, newsmen and -women will be given prints from the photographer's enormous collection. The approvals, of course, are dispensed by a separate senior staff officer who guards the president's "image." When President Reagan, for instance, was first told of the explosion of the Challenger, a White House photographer quickly came into the Oval Office and snapped the president's sad countenance. "He also looked extremely old," Larry Speakes remembered, adding "That photograph was so unflattering that I refused to release it to the press."[8]

The politics and public relations are left to the image guardian; the photographer's job however, is professional: record the president and everything he does, for history.

ADMINISTRATIVE SUPPORT

To make the White House staff appear smaller, President Carter transferred a group of White House administrative functions to a new, non–
White House "Office of Administration." Payroll, accounting, purchasing,
printing, computing, moving, and painting, and the White House Reference and Law libraries were "subtracted" from the White House staff in
1977. The switchover was a paper change; dozens of professionals continue
their former White House support duties while wearing a hat labeled OA.

The White House Reference Center, for example, has fifteen professionals and ten interns who use a modest in-house library featuring materials
on the presidency but have immediate access to commercial data banks.
The Center aims at doing for the White House what the Congressional
Research Service does for the Congress: quick-response research. When
Carter moved to normalize diplomatic relations with China, the Reference
Center compiled a hundred-page information kit on that country—its
history, the pertinent American statutes, UN documents, biographies of its
leaders—and delivered it to senior White House staff members. The center
was caught napping once, however. On the day in 1981 when President
Reagan was shot, one of the assistant counsels rushed in looking for the
legislative history (House and Senate hearings and reports) on presidential
succession. The Reference Center didn't have them; the director had to
sprint to a nearby library for the full texts.

THE MILITARY OFFICE

Since the president is commander in chief, military support for the presidential office is everywhere in the White House establishment. It is quiet,
professional, and, except on a few occasions, almost out of sight. The
military group is also the largest part of the White House staff family.

Thirteen hundred military men and women serve the White House
daily; twenty-five hundred more support the president and his staff on a
less frequent basis. In keeping with the concept of the presidency as a
civilian office, uniforms are rarely worn during daytime hours. This under-
statement of the military staff is significant when the president travels
abroad; some host nations resent any visible presence of U.S. armed forces.

There are currently five military aides, one from each service, including the Coast Guard. The five are career officers; their White House assignments, however, are at the president's pleasure. Each advance team includes a military aide; one is always on duty with the president.

It is the military aide who constantly has the "presidential emergency satchel" in hand, colloquially known as "the football" (because it is passed around). The satchel carries authentication codes and presidential emergency declarations; the aide who carries it has been trained in emergency drills and facilities and is competent not only to open the bag, but to explain to a chief executive exactly what each of its contents is and does.

Some of the military aides—at least in the past—have succumbed to the temptation to intervene in personnel or other aspects of their respective service's work, or, vice versa, to elevate parochial service concerns into the environment of the White House. Truman's military aide, General Harry Vaughan, so vexed Army Chief of Staff Dwight Eisenhower with intercessions that the latter "had to go right to the President to get who was running the Army straightened out."[9] When Ike became president, he was determined not to have flag-rank officers as military aides. Eisenhower's second Naval aide, Captain "Pete" Aurand, however, lost no opportunity to foist Navy propaganda upon his White House colleagues, including even the president. John Eisenhower observes: "Dad would go back for lunch every noon . . . for an hour's rest. Well, Pete would sail into the office every noon . . . walked Dad over and practically put him into bed for his nap singing 'Anchors Aweigh' all the way over to the mansion."[10]

In December 1959, on the way back from his trip to India, Eisenhower went aboard the cruiser Des Moines in Greek waters and sailed through the Mediterranean to Tunisia. Aurand arranged for the Sixth Fleet to be on parade, complete with firing displays. "Boom, boom, boom, with a puff for every boom," Aurand recalled, ". . . of course he was pretty impressed when the whole Sixth Fleet passed by."[11]

In August of 1960, however, Staff Secretary Goodpaster sent a stiff note to all the military aides: "When, as and if" there were going to be any "spectaculars involving Presidential participation," Goodpaster and the top level at Defense were to be informed "before White House action begins."[12]

First Carter, then Reagan, specified that the Military Office be headed by a civilian.

The military staff is not involved in defense policy matters; these, as described in chapter 7, are the exclusive province of the national security assistant. The Military Office does, however, review the four hundred to seven hundred letters a week to their commander in chief from men and women in the armed forces, helping the services to untangle hardship cases, making sure that the petitioners or their families are treated fairly.

There are eleven principal White House support units that the Military Office supervises:

1. *Air Force One* and the 89th Military Airlift Wing

Two new Boeing 747s are being outfitted as presidential aircraft for 1989, each to carry eighty passengers and twenty-three crew members. *Air Force One* will then be in effect a flying White House, complete with offices and their equipment, sleeping quarters, medical facilities, food service, and communications. A new hangar, eleven stories high, four hundred yards across, is being built at Andrews Air Force Base to accommodate the new presidential planes, either one of which is *Air Force One* when the president is aboard.

The huge blue and silver plane is symbol as well as transportation; as the advance men report, crowds come to presidential arrivals as eager to see *Air Force One* as to see the chief executive himself.

2. Marine Helicopter Squadron One

The squadron, using a variety of helicopters, is based only minutes downriver from the White House. *Marine One*'s helipad is the South Lawn of the White House; three bright discs are placed on the grass where its wheels must land, and a portable control tower is trundled into position when the big green bird is approaching. A larger helicopter was tested a few years ago; the blast from its blades, however, blew limbs down from treasured White House trees and the experiment was not repeated.

3. The Staff Mess

Managed by the Navy, the three adjacent dining rooms in the lower level of the West Wing seat 45, 28, and 18 respectively in paneled decorum, for each of two midday shifts. Two hundred staffers (and the Cabinet) are eligible. Private luncheons in their own offices are available for West Wing senior staff and tray carry-outs are provided to harried aides on the run. The Mess is staffed by over fifty Navy personnel and, hanging noiselessly under glass, a hallowed symbol is at its doorway: the 1790 mess gong from the USS *Constitution*.

The Presidential Watch serves lunches in the Oval Office, and occasionally breakfast or other meals in the Cabinet Room. It is entirely separate from the first family's kitchen and dining facilities in the Residence. The Mess and Watch are run by the presidential food service coordinator, who has been in the White House since 1965.

4. Camp David

A favorite retreat of presidents in the Catoctin Mountains, the camp is a hideaway rest and recreation spot, but much more. Since presidents have also chosen to hold Cabinet meetings and to host gatherings of international leaders there, a new conference center has been added to its traditional sports, communications, and support facilities. The camp is managed by the Navy, and when the president is on the scene, the security and related staffs number close to four hundred.

5. The White House Medical Unit

The president's personal physician and some thirteen military assistants and nurses use a principal medical suite in the Residence and a second in the Executive Office Building, where new exercise rooms have also been added. A dental suite is available for an officer who makes periodic visits. The physicians' first objective is to see to it that, when needed, the president gets specialized care, usually at one of Washington's military hospitals rather than trying to provide it themselves in their limited facilities at the White House.

A medical staffer is on each advance team and visits nearby hospitals at every planned presidential stop, asking, for example, if blood supplies of the president's type are available. In those which have the best emergency facilities, a temporary White House telephone may be installed, but the hospital is warned against then advertising itself as "the president's hospital."

Like any other staff officer known to have direct access to the president, the physician is occasionally the target of groups or individuals who would exploit his entré to the chief executive. Eisenhower, for example, had planned to come out with a proposal for nationwide medical insurance linked to social security, but Ike's doctor, General Howard Snyder, lobbied the president to adopt a position more amenable to the American Medical Association. In any White House, *ex parte* pressures are omnipresent.

A presidential illness becomes not only a medical problem, but instantly injects the president's physician into a crosshatch of internal strains within the White House. There is likely to be a gritty three-way tension among the physician, the press secretary and the first lady, the three of them struggling to balance the nation's need for straightforward information with the protection of the first family's privacy. "We should not be yakkers," commented a former White House doctor. "The public should know if the president is or is not able to go back to work, but they don't have to know his blood count or his urine specific gravity."[13]

If the presidential illness is serious—with general anesthesia in prospect—the most elemental question is presented: should the president act to transfer his powers, for the time being, to the vice president, in conformity with the Twenty-Fifth Amendment? And when is the president lucid enough to reassume them? In counseling the president, the physician, the first lady, the chief of staff, and the vice president may be swayed by different professional or even personal viewpoints. How will the nation's interests be safeguarded from the potential dangers lurking in their individual biases? One observer proposes that the physician to the president be confirmed by the Senate—in order that the Congress would have "one sure source of direct information about the president's health"; other experts emphasize that "a president must have a close, personal relationship with his physician and the selection of that person should not be subject 'to approval by any other body, medical or otherwise.' "[14]

The physician's necessary involvement in issues of such import is but another illustration of the borderless swamp, in the White House, in which both professional skills and political issues are inextricably submerged.

6. The White House Emergency Planning Group

A twelve-person group reviews and keeps current the varying options a president has for evacuation and security in emergency situations. It was Eisenhower who took this planning the most seriously of any president; annually, he would move his whole Cabinet to relocation centers and convene them to discuss hypothetical postattack recovery actions. "After a nuclear exchange, it would be the blind leading the blind," he used to remind them. "If you just knew where your desk was, you would at least be ahead of chaos."[15]

7. The Naval Imaging Command

Created in 1963, a technical crew makes documentary television tapes of most of the president's White House activities and of all of his trips. The videotapes end up in the presidential libraries, but each week's "take" is edited for showing on Thursday afternoons over the White House closed-circuit system.

8. The White House Garage

Fifty military chauffeurs, on rotating duty, drive cars for White House staff members on official business; the former privilege of home-to-office transportation is now rarely if ever provided. The radio-equipped cars put every staffer within reach of every other one. When trips begin or end, the garage complement are the baggage coordinators for the first family, guests, staff, and press.

9. The White House Social Aides

A pool of some fifty young, single men and women officers is assembled from the five services for assisting the social secretary at formal functions in the Residence. Thirty-five of them are used at a state dinner, three or four at a reception. "Being a social aide was like being a potted plant," Truman's White House assistant Clark Clifford once remarked, but that may have been an unfair jibe. The aides announce the guests in the receiving line, are expected to have studied the history of the White House itself and perhaps be fluent in a foreign language. They volunteer their time, and pay for their own formal uniforms.

10. The *Sequoia*

Presidential yachts have recently come on hard times. Truman's *Williamsburg* has been rotting at a Washington pier; President Carter ordered the smaller ship, the *Sequoia,* sold. A private organization, the Presidential Yacht Trust, repurchased the latter, has reconditioned it, and, if the Navy accepts it, and the White House wants it back, presidents of the future may again be able to take senators or friends or cabinet members to settle strategy under the Potomac summer sunsets.

When Nixon used the *Sequoia,* as he did often, a Navy support crew of forty would have the ship ready on thirty minutes' notice. Two Secret Service chase boats would escort it on the often-crowded river. Cabinet members could reserve it or a senior White House officer could (at his cost) take his whole staff and their spouses for a morale-building dinner and evening to Mt. Vernon and back.

11. The White House Communications Agency

Largest and necessarily the most secretive of the White House support groups, the WHCA is an elite unit of close to eight hundred military professionals. Within the White House, they operate the Signal Board, which connects the president with all of the nation's military and diplomatic communications nets. Each senior staff member has a Signal Board telephone at home. A parallel WHCA facility is the Secure Voice Board, also with worldwide capability. Secure voice is of especial importance because, in addition to the espionage threat, there are radio amateurs whose personal hobby is to monitor presidential radio nets and notify news media of what they hear.

WHCA's radio console, with the call sign "Crown," is the switch for radio traffic among, for example, the staff cars in Washington. WHCA runs the National Security Council's classified computer center, supplies the Secret Service with its communications, including hand-held secure radios, and operates the White House paging system, which reaches staff members anywhere in town.

The Communications Agency supplies all of the audiovisual equipment for the president's public appearances: mikes, lights, PA systems, teleprompters, and even the lectern. Every advance team has a WHCA member, and if the president is somewhere else than 1600 Pennsylvania Avenue, WHCA's job is, as one veteran put it, "to duplicate the White House communications environment, anywhere the president happens to be."[16] Multiextension switchboards, automated satellite-relay base stations, two-way radios, and pagers are all deployed; even if the president flies in a Chinese or Soviet airplane (as Nixon did), portable communications equipment ties him to the White House. As soon as *Air Force One* parks, a landline is plugged in and the blue "bat phone" is connected at the foot of the ramp. There is a Signal Board extension concealed at every wreath-laying; WHCA even had a telephone at the Great Wall of China. The presidential limousine has four fender jacks for loudspeakers should he want to stop and make remarks en route.

When President Carter rafted down the Salmon River in 1978, portable satellite links had not yet been developed; to keep in touch with the president on his raft for three days, WHCA had to install manned base stations on seven riverside mountaintops. The crews went in by helicopter, camped out, and leapfrogged from early sites to later ones. Since Secretary of State Vance was preparing for the Camp David summit meetings, four or five calls each day were exchanged between Foggy Bottom in Washington and the river-bottom White House in the Idaho wilderness.

When President Reagan went trail-riding at his Santa Barbara ranch, Larry Speakes recounts, a four-wheel-drive communications van followed him. The president could "talk from horseback to anywhere in the world."[17]

THE EXECUTIVE RESIDENCE

"The White House" of pictures and tourists, the famous mansion has a problem: it may be famous for too much. It is a home, for husband and wife, children, grandparents, grandchildren, guests, and pets (including ponies). It is also a museum of American history and culture, an exhibition gallery, a collection of presidential furnishings, a magnet for tourists and a secure redoubt. The Residence has seen service as a wartime map and command post, a wedding chapel, a funeral parlor, a nursery, and a church. Today it is simultaneously a backdrop for TV productions, a press-conference auditorium, a concert hall, and a banquet center (75,000 were served there in 1980). The mansion or parts of it serve as a flower stall, performing-arts center, physical fitness emporium, Easter-egg-rolling yard, movie theater, heliport, parade ground, carpentry shop, art gallery, library, arboretum, clinic, office building, conference center, and sophisticated communications hub. (Some reports allege that it is a missile base as well, though officials there deny it.)

Can the same place meet all these demands? Its staff do their damnedest.

The chief usher is the manager of the Executive Residence. While all who work there serve at the pleasure of the president, the entire staff is proud of its tradition of being career professionals. There have been only five chief ushers since 1891; the staff average has been twenty years of service on the job and two recent employees served forty-four years apiece.

The staff inside the Residence numbers ninety-three; in addition, thirty-six National Park Service experts take care of the grounds and manage the outlying greenhouse and storage warehouse. Volunteers help arrange cut flowers and decorate the Residence at Christmas.

The food-service group, led by world-class chefs, is augmented by contract help to serve a state dinner's thirteen tables of ten (the thirteenth table is called Number 14), or, as has happened at least twice, a South Lawn outdoor sit-down dinner for thirteen hundred (they were under tents and each of those dinners required setting out thirty-seven thousand pieces of tableware.) Twelve work-years of overtime are included in the mansion's $5.4 million budget, but many thousands of hours beyond that are gifts to the United States from a staff whose dedication is legendary. "When I hired them," commented one former supervisor, "I said, 'Don't plan on celebrating any anniversaries or birthdays with your family.'"[18] They have no job descriptions; the unpredictable is routine. Are the cut rosebuds not sufficiently unfolded? Some warm whiffs from a hair dryer will get them ready for the party. Does orange pollen from the lilies stain white uniforms? Fetch towels and shake out each bloom before the guests arrive.

Some presidents have brought personal servants, but no staff now live in the mansion, nor are they responsible for any of the president's out-of-town residences. Presidential overnight guests at the White House are personal; visiting chiefs of state usually stay at Blair House across the street.

Close to the north foyer, the usher's small office is crammed with noiseless reminders of both the present and the past. A digital screen flashes the location of each member of the first family; computer terminals blink out the details of the fine-art collections, menus, supplies, and the budget. But above them on the wall hangs a piece of charred wood from the British fire of 1814.

"The growing fringe of precedent" is everywhere in the White House, and the old mansion almost trembles under its new uses. The East Room floor, new in 1950, was nearly worn through by 37 million tourists when it was relaid in 1978. In a recent musicale, heretofore the occasion for decorum and calm, the usher counted 27 two-person Minicam news teams.

Events started by one president become "traditions," hard if not impossible to change. The Easter egg roll is now a "tradition" (30,000 tots and parents scramble in), so are the spring and fall garden tours (15,000 inspect the blooms), as well as the three nights of candlelight tours each Christmas (20,000 view the decorations).

For each press conference, the technical crews monopolize the East Room, jamming the stately ballroom with mikes and lights. The hosting of a huge outdoor dinner means resodding the lawn. The helicopter blades whoosh the petals off the spring flowers.

Can the new presidency preserve the old graciousness? The mansion staff's loyalties run in two directions: to serve the house's masters who are there, and at the same time to stand in trust for a revered place that belongs to all the American generations.

THE FAMILY THEATER

Like most other Americans, presidents enjoy relaxing at the movies, but absent a presidential box, a trip to the local cinema means unwanted disruption. The Family Theater was incorporated in the East Wing in 1942. When a union operator did not show up one night during the Roosevelt administration, the Naval aide commandeered a substitute from the Navy—and started the practice of having a White House projectionist on duty. One aide served for thirty-three years in that role. Groups of films are borrowed from the Washington area's central booking service, and synopses sent to the first family for their selection. The movies are then shown in the White House or at Camp David. President Carter so far holds the record for nights at the movies: he viewed 564 showings during his term.

THE CURATOR

Not only is the White House the people's property, but so are most of its furnishings. A statute of 1961 ended the practice of some early presidents of bringing in, and then taking out, furniture, paintings, silver, glassware, and china. Today once any president declares White House articles to be "of historic or artistic interest," they become forever "inalienable" and must be used, displayed, or stored but never sold.[19] Every June the law requires "a complete inventory" of all "plate, furniture, and public property" in the White House to be made by the National Park Service.

To help the president with these duties, Lyndon Johnson established a new position on the staff: the Curator of the White House.[20] There have been five curators and their mission has been much more than preserving what is there; they have gone on the prowl for furniture and paintings that should be added to the White House collections. On the U.S. East Coast, in England, and in France, auctions, antique shops, and even private homes were visited, donors contacted; an "adopt a room" program was initiated for patriotic benefactors. Fourteen portraits of first ladies, for instance, had been missing; seven have now been acquired. One of the curators found a Dolley Madison portrait in a museum basement, and a painting by Gilbert Stuart of Mrs. John Quincy Adams was located in a private collection. One curator (who served sixteen years) raised $7 million in cash and collected donations in kind worth $15 million.[21]

"The principal public rooms on the first floor," says the law, are of "museum character." The curator and his staff are there to help them remain so.

THE VISITORS' OFFICE

In a striking mixture of traditions, Americans exalt the presidency but they own his home. His office is respected but his house is open for visitors; every tourist coming to Washington expects to walk through it.

The tradition of dropping by to shake hands with the president stopped with Hoover, but a new one began with Truman: fixed hours for public tours. Still another practice started under Eisenhower: "special" guided tours at the beginning of the morning. Like other "traditions" noted in this book, both practices have grown to press against the very limits of what is possible without degrading the experience itself. The public tour now averages 1,250,000 people a year (Johnson let 2,000,000 come through in 1964). The "special" tour has mushroomed from 150 to 1,300 participants a day; here, specially trained Executive Protection Service officers escort the appreciative contingents of visitors, explaining as they go the history of the famous State Rooms and of the White House collections.

The Visitors' Office, with a seven-person staff in the East Wing, is responsible for the public admissions to the Residence (as opposed to entrants on official business) and for any group over twenty-five in number, except the formal state dinners and similar functions managed by the social secretary. Theirs is the unenviable chore of allocating the prized "special" tour slots among congressional and senior White House staff offices. The legislative affairs staff has a heavy influence in such allocations. Admission slots are privileges; supporters are rewarded and opponents penalized, although rarely cut off altogether. "You talk about doing all of this stuff politically versus serving the office of the President," recalled one veteran; "in my opinion you cannot divorce one from the other."[22]

"Crowd-raising" is a Visitors' Office assignment; if an arrival ceremony for a distinguished visitor is planned on the South Lawn, several thousand admission cards will be distributed to congressional invitees, school groups, and friendly associations like the Future Farmers of America. The list may be six thousand names long; each person's Social Security number is obtained and brief security checks made ahead of time. Physical security is not the only reason for all this work; if Gorbachev or Hirohito had heard some "boos" on the White House South Lawn, nothing would have convinced them that the disrespect was not planned ahead of time.

Like other staff units described here, the Visitors' Office, too, labors on the thin edge between accommodating the pressures of accumulated expectations and preserving the dignity of the presidential office.

THE SECRET SERVICE

It regards itself as "the premier law-enforcement agency in America" and it has the premier task: protecting the nation's executive political leadership. The Service has other responsibilities, too, including tracking down forgers and counterfeiters and protecting the embassies of other nations as well as foreign leaders when they are in this country. Candidates for president and former presidents are protected (although they may decline the privilege) as are senior White House staff officers who may have received threats.

The 36,000-person Service has 1,800 agents in Washington and in sixty-five field offices; it borrows heavily from Treasury and the Park Service when, as in a campaign year, its regular force is overwhelmed with demands. "Sometimes," observed the author of a recent book on the Secret Service, "during a presidential campaign year, there are more non–Secret Service Treasury Department personnel doing protective work than there are Secret Service agents."[23] The director of the Secret Service is appointed by the secretary of the treasury but always from its career ranks.

At the White House, five hundred—one half—of the Service's Uniformed Division officers are on duty (in shifts) in the outer perimeter of guard stations, others in the middle perimeter, within the buildings. A separate telephone switchboard, the "Police Board," is on twenty-four-hour duty.

On the inner protective perimeter are the agents in civilian clothes; there are over a hundred on the White House detail, another hundred with the vice president, and their total is augmented by field-office agents when either of the leaders is traveling. While a president can request a specific head for his own group, the protective details are all professionals; there was not a "Carter" nor a "Reagan" detail since the agents' assignments are usually longer than four years.

A hundred-person Technical Security Division, located within the White House area, includes experts in detection of bugs, weapons, and radioactive or other materials that could endanger those being protected; it has installed gamma radiation detectors to supplement the regular magnetometers that screen visitors to the White House. At the White House gates, some four hundred weapons are detected every year, almost all of them being carried by people who have state permits to do so. Unless they are among the very few who have District of Columbia permits, however, pistol-packers are taken to local police headquarters for embarrassing arraignment, the D.C. felony charges usually reduced to misdemeanors. Mentally disturbed people walk in off the street demanding to see the president; about 250 each year are taken to St. Elizabeth's Hospital for observation.

In a recent year, besides the more than 1,250,000 tourists, there were over 216,000 official visitors, more than 18,000 guests, and 88,000 couriers, deliverymen, and messengers who were admitted to the White House complex. Over 5,400 people hold passes to the White House or the Executive Office Building (2,000 of them are press), and another 6,900 are on the "access list" of tradesmen and technicians who can be cleared for admission by a phone call.

The Service's presidential protective command post is immediately under the Oval Office; throughout the White House establishment, electronic locator boxes tell agents and others, including the chief of staff, exactly where the principal protectees are every minute of the day or night. "Red teams" practice penetration to make "vulnerability assessments"; packages are X-rayed, bomb squads are on call. Fixed-based ground-to-air missiles are reportedly in the White House area, and shoulder-fired Redeye antiaircraft weapons are stored for use.[24]

Is the White House a museum that welcomes tourists or a forbidding armed camp? It has to be both—a grating challenge for the contrasting missions of the Visitors' Office on the one hand and the Secret Service on the other.

Psychiatric consultant services are used by the Service, to study agent stress and (with the help of artificial-intelligence computer software) to experiment in constructing profiles of possible assassins. "There's no hard and fast way yet to make predictions as to which oncoming stranger will be a threat to the president," explained one agent, "intuition still plays a major role."[25]

The Service's Protective Research Division lists forty thousand Americans who are potential threats. Some four hundred of them are on a "Watch List" of known dangerous individuals, and agents from the Service's field offices will periodically check to see where they are and what they are doing. The agents may visit the person's relatives and ask "How is Joe these days?" The families themselves are often cognizant of the danger and genuinely cooperative.

A presidential trip requires extra mobilization of the Secret Service's resources. "Our mission is to duplicate the White House protective environment," declared one agent. The Secret Service is always represented on the preadvance and advance teams. If the trip is domestic, the whole Protective Research collection of forty thousand names, and especially the Watch List, is combed according to each area the president will visit; for each stop a "trip file" of perhaps one hundred names is assembled. State and local police are then asked to help account for all of those individuals. Some on the "trip list" who have demonstrably threatened the president may already have been prosecuted and jailed. If detention is not possible and a presidential trip is imminent, the agents may start a temporary surveillance. "We will sit on them for a day," one agent explained. Another remembered, "I have been sued sixty times for invasion of privacy or false arrest, and won every time." Just before the trip starts, a photo album is made up of individuals judged truly dangerous but who have not been located; agents try to memorize the pictures.

If the trip is abroad, the advance preparations, as chapter 19 described, are innumerable. Will the presidential limousine fit through the palace gates? It will be flown abroad and tested. (There are in fact several limousines and in some motorcades two identical presidential cars are used, to foil possible attackers.) Is a bundle of roses to be handed to the president? The welcoming committee will be informed it can't be done. When one host government raised too many objections, it was told, "Meet our minimum protective standards or the president isn't coming." The KGB, the Service agents find, are equally professional—and more relaxed in recent years. At the Geneva summit in November 1985, an agent complimented his KGB opposite number about the fine fur hat he was wearing. "L. L. Bean," the Russian grinned.

The treatment of two different groups of citizens who are not dangerous—professional press, and orderly demonstrators—has raised recent controversy about what the White House staff expects of the Secret Service. A White House Correspondents Association report of 1985 accused the Secret Service of letting itself be used by the staff to keep the press away from the president, not for security reasons, but to protect the president from questions. This practice, wrote White House reporter Lou Cannon, "keeps the Secret Service preoccupied with the busy work of distancing the news media and saving the President from annoying questions. This inevitably diverts the Secret Service from its real job."[26] An arrangement has now been agreed upon that the host committee or the White House press secretary will decide where the press is to stand; the Service will stay out of that decision entirely.

In an arrival crowd, demonstrators are anathema to PR-conscious White House aides; there have been instances in which the staff have tried to use the Secret Service to move them out of the way—"for security reasons." The Service rightly resists this manipulation; demonstrators' yells are much less of a concern than perhaps the sticks on which their signs are mounted. It is the staff who sometimes have to be reminded of the First Amendment's consequences.[27]

The Secret Service must be an adaptable outfit, and always a professional one. If the president rides, they will be horsemen; if the vice president jogs or enjoys superpowered speedboats, they will don sneakers or purchase 495-hp engines. They know they must never recount to one president the privileged confidences of a predecessor, nor can an agent even do the president's bidding to "please hold my coat for a second" or "find me some change for the collection plate." Kennedy, at Hyannisport, once spotted the agent outside his door. "Why stand out there?" he queried. "Come on in and watch the ball game with us." The answer was no; from the professionals' viewpoint, even new presidents need training.

The White House, then, is not empty at the Inaugural noon. Throughout its expectant halls, in its foyers, kitchens, switchboards, and guard posts, men and women are on duty who will serve tomorrow as they served yesterday. For some, they have walked taller in the mornings of two, three, or four decades—skilled, committed, and proud—to support the office that they honor and the house that they revere. They will continue to be unknown to their countrymen and some of them even to their president, who years later will depart, as they again remain. Their respectful loyalty is always transferred to each new chief executive, and president after president is rewarded by their service.

PART IV

Conclusion:
The Essence of
White House Service

The time when Presidents and their aides were regarded as upright citizens devoted to the service of the nation had long since passed. Since Vietnam and Watergate much of the big-time media have tended to regard every public official, elected or appointed, as a suspect from the day he takes office, and public service as a crime waiting to happen.
—Donald Regan

I pray Heaven to bestow the best of blessings on this House and all that shall hereafter inhabit it. May none but honest and wise men ever rule under this roof.
—John Adams

Why there is a White House staff, what it does, what its elements are—the previous chapters have given a photomontage of the ring of power that supports the modern president.

Questions now arise. How large is the staff, and what limits its size? What principles govern the staff's use of its influence?

THE WHITE HOUSE STAFF COMMUNITY

What is the size of the entire White House staff family? Its major elements are totaled as of the fall of 1987.

TABLE 2

Major Units of the White House Staff Community

The White House Office	
(Including the Office of Policy Development)	568
The National Security Council staff	190
The Office of the Vice President	98
The 45 percent of the Office of Administration that directly supports the White House	91
The Executive Residence	
(Including National Park Service staff regularly on the grounds)	129
The Military Office	1,300
U.S. Secret Service:	
Uniformed Division (White House Police)	500
Presidential Protective Detail	100
Vice Presidential Protective Detail	100
White House Technical Security	100
Engineering and Maintenance	
(From the General Services Administration, the Telephone Company)	190
Full-time Total	3,366[1]
Part-time staff:	
Military personnel who support the White House on a less than full-time basis	2,500
Regular volunteers	500

Such is the community which de facto is the White House environment and which serves the presidency of today.

It never stays still; any table of figures (including this one) is but a stroboscopic photograph of a buzzing, swiftly altering scene. Staffers, consultants and advisers, both high and low, continually join and leave the ranks; the numbers and totals change daily.

As the table makes clear, the security and military support staffs are the largest part of the White House establishment. These men and women are not on the White House payroll, nor are they "detailed" there in the sense of being borrowed away from their regular duties in other agencies; the White House is their duty station. They, the Residence staff, and many others are career professionals; while their presence in the White House is at the president's pleasure, they serve every succeeding president with equal and neutral competence. They are not policy officers, of course, but are an indispensable underpinning of the immediate presidential community.

The practice of borrowing personnel is decades old at the White House. Some 200 of the 947 employees in the first four of the elements listed are detailees; 85 of the 190 NSC staffers, for instance, are from outside the White House. Former President Ford disapproves of the practice of details:

> Having somebody from a department in the White House—on the staff—tends to project a departmental view more than an independent White House view. . . . If you bring somebody in from a department, that department has a foot in the door and is undermining the independent judgment of the White House itself.[2]

Ford's apprehensions are justified. In the first Reagan term, a staff officer on detail from one of the agencies told the author that his agency head made it clear to him: "Represent *my* interests over there at the White House or your promotions are in jeopardy." The staff officer in question refused to play the advocate role and the vindictive agency head aborted the promised raise.

Notwithstanding Mr. Ford's warning, presidents continue to use detailed employees, masking the true size of the staff. In July of 1987, the General Accounting Office issued a public reminder that many detailees at the White House were not being reported to the Congress, as a 1978 law requires.[3]

In addition to detailees, White House staff offices in the Executive Office Building regularly use volunteers, and student interns, to pinch-hit in cases of illness but also to help relieve the inexorably increasing workloads.

Considerations of security underlie the general rule that volunteers are not used in the West Wing, the East Wing, or the Residence, but the rule has been bent; volunteers, for instance, have assisted the first lady's staff in her Press and Advance Offices.

As the reader will now be observing, there is probably no ready answer for one who might ask: what is the total budget of the White House? The published figures for the White House Office, the vice president, the Office of Policy Development, the National Security Council, and the Executive Residence would have to be augmented by a substantial percentage of Treasury's uniformed and civilian Secret Service totals, by significant National Park Service and General Services Administration contributions, and by Defense's outlays for White House communications, facilities and aircraft, and the military personnel to support them. Even that cumulative total would have to be enlarged by gleaning, one by one, the costs of the many detailees, which are imbedded in the budgets of a dozen odd departments and agencies.

However large are the gross numbers of dollars or people, the ring of power itself is smaller. There are one hundred White House staff members with presidential commissions. Among them is the senior circle, the heads of the twenty major offices described in part II (and depicted on pages 90–91). Even within that ring, there are, in every White House, a very few who are the president's most intimate associates.

The size of the contemporary White House staff is not the result of mindless, willy-nilly empire-building; it is a direct consequence of the presidential demand for the tasks the staff performs. The threat of terrorism, for example, leaves the president no choice but to require security support in depth. The president's pastoral role, quantified in the volume of mail, telephone calls, tourists, hardship cases, messages, cards, and gifts, nearly overwhelms the place; the five hundred volunteers are used to keep the staff's heads above the flood.

Services added by earlier presidents as useful innovations—the Situation Room, the News Summary, the photographer, for example—have now proven their worth, and are standard White House elements. With more and more institutions reaching *in* to the presidency, and affording additional avenues of persuasion (interest groups, state and local officials, political coalitions), the White House has organized itself—and grown—to reach *out* to exploit those opportunities. As other authors have so well demonstrated, the president puts great store in "going public"; the "White House bubble machine" is a staff apparatus that no future president will forgo.[4]

Above all else, the centrality of the president's personal role in leading and coordinating the Executive Branch, detailed in part I, has occasioned the increase in his own staff resources. The thirty Cabinet departments and agencies are every chief executive's proud professional resource, but their disparate priorities must be marshaled and synchronized—a task the Constitution itself implies that presidents must do. As a Brookings scholar recently wrote:

> ... over time the built-in advantage of the White House will prevail: presidents will incrementally enhance its competence, problems and issues will be increasingly drawn into it for centralized coordination and control, expectations surrounding previous patterns will slowly break down, new expectations will form around a White House-centered system, and the new expectations will further accelerate the flow of problems and issues to the White House—thus enhancing the need for still greater White House competence.[5]

The more centrifugal the inevitable cacophony outside the White House gates, the more potent becomes the centripetal strength within.

Presidents have sworn to try to slice down the White House staff—but none have really done so. Can the staff be trimmed? One searches first for do-nothing hangers-on at the White House. There are few if any.

Are there superfluous offices? Only if a president is willing to deprive himself of functions already being performed. While in theory a new president has a clean slate, outside the White House there are expectations that condition his choices. Governors, legislators, state party chiefs, interest groups, and the news media would be the first to decry an "isolated" presidency if the intergovernmental, legislative, political, public liaison, or communications staffs were abolished.

Short of abolition, a president could ordain that the core functions continue but their staffs be smaller. He might pare his Public Liaison Office, cutting back its policy briefings, for instance, for the Business Roundtable or the Urban League. The president, however, needs the informed influence of just such groups in the halls of Congress. He could delegate sub-Cabinet patronage to his Cabinet members, shrinking his presidential personnel staff. President Carter tried that and recognized too late that he was giving up too much authority.

Reduce the Residence staff? Abandon Camp David? Instruct the first lady to be less active? Size per se is not the true issue in the management of the White House. As former Chief of Staff Richard Cheney urges,

> I don't think we should place artificial constraints on the President. If the President says he needs 500 people to do the job, give him 500; if he thinks he needs 700, give him 700. It's a minor price to pay for having a president who

is the leader of the free world. . . . A trillion dollar federal budget, 4.2 million federal civilian and military employees—we can afford to give the President of the United States however many persons he needs on his personal staff.[6]

"The president is the best judge of what he needs to do his job," added a House appropriations staff officer. "We give him what he asks for and then, if he screws up, we can criticize him. We have made very, very few cuts in the White House Office requests."[7]

To be a countervailing magnet to the atomizing particles in the polities of the nation and the world, the American president needs and deserves all the personal staff resources he can control. "Control" is the nub. The limit on White House staff size is the point at which the president senses that he can no longer govern what the least of his staff do or say. This limit is a dynamic arrangement, not an arbitrary figure. It should not be an imposed number, but will depend on the internal communications and disciplinary systems that the president and his chief of staff establish. If information flows readily from senior staff to mid-level officers, if the latter, for instance, are invited as experts or note-takers to presidential meetings, they can accurately relay the president's priorities, and a large staff is manageable. As the assistant Cabinet secretary attending Eisenhower Cabinet meetings, the author could and did convey to other White House colleagues or to inquiring departmental experts the precise thrust and emphasis of the presidential decisions rendered in those sessions. If there is constipation in communications, however, even a small staff would lack direction.

Is the staff now beyond control?

ACCOUNTABILITY

The Iran-contra escapade has indeed given the public the impression that the White House staff is a freewheeling bunch, pursuing not the president's agenda but their own. Some may seemingly have interposed themselves—the president allegedly unknowing—between the chief executive and his line subordinates.

That impression is understandable but wrong. No major enterprises take place in the White House environs without the president's knowledge and consent. The seniormost ring of White House staff are close to the president, and he to them, their confidences intimately shared, the mutual respect intense. The chances that they would keep secrets from one another—especially they from him—are close to zero.[8]

The senior staff will constantly be the transmitters of the chief executive's wishes; on occasion they will—or will be told to—mask the president's hidden hand behind a directive ostensibly their own. Some disgruntled recipients of such orders may mistakenly believe—or may choose to believe—that the instructions emanate not from the president's choice but from the staff's own arrogance. They, too, are wrong. "If Bob Haldeman tells you something, you are to consider it as a communication directly from me and to act on that basis," President Nixon once told J. Edgar Hoover.[9] "If Ham or Stu or Jack calls on my behalf, take their word as coming directly from me," President Carter told his Cabinet. "You have been overly reluctant to respond when the White House staff calls you."[10] For their part, rarely do senior staff need the kind of reminder President Johnson often gave: "You make sure you know what I think before you tell . . . [an outsider] what you think I think."[11]

It is the use by lower-ranking aides of the presidential "we" that most quickly provokes challenges to the staff's reliability. "If you have hundreds of people doing that, there is no way you can keep them out of mischief," commented Kennedy assistant Ted Sorensen.[12] Neustadt adds:

> Only those who see the President repeatedly can grasp what he is driving at and help him or dispute him. Everybody else there is a menace to him. Not understanding they spread wrong impressions. Keeping busy, they take their concerns for his.[13]

There is, however, a sharp, fast antidote to mischief-making by the more junior staff, a kind of pruning saw that rests in the hands of any on the receiving end of White House badgering. Should a query fired back to a White House superior produce the response that the original caller was not close to the presidential trunk, but out on a limb of his own, the saw cuts quickly, the limb is severed and with it collapses the aide's credibility if not his employment. Among Cabinet officers, governors, ambassadors, or legislators, the pruning saw is likely to be unsheathed whenever they hear "the White House calling." At the White House, every mid-level or junior assistant soon learns that he or she operates under that sharp-toothed discipline.

The disciplinary saw also cuts two ways. Johnson assistant Califano tells of the evening when he asked his associate, Lawrence Levinson, to pass on a presidential request to Secretary of Labor Willard Wirtz. The secretary doubted the younger aide's authenticity and paid the request no heed. Explaining his hesitation to an irritated president the next morning, Wirtz received the following admonition: "If you get a call from anyone over here, if you get a call from the cleaning woman who mops the floors at three A.M. and she tells you the President wants you to do something, you do it!"[14]

Johnson, however, followed a very different principle where Secretary of Defense McNamara was concerned. In a 1965 interview, he declared, "I've told Bob McNamara if anybody calls him and says he speaks for me, let me have the name of that man right away and I'll fire him."[15]

NO ROOM FOR SPECIAL PLEADERS

President Carter's experience with Midge Costanza and Nelson Cruikshank, detailed earlier, illumines another principle at the heart of White House service: there is no place in the White House for narrow advocates; crusaders are ultimately forced out. What Costanza did in the Roosevelt Room and Cruikshank before a House committee, Reagan aide Pat Buchanan repeated in Lafayette Park: pushing a cause beyond the president's own priorities. There is only one route in the White House for the man or woman who climbs on a white horse: out the back door.

THE PASSION FOR ANONYMITY

There is a maxim of staff conduct that governs throughout the institution: the staff is to do its work behind the scenes. Part I catalogued the assignments that White House staff undertake—policy development, implementation enforcement, information-gathering, crisis management—missions that unavoidably breed polarities between them and Cabinet officers. Such tensions are inherent in the methods presidents now use in administering the Executive Branch.

While the polarities are unavoidable, they are exacerbated manyfold if the White House staff member is in the newspapers, implying that he or she is the centerpoint of the action. Louis Brownlow's advice, given over fifty years ago, is still valid today: White House staff should stay out of the limelight.

Occasional background briefings by senior White House officers may be appropriate; perhaps sufficient visibility could be permitted to offset a false mystique of "sinister forces" behind the presidency. If, however, White House men and women become featured speakers, TV personalities, and press-conference performers, the public will wonder and Cabinet officers will rightfully complain: "Who is running the place?" In the end, the president will ask the same question.

THE UNFORGIVING ETHICAL STANDARD

New recruits may chafe at the ethical requirements for government service—conflict-of-interest statutes and financial disclosure requirements. At the White House, those are merely the minima. The White House is a glass house, shot through with floodlights of scrutiny from a skeptical press and a hostile political opposition, watched by a changeable public. It is expected to be a model for public service and it cannot help but be a target for attack on even the least of pecadilloes. Its rules of conduct reflect its honored—and vulnerable—circumstance. The basic ethical standard in the White House is so old and clear that it still comes as a surprise to see any staff officers falling afoul of the rule. The *appearance* of impropriety is itself the impropriety. Will a staffer's acceptance of favors from outsiders, for instance, in fact compromise his or her judgment? No matter; it will look that way—enough to fail the test. The "appearance" rule is not in any law; it is tougher than law. It is the unrelenting standard for men and women who serve near the presidency.

White House staff can have no personal agendas other than helping the president. Political, professional, or financial ambitions in their years ahead have to be put aside, or one runs the risk of using the office for personal gain and of putting selfish priorities ahead of presidential objectives, instead of the other way around.

Even after leaving the staff, some officers have disregarded the proprieties of their relationship with the president. Many have rushed into print with one-sided, first-person accounts of their erstwhile internal feuds, even before their president has left office. In thus undermining the confidences of a sitting president, they weaken him before the world and, in turn, ever so little undermine the trust which future presidents and their staffs must try to reestablish. A few former aides have even been convicted of violating the conflict-of-interest laws, tainting their own White House service with the stain of avarice.

THE WHITE HOUSE OF THE FUTURE

As Hamilton would remind us, the raucous pluralism of American society will long continue to be the frustrating environment for those who govern. In a world balanced between peace and war, and in a nation buffeted by competing prescriptions for the division of its resources, parties, legislators, Cabinets, and presidents will forever be making their decisions in an environment of supercharged advocacies and pressures.

Can anything "bring us together"?

John Gardner looks at the White House:

> Whatever may be said for the parties and for Congress, the best present hope of accomplishing the orchestration of conflicting interests, the building of coalitions and the forging of coherent national policy is the President. It is his natural role. He begins the process long before election as he seeks to put together the constituencies he needs. In this day of media-dominated campaigns, the coalition of constituencies may appear to be less needed to gain electoral victory; but it is as needed as ever if the President is to govern effectively after victory.
>
> The President's capacity to balance conflicting forces and forge coherent policy and action should be substantially strengthened.[16]

It is the thesis of this book that the development of the modern White House staff has become a necessary part of that strengthening.

Presidents will continue to rely on such strength, yet they do so wrenched by two apparently contradictory imperatives: on the one hand, the presidential staff, both structure and people, must be kept loose and flexible, a president never encumbering himself with formal White House machinery incompatible with his style of governing; on the other hand, the core functions of the contemporary White House, which this book describes, are inescapably a part of the modern presidency—no chief executive can permit himself to be without them. The answer to the dilemma lies in choosing an incoming staff who can do the old work in new ways, who will be able to fulfil the conventional responsibilities with unconventional innovation.

The path through this contradiction is narrow. The innovations must be dramatic enough for a new president to boast that he has "reformed" White House operations, without actually diminishing the powers of governance which the existing systems afford him. A new president, for instance, will want changed diplomatic and military policies; he will have a new national security assistant and staff to help develop them. There is no alternative, however, to a coordination system *at* the White House for national security affairs; to disestablish the entire role is to guarantee chaos. Multiply that illustration twentyfold and the "reformed" White House will look a great deal like what part II has described.

Apropos of dramatic innovation, thoughtful observers have recently been asking a challenging question: must the top staff all be ejected when a new president arrives? Why should not the White House of the future preserve more than its professional administrative cadre—why not set up a permanent core of senior civil servants in its policy ranks?[17]

Former domestic assistant Stuart Eizenstat recommends retaining perhaps ten career men and women, in the form of a permanent secretariat, directly responsible to the chief of staff. Such officers would be experienced in government, neutral in politics, have at hand copies of the policy papers of the recent presidents, and be linked to all the agencies' information systems. Half of this continuing secretariat, Eizenstat suggests, would concentrate on national security issues, half on domestic affairs. They would be expected to say to a new president—supplementing the policy memoranda to him from his incoming staff—"Here is the inner story of what the former president(s) did and why; here is the historical precedent; here are the risks involved in changing the past policies."[18]

Is this a realistic suggestion? Amid the competitive tumult of a new president's first months, would careerists be welcome or their voices be heeded? In the modern White House, there have been very few cases from which to learn, and two of the highly regarded officers who personified such bridging between administrations of different parties come to differing conclusions. One distinguished career officer, General Andrew J. Goodpaster, overlapped for eight weeks from Eisenhower's into Kennedy's White House. From that experience he believes there is little in the past to give encouragement for the success of a senior "permanent secretariat" in the White House staff itself. A second careerist, Harold Saunders, served on the NSC staff from 1961 (Kennedy) to 1974 (Nixon) and advocates a repetition of that transition model in future NSC staffs.

Eizenstat's suggestion may be visionary; certainly it would be realizable only if the incoming president is convinced that it would be in *his* interest to insist on having a stanchion of continuity in such a swirl of impermanence. More likely, the White House of the future will continue to rely on the informal counsel of former presidents or senior staff alumni in person, rather than inject formal rigidities into what must always be a flexible policy environment.

Before launching any innovations, a future White House staff needs to know what it is they are reforming. Presidential public administration here enters virgin territory. With few exceptions, postelection communication between incoming and outgoing White House staff members has been at best perfunctory. Transition briefings are of course provided for newcomers within the Cabinet departments, but conversations among new and old White House office heads have often not gone beyond handing over the floor plans. Such communication gaps are harmful to good government. Between election and inauguration, therefore, private forums are needed where newly designated staff leaders can put their inherent superciliousness aside and give a hearing to the observations of those who have preceded them. Each White House of the future deserves the benefits of the experience each presidency has accumulated.

After a presidential change, the alumni of the years just gone begin to draw together to recall—and celebrate—the unforgettable intensities they shared. Eisenhower administration veterans gather in reunion luncheons and dinners; the Judson Welliver Society includes all the speechwriters present and past; the 1600 Club welcomes the White House Communications Agency insiders. Every few months the February Group of Nixon-Ford alumni convenes, its national directory of names and addresses kept current, its newsletter chatty with nuggets about new promotions, new marriages, old memories.

Within weeks of inauguration, a new White House staff comes to reflect, as did its predecessor, the president's own policies, priorities, and style. The older core functions continue, juggled perhaps into different hierarchies, adorned with new labels. Fresh adjustments are frequently made, practices fine-tuned, faces often changed. The White House staff then becomes no more than and no less than what the chief executive wants it to be; the instructions it gives are his orders and the procedures it specifies are the ones he desires.

If the Cabinet, the Congress, or the country are persistently offended by what a White House staff says and does, there is just one person in whose hands to heap their woe: the president of the United States. Ask not the White House staff to be what he is not. Should a president, fully informed, insist on unwise decisions, it is not they who will reverse him. Should he be malicious or dishonorable, it is only the more independent institutions of our nation—the Congress, the courts, the press—not the White House staff, who must guard the republic.

The essence of White House service, however, is not the notorious dishonor of a few, but the quiet honor of thousands. The newest staff intern remembers what the oldest White House veteran never forgets—John Adams' prayer inscribed over the fireplace in the State Dining Room and quoted at the beginning of this part. That invocation reaches staff members as well; few of them fail to be humbled by the sense of obligation that those words instill. Implied within them is a further admonition: whether high or low in the staff, even in the midst of partisanship, one's duty is not only to the ruler of the present, but to the White House of the future, to the president of today and to the presidency of tomorrow.

The true reward of White House service reaches, also, beyond the excitement of the moment, is deeper than the seductive allure of the trappings of office. The energetic and intellectually aggressive men and women who make up the White House staff are driven not so much by the thirst for fame in the present but by the prospect of nudging the future—of "hacking a few toeholds on history," in the words of one.

A president is elected to effect a coherent program of change, battling all the while the incoherencies of pluralism beyond the White House gates. The White House staff are his ring of power in this battle, tolerating the personal pressures and accepting anonymity as lesser sacrifices for a larger goal.

NOTES

Chapter 1

1. *Washington Post,* July 28, 1987, p. A-15.
2. Alexander Hamilton, *The Federalist Papers—The 70th Federalist* (New York: Mentor Books New American Library, 1961), p. 427.
3. Lemuel A. Garrison, *The Making of a Ranger* (Sun Valley, Idaho: Institute of the American West, 1983), p. 304.
4. *Washington Post,* July 3, 1986, p. A-21.
5. *New York Times,* December 9, 1986, p. A-1.

Chapter 2

1. Joseph Califano, *A Presidential Nation* (New York: Norton, 1975), p. 25.
2. *Papers Relating to the President's Departmental Reorganization Program, A Reference Compilation* (Washington, D.C.: Government Printing Office, 1971), p. 11.
3. Califano, *A Presidential Nation,* p. 52.
4. Henry M. Kissinger, *Years of Upheaval* (Boston: Little, Brown, 1982), p. 435.
5. Nineteen months before he might become president, Democratic Governor Michael Dukakis, speaking to the League of United Latin American Citizens in Corpus Christi, Texas, was asked if he would name a Hispanic to his Cabinet. *"Sin duda,"* [without question] he promised. *The Washington Post,* June 29, 1987, p. A-3.
A year before his possible inauguration, Republican presidential candidate Pat Robertson, campaigning in Storm Lake, Iowa, said, "I promise in the Cabinet I'm going to have an Asiatic, a black—at least one or two—a Hispanic, a woman, every segment of the population." *The Washington Post,* January 24, 1987, p. A-10.
6. The supposed irrelevancy of the postmaster general's attendance is often cited by those who argue that the Cabinet is too big for focused policy discussions. Arthur Summerfield nonetheless contributed to the dialogue in Ike's sessions; he had been the party's national chairman and also helped run the 1952 campaign. Few matters on any Cabinet agenda are sterilized from that kind of political judgment. The Postal Service being now a semi-independent corporation, however, the postmaster general no longer holds a Cabinet seat.
7. Bradley H. Patterson, draft of a memorandum for the president, February 11, 1960, personal files.
8. Margaret Truman, *Harry S. Truman* (New York: Morrow, 1973) pp. 551–52.
9. Comments of the President at the Cabinet Meeting of Friday, April 18, 1958, Dwight D. Eisenhower Library.
10. Ann Whitman Series, Cabinet, Box 1, Dwight D. Eisenhower Library.
11. Martin Anderson, *Revolution* (San Diego: Harcourt, Brace Jovanovich, 1988), p. 228.
12. Theodore C. Sorensen, *Kennedy* (New York: Bantam Books, 1965), pp. 317–18.
13. *The Ford White House* (Lanham, Md.: University Press of America, 1986), p. 19.
14. Richard M. Nixon, *The Memoirs of Richard Nixon* (New York: Warner Books, 1978), 1:418.
15. Stuart Eizenstat, Memorandum for Cabinet Heads entitled "Interagency Review of Nonfuel Minerals-Related Policy Issues," December 12, 1977, author's personal collection.

16. Robert A. Goldwin, Special Consultant to President Ford, as quoted in *The Ford White House,* p. 49.

17. Theodore Sorensen, as quoted in Samuel Kernell and Samuel Popkin, eds., *Chief of Staff* (Berkeley: University of California Press, 1986), pp. 145–46.

18. Dom Bonafede, "Stuart Eizenstat—Carter's Right-Hand Man," *National Journal,* June 9, 1979, pp. 944, 946. Emphasis added.

19. Edwin Harper, interview with the author, Camden, N.J., August 12, 1986.

Chapter 3

1. *Alexander* v. *Holmes County Board of Education,* 396 U.S. 19 (1969).

2. Spiro Agnew, as quoted in William Safire, *Before the Fall* (New York: Belmont Tower Books, 1975), p. 234.

3. John D. Ehrlichman, interview with the author, Washington, D.C., September 6, 1987.

4. Manifesto by School Board Citizens Committee, Dr. E. E. Harrill, Temporary Chairman, Leonard Garment Papers, Box 7, Manuscript Division, Library of Congress. Used with permission.

5. As quoted in Safire, *Before the Fall,* p. 239.

6. Elwood R. Quesada, Oral History (hereafter OH) 308, Columbia Oral History Project, Dwight D. Eisenhower Library, p. 17. Used with permission.

7. Stuart E. Eizenstat, Case Note for the John F. Kennedy School of Government, Harvard University, author's private collection.

8. Henry A. Kissinger, *White House Years* (Boston: Little, Brown, 1979), pp. 29–30.

9. Kissinger, *White House Years,* p. 30.

Chapter 4

1. Andrew J. Goodpaster, Memorandum of July 5, 1956, Staff Notes File, Dwight D. Eisenhower Library. Emphasis added.

2. Albert P. Toner, OH 491, Dwight D. Eisenhower Library, p. 67. Used with permission.

3. Ibid.

4. Christopher H. Russell, OH 406, Dwight D. Eisenhower Library, p. 132. Used with permission.

5. Ibid., p. 97.

6. Ibid., p. 121.

7. Frederick Dutton, interview with the author, Washington, D.C., May 12, 1986.

8. Arthur Schlesinger, Jr., as quoted in Richard E. Neustadt, *Presidential Power* (New York: John Wiley & Sons, 1960), p. 156.

9. Kernell and Popkin, eds., *Chief of Staff,* p. 80.

Chapter 5

1. Nixon, *Memoirs* 1:476.

2. Sorensen, *Kennedy,* p. 316.

3. Califano, *A Presidential Nation,* p. 25.

4. Anderson, *Revolution,* p. 227.

5. Kenneth Cole, White House Memorandum of April 17, 1970, author's private collection.

6. Richard M. Nixon, Message to the Congress, July 8, 1970 (Washington, D.C.: National Archives, Public Papers of the Presidents, 1970), p. 573.

7. *Stevens* v. *Commissioner of Internal Revenue,* 452 F.2nd 741 (9th Cir. 1971).

8. Kissinger, *White House Years,* p. 154.

9. Zbigniew Brzezinski, *Power and Principle* (New York: Farrar, Straus & Giroux, 1985), p. 73.

10. As quoted in Roger Hilsman, *To Move a Nation* (Garden City, N.Y.: Doubleday, 1967), p. 24.

11. McGeorge Bundy to Douglas Dillon, February 20, 1961, author's personal collection.

12. Ibid. Emphasis added.

13. Donald J. Devine, in "Where We Succeeded, Where We Failed," Washington, D.C., *The Heritage Foundation, Policy Review,* Winter, 1988, no. 43, p. 49.

Chapter 6

1. Major R. Hargreaves, "The Mechanics of Communication," *Military Review,* December, 1965, vol. 45, no. 12.

2. This chapter is discussing crises which result from conflicts. Accidents and natural disasters can of course also cause crises requiring federal intervention, as illustrated in chap. 20.

3. Kissinger, *Years of Upheaval,* p. 451.

4. Kissinger, *White House Years,* p. 321.

5. *Washington Post,* August 23, 1981, p. A-3.

6. See the advertisement for the Lightweight ELF Terminal (LET) by the TRW Electronic Systems Group, *National Journal,* April 4, 1987, p. 827.

7. Dwight D. Eisenhower, interview with the author, Gettysburg, Pennsylvania, October 12, 1965. The author's opening question to Eisenhower was whether Roosevelt had, as Churchill apparently did to his commanders, given Ike detailed instructions during World War II. "If I had gotten anything more than a birthday card from FDR," Eisenhower exclaimed, "I would have thought the world was coming to an end." Ike then recounted a wartime experience from the Casablanca Conference. Roosevelt did make one tactical suggestion: send a regiment of troops to capture Dakar. Eisenhower flatly told Roosevelt, he remembered, that if the president wanted serious attention given to such a suggestion, he should make it to the Combined Chiefs of Staff; they were the ones from whom Eisenhower took his orders. "I never heard anything more about Dakar," Ike added.

8. Michael Beschloss, *May Day* (New York: Harper & Row, 1986), p. 140.

9. Ibid., p. 144.

10. Ibid., p. 251.

11. Ibid., p. 257.

12. Graham T. Allison, *Essence of Decision* (Boston: Little, Brown, 1971), pp. 127–28.

13. Essay: "The Lessons of the Cuban Missile Crisis," *Time,* September 27, 1982, pp. 85–86.

14. Theodore Sorensen, Oral History, John F. Kennedy Library, pp. 126–27.

15. Townsend Hoopes, *The Limits of Intervention* (New York: David McKay, 1969), p. 62.

16. Kissinger, *White House Years,* p. 603. Emphasis added.

17. Gerald R. Ford, *A Time to Heal* (New York: Berkley Books, 1980), p. 270; and Kernell and Popkin, *Chief of Staff,* pp. 56–57.

18. See Gary Sick, *All Fall Down* (New York: Penguin Books, 1986), pp. 84–87.

19. See Hamilton Jordan, *Crisis* (New York: G. P. Putnam's Sons, 1982); and Sick, *All Fall Down.*

20. *Washington Post,* April 22, 1988, pp. A–1 and A–18.

21. In using the theatrical metaphor in the descriptions which follow, the author is signaling the difference between the noisy confrontational methods of the American Indian Movement in those years and the true issues affecting native American progress—which were and are daily being grappled with by responsible, elected Indian tribal leadership. When the last of the three confrontations was past, even the news media came to resent the degree to which they had been maneuvered into being part of the A.I.M. theatrics. Free-lance writer Terri Schultz wrote in the June, 1973 issue of *Harper's* magazine, an article entitled "Bamboozle Me Not at Wounded Knee," and Neil Hickey followed with a four-part series in *TV Guide* (December 1973), the first of which was titled "Was TV Duped at Wounded Knee?"

22. *Time,* April 12, 1971, p. 21.

23. *San Francisco Examiner,* June 15, 1971, p. 30.

24. Statement of Deputy Director Frank Carlucci before the Subcommittee on Indian

Affairs of the House Committee on Interior and Insular Affairs, Washington, D.C., Office of Management and Budget, Press Release of December 5, 1972.

25. Arthur S. Hoffman, Memorandum to the Director of the United States Information Agency, Washington, D.C., March 8, 1973, author's personal collection.

26. U.S. Court of Claims, Washington, D.C., Congressional Reference Case 4-76, Opinion of Trial Commissioner Lydon, filed June 10, 1981, pp. 3, 8–9; also Findings of Fact to Accompany the Opinion, p. 24.

Introduction to Part II

1. Extract from a "letter" (number LXII) by political satirist Seba Smith (whose pseudonym was a fictional "Major Jack Downing"). Dated August 17, 1833, the "letter" was printed in the Portland (Maine) *Daily Courier* and reprinted in the book *The Select Letters of Major Jack Downing* (Philadelphia, 1834), pp. 160–63. The author acknowledges the assistance given by John McDonough of the Manuscript Division of the Library of Congress.

Chapter 7

1. Robert Kimmitt, interview with the author, Washington, D.C., October 15, 1986.

2. Even such a chairmanship role can be a matter of sensitive turf relationships, however; at least one strong secretary of state has challenged it.

3. Robert Cutler, Memorandum to the President, April 7, 1958, Ann Whitman Diary File, Dwight D. Eisenhower Library.

4. Les Janka, "The National Security Council and the Making of American Middle East Policy," *Armed Forces Journal International,* March 1984, p. 84.

5. Kimmitt interview.

6. Lou Cannon, "Why Reagan Is Finally Winning in Foreign Policy," *Washington Post,* March 27, 1988, p. C-1.

7. Report of the President's Special Review Board (Washington, D.C.: Government Printing Office, February 26, 1987), p. V-6. (Referred to hereafter as the Tower Commission Report.)

8. The White House, Washington, D.C., National Security Decision Directive 286 of Summer 1987; declassified December 15, 1987, author's personal collection.

9. *Tower Commission Report,* p. V-6.

10. James S. Lay, Jr., Memorandum for the National Security Council, July 1, 1959, National Security Council, Washington, D.C., author's personal collection.

11. *Tower Commission Report,* p. IV-4.

12. Robert L. Dennison, Oral History, Harry S. Truman Library, p. 12.

13. Brzezinski, *Power and Principle,* p. 70.

14. President Ronald Reagan to the Special Review Board, Washington, D.C., February 20, 1987, as quoted in the *Tower Commission Report,* p. III-7.

15. *Tower Commission Report,* p. V-2-3.

16. The White House, Washington, D.C., National Security Decision Directive 266 of March 31, 1987.

17. The White House, Washington, D.C., Message to the Congress of March 31, 1987.

18. Beginning with the Reagan papers, in 1989, a law (PL 95–591 of November 4, 1978) takes effect which transforms this custom of comity into statute. The incumbent president will have access to the records of his predecessors when "needed for the conduct of current business of his office" (Title 44 of the U.S. Code, Section 2205(2)(B)). The Archivist of the United States must notify the former president (Section 2206(2) and (3)) and the latter may contest the loan (Section 2204(c)(2) and (e)).

19. *Strengthening U.S.-Soviet Communications: Report of the National Academy of Public Administration,* Washington, D.C., 1987, p. 9.

20. Clark Clifford, Oral History, Harry S. Truman Library, p. 185.

21. Ibid., pp. 95–106; Robert Donovan, *Conflict and Crisis* (New York: Norton, 1977), pp. 381–82.

22. Oscar Ewing Oral History, Harry S. Truman Library, p. 298.

23. Nixon, *Memoirs* 2:86.

24. Jimmy Carter, *Keeping Faith* (New York: Bantam Books, 1982), p. 53.

25. Kissinger, *White House Years*, p. 666.

26. Sorensen, *Kennedy*, pp. 333, 342, 343, 726.

27. Ibid., p. 711.

28. Robert S. McNamara, interview with the author, Washington, D.C., June 1, 1987.

29. Frank Carlucci, informal remarks at the conclusion of the Brookings Institution Trustees Dinner, Washington, D.C., February 26, 1987.

30. *Tower Commission Report*, p. IV-10.

31. National Security Decision Directive 266, p. 4.

32. Dwight D. Eisenhower, *Mandate for Change* (Garden City, N.Y.: Doubleday, 1963), p. 477.

33. David Halberstam, *The Best and the Brightest* (New York: Random House, 1972), p. 168.

34. Stanley Karnow, *Vietnam, A History* (New York: Viking, 1983), p. 411.

35. John D. Ehrlichman, *Witness to Power* (New York: Pocket Books, 1982), pp. 76–77.

36. Elmer B. Staats, interview with the author, Washington, D.C., August 1987.

37. Robert Huyser, *Mission to Tehran* (New York: Harper & Row, 1986), p. 273.

38. Constantine C. Menges, in the *Heritage Foundation, Policy Review*, Winter 1988, p. 52.

39. Off-the-record interview with the author, Washington, D.C., April 1987.

40. National Security Decision Directive 266, p. 4.

41. *Washington Post*, May 5, 1980, p. A-21.

42. Talking Paper, January 6, 1981, as printed in the *Washington Post*, July 11, 1982, pp. C-1, C-5.

43. Off-the-record interview with the author, Washington, D.C., May 1987.

44. Richard M. Nixon, interview with David Frost, condensed text printed in the *Washington Post*, May 13, 1977, p. A-19.

45. Kissinger, *White House Years*, p. 138.

46. Hilsman, *To Move a Nation*, p. 67.

47. As quoted in the *New York Times*, December 18, 1986, p. A-22.

48. Brzezinski, *Power and Principle*, pp. 153, 226.

49. Ibid., p. 207.

50. Ibid., p. 41.

51. Carter, *Keeping Faith*, p. 197.

52. Alexander Haig, *Caveat* (New York: Macmillan, 1984), p. 290.

53. Ibid., p. 356.

54. Bromley K. Smith, interview with the author, Washington, D.C.

55. Karnow, *Vietnam*, p. 516.

56. Kissinger, *White House Years*, pp. 315, 601.

57. For the description of an important possible additional use for Room 208, the reader is referred to n. 11 of chap. 20.

58. As quoted in Haig, *Caveat*, p. 145.

59. A vice president with as much experience in foreign affairs as George Bush would be valuable as a foreign policy adviser at any time, crisis or not. In March of 1981, the president's problem was not crisis management but how to handle his secretary of state. Secretary of Defense Weinberger would not concur in seeing Mr. Haig designated as "crisis manager" and neither Weinberger nor Haig would concur having the then national security assistant, Richard Allen, so named. Bush embodied the compromise. On the next day, March 25, Haig wrote out a letter of resignation.

60. Kissinger, *White House Years*, p. 21.

61. Brzezinski, *Power and Principle*, p. 77.

62. Dick Kirschten, "McFarlane's Openness Sends Press the Signal: This Bud's For You," *National Journal*, November 2, 1985, pp. 2492–93.

63. *Time*, June 25, 1965.

64. Kissinger, *White House Years*, p. 21.

65. Dick Kirschten, "His NSC Days May Be Numbered, but Allen Is Known for Bouncing Back," *National Journal*, November 28, 1981, pp. 2114–17.

66. *National Journal,* November 2, 1985.

67. Sunday, December 20, 1987.

68. Nixon, *Memoirs* 1:620–21.

69. H. R. Haldeman, with Joseph DiMona, *The Ends of Power* (New York: New York Times Books, 1978), p. 195.

70. Robert Cutler, *No Time for Rest* (Boston: Little, Brown, 1966), pp. 295–6.

71. Kissinger, *Years of Upheaval,* p. 95.

72. In Public Law 95-570, Section 108(a), Congress authorizes the president to have an annual contingency fund of $1,000,000 "for unanticipated needs for the furtherance of the national interest, security or defense." Expenditures under this section must be reported to the Congress annually. In FY 1987, $250,000 of the fund, for example, financed the work of the Tower Commission.

73. Oliver L. North, *Taking the Stand* (New York: Pocket Books, 1987), pp. 442–43.

74. *Tower Commission Report,* p. V-4.

75. *Report of the Congressional Committees Investigating the Iran-Contra Affair* (Washington, D.C.: Government Printing Office, 1987), p. 18.

76. *Tower Commission Report,* p. V-4.

Chapter 8

1. Richard E. Neustadt, in Francis H. Heller, ed., *The Truman White House: The Administration of the Presidency* (Lawrence: Regents Press of Kansas, 1980), p. 99.

2. Ibid.

3. Robert E. Merriam, OH 118, Dwight D. Eisenhower Library, pp. 180–81. Used with permission.

4. Califano, *A Presidential Nation,* p. 47.

5. Richard M. Nixon, Message to the Congress, March 12, 1970 (Washington, D.C.: National Archives, Public Papers of the Presidents, 1970), p. 259.

6. Margaret J. Wyszomirski, "A Domestic Policy Office: Presidential Agency in Search of a Role," *Policy Studies Journal* 12, no. 4 (June 1984): 707.

7. Ehrlichman, *Witness to Power,* p. 216.

8. Jimmy Carter, Memorandum for Six Cabinet Heads, March 21, 1977, author's personal collection.

9. The material for this chapter's description of President Carter's urban development initiative, and the short quotations included in this material, are from a series of off-the-record interviews by participants in that policy process with the author, and from private papers made available to the author that are presumably destined for subsequent inclusion in the Carter Library.

10. David Broder, *Washington Post,* March 29, 1978, p. A-23.

11. John D. Ehrlichman, interview with the author, September 6, 1986.

12. Stuart Eizenstat, Memorandum for the President, July 18, 1977 (Washington, D.C.: National Archives, Papers of Stuart Eizenstat, Chronological Files, box 10, July 17–23).

13. Griffin B. Bell, with Ronald J. Ostrow, *Taking Care of the Law* (New York: Morrow, 1982), pp. 29–30.

14. For example, Section 1115 of the Social Security Act, codified as 42 USC 1315.

Chapter 9

1. Note the previous chapter's discussion of the Justice Department/White House tug-of-war over the brief in the *Bakke* case and the fuller discussion of this issue in Griffin Bell, *Taking Care of the Law,* pp. 26–45.

2. From several off-the-record interviews with the author.

3. Mr. Cutler attributes this aphorism to former Under Secretary of State George Ball. Interview with the author, Washington, D.C., October 22, 1986.

4. *The White House Office Handbook,* "Standards of Conduct for the White House Staff," February 1975, Tab E, p. E-7, author's personal collection.

5. Lloyd Cutler, interview with the author, Washington, D.C., October 22, 1986.

6. Ann Whitman Diary, January 11, 1955, Dwight D. Eisenhower Library.

7. *New York Times,* December 9, 1986, p. B-14.

8. Fred Fielding, Testimony to the Commission of September 30, 1986, as quoted in the *Report of the Miller Center Commission on Presidential Disability and the Twenty-Fifth Amendment* (Lanham, Md.: University Press of America, 1988), p. 7.

9. Philip W. Buchen, interview with the author, Washington, D.C., May 16, 1986.

10. Philip Buchen, Memorandum for All Employees of the White House Office, Washington, D.C., October 28, 1974, p. 4, author's personal collection.

11. Dwight D. Eisenhower, Press Conference of May 4, 1956 (Washington, D.C.: National Archives, Public Papers of the Presidents, 1956), p. 457.

12. Bernard Shanley, OH 348, Dwight D. Eisenhower Library, pp. 83–84.

13. Griffin Bell, *Taking Care of the Law,* p. 42.

Chapter 10

1. Memorandum from Charles S. Murphy to President Truman, March 11, 1948, Charles Murphy Papers, President's General Files, Harry S. Truman Library.

2. Charles S. Murphy Oral History, Harry S. Truman Library, pp. 236–37.

3. Off-the-record interview, Washington, D.C., August 26, 1986.

4. Max L. Friedersdorf, interview with the author, Washington, D.C., April 29, 1987.

5. Off-the-record interview with the author, Washington, D. C., Spring 1987.

6. Memorandum from Frank Moore to President Carter, April 8, 1980, author's personal collection.

7. The letter appears in the *Congressional Record—Senate,* October 28, 1981, p. S-12349.

8. Friedersdorf interview.

9. Charles U. Daly Oral History, John F. Kennedy Library, pp. 43–46.

10. Warren Cikins, former legislative assistant to Presidents Kennedy and Johnson, interview with the author, Washington, D.C., August 26, 1986.

11. Off-the-record interview, Washington, D.C., Spring 1987.

12. Charles S. Murphy Papers, President's General Files, Harry S. Truman Library.

13. Ann Whitman Diary, July 25, 1957, Dwight D. Eisenhower Library.

14. Sorensen, *Kennedy,* p. 400.

15. "Turning Screws: Winning Votes in Congress," *Congressional Quarterly,* April 14, 1976, p. 947.

16. *Washington Post,* May 21, 1979, p. A-4.

17. *Washington Post,* February 12, 1982, p. A-18.

18. Off-the-record interview with the author, Washington, D.C., Spring 1987.

19. Dom Bonafede, "Carter's Relationship with Congress—Making a Mountain out of a 'Moorehill,' " *National Journal,* March 26, 1977, p. 459.

Chapter 11

1. The White House issues some 1,700 press credentials but many are to technicians. Augmenting the 50 regulars, others come in and out of the press room sporadically.

2. George Herman, in the Herman-Lisagor-McGrory Oral History, August 4, 1964, John F. Kennedy Library, p. 74.

3. Ehrlichman, *Witness to Power,* pp. 237–38.

4. Jimmy Carter, *Keeping Faith,* p. 117.

5. A Ford administration official, quoted in Michael B. Grossman and Martha J. Kumar, *Portraying the President* (Baltimore: Johns Hopkins University Press, 1981), p. 227.

6. Larry Speakes, with Robert Pack, *Speaking Out: Inside the Reagan White House* (New York: Charles Scribner's Sons, 1988), p. 271.

7. James C. Hagerty, as quoted in R. Gordon Hoxie, ed., *The White House: Organization and Operations* (New York: Center for the Study of the Presidency, 1971), p. 4.

8. Ron Nessen, *It Sure Looks Different from the Inside* (Chicago: Playboy Press, 1978), p. 224.

9. Speakes, *Speaking Out*, p. xiii.

10. Speakes, *Speaking Out*, p. 171.

11. As quoted in the *Washington Post*, July 18, 1987, p. G-9.

12. Nessen, pp. 124–26.

13. *New York Times*, October 10, 1986, pp. 1 and 8.

14. Ibid.

15. Ibid.

16. Speakes, *Speaking Out*, p. 136.

17. Off-the-record interview with the author, Washington, D.C., June 17, 1987.

18. David Broder, from Remarks to the National Academy of Public Administration, Washington, D.C., April 21, 1987.

19. Off-the-record interview with the author, Washington, D.C., June 17, 1987.

20. Speakes, *Speaking Out*, p. 153.

21. Nessen, *It Sure Looks Different*, p. 203.

22. *Washington Post*, January 29, 1979, p. B-9.

23. Robert E. Merriam OH 118, Columbia Oral History Project, Dwight D. Eisenhower Library, pp. 200–201. Used with permission.

24. *Washington Post*, January 31, 1987, p. A-3.

25. Jody Powell in "The President and the Press," The Virginia Papers on the Presidency, vol. 6 (Washington, D.C.: The University Press of America, 1981), p. 76.

26. *Washington Post*, June 3, 1985, p. A-4.

27. Off-the-record interview with the author, Washington, D.C., June 17, 1987.

28. George Elsey Oral History, Harry S. Truman Library, pp. 77–78.

29. Sorensen, *Kennedy*, p. 362.

30. Frederick G. Dutton Oral History, John F. Kennedy Library, p. 39.

31. Speakes, *Speaking Out*, p. 149. On pp. 148–49 Speakes gives the details of the post-summit "news blitz" which he engineered.

32. George Reedy, "The White House: The Media and the Man in the Middle," in Kenneth W. Thompson, ed., *Three Press Secretaries on the Presidency and the Press* (Lanham, Md.: University Press of America, 1983), p. 98.

33. Ehrlichman, *Witness to Power*, p. 247.

34. *Washington Post*, January 20, 1977, p. E-1.

Chapter 12

1. Publicist John R. (Tex) McCrary is said to have coined the "HPCQ" aphorism.

2. A superb description of how Nixon, Ford, and Carter organized what is well termed the "White House Bubble Machine" is given in Michael Grossman and Martha Kumar, *Portraying the President* (Baltimore: Johns Hopkins University Press, 1981).

3. Herman-Lisagor-McGrory Oral History, p. 82.

4. Ibid.

5. Emmette Redford and Richard McCulley, *White House Operations: The Johnson Presidency* (Austin: University of Texas Press, 1986), p. 172.

6. Ehrlichman, *Witness to Power*, p. 248.

7. Donald Regan, *For The Record—From Wall Street to Washington* (San Diego: Harcourt Brace Jovanovich, 1988), p. 257.

8. Martin Schram, *The Great American Video Game: Presidential Politics in the Television Age* (New York: Morrow, 1987), p. 57.

9. For an additional first-hand description of the "orchestration" of presidential events, see

the recent book by former Chief of Staff Donald T. Regan, *For the Record—From Wall Street to Washington* (San Diego: Harcourt Brace Jovanovich, 1988), pp. 247–48.

10. Anonymous senior White House staff member, quoted in Dick Kirschten, "Communications Reshuffling Intended to Help Reagan Do What He Does Best," *National Journal,* January 28, 1984, p. 154.

11. Ibid.

12. As quoted in Grossman and Kumar, *Portraying the President,* p. 46.

13. Kirschten, "Communications Reshuffling," p. 153.

14. David Broder, "How Press Secrecy Backfired on Reagan," *Washington Post,* March 22, 1987, p. C-4.

15. Jane Mayer, "It Took Work to Get Reagan into Grenada for 4 Hours Today," *Wall Street Journal,* February 20, 1986, p. 1.

16. Ron Nessen, "Always on Saturday?" *Washington Post,* August 20, 1986, p. A-19.

17. Bill Plante, "Why We Were Shouting at the President," *Washington Post,* October 11, 1987, p. H-7.

18. *Washington Post,* July 11, 1984, p. A-3.

19. Speakes, *Speaking Out,* p. 40.

20. Grossman and Kumar, *Portraying the President,* p. 92.

21. Robert Montgomery, *Open Letter from a Television Viewer* (New York: Heineman Paperbacks, 1968), p. 64.

22. *Washington Post,* August 8, 1978, p. A-17.

23. *Washington Post,* December 22, 1986, p. A-16.

24. Jerry terHorst, in Thompson, ed., *Three Press Secretaries,* p. 41.

25. Speakes, *Speaking Out,* p. 79.

26. *Washington Post,* December 22, 1986, p. A-16.

27. Ibid.

28. Grossman and Kumar, *Portraying the President,* p. 102.

29. Jody Powell, in Thompson, ed., *Three Press Secretaries,* p. 44.

Chapter 13

1. Raymond K. Price, Jr., interview with the author, New York, December 10, 1985.

2. Theodore C. Sorensen, "Dearth of Eloquence at the Top," *Chicago Tribune,* August 23, 1979, p. 18.

3. Raymond K. Price, Jr., *With Nixon* (New York: Viking, 1977), p. 166.

4. Sorensen, "Dearth of Eloquence."

5. Sherman Adams, *First-Hand Report* (New York: Harper & Brothers, 1961), p. 81.

6. As quoted in Stephen E. Ambrose, *Eisenhower: The President* (New York: Simon & Schuster, 1984), p. 346.

7. Speech of May 29, 1986 (Washington, D.C.: National Archives, Weekly Compilation of Presidential Documents, week of May 30, 1986), vol. 22, no. 22, p. 714.

8. Clark Clifford Oral History, Harry S. Truman Library, pp. 350, 359.

9. Bryce N. Harlow, OH 214, Columbia Oral History Project, Dwight D. Eisenhower Library, p. 97. Used with permission.

10. Sorensen, *Kennedy,* p. 370.

11. Gerald R. Ford, Address of August 30, 1974, in *Public Papers of the Presidents of the United States: Gerald R. Ford, 1974* (Washington, D.C., National Archives and Records Service), p. 71.

12. Peggy Noonan, interview with the author, McLean, Va., October 2, 1987.

13. Address to the Nation, January 28, 1986 (Washington, D.C.: National Archives and Records Administration, Weekly Compilation of Presidential Documents, week of January 31, 1986), vol. 22, no. 5, p. 104.

14. Will Sparks, *Who Talked to the President Last?* (New York: W. W. Norton, 1971), p. 54.

15. Raymond K. Price, Jr., interview with the author, New York City, December 10, 1985.

16. Richard Nixon, Speech of June 25, 1971, in *Public Papers of the Presidents: Richard Nixon, 1971,* p. 781.

17. Noonan interview.

18. Price interview.

Chapter 14

1. Gerald R. Ford, Remarks to the Republican National Hispanic Assembly, July 29, 1976, in *Public Papers of the Presidents: Gerald R. Ford, 1976–77*, 3:2106–7.
2. E. Frederic Morrow, *Black Man in the White House* (New York: Coward-McCann, 1963), p. 266.
3. Califano, *Governing America*, p. 389.
4. David Silverberg, "The Quest for Access to the White House," *Jewish Monthly*, February 1984, p. 8.
5. *Washington Post*, September 28, 1972, p. A-16.
6. *Washington Star*, December 12, 1976, p. F-4.
7. Silverberg, "The Quest for Access," p. 11.
8. *Wall Street Journal*, February 25, 1975, p. 1.
9. Anne Wexler, interview with the author, Washington, D.C., October 30, 1986.
10. Anne Wexler, Activities Report—Week Ending March 21, 1980, Washington, D.C., p. 3. Ms. Wexler's private files. Used with permission.
11. Wexler interview.
12. Wayne Valis, interview with the author, Washington, D.C., May 12, 1986.

Chapter 15

1. Appointments secretaries have not always been above using their position for personal or policy leverage. Truman confidant George Allen tells of his 1944 conspiracy with Roosevelt Appointments Assistant Edwin M. "Pa" Watson "to arrange appointments with Roosevelt for all potential convention delegates who were opposed to Wallace. . . . This went on month after month . . . little by little, they began having their effect." Allen alleges that these machinations led up "to the selection of Harry S Truman as candidate for Vice President in 1944." George Allen Oral History, part I, Harry S. Truman Library, p. 59.
2. Frederick Ryan, interview with the author, Washington, D.C., February 18, 1987.
3. Nixon reportedly did not enjoy such protocol formalities, but recognized that U.S. envoys abroad needed the reciprocity to establish their own access. The new ambassadors in Washington are now often brought in to the Oval Office as a group rather than singly.
4. Speakes, *Speaking Out*, p. 220.
5. Bryce N. Harlow, OH 214, Columbia Oral History Project, Dwight D. Eisenhower Library, p. 101. Used with permission.

Chapter 16

1. Executive Order 11455 of February 14, 1969, in *Public Papers of the Presidents: Richard Nixon, 1969*, p. 96.
2. In his book *American Intergovernmental Relations, Their Origins, Historical Development and Current Status* (New York: Scribners, 1964), p. 886, W. Brooke Graves tells that Roosevelt had first James McReynolds and later Guy Moffat on his personal staff "to coordinate Federal programs involving intergovernmental relations." No record exists of their work, reports Graves, but both attempts "were short-lived, partly because the administration did not back the efforts of the coordinators and partly because of the almost unlimited ingenuity of department and agency administrators in finding means of resisting any attempts to develop uniform policies and procedures and to coordinate programs. This resistance, incidentally, is the root of much of the present difficulty, and it is not unreasonable to assume that it will continue to be a problem far into the future."
3. Commission on Intergovernmental Relations, *A Report to the President for Transmittal to the Congress* (Washington, D.C.: Government Printing Office, 1955), p. 87.

4. Howard Pyle, OH 120, Columbia Oral History Project, Dwight D. Eisenhower Library, pp. 124–25. Used with permission.

5. The Kennedy instruction was later the subject of a Budget Bureau circular and was reaffirmed in Reagan Executive Order 12372 of July 14, 1982, in *Public Papers of the Presidents: Ronald Reagan, 1982* 2:926–28.

6. Jean Appleby, *The Office of Intergovernmental Relations: A Study of an Organization,* (M.A. diss., University of Virginia, 1980).

7. Eugene Eidenberg, interview with the author, July 16, 1987.

8. Jack Watson, interview with the author, Rio de Janeiro, February 4, 1986.

9. Executive Order 12075 of August 16, 1978, in *Public Papers of the Presidents: Jimmy Carter, 1978* 2:1433–34.

10. Jay Solomon, Memorandum for the President, Weekly Report of GSA Activities, June 9, 1978 (Washington, D.C.: National Archives, Papers of Stuart Eizenstat, Cabinet Summaries, Status Reports 1977–1978, box 24).

11. Eidenberg interview.

12. In chaps. 2, 5, and 6, examples have been given of the role the Indian Affairs Office played throughout the Nixon administration.

13. The ACIR is a statutory body established twenty-five years earlier at Eisenhower's urging, based on the Kestnbaum Commission's recommendations.

14. Richard S. Williamson, interview with the author, August 14, 1986.

15. Linda E. Demkovich, "Team Player Schweiker May Be Paying a High Price for His Loyalty to Reagan," *National Journal,* May 5, 1982, p. 849.

16. Stephen B. Farber, interview with the author, July 29, 1986.

17. *Washington Post,* June 23, 1983, p. A-21.

18. David S. Broder, "Governors Relent, to Seek Accord on Federalism with Reagan," *Washington Post,* August 11, 1982, p. A-8.

19. Stephen B. Farber, "The 1982 New Federalism Negotiations: A View from the States," *Publius, The Journal of Federalism,* Spring 1983, p. 38. The author acknowledges the indispensable help he received for this section of chap. 16 from interviews with Messrs. Williamson and Farber and from several of the Williamson associates, as well as from the Williamson article "The 1982 New Federalism Negotiations," in the above-cited issue of *Publius.*

Chapter 17

1. Matthew J. Connelly Oral History, Harry S. Truman Library, pp. 129–30.

2. Ken Hechler, *Working with Truman* (New York: Putnam, 1982), p. 68.

3. William L. Batt, Jr., interview with the author, August 1987.

4. Howard Pyle, OH 120, Columbia Oral History Project, Dwight D. Eisenhower Library. Used with permission.

5. Robert Merriam, OH 118, Columbia Oral History Project, Dwight D. Eisenhower Library, pp. 134ff. Used with permission.

6. Redford and McCulley, *White House Operations* (see chap. 12, n. 5), p. 175.

7. Harry S. Dent, *The Prodigal South Returns to Power* (New York: Wiley, 1978), p. 229.

8. Dent, interview with the author, Columbia, South Carolina, October 14, 1985.

9. *Washington Post,* October 5, 1982, p. A-5.

10. Clark Clifford Oral History, Harry S. Truman Library, p. 317.

11. Off-the-record interview with the author.

12. Ibid.

13. It was H.R. 1562, vetoed December 17, 1985. *Congressional Quarterly Almanac* 16 (1985), p. 40-D.

14. Califano, *Governing America,* p. 103.

15. Ibid., p. 277.

16. Dent interview.

17. Ambrose, *Eisenhower: The President,* pp. 218–19.

18. Dick Kirschten, "Reagan on the Road," *National Journal,* October 18, 1986, p. 2490.

19. Mitchell Daniels, interview with the author, Washington, D.C., May 29, 1987.

20. Donnie Radcliffe, "The Notable Nofziger," *Washington Post,* April 12, 1981, p. L-8.

21. Dent, *The Prodigal South,* pp. 237–38.

22. Charles Masterson, OH 120, Columbia Oral History Project, Dwight D. Eisenhower Library, pp. 69ff. Used with permission.

23. Califano, *Governing America,* p. 420.

24. Daniels interview.

25. Mitchel Daniels, in "Where We Succeeded, Where We Failed—Lessons from Reagan Officials for the Next Conservative Presidency," *The Heritage Foundation, Policy Review,* Washington, D.C., Winter 1988, pp. 47–48.

26. Radcliffe, "The Notable Nofziger."

Chapter 18

1. Bruce Adams and Kathryn Kavanagh-Baran, *Promise and Performance: Carter Builds a New Administration* (Lexington, Mass.: Lexington Books, 1979), p. 64.

2. The specific duties of certain of the senior departmental positions, such as some assistant secretaries, are not set forth in statute but are left for each Cabinet head to determine; there is thus flexibility—and variability—from administration to administration.

3. Ms. Katja Bullock, assistant director of the Presidential Personnel Office, interview with the author, Washington, D.C., February 10, 1988.

4. E. Pendleton James, former assistant to President Reagan and former director of the Office of Presidential Personnel, interview with the author, New York City, June 23, 1987.

5. E. Pendleton James, quoted in "Recruiting Presidential Appointees—A Conference of Former Presidential Personnel Assistants," Fourth in a Series of Occasional Papers on American Governance (Washington, D.C.: National Academy of Public Administration, December 13, 1984), p. 11.

6. Ibid., pp. 20–21.

7. James interview.

8. Charles F. Willis, Jr., "Memorandum for Special Assistants" of November 29, 1954, Charles Willis Papers, Box 4, Dwight D. Eisenhower Library, p. 3; and set of half-page attachments on the Personnel Management Program, pp. 17–19a.

9. Presidential Press Conference, October 27, 1954, in *Public Papers of the Presidents: Dwight D. Eisenhower, 1954,* pp. 966–67.

10. Dwight D. Eisenhower, Diary Note for January 5, 1953, *The Eisenhower Diaries,* ed. Robert H. Ferrell (New York: Norton, 1981), p. 218.

11. Robert Keith Gray, *Eighteen Acres Under Glass* (Garden City, N.Y.: Doubleday, 1962), pp. 77–79.

12. Nixon, *Memoirs* 1:440.

13. Ibid., p. 441.

14. William J. Hopkins, interview with the author, Washington, D.C., Summer 1987.

15. Nixon, *Memoirs,* 2:285.

16. Hamilton Jordan and Stuart Eizenstat, Memorandum for the President, July 26, 1977, "Holdover Republican Appointees in Federal Positions" (Washington, D.C.: National Archives, Papers of Stuart Eizenstat, Chronological Files, box 10, July 24–31, 1977).

17. Arnie Miller, NAPA Fourth Occasional Paper, p. 13.

18. William N. Walker, NAPA Fourth Occasional Paper, p. 34.

19. Ibid., p. 42.

20. The Goldwater-Nichols Department of Defense Reorganization Act of 1986, Section 102(f) (Washington, D.C.: U.S. House of Representatives, 99th Cong., 2nd Sess., Report 99-824, September 12, 1986), p. 5.

21. Walker, NAPA Fourth Occasional Paper, p. 35.

22. Carter, *Keeping Faith,* p. 61.

23. Miller, NAPA Fourth Occasional Paper, p. 22.

24. John W. Macy, Jr., NAPA Fourth Occasional Paper, p. 34.

25. James, NAPA Fourth Occasional Paper, p. 19. Reading the account of Griffin Bell, Carter's attorney general, however, reveals that even in the Carter administration, moves were made to transfer the evaluation process for judicial nominations from the Justice Department to the White House, an initiative stoutly but vainly resisted by Bell (see chap. 9).

26. President Reagan's nomination of Judge Ginsburg to the Supreme Court was not an outstanding illustration of such staff work.

27. Walker, NAPA Fourth Occasional Paper, p. 33.

28. Becky Norton Dunlop, "The Role of the White House Office of Presidential Personnel," in Rector and Sanera, eds., *Steering the Elephant* (New York: Universe Books, 1987), p. 149.

29. James interview.

30. Walker, NAPA Fourth Occasional Paper, p. 23.

31. See Edward Preston, "Orienting Presidential Appointees," *The Bureaucrat,* Fall 1984.

32. *Washington Post,* July 19, 1979, p. A-1.

33. Miller, NAPA Fourth Occasional Paper, p. 30.

34. Off-the-record interviews with the author.

35. Douglas Bennett, interview with the author, Washington, D.C., Spring 1987.

36. Dunlop, in Rector and Sanera, eds., *Steering the Elephant,* p. 152.

37. Rector and Sanera, "The Reagan Presidency and Policy Change," in *Steering the Elephant,* p. 331.

38. 5 USC 1102, Public Law 95-454, Title II, 201(a), October 13, 1978.

39. Former Reagan Secretary of Education Terrel Bell, especially on pages 38 and 41 of his new book, *The Thirteenth Man* (New York: Free Press/Macmillan, 1988), is only the latest in a long line of Cabinet officers who "wanted to select [departmental executive] leaders on the basis of their qualifications without concern for political ideology . . ." and who blame the senior White House staff, or even "second- and third-level staff people," rather than the president, for White House actions of which they disapprove. The then director of the Presidential Personnel Office, E. Pendleton James, has confirmed to the author that Bell's allegations that lower-level White House staffers had "the power to reject cabinet-level recommendations" are incorrect. The personnel decisions which Bell describes were, in fact, appealed through James to the president, and were made by the president.

40. Miller, NAPA Fourth Occasional Paper, p. 39.

Chapter 19

1. The White House cooperation with the dedication of the Cordell Hull Dam was firm, but the president's scheduled participation fell victim to the Yom Kippur War in the Middle East that October. Tricia Nixon Cox represented her father and a creative and energetic young singer added her then almost unknown talents to the ceremonies. Her name: Dolly Parton.

2. The White House advance manuals with their appendices and attachments are in a private collection that was shown to the author; the quotations therefrom are with permission. The author wishes to express his appreciation for this opportunity and for the off-the-record interviews with several alumni of the Advance Office, all of which provided the greatest part of the information base for this chapter.

3. See n. 2 above.

4. CBS newswoman Susan Zirinsky, as quoted in Martin Schram, *The Great American Video Game* (see chap. 12, n. 8), p. 55.

5. Ibid.

6. See n. 2 above.

7. Ibid.

8. Off-the-record interview with the author.

9. Kissinger, *White House Years,* p. 769.

10. Red Cavaney, interview with the author, New York City, Spring 1987.

11. Ibid.

12. See n. 2 above.

Chapter 20

1. In November of 1986, Section 1311 of the Defense Authorization Act for FY 1987 (Public Law 99–661) told the Chief Executive that it was "the sense of Congress that the President should designate," under his White House national security assistant, a "Deputy Assistant for Low Intensity Conflict." Reagan complied, designated retired Vice Admiral William Cockell, and this second-magnitude czar was on duty, as of February 1988, with a staff of seven.

2. James R. Killian, Jr., *Sputnik, Scientists, and Eisenhower* (Cambridge, Mass., MIT Press, 1977), p. 7.

3. Dwight D. Eisenhower, Address to the Nation, November 7, 1957, in *Public Papers of the President, Dwight D. Eisenhower, 1957,* p. 796.

4. Killian, *Sputnik, Scientists, and Eisenhower,* p. 32.

5. Ibid., pp. 34, 205.

6. Ibid., p. 205.

7. Ibid., p. 152.

8. George Kistiakowsky, OH 412, Dwight D. Eisenhower Library, p. 19.

9. Dwight Ink, interview with the author, Washington, D.C., June 13, 1987.

10. *Response to Disaster,* Report of the Federal Reconstruction and Development Planning Commission (Washington, D.C., Government Printing Office, September 1964), p. v.

11. On January 19, 1988, with the approval of President Reagan, Domestic Policy Council Chairman Edwin Meese issued (on White House stationery) a memorandum proclaiming a "National System for Emergency Coordination," to be used "in extreme catastrophic technological, natural or other domestic disasters of national significance." The memorandum specifies that in such a case, the president, and only the president, would activate the system; the official at the head of the Office of Cabinet Affairs at the White House would start consultations with the NSC and the other appropriate agencies to "develop specific action plans for consideration by the President"; and the White House Cabinet Affairs Office would "be responsible for apprising the President of developments and decisions that may be needed." A "National Coordinator," probably a Cabinet member, would likely be designated by the president "to coordinate Federal support operations" to assist state and local governments. The National Coordinator would activate the needed "interagency functional groups," e.g., medical, environmental, telecommunications, etc.

Coming in parallel with this decision to formalize a major White House staff role in domestic disasters is the capability of the newer and larger of the two national security Situation Rooms at the White House to function as a Cabinet-wide communications and command center. Thus, in another precedent-making step, the White House will apply to domestic crisis management, and to the domestic agencies, arrangements and disciplines similar to those heretofore used in the national security area.

12. Ronald Reagan, Remarks on Signing Executive Order 12368, June 24, 1982, in *Public Papers of the Presidents: Ronald Reagan, 1982* 1:836.

13. Ibid.

14. Carlton E. Turner, telephone interview with the author, May 6, 1987.

Chapter 21

1. Rosalynn Carter, *First Lady from Plains* (Boston: Houghton Mifflin, 1984), pp. 183–84.

2. Michael K. Deaver, with Mickey Herskowitz, *Behind the Scenes* (New York: William Morrow, 1987), pp. 39, 120. In his recent book, *For the Record,* former Chief of Staff Donald T. Regan depicts First Lady Nancy Reagan as relying on an astrologer in San Francisco for advice on the president's schedule—advice which the first lady insisted be followed. Of the president's own role in this bizarre and demeaning circumstance, Regan notes:

"The fact that he permitted it to exist, and that he never reversed any of the situations created by his wife's intervention, was regarded as sufficient evidence that he was willing to tolerate the state of affairs." (p. 292)

Regan's book also details Mrs. Reagan's aggressive interest in Cabinet and White House staff appointments and in the texts of the president's speeches. She "regarded herself as the President's alter ego not only in the conjugal but also in the political and official dimensions, . . ." Regan wrote, in a "genuine belief that she was the best judge of her husband's interests." Regan summed up his opinion of her role: a "shadowy distaff Presidency."

3. Julie Nixon Eisenhower, *Pat Nixon: The Untold Story* (New York: Zebra Books, 1986), p. 527.

4. The statute is Public Law 95–570 of November 2, 1978, which sets forth Section 105(e) of Title 3 of the U. S. Code. See part IV, note 3. Section 106(c) in the same statute authorizes staff help to the spouse of the vice president as well.

5. Ford, *A Time to Heal,* (see chap. 6, n. 17), p. 183.

6. James S. Rosebush, *First Lady, Public Wife* (Lanham, Md: Madison Books, 1987), p. 61. Rosebush's book (he was Nancy Reagan's chief of staff) is an excellent description of the historical growth of the first lady's responsibilities and how different first ladies have discharged them.

7. Off-the-record interview with the author.

8. Betty Ford, with Chris Chase, *The Times of My Life* (New York: Ballantine Books, 1978), pp. 242–43.

9. Off-the-record interview with the author.

10. Helen Lempart Oral History, John F. Kennedy Library, p. 50.

11. Sorensen, *Kennedy,* p. 297.

Chapter 22

1. For excellent, detailed analysis of the role of the postwar vice presidents, see Paul C. Light, *Vice Presidential Power* (Baltimore: Johns Hopkins Press, 1984), and Joel K. Goldstein, *The Modern American Vice Presidency* (Princeton: Princeton University Press, 1982).

2. Robert E. Cushman, OH 379, Dwight D. Eisenhower Library.

3. Christopher H. Russell, OH 406, Dwight D. Eisenhower Library, p. 126. Used with permission.

4. Off-the-record interview with the author.

5. Ambrose, *Eisenhower: The President,* p. 513.

6. Light, *Vice Presidential Power,* p. 68.

7. Myer Feldman Oral History, John F. Kennedy Library, pp. 51ff. Used with permission.

8. George Reedy, quoted in Kenneth W. Thompson, ed., *The Johnson Presidency: Twenty Intimate Perspectives of Lyndon B. Johnson* (Lanham, Md.: University Press of America, 1986), p. 100.

9. David Halberstam, *The Best and the Brightest* (New York: Random House, 1972), p. 534.

10. In Thompson, ed., *The Johnson Presidency,* p. 149.

11. Halberstam, *The Best and the Brightest,* p. 533.

12. Light, *Vice Presidential Power,* pp. 32–33.

13. *The Appendix to the Budget of the United States for FY 1971* (Washington, D.C.: Government Printing Office, 1970), p. 53.

14. Nixon, *Memoirs,* 1:421.

15. Ehrlichman, *Witness to Power,* p. 124.

16. Memorandum for the Vice President and 17 Cabinet and Agency Heads, February 13, 1975, in Archives, *Public Papers of the Presidents: Gerald R. Ford, 1975* 1:256–58.

17. Statement by the Press Secretary, New York City, February 13, 1975, author's personal collection.

18. Light, *Vice Presidential Power,* pp. 49–50.

19. Carter, *Keeping Faith,* p. 40.

20. Lou Cannon, Interview with Ronald Reagan, *Washington Post,* February 26, 1988, p. A-18.

21. *Newsweek,* October 19, 1987, p. 36.

22. Gerald R. Ford, interview with the author, New York City, November 18, 1987.

23. Ryan J. Barilleaux, "The Post-Modern American Presidency," in *Presidency Research X,* no. 1 (Fall 1987):18. Adapted from his book, *The Post-Modern Presidency: The Office After Ronald Reagan* (New York: Praeger, 1988).

Chapter 23

1. Richard E. Neustadt, in Francis H. Heller, ed., *The Truman White House* (Lawrence: Regents Press of Kansas, 1980), p. 114.

2. Morrow, *Black Man in the White House,* p. 102.

3. Nixon, *Memoirs* 2:272.

4. See "Ronald Reagan, On Cue," *Washington Post,* February 29, 1988, p. A-15.

5. Donald Regan, *For The Record*, p. 84.

6. The author, then newly appointed as the assistant cabinet secretary, was assigned by White House Chief of Staff Sherman Adams to visit each of the Cabinet departments and explain Eisenhower's new staff and Cabinet secretariat system to the Cabinet officers and their top associates. There was even a handbook distributed: *Staff Work for the President and the Executive Branch.* The message conveyed was "Here is the way the president is going to run his White House; you may want to try it yourself." Over thirty-four years, most of them have done so.

7. Off-the-record interview with the author.

8. Ambrose, *Eisenhower: The President,* pp. 29–30.

9. Off-the-record interview with the author.

10. Steve Bull, interview with the author, Washington, D.C., July 25, 1986.

11. Stuart Eizenstat, "Year-End Summary" Memorandum to the President, December 27, 1977, Eizenstat personal collection.

12. Kernell and Popkin, eds., *Chief of Staff,* p. 143; and Richard E. Neustadt, "Does the White House Need a Strong Chief of Staff?" *Presidency Research* X, no. 1 (Fall 1987): 10.

13. Donald Rumsfeld, interview with the author, Washington, D.C., June 1, 1987.

14. Ibid.

15. Quotes are from declassified National Security Decision Directives 266 of March 31, 1987; 276 of June 9, 1987; and 286 of Summer 1987, author's personal collection.

16. Kernell and Popkin, eds., *Chief of Staff,* p. 182.

17. CBS Special, "Five Presidents on the Presidency," a production of CBS News, 1973, as quoted in Fred I. Greenstein, *The Hidden-Hand Presidency* (New York: Basic Books, 1982), p. 43.

18. Haldeman, *The Ends of Power* (see chap. 7, n. 69), p. 112.

19. Califano, *A Presidential Nation,* p. 45.

20. Robert J. Donovan, *Conflict and Crisis: The Presidency of Harry S. Truman, 1945–1948* (New York: Norton, 1977), p. 223.

21. Haldeman, *The Ends of Power,* pp. 155, 320, and 319.

22. *Washington Post,* July 31, 1987, pp. A-10 and A-9.

23. *Tower Commission Report,* p. IV-11.

24. Congressman Lynn Martin (R.-Ill.) as quoted in the *Washington Post,* January 30, 1986, p. B-1.

25. Gerald R. Ford, interview with the author, New York City, November 18, 1987.

Part III

1. Informal paper entitled "The Office of the Executive Clerk—The White House," authored by the Executive Clerk's Office, March 1986, pp. 12–13, author's personal collection.

2. Off-the-record interview with the author.

3. Off-the-record interview of a White House volunteer by the author.

4. Off-the-record interview with the author.

5. A letter-writing campaign about school prayer sent the 1985 total to 8,204,653. Off the record interview with the author.

6. Frederic E. Fox, former staff assistant to President Eisenhower, undated memorandum entitled "The Pastoral Duties of the President," author's personal collection.

7. Off-the-record interview with the author.

8. Speakes, *Speaking Out,* p. 93.

9. Evan P. Aurand, Naval aide to President Eisenhower, Oral History 127, Columbia Oral History Project, Eisenhower Library, p. 4. Used with permission.

10. John S. D. Eisenhower, Assistant Staff Secretary to the President, OH 15, Dwight D. Eisenhower Library, p. 32.

11. Auraud Oral History 127, pp. 113ff.

12. Andrew J. Goodpaster, Memorandum for the three military aides, August 19, 1960; Dwight D. Eisenhower Library, White House Office Collection, box 4.

13. Off-the-record interview with the author. For an especially candid illustration of the "gritty, three-way tension," the reader is referred to pages 189–202 of Larry Speakes' book.

14. As described in Bill McAllister, "The Precarious Role of the President's Physician," Health Section, *Washington Post*, February 9, 1988, pp. 12–15.

15. Author's recollection of statement made several times by President Eisenhower during Cabinet evaluations of the annual "Operation Alert" exercises.

16. Off-the-record interview with the author.

17. *Speakes, Speaking Out*, p. 110.

18. Off-the-record interview with the author.

19. Public Law 87-286.

20. Executive Order 11145 of March 7, 1964 (Washington, D.C.: United States Code, Title 3), pp. 256–67.

21. Off-the-record interview with the author.

22. Off-the-record interview with the author.

23. Philip H. Melanson, *The Politics of Protection* (New York: Praeger, 1986), p. 40.

24. Ibid., pp. 95, 97–98.

25. Off-the-record interview with the author.

26. *Washington Post*, May 20, 1985, p. A-2.

27. The reader is also referred to pages 99–100 of Larry Speakes' book wherein he describes the intense pressure he received on one occasion from First Lady Nancy Reagan to force the Secret Service to move the press away from positions from which reporters and photographers could intercept the president's son, Michael.

Part IV

1. The figures in this listing come from confidential sources on whom the author relies, although the numbers given here exceed those in published reports. The figures given for the Secret Service protective details are rounded off; the precise totals are not made public.

2. Gerald R. Ford, interview with the author, New York City, November 18, 1987.

3. Report GGD-87-102BR (Washington, D.C.: General Accounting Office, July 1987). See also Report GGD-88-33 of March 1988.

The statute referred to is Public Law 95-570 of November 2, 1978. This statute clarifies Congress' authorization for the president to appoint a White House staff and authorizes the vice president to appoint a staff as well. The statute puts limits on the numbers of presidential and vice presidential assistants paid at or above the GS-18 maximum level, but gives them open-ended authority to hire staff at or below the minimum rate of GS-16. The use of "temporary or intermittent" experts and consultants is authorized, as well as the use of detailees, but the loaning agencies must be reimbursed for the salaries of detailees who spend more than 180 days a year at the White House. An annual report is required to the Congress (it is submitted near the beginning of each December) on the numbers of White House staff, including detailees serving there over 30 days. PL 95-570, however, did not apply to the National Security Council. The Iran-contra Investigating Committees recommended, on page 425 of their majority report, that the president should be required to "report to Congress periodically on the organization, size, function, and procedures of the NSC staff," including civilian and military detailees.

Congress then, in December of 1987, added a new enactment (PL-100-202, 101 STAT. 1329-427, Section 621) which requires every detailing agency (except the intelligence community) to report annually to the Senate and House Appropriations Committees the grade,

position, and offices of each federal employee and each member of the armed services detailed
to any other Executive Agency, specifically including "the White House Office, the Executive
Residence, and any office, council, or organizational unit of the Executive Office of the
President."

4. See Samuel Kernell, *Going Public* (Washington, D.C.: *Congressional Quarterly* Press, 1986),
and Grossman and Kumar, *Portraying the President.*

5. Terry M. Moe, "The Politicized Presidency," in John E. Chubb and Paul E. Peterson,
eds., *The New Direction in American Politics* (Washington, D.C.: Brookings Institution, 1985), pp.
244–45.

6. Richard Cheney, interview with the author, Washington, D.C., April 27, 1987.

7. Off-the-record interview with the author.

8. While former Security Assistant Admiral John Poindexter testified to a congressional
committee that he did not tell the president about the NSC staff's diversion of funds to aid
the Nicaraguan contras, the author's own past experience at the White House makes him
unable to put credence in that story. Even the committee itself commented, "Preempting a
decision by the President to provide political deniability—which Poindexter testified that he
did—was totally uncharacteristic for a naval officer schooled in the chain of command."
(Iran-contra Report, p. 272).

9. H. R. Haldeman, interview with the author, Santa Barbara, Calif. April 16, 1986.

10. Califano, *Governing America,* p. 411.

11. Ibid., p. 50.

12. Sorensen, in Kernell and Popkin, eds., *Chief of Staff,* p. 106.

13. Richard Neustadt, "Presidential Leadership: The Clerk Against the Preacher," James
Sterling Young, ed., *Problems and Prospects of Presidential Leadership,* Vol. 1 (Lanham, Md: The
University Press of America, 1982), p. 33.

14. Califano, *Governing America,* p. 412.

15. "An Interview with LBJ," *Newsweek,* August 2, 1965.

16. John W. Gardner, *Toward a Pluralistic but Coherent Society* (Queenstown, Md.: Aspen
Institute for Humanistic Studies, 1980), pp. 20–21.

17. A panel of the National Academy of Public Administration made this recommendation
in 1980 in its report, *A Presidency for the 1980's* (Washington, D.C., November 1980), pp. 16,
18, and 21. The Tower Commission raised a similar possibility in its 1987 Report, previously
cited (p. V-4).

18. Stuart E. Eizenstat, Testimony before the Senate Committee on Governmental Affairs,
September 17, 1987. Eizenstat points out that the current practice for an incoming president
of the opposing party is to make sure not only that the former policy officers depart, but that
secretaries are ejected as well.

INDEX